Sideshows of the Indian Army in World War I

Harry Fecitt, MBE, TD

(Established 1870)

Centre For Armed Forces Historical Research
United Service Institution of India
New Delhi

Vij Books India Pvt Ltd

New Delhi (India)

Published by

Vij Books India Pvt Ltd
(Publishers, Distributors & Importers)
2/19, Ansari Road
Delhi – 110 002
Phones: 91-11-43596460, 91-11-47340674
Fax: 91-11-47340674
e-mail: vijbooks@rediffmail.com

Copyright © 2017, United Service Institution of India, New Delhi

ISBN   : 978-93-86457-23-3 (Paperback), 2018

All rights reserved.

No part of this book may be reproduced, stored in a retrieval system, transmitted or utilised in any form or by any means, electronic, mechanical, photocopying, recording or otherwise, without the prior permission of the copyright owner. Application for such permission should be addressed to the publisher.

Sideshows of the Indian Army
in World War I

CONTENTS

Introduction		ix
1.	Military Operations in Aden during 1914 and 1915	1
2.	Military Operations on the North-West Frontier and in Baluchistan – October 1914 – March 1917	15
3.	The Actions at Shimber Berris, Somaliland, November 1914 to February 1915 Indian Sepoys fighting with the Somaliland Camel Corps	30
4.	The 36th Sikhs at the fall of Tsingtao, China October to November 1914	41
5.	The Suez Canal 1914-15	48
6.	The Hong Kong-Singapore Mountain Battery in Egypt, Sinai and Palestine 1915 – 1918	55
7.	The East Persia Cordon and the Sarhad Operations, 1915 – 1917	72
8.	Indian Military Transport units in Macedonia 1916 – 1918	82
9.	The 25th Cavalry (Frontier Force) in German and Portugese East Africa– September 1917 – February 1918	91
10.	Operations in Transcaspia 1918 – 1919 Sowars, Sepoys and Guides fight the Bolsheviks	99
11.	Fighting The Tangistanis Bushire, Persia, July – September 1915	120

12.	The Gurkha Action at Tor, Sinai The 2/7th Gurkhas in action on 12th February 1915	134
13.	Atonement: The 5th Light Infantry in German Kamerun August 1915 to February 1916	140
14.	The 5th Light Infantry in East Africa March 1916 – January 1918	159
15.	Lake Victoria, German East Africa, 6th December 1915	166
16.	The 15th Ludhiana Sikhs and the Senussi The Egyptian Western Desert, November 1915 to February 1916	173
17.	The 40th Pathans in action in East Africa January 1916 to February 1918	181
18.	Indian Army Units in Action, March to mid-June 1916	195
19.	Kisangire and Kisiju – Operations north of the Rufiji River Delta, German East Africa October and November 1916	210
20.	The 129th DCO Baluchis at German East Africa October 1916 to January 1917	216
21.	The 22nd Derajat Mountain Battery (Frontier Force) in East Africa – December 1916 to December 1918	231
22.	Indian Army Battalions in the Battle of Ramadi, Mesopotamia, 27-29 September 1917; Gurkhas, Garhwalis and Punjabis in action	238
23.	The 30th Punjabis at Tandamuti Hill and Nakadi Ridge, East Africa – February – October 1917	247
24.	The Kuki Rising 1917-1919 Insurrection in north-eastern India and Burma	255
25.	Fighting the Marris and the Khetrans February to April 1918	271
26.	Indian Army units in Dunsterforce North-West Persia in 1918	280

27.	Reforming and Redeploying	
	The 120th Rajputana Infantry in southern Persia and Seistan 1918 – 1920	292
28.	Death on a Dark Desert Night	
	Manchester Column disaster., Mesopotamia, July 1920	300

Bibliography — 307

Index — 325

Maps

Chapter Location Map	xi
East Africa Map	xii
Middle East Map	xiii

Introduction

Thanks to a number of dedicated enthusiasts who over the last two years have been writing and speaking on the subject, the interested public is now more aware of Indian Army involvement and sacrifice on the Great War battlefields of France and Gallipoli in Turkey. What is not widely known is the extent of sepoy and sowar involvement in other Great War and post-Great War battlefields around the world.

As can be seen by a glance at the Chapter Location Map sepoys and sowars were involved in military actions in Macedonia and the Egyptian Western Desert, and from West Africa to China. The enemies were varied – Germans, Bulgarians, Turks, enemy African Askari and Arab irregular troops, Mesopotamian insurgents, Somali, Senussi, Baluchi and Persian tribesmen, and Russian Bolsheviks who used Austrian and Hungarian former prisoners of war in their forces. But the regiments operating in these far-flung outposts of European Empires did not falter, and every campaign that they were involved in was successfully concluded or drawn to a close for political reasons.

A particularly interesting regiment is the 5th Light Infantry which after half its strength had mutinied in Singapore (due to provocations caused by inadequate leadership, misinformation and intrigue by enemy prisoners of war) was re-formed and sent to fight in German Kamerun in West Africa. When the Allies won that campaign the regiment was despatched to East Africa where it had a tough time against a determined and aggressive foe. Finally it went to British Somaliland where many sepoys, already weakened by tropical diseases and strenuous operational conditions, died due to Somaliland's harsh climate. The regiment was disbanded in 1922. Let us not forget those courageous sepoys of the 5th Light Infantry who served in Africa.

Where possible citations for gallantry awards have been quoted, and as these were written by officers who were fighting alongside their men, often the urgency of the tactical situation and the gallant responses of the sepoys and sowars are conveyed in the citations. To the discerning reader what is apparent is that once combat had commenced the men were not fighting for an Allied ideology but for their regiment, their comrades and their honour. That is how it was.

The contents of this book could not have been compiled without the generosity of the Director of the United Services Institute of India who gave free access to the Institute's magnificent library. Many of the regimental histories in the library are unobtainable elsewhere. Also gratitude for sponsorship is given to the youthful and energetic team comprising the Centre for Armed Forces Historical Research; their cheerful support is matched by their willingness to innovate and develop fresh ways of bringing military history into the public domain.

Please pick and choose your way through the contents of this book, and at the end I hope that you feel a strong sense of pride in the battlefield achievements of a generation of warriors who all volunteered to serve, wherever in the world that service took them.

– Harry Fecitt

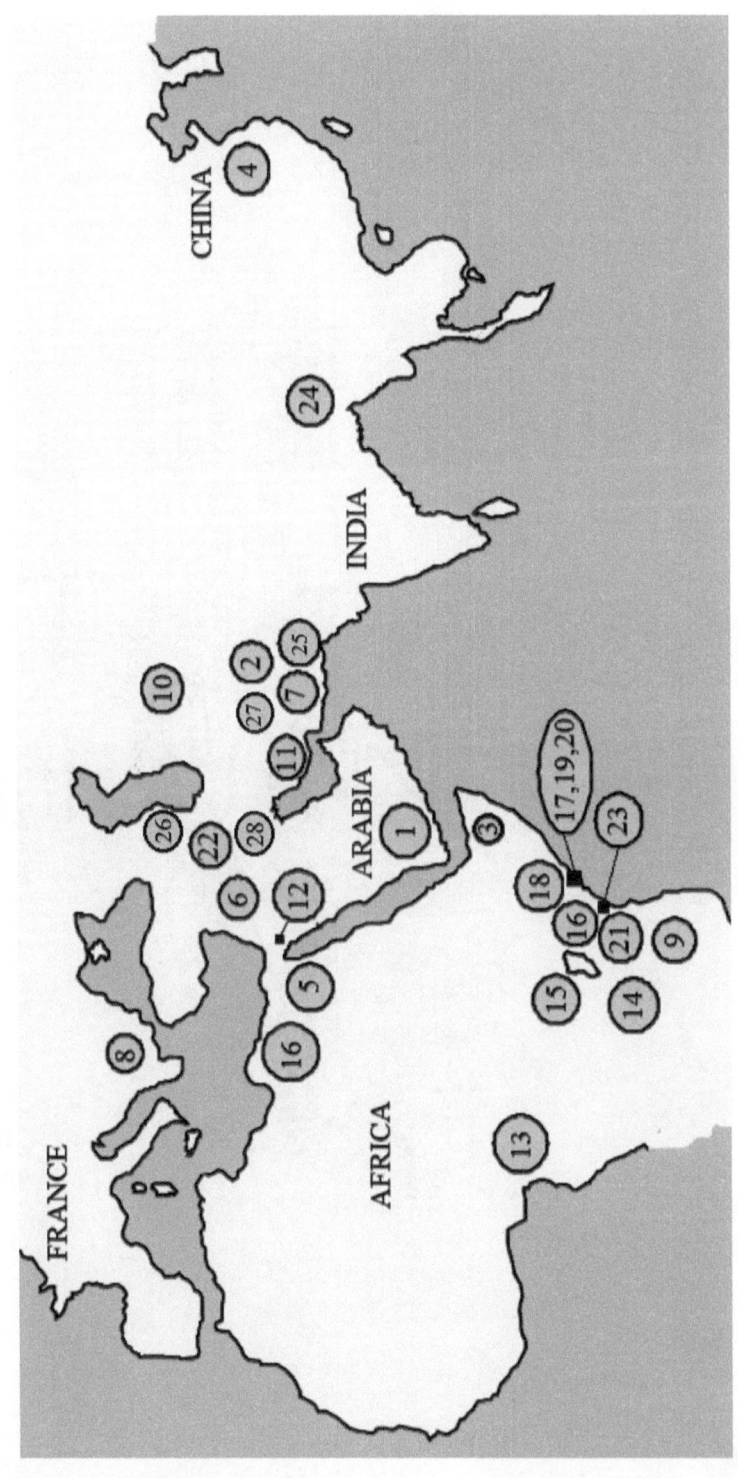

Middle East Map

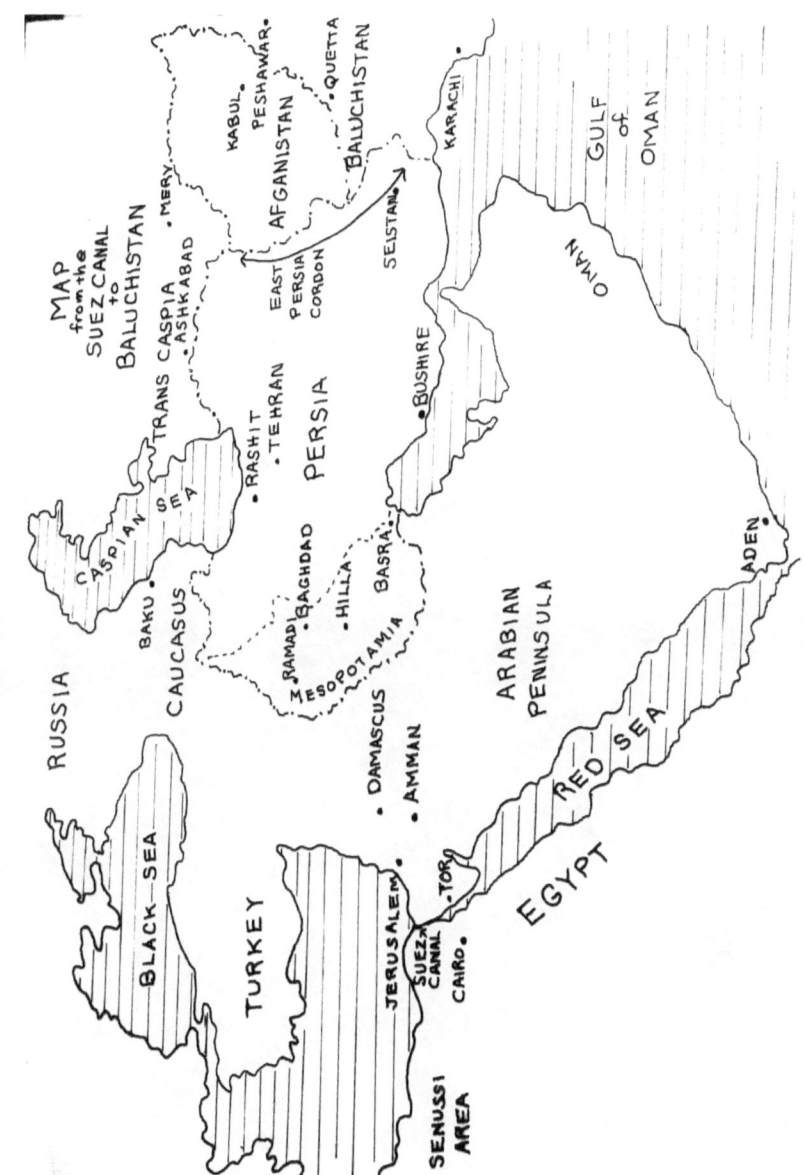

Military Operations in Aden during 1914 and 1915

Aden and Yemen in 1914

When Turkey entered the Great War as a German ally in early November 1914 Britain was faced with defending two frontiers against Turkish aggression, one in Egypt and the other in Aden and its hinterland. The Turks had invaded Yemen in 1872 and they garrisoned the capital Sanaa and the coastal ports with an army corps of unknown strength. A joint Boundary Commission in 1904[1] had established a border between Yemen and the Protectorate that Britain had established in the Aden hinterland and Turkish troops also garrisoned tactical points near this border.

Aden was a strategically important coaling port and harbour for the British Empire as it lay on the shipping route between the Antipodes and Europe, and it was near the entrance to the Red Sea that led to the Suez Canal. However the administration of Aden by Britain was marked by confusion and complication, and it was left to the Government of India to administer the territory through a Political Resident who usually was the military commander in Aden. The Aden garrison consisted of one British and one Indian infantry battalion and the Aden Troop, which was a cavalry squadron of both horse and camel-mounted sowars, manned by volunteers from Indian cavalry regiments. The hot harsh climate and rugged terrain in Aden's hinterland presented strong challenges to both European and Indian soldiers.

As troops were needed for France the British battalion in Aden had been sent to Europe and initially a mixed force was hurriedly assembled and sent from India to replace it. Later the 23rd Sikh Pioneers who had been

---
[1] See article at: http://www.kaiserscross.com/304501/462522.html

earmarked for service in Egypt were re-assigned to be part of the Aden Garrison, arriving there on 9th November.

The Attack on Sheikh Said

The first confrontation with the Turks occurred near the island of Perim lying 145 kilometres west of Aden in the Straits of Bab El Mandib at the mouth of the Red Sea. Volcanic and waterless Perim Island, 13 square kilometres in area and a part of Aden territory, housed an important lighthouse, a coaling station and a small garrison of around 50 Indian soldiers. The African coast lay 18 kilometres away but the Yemen mainland opposite the island lay only 2.5 kilometres distant. On a knoll opposite Perim, at a location named Sheikh Said, the Turks had constructed Fort Turba, which commanded both Perim Island and the straits of Bab El Mandib. Strong gun positions had been built using granite and concrete; these housed two Krupp's guns with a range of around 20 kilometres, and two more light but more mobile field guns. Good ammunition magazines, stores and barracks had also been constructed and a Turkish garrison of around 500 men was deployed in and around the fort. More field guns in well-camouflaged positions were positioned in the area behind the fort. A few small fishing villages in the area were inhabited by Yemeni civilians.

During the first week of November the officer commanding Perim garrison alerted Aden about a new camp that the Turks were building six kilometres from Sheikh Said. The Indian Army was obviously anxious to keep open the shipping lane that was being used to reinforce France and Egypt and Delhi authorised a 24-hour operation against Sheikh Said by troops on their way to Egypt. This decision to make a pre-emptive attack appears to have been one known only to military commanders in India and Aden, politicians being left out of the picture until afterwards. This secrecy undoubtedly prevented questions or obstruction from above.

On 3rd November the 29th Indian Infantry Brigade under Brigadier-General H.V. Cox had sailed from Karachi for Egypt in a convoy and it was decided to use this brigade to attack Sheikh Said. Four battalions were in the brigade, 14th (King George's Own) Ferozepore Sikhs, 69th Punjabis, 89th Punjabis, and 1st Battalion of the 6th Gurkhas. For the attack the Gurkhas were to be left on board their ship and the 23rd Sikh Pioneers were to join the brigade at Aden; the Pioneers were needed because of their demolition skills. A plan was made at Aden by the General Staff Officer there, Major

C.R. Bradshaw, 9th Gurkha Rifles. When the convoy reached Aden he joined Brigadier Cox's headquarters with maps, appreciations and a draft plan. Lieutenant Colonel H.F. Jacob, the acting political resident, had requested to Delhi that a political officer accompany Major Bradshaw so that the tribes at Sheikh Said could be assured of Britain's friendly intentions towards them, but no reply came to the request and Bradshaw went alone.

Brigadier Cox and Captain H. Blackett, Royal Navy, captain of the supporting cruiser *HMS Duke of Edinburgh*, agreed a combined-operations plan to arrive off Sheikh Said at 0100 hours, make a covert landing in darkness, and then attack Fort Turba at dawn under the supporting fire of the cruiser's six 240mm (9.2-inch) and ten 152mm (6-inch) guns. Meanwhile the remainder of the convoy would anchor off Aden for 24 hours.

In the event when the brigade in their transports and the cruiser arrived off Sheikh Said in the early hours of 10th November they encountered rough seas. The cruiser's picket boat made a reconnaissance and returned, the Beach Master reporting that the sea was too rough to make a landing and that the picket boat had been observed and had attracted Turkish rifle fire. The plan was changed to one where the cruiser shelled Fort Turba at dawn and then took the convoy to the western side of Sheikh Said where a daylight landing would be made supported by naval gunfire. The disadvantages of this new plan were that the line of Turkish retreat could not be cut off from the west, and fringes of rocks along the shore meant that the transports had to anchor well out to sea.

The new plan was put into effect and went well until the troops started disembarking when it was found that the transports' gangways were not suitable for laden soldiers entering small boats. Many sepoys had never seen the sea before this voyage and took some time to adjust to the landing boats that were being towed towards the shore. The landing boats from the transports were found to be leaking and often rudderless and were quickly replaced by naval boats. The tugboats were crewed by civilians from Perim Island and Aden and these crews were unhappy at receiving heavy Turkish shrapnel fire. Strong winds also hampered the landings.

By 1100 hours landings had been made but only the 89th Punjabis and a double-company and the machine guns of the 69th Punjabis were ashore and digging-in to secure the beach-head. Realising the shortage of time remaining for the operation Brigadier Cox ordered these troops to attack towards Fort Turba whilst the remaining troops from his brigade were brought from the transports. The Punjabis fought slowly forward over ground providing little cover whilst the Turks engaged them with machine gun and rifle fire and shrapnel from field guns. During this fighting a machine gunner of the 69th Punjabis, No. 765 Naik Labh Singh, displayed gallantry whilst providing covering fire from exposed positions and he later received an **Indian Distinguished Service Medal**. The naval gunfire was effective in encouraging the Turks to withdraw, and the Punjabis continued their advance throughout the night with the aim of being at Fort Turba by 0600 hours on 11th November.

After dusk the cruiser sailed eastwards and at dawn provided covering fire whilst Fort Turba was taken without a fight. The naval lyddite shells had caused extensive damage to the fort and its gun positions but had not detonated the Turkish ammunition magazines. Whilst the two Punjabi battalions re-embarked, the 14th (King George's Own) Ferozepore Sikhs[2] occupied positions to cover the 23rd Sikh Pioneers. The Pioneers, assisted by a naval demolition party, successfully destroyed the 2 Krupp guns, 4 field guns, 1 brass cannon, about 10,000 rounds of small arms ammunition, gun emplacements and large quantities of artillery shells and cordite. The 3,000 men that had been landed were all back on board by 1730 hours; the 29th Indian Infantry Brigade re-joined its convoy and sailed for Egypt whilst the 23rd Sikh Pioneers sailed back to Aden. Six dead Turks and a few wounded had been found on the battlefield and two wounded prisoners had been taken; the Turks had removed their other casualties when they withdrew. Brigadier Cox's force had lost 5 men, killed or died of wounds and around a dozen wounded during a very successful combined operation. But due credit must be given to the Royal Navy who provided the seamanship skills and firepower that ensured success.

On 29th May 1915 No. 1 Company of the 23rd Sikh Pioneers under Captain H.S. Hutchison was garrisoning Perim Island. That night a sepoy shot dead in their beds the two senior Indian officers in the battalion, Subedar Major Balwant Singh and Subedar Paritam Singh. No. 3886 Havildar

---

2   A sepoy from the 14th (KGO) Sikhs, fed up with the problems of cooking on board using coke, chopped the Turkish flagpole down in the fort to take back to his transport. He discarded the Turkish flag, which he saw no use for but the flag was recovered and later was displayed in the battalion Officers' Mess.

Uttama Singh[3] closed with the murderer, No. 4510 Sepoy Basakha Singh, and although fired at, arrested him. Basakha Singh was tried, found guilty, and hanged in Aden Special Prison on 7th June.

The Turks reoccupied Sheikh Said and they attacked Perim Island on 13th June firing around 300 shells from a 4.1-inch gun and two lighter guns. The lighthouse was hit several times but not badly damaged. The following night at 0100 hours the enemy launched dhows full of soldiers in an attempted landing on the island. Most of the dhows were discouraged by effective defensive fire but some Turkish troops landed successfully. However after being illuminated by a British star shell the Turks rapidly withdrew.

The disastrous attempt to defend Lahej

In early 1915 the Aden garrison was increased with the Territorial 4th Battalion, South Wales Borderers (Brecknockshire Battalion) arriving from Britain as a replacement for the departed Regular Army battalion. However the Brecknocks were not fully trained and needed to acclimatize to Aden's unrelenting severely hot weather. The Indian battalions in theatre were the 23rd Sikh Pioneers, the 109th Infantry and half of the 126th Baluchistan Infantry, but the Sikh Pioneers and the Baluchis were sending reinforcement drafts to battalions in France whilst the 109th Infantry and some of the Sikh Pioneers were manning outposts such as Perim and also Kamaran Island off the Yemen Red Sea coast. On the political front the new garrison commander and Political Resident, Major-General D.L.B. Shaw, made a treaty with a tribal leader outside Aden and supplied him with money, rifles and ammunition. The pro-British Sultan of Lahej, north of Aden port, was presented with four field guns and a British officer was seconded to teach gunnery to the Sultan's soldiers. General Shaw hoped that these arrangements would provide him with security outside Aden town. The Aden Troop patrolled to the north of Lahej.

Meanwhile the Turks were preparing to advance with 2,000 men and 6 guns on Lahej, and they received the co-operation of the Adeni tribes whose land they would cross. The Turkish advance was made in late June when the power of the sun was approaching its strongest, but General Shaw had to despatch a Moveable Column to defend Lahej. This column concentrated

---

3   Later Uttama Singh received the Indian Meritorious Service Medal and was promoted to Jemadar.

at the oasis of Sheikh Othman, just north of Aden port, on 3rd July and contained:

- 15-pounder Camel Battery, Royal Garrison Artillery (6 guns).

- 10-pounder Mountain Battery, Royal Garrison Artillery (4 guns packed on camels).

- Elements of the 23rd (Fortress) Company, Bombay Sappers & Miners.

- A Wing (half a battalion) of Brecknocks.

- A company of 23rd Sikh Pioneers with two .450-inch machine guns and two .303-inch machine guns.

- A Wing of the 109th Infantry with two .450-inch machine guns and two .303-inch machine guns.

- Two companies of 126th Baluchistan Infantry.

The column departed at 0300 hours the following day and as the sun rose higher in the sky cases of dehydration and heat stroke began to occur in the column. The fitter elements marched on whilst undisciplined chaos set in amongst the rest of the column. Meanwhile a flying advanced guard of machine gunners in cars had set out ahead of the marching men, arriving in Lahej at 0800 hours. By 1030 hours the first 100 of the 109th Infantry under their commanding officer, Lieutenant Colonel H.C. Wooldridge, and the Sappers & Miners under Captain C.F. Stoehr, Royal Engineers, had marched the 45 kilometres into Lahej; the remainder of the battalion and company trickled in by 1730 hours. Colonel Wooldridge briefly rested the men and commenced planning a defence.

The company of 23rd Pioneers arrived at Lahej at 1330 hours; the Pioneers' commanding officer, Lieutenant Colonel H.F.A. Pearson, was the commander of the Moveable Column and his Adjutant, Captain F.C. Squires was the Column Staff Officer. Colonel Pearson took over command of the British force from Colonel Wooldridge. The camel-packed mountain battery arrived at Lahej in good order but the 15-pounder guns being hauled by camels were stuck in the sand on the track. Fitter men of the Baluchis and the Brecknocks also trickled in. To the rear on the track from Sheikh Othman the logistical side of the operation had collapsed as the Adeni camel drivers carrying water, ammunition and supplies abandoned their tasks and retired with their camels[4]. Not all the allocated medical units were in place on the line of march and men were dying of heat stroke.

In Lahej, which was the size of a village, Colonel Pearson organised a defence based on the northwest edge as the Turks attacked. To the rear were two gardens where the British and Indian troops respectively had rested after their march. Three awards of the **Indian Order of Merit, 2nd Class**, were later made for gallantry displayed during the Lahej fighting:

No. 2007 Havildar Shah Nawaz, 109th Infantry: *For gallantry on the 4th and 5th July 1915 while in charge of a machine gun section. It was mainly owing to his exertion that the guns were got up to Lahej. He handled his men well throughout the action and showed much discretion in checking one or two rushes.*

No. 3979 Lance Naik Gil Baz, 126th Baluchistan Infantry: *This non-commissioned officer, while wounded, was of the greatest assistance in steadying the men during the action on the 4th and 5th July 1915.*

The third award was made in 1920 after the recipient had escaped from captivity[5]. Sepoy Sohan Singh, 1st Battalion 23rd Sikh Pioneers: *For conspicuous gallantry and devotion to duty on 4th July 1915 when he carried messages between his machine gun section and the officer commanding the unit. Sepoy Sohan Singh also showed the greatest pluck and determination when he escaped from captivity. He made his way through 350 miles* (560 kilometres) *of strange country and after undergoing many privations due to lack of food and water and a bad climate, rejoined the British forces.*

The British held their line during the hours of daylight mainly due to effective use of the mountain guns, one of the Sultan's guns, and the machine guns. However after dusk the enemy fired huts that illuminated the British positions and the Turks and their local Arab allies started to turn both British flanks. Colonel Pearson had to withdraw to the garden area 550 metres to his rear, abandoning two of the mountain guns, which were first disabled. Close quarter fighting took place in the village main street in which Captain Squires was mortally wounded; men of the Sappers & Miners were prominent in the

---

4   Whenever it was tactically possible experienced battalions would march in hot regions with an escorted water supply at the head of the column; this discouraged men from dropping out further back in the column.

5   The 1st Battalion 23rd Sikh Pioneers later fought in Palestine and Sohan Singh was probably taken prisoner there.

fighting at this time and Captain Stoehr was very active with his revolver. Meanwhile the Sultan of Lahej's artillerymen had fled but his remaining loyal riflemen cheerfully fired from rooftops at anyone who moved. Unfortunately the Sultan himself was shot by a British bullet, a case of mistaken identity, whilst he observed the battle from a balcony of his palace. The British fought and held the garden line until 0300 hours 5th July, when the Turks withdrew after suffering around 250 casualties. The British wounded were then evacuated on all the available camels.

At dawn Colonel Pearson made an appreciation of his situation and decided that without ammunition and supplies he must withdraw to Sheikh Othman; this was achieved but the 450 machine guns had to be disabled and abandoned because of the lack of pack animals. The Turks did not immediately follow-up the British withdrawal. At Sheikh Othman General Shaw decided that his troops were not in a fit state to defend the oasis, which was the main water supply for Aden, and a further withdrawal was made to the Khor Maksar line at the outskirts of the port. Local inhabitants gleefully looted Sheikh Othman and the Turks occupied it, cutting off Aden's water supply; British prestige was at its lowest point and in Aden drinking water had to be produced from condensers on ships in the harbour. British casualties on the Lahej operation were: Captain Squires died of wounds, 6 British and 6 Indian soldiers killed or missing, 5 British and 10 Indian soldiers wounded and 35 men dead from heatstroke, most of them from the Brecknocks.

The arrival of the 28th (Frontier Force) Brigade

Swift action was called for and on 8th July half of the 108th Infantry arrived in Aden as reinforcements, and the 4th Battalion The Buffs (East Kent Regiment), another Territorial unit, relieved the Brecknocks. The most important development was the arrival in Aden of a new commander and an infantry brigade from Egypt; Major General Sir George Younghusband replaced General Shaw, bringing with him the 28th (Frontier Force) Brigade and two British Territorial batteries, the Berkshire Battery, Royal Horse Artillery and 'B' Battery, Honourable Artillery Company. The battalions in the 28th (Frontier Force) Brigade were: the 51st Sikhs (Frontier Force), the 53rd Sikhs (Frontier Force), the 56th Punjabi Rifles (Frontier Force) and the 62nd Punjabis; the Brigade disembarked at Aden on 20th July and marched to bivouac at Khor Maksar.

General Younghusband quickly appreciated that Sheikh Othman had to be held by the British but that there would never be sufficient troops to occupy other locations in the hinterland, therefore an 'aggressive defence' had to be practised from Aden. This meant that a Flying Column was to be on standby as a quick-reaction force and a Moveable Column was to be quickly formed when a short expedition was mounted against a Turkish post. The basic factor that underlay all tactical planning was that columns had to carry sufficient water with them for both the outward and return journeys, and this factor limited the distance that operations could be mounted from Aden.

At 0300 hours on 21st July the 28th (Frontier Force) Brigade, with the Aden Troop in support, marched the six kilometres to Sheikh Othman under the temporary command of Lieutenant Colonel A.M.S. Elsmie, 56th Punjabi Rifles. The 53rd Sikhs were on the left, the 56th Rifles on the right, the 51st Sikhs marched in support and the 62nd Punjabis were in reserve at Khor Maksar. The sepoys approached Sheikh Othman at dawn and firing broke out from enemy troops shooting from houses and over walls. However surprise had been achieved and the Brigade maintained momentum, attacking the Turkish positions. An enemy counter-attack was mounted onto the British left but was beaten back, and brisk fighting developed in the oasis during which Lieutenants V.W.K. Mackinnon and G.C. Southern, both of the 53rd Sikhs, were killed along with 3 sepoys, 22 other sepoys were wounded. The Turks did not defend Sheikh Othman for long before withdrawing towards Lahej, harassed by the Aden Troop. The Brigade then occupied the oasis, supported by an artillery battery.

Subedar Molar Singh, 53rd Sikhs (Frontier Force), was awarded an **Indian Order of Merit, 2nd Class**: *On the 21st July 1915 this officer led a platoon in action with great coolness and conspicuous gallantry and gave an excellent example to his men at a time when they had several casualties in the space of a few minutes.*

The action at Fiyush and the reconnaissance of Waht

The water supply from Sheikh Othman to Aden was restored within 24 hours of the oasis being captured, and the policy of 'aggressive defence' was implemented. An attack by a small column was mounted against Fiyush, a Turkish post on the eastern camel track to Lahej. The column consisted of the Aden Troop, two guns of the Berkshire Battery, Royal Horse Artillery, two guns of the Honourable Artillery Company, Royal Horse Artillery and the 56th Punjabi Rifles. On 25th August the 56th Rifles attacked the village frontally whilst the cavalry rode around to the Turkish rear where 16 Arab irregulars, 7 rifles and 8 camels were captured. In the village the 56th Rifles had lost, 5 sepoys dead and 3 wounded, but enemy casualties were estimated at 12 dead and 20 wounded.

On 28th August Aden Troop was out again with the 53rd Sikhs under Lieutenant Colonel C.H. Davies DSO. The mission was to reconnoitre Waht under cover of darkness. As the cavalry rode to the rear of the village, greatly impeded by flooded fields, stone walls and steep banks, a commotion was seen and heard in the village. A couple of villagers advised that 2,000 enemy troops, 100 horsemen and 14 guns with 200 mules had just arrived from Lahej. A mounted orderly rode to alert Colonel Davies but he was already in contact with the enemy. As the new day dawned Colonel Davies realised the overwhelming strength of the Turks, and made a fighting withdrawal.

Three men of the 53rd Sikhs (Frontier Force) were awarded the **Indian Order of Merit, 2nd Class**, for gallantry displayed at Waht. The joint citation for No 3543 Naik Bahadur Shah and No. 3218 Sepoy Allah Khan read: *For conspicuous gallantry on the 28th August 1915 during operations in the vicinity of Aden. After three other signallers had been shot down these men, in spite of a heavy fire directed at them, succeeded in correctly transmitting a message to their commanding officer.*

During the fighting a subaltern, Indian Army Reserve of Officers attached to 53rd Sikhs, was severely wounded. Jemadar Faiz Talab, 53rd Sikhs (Frontier Force) rescued the subaltern, receiving the **Indian Order of Merit, 2nd Class**: *For conspicuous gallantry in operations in the vicinity of Aden on the 28th August 1915. When 2nd Lieutenant P.F. Durand was wounded, Jemadar Faiz Talab carried him on his shoulders across an open field under a heavy fire to a place of safety. By his devotion he undoubtedly saved 2nd Lieutenant Durand's life.*[6]

Colonel Davies withdrew his battalion to Sheikh Othman, struggling in deep sand and excessive heat. The camel-mounted sowars of the Aden Troop provided security against the enemy horsemen and several wounded and exhausted Sikhs were brought in on the camels. Enemy losses were not known but one sowar was wounded whilst the Sikhs suffered 2 sepoys killed, 2 officers and 18 sepoys wounded and 2 sepoys missing. Missing men were rarely seen again.

---

6   Jemadar Faiz Talab later also received the French Croix De Guerre.

This was the last action before the 28th Brigade (Frontier Force), less the 56th Punjabi Rifles, left Aden on 7th September to return to Egypt. Major General J.M. Stewart took over command of the British forces in Aden. Colonel Elsmie and his 56th Punjabi Rifles remained in Aden until mid-October when the battalion returned to Egypt. A newly arrived unit, the Malay States Guides[7], then took over the role performed by the 56th Punjabi Rifles.

The attack on Waht

A much bigger column attacked Waht on 28th August. The British forces were:

- Aden Troop.
- Hampshire Battery (4 horse-drawn 5-inch howitzers).
- 15-pounder Camel Battery (6 guns).
- 10-pounder Camel-packed Mountain Battery (2 guns).
- 5th Company, 1st Sappers & Miners.
- One section, 23rd Fortress Company, Sappers & Miners.
- Royal Navy Machine Gun Section.
- One Wing of the 1st Battalion, 4th Buffs (East Kent Regiment).
- One Wing 23rd Sikh Pioneers.
- 109th Infantry.
- 56th Punjabi Rifles.
- 62nd Punjabis.

The Turkish forces at Waht consisted of 700 Turks, 1,000 Arab irregulars and 8 guns. Hostilities commenced at dawn on 25th September when the Aden Troop on the British right came into contact with a Turkish picquet; the subsequent firing alerted the enemy force. The well-acclimatised 62nd Punjabis under Lieutenant Colonel E.W. Grimshaw led the initial attacks,

---

7   See article at: http://www.kaiserscross.com/304501/514322.html

seizing some small villages. The 23rd Sikh Pioneers were then deployed to the British right to secure Sharj village that had been taken by the Punjabis. Colonel Grimshaw pushed on, entering the south of Waht village as Turkish reinforcements from Lahej entered from the north, but as the Punjabis pushed the Turkish defenders back the enemy reinforcements fell back as well, forming a line in thick scrub 1200 metres north of Waht. Turkish officers were seen urging their men forward but British shrapnel dissuaded any forward movement.

A stalemate developed as the well-handled Turkish artillery, always in superior numbers, prevented any further British advance. Having occupied Waht for a couple of hours Colonel Elsmie withdrew to Sheikh Othman. No. 437 Havildar Bishen Singh, 62nd Punjabis, was awarded an **Indian Distinguished Service Medal**: *(He) led the attack on Sharj Village, and was of great assistance in leading and urging on the men of his section throughout the day.*

This attack had failed to kill many Turks and reading between the lines of after-action reports and regimental histories it is apparent that once again the effects of the climate were under-estimated by the planners, as 11 British soldiers and one sepoy died of heatstroke. It is probable that many of the men in this large column were incapacitated on the battlefield by dehydration and heat exhaustion. Other British casualties were one British soldier who died of wounds, and one officer, 3 British and 13 sepoys who survived wounds.

The arrival of the 26th (King George's Own) Light Cavalry, Indian Army

On 19th September 1915 the 26th (King George's Own) Light Cavalry arrived in Aden where it was to stay until 1922; during those seven years the regimental war diary recorded 239 actions against the Turks and their irregular Arab allies. This was a four-squadron Class Squadron Regiment with a squadron each of Madras and Dekhani Mussalmans, Punjabi Mussalmans, Rajputana Rajputs, and Jats. The commanding officer was Lieutenant Colonel A.S. Arnold and his 2nd in Command was Lieutenant Colonel R. de L. Faunce. The arrival of this regiment relieved the strain on the Aden Troop, which had less than 90 sowars on strength yet had been performing the tasks of a regiment since the Turkish advance on Lahej.

The 26th Light Cavalry wasted no time in getting out on patrols and missions such as the arresting of enemy agents known to be in outlying villages. On 7th October 'D' Squadron under Captain J.A. Collum deployed on an operation with the 15-pounder Camel Battery. 'D' Squadron used darkness to covertly occupy a concealed position 1,000 metres north-east of As Sela Village where enemy irregular troops were known to be based. At dawn the Camel Battery shelled As Sela resulting in around 40 of the enemy retreating towards Al Darb Village on the track to Lahej. The enemy group was mostly mounted on camels and fled to the north-west. Captain Collum ordered the troop commanded by 2nd Lieutenant R.A. O'Connor to pursue at the gallop and attack. Collum brought up his other three troops as quickly as he could.

When the enemy group was about 2.5 kilometres south of Al Darb, Connor's troop caught up with them and charged straight in with the lance, killing or wounding around 20 of the enemy. The other three troops were only 200 metres behind but the surviving enemy moved into thick brush and engaged the cavalry with rifle fire, supported by a strong concealed picquet. Captain Collum ordered dismounted fire action until the enemy from As Sela withdrew with their casualties; the enemy picquet remained in place. The squadron then advanced on foot in extended order and under fire to recover the body of an Indian officer who had been killed in the fighting. This was accomplished and as it was not in Collum's orders to attack fixed positions he withdrew his squadron.

The dead officer, Jemadar Muhammad Khan, 26th (King George's Own) Light Cavalry, was awarded a posthumous **Indian Order of Merit, 2nd Class**, with the citation: *For conspicuous gallantry and courage in a skirmish near As-sela in the vicinity of Aden on the 7th October 1915. He showed great dash and gallantry in leading an attack on the enemy and he himself attacked a group of Arabs armed with rifles. He killed three and wounded another but was shot by the fifth.*

Until the end of 1915 General Stewart did not order any large operations with a Moveable Column, but low-level patrolling and skirmishing continued aggressively. Neither side was strong enough to eject the other, but both sides wanted to skirmish, and needed to do so in order to retain the support of their respective groups of allied local tribes.

Turkish spies in Aden

In his book *40 Years a Soldier* General Younghusband describes the apprehension of a Turkish spy in Aden port. The man was a leading

Arab merchant who regularly corresponded with Said Pasha, the Turkish commander in Lahej. The letters containing information were entrusted to local camel drivers who went into the hinterland to bring supplies back into Aden; doubtless these camel drivers then passed the letters on to others who would deliver them to Lahej. One night a camel driver with a letter noticed that at the postern gate exit from Aden town everyone was being carefully searched.

Slipping away from the camel train for a few minutes the driver found a British red-letter box and deposited the letter there. The following day after the letter box had been opened the contents were taken to the Postal Censor, Colonel Cleveland. The letter to Said Pasha was opened and found to contain an accurate plan of Aden showing all the defences and gun positions. Exact ranges were marked in red ink between all the important points in Aden and landmarks on the mainland. The signed letter also mentioned the fact that the writer was owed 100 rupees for his last letter, and he asked for another 100 rupees for the information he was sending now. After being found guilty by court martial the writer was executed by firing squad in front of a group of the leading citizens of Aden.

In a similar vein the war diary of the Aden Troop mentions that local Arab and Somali deserters from the British force who were later captured whilst in the service of the Turks, were also court martialled and shot when found guilty.

Military Operations on the North-West Frontier and in Baluchistan
October 1914 – March 1917

(This should be read as a continuation of the article TOCHI VALLEY OPERATIONS, WAZIRISTAN, 1914-1915.)

The North-West Frontier

As described in the Tochi Valley article, military operations continued on the North-West Frontier during the Great War. They were a result of religious appeals to potentially dissident tribesmen for a Jihad or Holy War against the British as well as the usual economic reasons that the tribesmen had for the accumulation of arms and wealth. At first the local militias dealt with the situation as seen in the Tochi Valley fight, and in fact the earliest notable incident was in October 1914 involving the Kurram Militia. This militia recruited Shia Turi tribesmen who lived in the Kurram Valley and who were surrounded by Sunni tribes.

Jagi tribesmen attacked a Post and wounded a British officer. For gallantry displayed in responding to this situation No. 4256 Sowar Sarwar Ali, Kurram Militia, was awarded an **Indian Order of Merit, 2nd Class**: *For his conspicuous bravery while under fire during an engagement between the Jagis and the Kurram Militia which took place at Lakkatigga Post on the 4th October 1914, when he dragged Lieutenant C.A. Boyle, Kurram Militia, for a considerable distance until they were under cover. This act was performed under close fire.*

Two of Sarwar Ali's companions in the Kurram Militia received the **Indian Distinguished Service Medal** as a result of gallant acts in skirmishes; they were Subadar Said Asghar in 1914 and Jemadar Faqir Hassan in 1915.

After the Tochi Valley fight British and Indian Army units were regularly deployed into hostile areas, as we saw in the Miramshah fight against the Khostwals.

The Tochi Valley, November 1915

In September 1915 the 45th Rattray's Sikhs had taken over a number of posts from the 87th Punjabis. One of these posts was Khajuri Kach in the Gomal Valley, and on 18th November a detachment of the Sikhs from that post moved to a picquet position where an Up Militia Convoy to Tanai could be protected. Around 100 Mahsuds were lying in wait and the picquet party was ambushed. The Sikhs held their ground losing five sepoys and 2nd Lieutenant S.F. Criper, Indian Army Reserve of Officers, and nine sepoys wounded. However all the wounded, bodies and weapons were brought back safely to Khajuri Kach and the Up convoy was passed through safely on that day; on the following day the Down convoy also passed through without interference. For gallantry displayed the **Indian Distinguished Service Medal** was awarded to Jemadar Mehar Singh and No. 1121 Sepoy Puran Singh, both of 45th Rattray's Sikhs.

Fighting the Bunerwals

In mid-August 1915 reports came in of a mullah named Haji Sahib of Turangzai who had collected several thousand Buner tribesmen in the Ambela Pass with the intention of invading British territory; some of the tribesmen were from the Wahabi sect known as the Hindustani Fanatics. Immediately a small column moved out from Mardan to Rustam, which was reached on 16th August. General S.F. Crocker commanded at Rustam and his force consisted of 143 lances of the 13th Duke of Connaught's Lancers (Watson's Horse), 328 lances of the 14th Murray's Jat Lancers and 440 rifles of the Guides Infantry under Major A.H. Buist MVO.

Crocker's men dug-in all night and next day at 1330 hours they observed a tremendous enemy lashkar[8] displaying 25 standards advancing towards them down the nullah[9] from Surkhawi. The lashkar was in a line about three kilometres wide and 50 metres deep, and it was advancing directly onto

---

8   Assembly of fighting men.

9   Watercourse, usually dry, often with steep sides containing gulleys.

Rustam. Crocker ordered an attack and moved the cavalry to both sides of the nullah; the Guides infantry also occupied both flanks of the nullah.

At that moment the 91st Field Battery, Royal Field Artillery, arrived with its horses in a very distressed state as it had force-marched to get to Rustam. The horses had just enough strength left to pull the guns onto a ridge 800 metres beyond the camp. The battery opened fire at 1,500 metres range and caused havoc amongst the lashkar, which scattered. The Guides infantry moved up to pick off enemy stragglers but became embroiled in close-quarter fighting with Buner ghazis[10] who laid in wait in gulleys. Despite this the Guides only lost two men killed and two wounded, but one of the killed was 2nd Lieutenant C.G.H.R. Macnamara, Indian Army Reserve of Officers, who was over-run by seven of the enemy. At nightfall the Buners withdrew and later acknowledged the loss of 70 men dead and 70 others wounded.

As the Guides withdrew from the foothills No. 4744 Havildar Kishan Singh, Guides Infantry, was suddenly attacked by three ghazis as he moved his section across a small nullah. Major Buist later reported: He turned about and closed with them. Having bayoneted two, although severely wounded by sword-cuts in four places, he succeeded in killing the third Ghazi with a downward blow of his rifle on the man's head, smashing his rifle in the act. His wounds are such as to make it very probable that he will be invalided out of the Service. Kishan Singh was awarded the **Indian Order of Merit, 2nd Class**.

After the Rustam action many more units were moved into the area. A feature of this little campaign was the tremendous heat, which affected many of the soldiers from British Army units. General Nigel Woodyatt later wrote in his book *Under Ten Viceroys*: So many British soldiers fell down with heatstroke that the rearguard could hardly move. The stretcher-bearers were so overcome themselves that they were useless. It was then that the splendid Guides, and later the 84th Pioneers, came forward and volunteered to carry the sick, while officers, mounted and dismounted, as well as men in the ranks, took over the rifles and accoutrements of those hors de combat.

---

10 Muslim warriors.

Actions around Hafiz Khor in 1915

Mullahs in Mohmand tribal areas began preaching against Britain in late 1914 and this resulted in a series of confrontations around the area of Hafiz Khor. In April 1915 some of the Mohmands began gathering with a view to raiding Shabkadar. The garrison of Shabkadar Fort was strengthened and Queen Victoria's Own Corps of Guides (Frontier Force) (Lumsden's) marched 100 sabres of its Cavalry and 100 rifles of its Infantry into the area. Shortly afterwards the Guides Cavalry under Lieutenant C.E.T. Erskine was reconnoitring the foothills near the Ali Kandi Pass when an assailant fired at close range and killed a horse. Despite the personal risk No. 2466 Sowar Sher Muhammad, a young recruit, brought away the dismounted rider and received an **Indian Distinguished Service Medal** for his bravery. Later it was discovered that the sniper was a well-known Mohmand raider, Muhasil of Khudu Khel, whose village had been destroyed by the Guides in the Mohmand Expedition of 1908.

The Khaibar Moveable Column under Major General C.F.G. Young took to the field and met the dissidents at Hafiz Khor on 18th April. A heavy engagement followed and the 21st and 72nd Punjabis on the left flank were ordered to withdraw. The 1st Duke of York's Own Lancers (Skinner's Horse) covered this flank and became involved in the fighting.

Risaldar Faiz Muhammad Khan, 1st Lancers, was awarded an **Indian Order of Merit, 2nd Class**: *For conspicuous gallantry at Hafiz Khor on 18th April 1915. In face of an advancing enemy, this Indian officer, with 2nd Lieutenant Harrison, searched a nullah in which two wounded sepoys had informed them that a wounded man was lying. They were unable to find the wounded man and came back to the spot where the two sepoys were awaiting their return. These two sepoys were exhausted and unable to move. Risaldar Faiz Muhammad Khan and a sowar lifted them onto their horses and galloped away. After going some 150 yards, the sowar's horse fell and Risaldar Faiz Muhammad Khan dismounted to help the sowar. They mounted again and rode off with the exhausted sepoys, under a close and heavy rifle fire.*

No. 1735 Sowar Nishan Ali was the sowar who assisted Faiz Muhammad Khan that day and he received the **Indian Distinguished Service Medal**.

For this action, another **Indian Order of Merit, 2nd Class**, was awarded to Kot Dafadar Muhammad Fazil, 6th Mule Corps: *For conspicuous gallantry at Hafiz Khor on 18th April 1915. This non-commissioned officer brought in a* *badly wounded man from the firing line, under fire from a distance of about 150 yards. He was cool and collected, showed great resource throughout and rendered valuable assistance in collecting ammunition mules which would otherwise have been lost.*

By late August 1915 the Mohmands were again concentrating for action and the 1st Infantry Brigade under Brigadier General L.C. Dunsterville, a formation of the 1st Peshawar Division commanded by Major General F. Campbell CB DSO, met the tribesmen near Hafiz Khor. On 5th September, after an artillery preparation, the infantry attacked the sangars that the tribesmen had built. The Risalpur Cavalry Brigade came up on the left flank where the 1st Infantry Brigade was fighting and started a dismounted action. The 1st Duke of York's Own Lancers (Skinner's Horse) also became embroiled in heavy fighting on the left.

The enemy strength was estimated at between 10,000 to 12,000 men and as the tribesmen had come down from their hills the British cavalry saw an opportunity. At 1110 hours two squadrons of the British Army 21st Empress of India's Lancers and one squadron of the 14th Murray's Jat Lancers charged. General Dunsterville later commented: 'It was one of those rare occasions on the frontier when the enemy comes down on to flat ground and give the cavalry a chance of which they cannot omit to take advantage, but unfortunately the cavalry in this case had to charge with their left on an almost impassable irrigation channel, on the other side of which were high sugar-cane crops concealing a body of the enemy who fired at short range into their left flank. It seemed to me to have been one of those unavoidable pieces of bad luck of which one has to take one's share in war-time.'

During the action a Shoeing Smith in the 21st Lancers, Private Charles Hull, saved an officer from certain death and for this act he was awarded a **Victoria Cross** with the citation: *For most conspicuous bravery. When under close fire of the enemy, who were within a few yards, he rescued Captain G. E. D. Learoyd, whose horse had been shot, by taking him up behind him and galloping into safety. Shoeing-Smith Hull acted entirely on his own initiative, and saved his officer's life at the imminent risk of his own.*

Three men of the 21st Lancers were awarded the **Distinguished Conduct Medal** and their citations show how serious the fighting was. No. 4815 Regimental Serjeant Major E. N. Ryder: *For conspicuous gallantry, when he picked up a comrade who was hanging by his foot from the stirrup, placed him on his own horse, and charged through the enemy, by whom he was surrounded.*

3764 Saddler Staff Serjeant W. A. Simpson: *For conspicuous gallantry. He dismounted and rescued a comrade by shooting a tribesman, and then went on foot to the assistance of an officer of his regiment and held off the enemy with his revolver. The officer was mortally wounded, and Serjeant Simpson was hit in the shoulder and badly hacked about by swordsmen before he was rescued by some other men of the regiment.*

No. 861 Lance-Corporal R. A. Ballard: *For conspicuous gallantry, when he endeavoured to save his commanding officer, whose horse had been shot, and afterwards kept the enemy away from his body until he could secure help to bring it in.*

It appears that Lance Corporal Ballard then rode up to the Commanding Officer of the 1st Lancers, Lieutenant Colonel P. Holland-Prior, for assistance and Holland-Prior took Captain A.A.H. Beaman (1st Lancers) and 2nd Lieutenant J.A. Ewart (Indian Army Reserve of Officers), to assist in the recovery of Lieutenant Colonel J.B. Scriven of the 21st Lancers. In fact Colonel Scriven was dead but his body was recovered and Pomeroy Holland-Pryor and Ardern Arthur Hulme Beaman were later admitted to Companionship of the **Distinguished Service Order**. James Alan Ewart received a **Military Cross**. Citations were not published for these three awards.

Meanwhile the sowars of the 1st Lancers were extricating wounded and dismounted troopers of the 21st Lancers from the battlefield, and Jemadar Ruknuddin and No. 961 Trumpeter Abdul Majid, both of the 1st Lancers, were awarded the **Indian Distinguished Service Medal** in recognition of their gallantry in these duties.

The squadron of 14th Murray's Jat Lancers that had also charged was in the thick of things and two men were awarded the **Indian Order of Merit, 2nd Class**, for bravery displayed. Jemadar Rati Ram's citation read: *For conspicuous bravery in action at Hafiz Khor on the 5th September 1915. When retiring from the hills, he saw a trooper of the 21st Lancers who had lost his horse and was thoroughly exhausted; he took him up on his horse and carried him away under very heavy fire. The ground was rough and the trooper fell off three times but Jemadar Rati Ram helped him up again each time.*

No. 2664 Sowar Dhan Singh received his similar award: *For conspicuous bravery in action at Hafiz Khor on the 5th September 1915. When retiring from the hills he saw a comrade whose horse had come down and was left 300 yards behind in the direction of the rapidly advancing enemy. He galloped back and brought in the man on the horse under a heavy fire.*

The British units had suffered over 100 casualties on 5th September, 24 of them fatal, but the Mohmands had been repulsed and the tribesmen withdrew to regroup, but not for long. In early October they came down from the hills again to Hafiz Khor where General Campbell attacked them with his 1st Peshawar Division. The Queen Victoria's Own Corps of Guides (Frontier Force) (Lumsden's) were now in the field at Hafiz Khor and Subadar Major Alam Khan *Bahadur* IOM, Corps of Guides Infantry, was promoted to the **Indian Order of Merit, 1st Class**[11]: *For exceptionally fine leadership in action, both on the Mohmand and Buner borders and for conspicuous bravery in action near Hafiz Khor on the 8th October 1915 when by his coolness, courage and good example he succeeded in getting away a large number of dead and wounded men of his company together with their rifles and equipment, whilst in an exposed position under heavy fire.*

Major Ivan Urmston Battye, Corps of Guides Infantry, was shot in the stomach whilst recovering wounded men in the same action; he probably survived because he was suffering from dysentery and so had not eaten anything that day. He was admitted to the Companionship of the **Distinguished Service Order**. No. 4442 Havildar Taj Muhammad and No. 5312 Sepoy Jagtu[12] were awarded the **Indian Distinguished Service Medal**. Subadar Romala and six men of the Guides had been killed or died of wounds and twelve sepoys had been wounded, but the enemy tribesmen had suffered 1,400 casualties and the survivors melted away back to their villages. After a British blockade prevented unauthorised movement the tribal leaders submitted to British authority in April 1916, and were fined Rupees 30,000.

The 30th Punjabis had also been in action as part of the 4th Infantry Brigade, and during operations around Hafiz Khor two men, Subadar Muhammad Khan, 29th Punjabis attached to 30th Punjabis, and No. 439 Havildar Sher Khan, displayed gallantry that resulted in the award of the **Indian Distinguished Service Medal**.

---

11 Alam Khan had been awarded an Indian Order of Merit, 3rd Class, for gallantry displayed during the Pathan Revolt near Inayat Kila, Bajour, in September 1897. He appears to have been the only officer or other rank who was advanced from the (pre 1912) 3rd Class directly to the (post 1912) 1st Class. This was an entirely rational progression following the move to a reduced two-class IOM structure in 1912.

12 Jagtu was also later awarded the French *Medaille Militaire*.

Fighting in the Swat Valley

On 20th August 1915 news came in of over 15,000 belligerent Swati tribesmen marching down from the Upper Swat Valley. To counter this the Malakand Moveable Column under Brigadier General W.G.L. Beynon CB DSO, moved from Chakdara up onto the Landakai Ridge and prepared defences. The Ridge controlled the Landakai Pass that the Swatis had to use. The left-half of the 2nd Battalion of the 1st King George's Own Gurkha Rifles (The Malaun Regiment) and the 46th Punjabis held the outer posts on the Ridge. All picqueting troops were under the command of Lieutenant Colonel G.H.G. Mockler, 46th Punjabis.

On the night of the 28th-29th August the whole line of the picquets was attacked from 2115 hours until dawn. One small picquet post commanded by Colour Havildar Jagatsher Gurung, 2/1st Gurkhas, was attacked by Swatis silently crawling up to the loopholes, but the Gurkhas fought off the attackers and when daylight arrived several dead bodies were found along with blood-trails showing that other bodies and wounded men had been dragged away. Jagatsher Gurung was awarded the **Indian Distinguished Service Medal**. In a report General Campbell had commended him: *For courage, coolness, and general military ability. He was in command of No. 3 Picquet of the outpost line, which owing to lack of time and material at hand, was in an uncompleted state. The picquet held 26 men, and it was here the enemy attack commenced at 10.15 PM, and the picquet was hotly engaged by superior numbers until 4 AM. Colour Havildar Jagat Sher repulsed four determined attacks when the enemy charged right up to the walls.*

Elsewhere on the picquet line the 46th Punjabis were involved in fierce fighting and three officers of that regiment were also awarded the **Indian Distinguished Service Medal**; they were Subadar Major Habibullah Khan, Subadar Badi-ul-Zaman and Subadar Abdul Ghafur Khan. At Subedar Major Habibullah's picquet an enemy standard bearer had been shot down at a distance of ten paces, and after first light the Punjabis seized the standard. General Campbell reported: *Subadar Major Habibullah Khan, 46th Punjabis, commanded No. 8 Picquet in the line of outposts. A large proportion of the 62 men in the picquet were young soldiers of less than one year's service, but under the leadership of the Subadar Major behaved admirably, and fire was kept well under control. The enemy left seven corpses and a standard next to the sangar.*

When dawn broke the right-half of the 2/1st Gurkhas and a wing of the 82nd Punjabis brought ammunition forward and reinforced the picquet line whilst No. 6 Company Sappers and Miners and two companies of the 94th Russell's Infantry strengthened the defences. The remainder of the Moveable Column destroyed Swati villages and fortifications and a section of the 25th Mountain Battery was deployed to disperse tribesmen who had located themselves above the northernmost picquet on Landakai Ridge. Later Jemadar Kehar Singh and No. 281 Naik Muhammad Khan, both of 25th Mountain Battery, and Subadar Major Afzal Khan, *Bahadur*, 82nd Punjabis, received a **Mention in Despatches**. The Swatis sniped the British positions for the next five days and nights and then withdrew. The Moveable Column returned to Chakdara on 5th September and deployed searchlights at night to deter snipers.

On 27th October the Malakand Moveable Column was in action again from Chakdara Camp; on this occasion the Temporary Column Commander was Lieutenant Colonel C.C. Luard, 1st Battalion The Durham Light Infantry. A lashkar of up to 3,000 Bajauras was advancing on Chakdara but Colonel Luard deployed his Durham Light Infantry as Advance Guard and when in a suitable position it used machine gun and musketry fire to cover an attack by the 46th Punjabis. An enemy standard was captured and the lashkar was dispersed. Chakdara Camp was not threatened again during the remaining months of 1915. Colonel Luard later received a **Mention in Despatches**.

Jemadar Indar Singh, 25th Punjabis, an officer who had received the Musketry Certificate (Indian Ranks) and who had passed the Course of Transport Instruction was detached from his regiment and employed on the North-West Frontier during 1915 to 1916, and he was awarded the **Indian Distinguished Service Medal**.

The 31st Duke of Connaught's Own Lancers was involved in operations in 1916 to 1917 and Captain W.G.H. Vickers, Risaldar Hakim Khan and Jemadar Abaji Rao Mahadik all received a **Mention in Despatches**. A similar **Mention** was given to Major C.R.S. Bradley, 4th Cavalry, who was attached to the Royal Flying Corps.

Fighting tribal raiders in Jhalawan, Baluchistan

In Baluchistan the Princely Ruler the Khan of Kalat did not possess sufficient power to enforce his rule throughout his state. During May 1915 the Khan's treasury at Khozdar, 180 kilometres south of Kalat, had been looted at the instigation of Sardar Khan Muhammad, the premier chief of Jhalawan.

Lieutenant Colonel Arthur Le Grand Jacob CIE DSO, commanding the 106th Hazara Pioneers, was ordered to take a small column of his Pioneers and a detachment of Sappers & Miners into Kalat to show the flag. Jacob fell sick and Major G.L. Carter, 106th Hazara Pioneers, took over command. Major Carter achieved his mission of reducing tensions and after six weeks of marching through Kalat in hot weather his column returned to Quetta on 19th June. Colonel Jacob later received a **Mention in Despatches**.

In early 1916 an aggressive band of Jhalawans again started marauding in Kalat and a stronger force was ordered to march into the state from Mastung Road to deal with the situation. The role of the troops was to escort the Political Agent in Kalat, Lieutenant Colonel A.B. Dew CSI CIE, and to assist him in restoring order. The new commanding officer of the 106th Hazara Pioneers, Lieutenant Colonel G.L. Carter, marched via Kalat to Jhalawan with 250 of his Pioneers, a section of two mountain guns, a section of a Field Ambulance and an officer and 29 men of the 3rd Gwalior Lancers (Imperial Service Troops).

On 29th June 1916 a small group of Pioneers and dismounted Gwalior Lancers, supported by Risaldar Khan Sahib Ghulam of the Kalat State Forces, tracked down a group of raiders and killed 21 of the 22 men that they surprised. Over-confidence appears to have set in with the Pioneers and they continued their search for the raider leader named Nuri. But the raiders confronted the Pioneers and Lancers in bushy country and the Pioneers' Adjutant, the Canadian Captain Elmes Pollock Henderson was shot dead; Captain R.B. Pargiter, Royal Garrison Artillery was wounded and evacuated. A Pioneer sepoy was mortally wounded and carried back to the British camp, further reducing the number of rifles available to engage the enemy.

A withdrawal was made and later three awards of the **Indian Order of Merit, 2nd Class**, were published:

- No. 1822 Sepoy Ghulam Hussain, 106th Hazara Pioneers: *For conspicuous gallantry in charging the enemy single handed.*

- No. 2796 Sepoy Kurban, 106th Hazara Pioneers: *For conspicuous gallantry when surprised by three of the enemy in low jungle. Although severely wounded, he killed two of them and put the third to flight.*

- No. 1120 Sowar Ibrahim, Gwalior State Lancers: *For conspicuous gallantry in standing by a wounded officer.*

Those three men also received a **Mention in Despatches**[13] as did Lieutenant Colonel G.L. Carter, Captain E.P. Henderson, No. 1465 Sepoy Abdul Hakim, No. 1437 Naik Abdul Karim, No. 2091 Sepoy Hajji Muhammad, No. 43 Havildar Kalbi Hussain, Subadar Muhammad Hassan and Subadar Wali Muhammad, all of the 106th Hazara Pioneers. Also **Mentioned** were Risaldar Khan Sahib Ghulam Nabi, Kalat State Forces, Captain R.B. Pargiter, Royal Garrison Artillery and Lieutenant Colonel A.B. Dew CSI CIE, the Political Agent.

This had been another operation undertaken in the hot weather, but by mid-August order had been restored in Kalat and the column returned to Mastung Road on the 22nd of that month. Lieutenant Colonel Godfrey Lambert Carter was appointed to be a Companion of the **Order of the Indian Empire** (CIE).

1916 – The Mohmand Blockade

During the first half of 1916 military activities on the North-West Frontier were confined to countering cross-border raiders from Afghanistan, as the large lashkars previously incited by Mullahs did not appear. However in the second half of the year Mohmand raiders began disturbing North-West Frontier Province again and so a permanent blockade line was erected. Lieutenant Colonel E.W.C. Sandes' comprehensive history *The Indian Sappers and Miners* describes it:'. . . so the blockade was reimposed from a line of defensible posts and barbed wire erected by the Sappers and Miners and Engineers along the Michni-Abazai front. The posts were 400 yards apart and connected by a double apron of barbed wire fence in front of which was a curtain of live wire supplied with electric current from a power house at Abazai.'

These defensive measures prevented lashkars from easily crossing the blockade line undetected, but they did not deter small groups of wily and energetic Mahsuds from crossing silently. In his autobiographical book *Under Ten Viceroys* Major General Nigel Woodyatt explains methods that were demonstrated to him of how tribesmen crossed the blockade line. As a preliminary operation before the Mohmand Blockade was under construction three towers were built on the Khazana Gund hills on the right bank of the Swat River overlooking the Lower Swat canal headworks. The

---

13 Ghulam Hussein, Kurban and Ibrahim were also awarded the French **Croix de Guerre.**

Guides infantry with the machine gun troop of the Guides cavalry, all under Lieutenant Colonel A.H. Buist MVO, provided protection supported by a wing of the 81st Pioneers and a section of 24th Hazara Mountain Battery (Frontier Force). On 27th October Captain D.G. Sandeman and the Afridi Subadar Khiyal Gul[14], both of the Guides Infantry, covertly reconnoitred the ground and then led the troops by night in a surprise occupation of the Khazana Ridge where picquet posts were swifly built before the Mohmands could react. Both men later received a **Mention in Despatches**. The Pioneers then built the three towers whilst the 1st and 2nd Infantry Brigades under Brigadier General Lionel Dunsterville built the Blockade line. The Mohmands gathered and observed but restricted their activities to desultorily sniping the British soldiers and sepoys.

Two weeks later, on 13th November, Mohmands began collecting again at Hafiz Khor and General Campbell decided to attack them. On 15th October the British artillery targeted the tribesmen whilst Royal Flying Corps aeroplanes bombed and machine-gunned them. Brigadier General W.G.L. Benyon's 2nd Infantry Brigade, comprising the 1st Battalion of the 4th Queen's Own (Royal West Kent Regiment), 1st Battalion Durham Light Infantry, 46th Punjabis and 95th Russell's Infantry, attacked at Subhan Khwar near Shabkadr. The Durham Light Infantry was on the left of the attack line with 'A' and 'D' Companies forward and 'C' Company in support. The tribesmen fell back until 1600 hours when the Brigade began its withdrawal; this triggered a swift enemy follow-up but 'C' Company laid down heavy covering fire and the withdrawal was completed with the loss of one of the Durhams being killed and ten men wounded.

Four men of the Durham Light Infantry received gallantry awards:

No. 7975 Company Sergeant Major J. R. Kilgour was awarded the **Distinguished Conduct Medal**: *For conspicuous gallantry and devotion to duty. He carried a badly wounded N.C.O. out of action under a hot fire for a considerable distance. He set a splendid example of fearlessness and devotion to duty.*

No. 8806 Serjeant E. Deveraux, No. 11104 Corporal F.E.P. Gordon and No. 10508 Private A. Lawty were all awarded the **Military Medal**. All four men received a **Mention in Despatches** as did Captain Arthur John Clifton

---

14 After the way Khiyal Gul was murdered for 'disloyalty in supporting the British' when he went on home leave.

of the same regiment who was later appointed to be an Officer of the **Order of the British Empire** (OBE).

Actions against raiders

Men of the Khyber Rifles were in action from 1914 to 1916 and three of them were awarded the **Indian Distinguished Service Medal**: Jemadars Gul Zir and Tans Khan, and No. 1888 Havildar Shamal.

A company of the 52nd Sikhs (Frontier Force) was in action in early 1917 as part of a Moveable Column that included a squadron of 25th Cavalry (Frontier Force), a section of 30th Mountain Battery and local Militia. On two occasions raiders were trapped in caves and smoked or grenaded out to be captured or killed. No. 471 Havildar Iman Ali Khan[15], 30th Mountain Battery, was awarded the **Indian Distinguished Service Medal**. Major C.R. Wilkinson and Jemadar Nihal Singh, both 52nd Sikhs (Frontier Force) and Jemadar Sher Ali Khan IDSM, 25th Cavalry (Frontier Force) received a **Mention in Despatches**.

The Northern Waziristan Militia was in the field in August 1916 against raiders, and after a successful contact Jemadar Gul Rakhim, Northern Waziristan Militia, was awarded an **Indian Order of Merit, 2nd Class**: *For conspicuous gallantry in an encounter with a gang of raiders on the 24th August 1916. This Indian Officer was entirely responsible for the success of the operations which led to the rounding up of the gang. Jemadar Gul Rakhim was himself wounded at a range of 70 yards from the raiders' sangars but continued to conduct the operations under a hot fire with coolness and skill until final success was achieved.* Also in 1916 two men of the Northern Waziristan Militia received the **Indian Distinguished Service Medal**: Jemadar Gul Amir and No. 167 Havildar Malang Khan.

In 1916 the 116th Mahrattas was located for three months in the Tochi Forts, being employed either by the Miranshah Field Force or Brigadier General B. Fane's Bannu Brigade. During an operation against raiders the Mahrattas killed or captured 20 of the enemy for the loss of two sepoys wounded. The introduction of Lewis light machine guns and hand grenades was coming as an unpleasant surprise to some of the tribesmen. Four Mahratta private soldiers received a **Mention in Despatches**: Lal Khan, Laxuman Chaudri, Goonid Daurekar and Keshaorao Sinde.

---

15 Iman Ali Khan was also later awarded the French *Medaille Militaire*.

The attack on the Sarwekai Fort

In late February 1917 Mahsuds began gathering around the Militia post at Sarwekai in South Waziristan, and on 2nd March 2,000 tribesmen advanced on the post. The garrison commander, Major F.L. Hughes, 20th Duke of Cambridge's Own Infantry (Brownlow's Punjabis) attached to the South Waziristan Militia, had moved 100 men out to occupy Garesi Sar, a hill 1,200 metres away that was being used by long-range enemy snipers. Hughes' problem now became one of supplying Garesi Sar and he reluctantly decided to withdraw the 100 men. Hughes took 50 rifles out to a mid-way point and ordered the men on the hill to withdraw to him. However the Mahsud were waiting for this move and swiftly rushed both parties, attacking with rifles and knives. Frederick Lee Hughes and 20 of his men were killed, ten others were wounded and eleven were captured and handed over to the Mahsud womenfolk for their unpleasant attentions.

For the Militia the situation was saved by the Jowaki Afridi Subadar Mohibulla *Sardar Bahadur* IOM[16], IDSM. Mohibulla fought a successful withdrawal into the fort and held it until the Derajat Moveable Column under Brigadier General G.M. Baldwin DSO relieved Sarwekai on 9th March.

The Northern Waziristan Militia again in action against raiders

Jemadar Pat[17] Khan IDSM, Northern Waziristan Militia, conducted a very successful manoeuvre on an operation in late March 1917 resulting in the award to him of an **Indian Order of Merit, 2nd Class**: *For conspicuous gallantry in the action at Dredoni on the 27th March 1917, when his personal leading was mainly responsible for the successful action of the party he commanded. During the pursuit of the enemy, it became necessary to seize a hill directly overlooking their line of retreat. This hill was held by the enemy and Jemadar Pak Khan, on his own initiative, advanced with a section and rushed the hill, he himself reaching the top at least fifty yards ahead of his men. From the position thus gained, he was able to bring an effective fire to bear on the retreating enemy thereby inflicting considerable loss on them.*[18]

---

16 Subadar Mohibulla had been awarded the Indian Order of Merit, 3rd Class, for gallantry displayed in an action near Sarwekai on 30th June 1905.

17 In his history *The Frontier Scouts* Charles Chevenix Trench uses the forename 'Pak' although compilers of medal lists use 'Pat'.

18 Pat Khan was also awarded the French Croix de Guerre, but he was a leader of mutinous Wazir Militiamen in 1919 and his awards were forfeited.

India's Western Frontier in March 1917.

Although since the war began all the British and Indian units on the western frontier had been continually tasked with sending drafts or specialists to other theatres of war, these units had quickly taken in more recruits and trained them, often "on the job". Also mechanisation had been introduced with the use of supply lorries, armoured cars and military aircraft. The frontier had not been allowed to erupt into open warfare. Similar operations against dissidents in Burma, Muscat and Seistan in south-east Persia had quelled problems in those locations. But this was becoming a longer war than many people had initially assumed it would be, and fighting on India's western frontier was to continue well beyond the 1918 Armistices with the Central Powers.

End note

If readers wish to understand more of operations on the North-West Frontier at this time an excellent book is *Frontier Fighters. On Active Service in Waziristan. The Memoirs of Major Walter James Cummings*. Edited by Jules Stewart and published by Pen & Sword Military in 2010.

The Actions at Shimber Berris, Somaliland
November 1914 to February 1915
Indian Sepoys fighting with the Somaliland Camel Corps

British Somaliland in 1914

During the latter half of 1914 millions of people around the world began to live in a state of war, but this was not the case for the people of the British Somaliland Protectorate. This territory, located 250 kilometres south of the strategic port of Aden, had been enduring savage periods of war for the previous 15 years whilst a renegade named the 'Mad Mullah' and his tribesmen-followers fought British troops. However this man was not mad, nor was he a Mullah, but he was an early type of 'freedom fighter' who possessed a vicious and cruel streak, particularly towards those of his fellow Somalis who did not immediately and openly support him in his aim of getting rid of the foreigners on Somali soil.

The "Mullah's" name was Mahomed Bin Abdulla Hassan, a Somali who declared himself to be the expected Mahdi (Guided One) and who declared jihad or religious war against the foreign occupiers of Somaliland. By a combination of strength of personality, military prowess, cruelty and guile the Mullah continued to survive despite five British military expeditions having been mounted against him and his followers who were named Dervishes. In 1910 the British authorities had, in desperation and in order to cut costs in a territory that had no integral wealth, adopted a 'Coastal Concentration' policy whereby the Mullah was left to roam the interior at will whilst the British defended the coastal ports with Indian troops from the Aden Garrison.

In 1911, in an attempt to halt the anarchy spreading throughout the Protectorate an armed force was re-constituted, the previous local force, 6th King's African Rifles, having been disbanded in 1910. The new organisation was a local camel-mounted police force named the Somali Constabulary. The Constabulary was not a military unit but regrettably it was used as one against a strong Dervish force in 1913 when the Dervishes killed the British commander and defeated the Constabulary detachment that opposed them in an action at Dul Madoba, south-east of Burao.

The Somaliland Camel Corps

That defeat led to a re-appraisal of what was needed, and a new unit named the Somaliland Camel Corps (SCC) was raised, and was categorised as being a military unit within the King's African Rifles. The SCC was designed to enforce government policies in the interior, and after an attempt to recruit Sudanese and Arab soldiers had failed it was eventually composed of:

- Two 150-man strong companies of camel-mounted Somalis.
- One 150-man company of Somalis mounted on ponies.
- One 150-man company of camel-mounted soldiers seconded from the Indian Army.
- 250 infantry soldiers seconded from the Indian Army and used primarily for garrison duties in the interior.
- The Somali companies had one machine gun each and the Indian mounted company had two machine guns.

The Somaliland Camel Corps was garrisoned at Burao (military headquarters), Las Dureh and Sheikh. A Temporary Contingent of 150 Sepoys from Aden garrisoned the chief town and port in the Protectorate, Berbera, and one or two of the minor ports. Experienced and proven European and Indian officers were seconded from both the British and Indian Armies.

The soldiers wore a khaki puggree (cloth head dress looking like a turban), a greenish-brown singlet, khaki shorts and blue puttees (cloth gaiters covering the lower legs). Initially the mounted Somalis did not wear boots. This dress provided excellent camouflage in the dry, dusty, thorn-bush scrub that covered much of Somaliland. Somali ponies were used and apart from one company mounted on Arab camels all the other riding camels were Egyptian. The leather saddlery for camels was the Bikaner pattern from India whilst the pony saddlery came from England.

The men were armed with modern short-pattern rifles and extra-long bayonets to compensate for the short length of the rifle. At first rifle magazine-loading was not taught, as single-shot loading conserved ammunition in situations when there were no supply columns to quickly replenish ammunition expenditure. Ammunition was standard British military issue and tampering with the bullet-heads to produce a 'dum-dum' expansion effect was prohibited. Each mounted man carried 260 rounds in his saddlebag and another 140 in three bandoliers worn around the waist and across both shoulders.

The mounted men carried a water bottle and animal watering gear; a haversack; two water chaguls (skin or canvas containers – for camels only); a blanket; a waterproof sheet; a Gudimo (bush axe); a hobble; rations for man and beast for 5 days; and in the bottle and chaguls water for himself for 3 days. To ensure that the pony men could react and move quickly their reserves of water, food and ammunition were distributed amongst the camels. The Somalis were used to living frugally on camel milk and a few dates if necessary, and when thirsty they often relished drinking spring or well water that was so brackish, saline or polluted by stock that the Europeans could not stomach it.

The Forts at Shimber Berris

By 1914 the 'Mullah' was no longer a young fleet-footed hawk of the desert, and he had both physical and mental impairments. It was believed that in his youth the 'Mullah' had received surgery on his head by a tribal doctor, and that resulted in an unsettled temperament; as he grew older a disease such as elephantiasis appears to have afflicted him, leading to obesity. But whatever the reasons, the 'Mullah' had decided to follow a more static and less-mobile lifestyle.

The Dervishes brought over experienced builders and masons from Yemen to construct fortresses that could withstand attacks by the British weapons that so far had been deployed against them. A massive fort was built at Tale, east of Jidballi and near the Italian border, but of more concern to the British were six small but strong forts built at Shimber Berris at the head of the Ain Valley that led into the large Nogal Valley. The stone fort walls were nearly 4 metres wide at the base and the three largest structures were each up to 9 metres high, with overhanging galleries supported by strong timber baulks. These forts were extensively loop-holed to allow defensive rifle fire to cover all the surrounding ground. The forts could each hold 50 or more defenders and were sited to cover the approaches to Shimber Berris. Below the forts was a very steep-sided valley a kilometre wide; at the valley base was the Shimber Berris well and the three smaller forts that guarded it. The steep valley sides were honeycombed with caves that provided good defensive positions and concealment for Dervish snipers.

Shimber Berris was used as a base that allowed the Dervishes to raid the herds of tribesmen friendly to the British who occupied the region nearer the Somaliland coast. On 12th March 1914 a Dervish party even raided the Somali residential and trading area of Berbera, forcing the British authorities to respond.

The first attack on Shimber Berris

In November 1914 a force was organised to attack the Dervishes at Shimber Berris. The British troop dispositions in Somaliland were:

Berbera - Garrisoned by 150 Sepoys of the 75th Carnatic Infantry from Aden (the Indian Temporary Contingent).

Las Dureh - Garrisoned by 100 infantry Sepoys of the Indian Contingent SCC.

Sheikh - Garrisoned by 50 infantry Sepoys of the Indian Contingent SCC.

Burao - Concentrated here were:
- Force Headquarters commanded by Lieutenant Colonel T. A. Cubbitt DSO, Royal Artillery;
- 'A' Company SCC – 100 Indian soldiers on camels;
- the two Somali camel companies and the one Somali pony company (a total of 450 men);
- the remaining 100 infantry Sepoys of the SCC as Burao garrison;
- the SCC Depot Company (50 Somalis).

Cubitt's offensive column left Burao on 17th November and two days later was within 5 kilometres of Shimber Berris before the Dervishes realised that it posed a threat. The column's animals were placed in a zareba (enclosure made of felled thorn bushes) on top of the ridge that was being used for the advance, and a guard of 200 men stayed with the animals. The three larger forts were visible, two on the ridge to Cubitt's front and one on another spur; as yet the British were unaware of the small forts below that guarded the Shimber Berris wells.

Cubitt ordered Lieutenant C.A.L. Howard, 32nd Lancers, to charge the nearest fort with his dismounted 'A' Company Indian Sepoys; this fort was secured, primarily because its standing garrison was taken by surprise and did not man the defences. But the next fort to be attacked, by Captain A. Carton de Wiart, 4th (Royal Irish) Dragoon Guards, and his dismounted 'C' Company of Somalis, proved to be a much tougher proposition. The defenders were ready and there was no easy access into the fort. Heavy machine gun fire supported the attackers but three British charges failed to get inside the fort; all the British junior officers joined in the final charge. Carton de Wiart was severely wounded in an eye, which he later lost, and Captain H.W. Symons, King's Own Yorkshire Light Infantry, was shot dead whilst within a metre of the fort doorway. Major A.S. Lawrence, 1st County of London Yeomanry, received an arm wound. Throughout these charges the Dervish defenders taunted their attackers.

Cubitt realised that he was under-resourced for this kind of fighting and he withdrew his force and camped at Little Bohotle 13 kilometres to the south. The Dervishes did not interfere with Cubitt's retirement as they were licking their many wounds from the machine gun fire that had entered fort loopholes, and were re-organising themselves. Meanwhile a messenger was speeding to Burao to order that one of the two 7-pounder mountain guns there be despatched as fast as possible to Cubitt's camp. In past encounters with the Dervishes these old guns had been packed on or pulled by camels, and had figured prominently as the only artillery pieces permanently in Somaliland. Why Cubitt, himself a horse-gunner, did not initially deploy one or both guns with his column is not known, but probably he had little idea of the strength of the Dervish forts until he saw them.

From Burao, Jemadar Feroze Khan of the 56th Punjabi Rifles, Indian Contingent SCC, rapidly marched a camel-mounted gun and 40 Sepoys to the British camp; the Naik (local Havildar) in charge of the gun was No. 293 Shan Khan, 76th Punjabis, Indian Contingent SCC. The gun arrived on the evening of 21st November and on the 23rd Cubitt ordered Captain H.C. Dobbs, 124th Duchess of Connaught's Own Baluchistan Infantry, to attack all three visible forts using the gun and two dismounted SCC Companies. Again the first fort was seized without a fight, and this time the second fort was abandoned after a few artillery rounds had been fired at it from 500 metres range. The approach to the third fort was difficult as a detour of over 6 kilometres had to be made around ravines, but again a few rounds into the fort walls from very close range, and one through an observation slit, made the garrison flee. Later interrogation of captured Dervishes found that although the artillery rounds hitting the forts were not killing or wounding the defenders, the concussive effects of the bombardments significantly demoralised them. Later the Mullah further significantly demoralised these unfortunates by castrating them for deserting their posts.

The gun then engaged a small fort that could be seen 250 metres below in the valley, and the defenders there fled once Shan Khan started hitting the walls and roof. By now Cubitt had several badly wounded officers and men on his hands but no doctor with him, and he did not have the explosives needed to properly demolish all the forts and blockhouses, so he withdrew his force to Burao. Within two weeks the Dervishes re-occupied all their defensive structures, but the Mullah ensured that only fresh men were in the new garrison. Cubitt had lost 1 officer and 5 Somalis killed, and 2 officers, 1 Indian Sepoy and 24 Somalis wounded; several of the wounds were serious. Over 21,000 rounds of rifle ammunition, over 10,000 rounds of machine gun rounds and 34 artillery shells had been fired. Cubitt had achieved as much as he could with the resources in his column; in his after-action report he commented that explosives and specialists were needed, and any future attacking column would need to occupy the Shimber Berris area for four or five days in order for all the structures to be effectively demolished.

Awards for the first action

Companion of the Distinguished Service Order

- Captain Adrian Carton de Wiart - For the gallantry that he had displayed when attacking on 19th November.

Indian Distinguished Service Medal

- Jemadar Feroze Khan, 56th Punjabi Rifles- Feroze Khan had been prominent in the seizing of the three forts on 23rd November.

- Naik (Local Havildar) Shan Khan, 76th Punjabis.

Mentioned in Despatches

- Major G.H. Summers, 26th (King George's Own) Light Cavalry.

- Captain H.C. Dobbs, 124th Duchess of Connaught's Own Baluchistan Light Infantry.

- Jemadar Feroze Khan, 56th Punjabi Rifles

- No. 293 Naik (Local Havildar), 76th Punjabis, both of the Indian Contingent Somaliland Camel Corps.

Preparations for the second move against Shimber Berris

Aden military headquarters was sympathetic to requests made by Cubitt and Captain W.A.H. Bird, 23rd Sikh Pioneers, was despatched to Somaliland with 29 of his Pioneers, gun cotton explosive and hand grenades. Bird and his men arrived at Burao on 29th January 1915, allowing Cubitt to advance a force against the Shimber Berris fortifications on the following day.

This time preparations were made to allow a longer stay on the objective. A Medical Officer, Lieutenant R.E. Drake-Brockman, Royal Army Medical Corps, accompanied the column; Lieutenant H.B. Davidson, 10th Gurkha Rifles[19], was the Transport Officer and Lieutenant G.J.J. Johnston, 32nd Lancers, commanded the Water Column. Cubitt's principal staff officers were unchanged: Brevet Major G.H. Summers, 26th (King George's Own) Light Cavalry and Captain H.L. Ismay, 21st Prince Albert Victor's Own Cavalry (Frontier Force), (Daly's Horse). His Majesty's Commissioner and Commander-in-Chief Somaliland Protectorate, G.F. Archer, accompanied the force.

Cubitt prepared two columns. The Mounted Column of 12 officers, 357 men, 5 machine guns and 5 days' rations moved with 388 riding camels and

---

19 The regiment still used the title '10th Goorkha Rifles'.

38 ponies; because of insufficient water on the route the remainder of the Pony Company SCC were dismounted. The Dismounted Column marched with 5 officers, 324 men, two 7-pounder guns, 1 machine gun, 8 ponies, 222 transport camels (8 of these camels being spares), and 6 days' rations. As always in Somaliland irregular pony-mounted scouts named Illalos were employed for reconnaissance and flank protection duties. Irregular riflemen from friendly tribes were engaged to garrison staging points and the objective after its capture.

To provide the necessary water at Ber, a staging point about half-way between Burao and Shimber Berris, 18 new wells were dug in advance. The tanks of water carried on the Water Column transport camels each held nearly 38 litres when full but the cans inevitably leaked. The water ration was: British Officers – 4 to a tank; Indians and Somalis of all ranks – 10 to a tank; ponies – 4 to a tank. Camels were watered when it was available from wells.

The standard load for a transport camel weighed 145 kilograms; all these camels were hired locally at Burao along with one attendant for each three camels. Six camels (plus two of the spares held ready for emergencies) carried the two 7-pounder guns whilst nine others carried 250 artillery shells; nine camels carried the force reserve rifle and machine gun ammunition and nine other camels carried the Pioneers' explosives and tools.

The second attack on Shimber Berris

On 2nd February 1915, Cubitt concentrated his force five kilometres from Shimber Berris. He had to destroy the top three forts before he could go down into the valley below to destroy the blockhouses; this job was made easy as the forts were not occupied, but the new foundations of a much larger fort were discovered on the ridge. The Dervishes had obviously hoped that the new fort, when completed, would withstand artillery shells. Whilst the 23rd Sikh Pioneers demolished the top forts the Dervishes sniped from caves below the plateau.

The morning of the following day was spent in moving the entire British force around to the other side of the valley in order to use a track that led down to Shimber Berris well. Friendly tribesmen secured the ridgeline and the nearest water holes. Once down in the valley Cubitt could see that two forts overlooked and flanked the water course and a third central one commanded the far end; Dervish snipers were also manning many of the caves that were now above the British troops on both sides of the valley. Whilst the two 7-pounder guns engaged the central fort the flanking forts were each attacked by a SSC company. Both flanking forts were captured by 1500 hours; they were not destroyed but used as cover for riflemen and machine gunners who supported attacks on the caves that the two attacking companies now made.

By 1600 hours many Dervishes could be seen fleeing from the caves and the remaining fort. Cubitt ordered a company to charge the fort, which it did, but it could not gain access. Whilst the company riflemen and supporting machine gunners provided covering fire the 23rd Sikh Pioneers laid charges at the fort doorway. Effective fire came from the fort's remaining defenders making the Pioneers' work extremely hazardous. No. 4584 Havildar Teja Singh and No. 4392 Naik Sher Singh of the 23rd Sikh Pioneers were later awarded the Indian Order of Merit, 2nd Class, for the gallantry that they displayed on 4th February 1915.

The effect of the explosives collapsed the top half of the fort onto the bottom half; burying and killing the 10 brave Dervish defenders who had remained to fight it out. Concurrently Lieutenant Howard and his 'A' (Indian) Company SCC were grenading and clearing the caves on the slopes above; whilst engaged in this activity Howard was wounded. Cubitt ordered the two flanking forts to be demolished, and after the dust had settled on those explosions the force withdrew to a zariba.

Whilst the Illalos had behaved as ordered the friendly tribesmen had come down off the ridge-lines during the cave clearances in attempts to get hold of Dervish rifles, and the presence of these friendlies had hampered Howard's men. But next morning when the force returned to the battleground all the caves were found to be empty of live Dervishes, although the bodies of 32 men were found there, including those of the Dervish commander and his second-in-command. Cubitt had lost three Other Ranks killed and three officers and ten other ranks wounded. Captain W. Lowry-Corry, 23rd Cavalry (Frontier Force), Indian Army, was one of those severely wounded. Only dead Dervishes remained under the rubble of the demolished forts.

The conclusion of the Shimber Berris actions

Cubitt marched his force back to Burao, leaving a garrison of friendly tribesmen at Shimber Berris. The platoon of gallant 23rd Sikh Pioneers returned to their regiment in Aden. Morale in British Somaliland was now high and groups of determined Illalos prevented the Dervishes from encroaching forward of their position at Jidballi, 100 kilometres to the east of Shimber Berris. The SCC was recognised as being an effectively trained and disciplined fighting force; nevertheless the Indian Contingent was to provide professional and vital stiffening to the Somaliland Camel Corps for many years to come.

Awards for the second action

Brevet Rank

Major and Temporary Lieutenant Colonel Thomas Astley Cubitt DSO, Royal Artillery, was awarded the Brevet rank of Lieutenant Colonel.

Indian Order of Merit, 2nd Class

- No. 4392 Naik Sher Singh -*For bravery in action on the 4th February 1915 at Shimberberris, Somaliland. In placing a charge of gun-cotton against the door of a fort, he was knocked over and rendered practically insensible by the discharge of dervish rifles through the door, but after getting clear, he returned and placed the box in the correct place.*

- No. 4584 Havildar Teja Singh - *For bravery in action on the 4th February 1915 at Shimberberris, Somaliland. He followed Naik Sher Singh to the door of a fort and coolly placed a charge of gun cotton, arranged fuzes correctly, fired the charge and enabled the demolition to be carried out successfully.*

Mentions in Despatches

- Brevet Major G.H. Summers, 26th (King George's Own) Light Cavalry.
- Captain W.A.H. Bird, 23rd Sikh Pioneers
- Captain H.L. Ismay, 21st Prince Albert Victor's Own Cavalry (Frontier Force).
- Lieutenant C.A.L. Howard, 32nd Lancers
- No. 4392 Naik Sher Singh, 23rd Sikh Pioneers
- No. 4584 Havildar Teja Singh, 23rd Sikh Pioneers

The Africa General Service Medal

Somaliland was not considered to be a theatre of the Great War, but a new Africa General Service Medal was struck in 1916, with the head of King George V replacing that of King Edward VII; the medal ribbon did not alter. A clasp to this medal titled **SHIMBER BERRIS 1914-15** was authorised for those who had been in the field during Cubitt's actions at Shimber Berris. Of the 821 clasps issued, 306 were awarded to members of the Indian Contingent SCC, indicating the involvement and importance of Indian soldiers in the actions. Today this medal and clasp is sought after by collectors, and is rarely seen at auction.

The 36th Sikhs at the fall of Tsingtao, China October to November 1914

European enclaves along the China coast

By the turn of the 20th Century the coastline and navigable rivers of China were dotted with small territories occupied by western nations who had acquired concessional rights to be there through treaties entered into with the Chinese. The Europeans wanted to trade openly anywhere in China but the Chinese authorities, whilst happy to export items such as silk, porcelain and rhubarb, wanted the trade to be controlled through a limited number of ports. The Europeans developed small temporary expatriate colonies in the areas that they controlled by treaty, and whilst trade was the real motivator, military strategy figured prominently in the decisions made, especially the requirements for European naval bases in the Far East.

In 1914, on the Shantung Peninsula south-east of Peking, there were two major foreign bases used as important naval stations. Britain leased Wei-hai-wei at the end of the peninsula and Germany leased Tsingtao that overlooked Kiaochow Bay. Both leased territories were surrounded on the landward sides by agreed respective spheres of influence. The Germans did not have any supporting military forces anywhere else in the area but the British had a garrison of two infantry battalions not far away in Tientsin, near Peking. In 1914 these battalions were the 2nd Battalion, The South Wales Borderers and the 36th Sikhs; both units supplied guards for local security duties and for the British Legation in Peking. The British commander in North China was Brigadier General Nathanial W. Barnardiston MVO.

Across the Yellow Sea to the east of the Shantung Peninsula lay Japanese-occupied Korea, and south of that peninsula lay Japan itself, who harboured imperial designs on Chinese territory. Japan had proved to be a very respectable military power by beating Russia on land and sea in Asia during the 1904 Russo-Japanese War. An Anglo-Russian treaty of alliance had been signed in London in 1902, the treaty having being expanded in 1905 and 1911. In 1914, German plans for war do not seem to have included the possibility that Japan might wish to attack German territory.

The outbreak of war

After the declaration of war in August 1914, German civilians working in China moved to Tsingtao to join the garrison as reservists. Eventually the senior German officer in Tsingtao, naval Kapitan Alfred Meyer-Waldeck, had around 5,000 soldiers and sailors and one aviator under his command. The largest unit was the 3rd *Battalion* of naval infantry that had on its strength 26 officers and 1,161 other ranks. The airman was the recently-qualified pilot Gunther Pluschow who had one Rumpler military aircraft known as a *Taube* (dove).

Britain's main concern was the presence of the powerful German naval Far East Squadron of five modern warships that frequented Kiaochow Bay; this squadron, commanded by Admiral Graf von Spee, was a potent threat to the Royal Navy. In the event von Spee and his squadron were in the Pacific Ocean when war was declared, and the German and Austrian warships that remained in Kiaochow Bay were fairly ancient and slow. After the declaration of war Meyer-Waldeck had few real concerns about the defence of Tsingtao as besides the firepower of his naval vessels Germany had constructed a complex of concrete defences to protect the hilly landward approach to the port; all these fortifications mounted naval guns or machine guns. It was not thought likely that the British would initially bother to concentrate sufficient forces to be in a position to successfully besiege Tsingtao.

However, although Japan was not yet involved in the war, Britain asked her to help in eliminating German naval activity in the region. The Japanese response was to the point but perhaps not what Britain had expected, as the Japanese solution offered was to attack and seize Tsingtao. Then events slipped rapidly away from British control as, after ascertaining that the United States of America would not object, Japan declared war on Germany on 23rd August, and on Austro-Hungaria 48 hours later; Japanese mobilization plans had been activated one week earlier. Tsingtao became an important Japanese military and political objective as the seizure of the German enclave would give Japan the base she needed to extend her influence on the Chinese mainland. The Japanese prepared to attack Tsingtao and agreed to the presence of a British military expedition consisting of the 2nd Battalion, The South Wales Borderers and a wing (half-battalion) of the 36th Sikhs; some medical and Army Service Corps support personnel accompanied the British infantry but no artillery or engineer units were involved. Brigadier General Barnardiston was the British commander and he was accompanied by a few staff officers.

The siege of Tsingtao

After diplomatic wrangling over China's neutrality that was solved by Chinese compliance, the Japanese began landing troops on Chinese territory at Lung Kow, about 160 kilometres north of Tsingtao. The Japanese commander was Lieutenant General Mitsuomi Kamio, and his force would eventually total around 57,000 men. The Royal Navy contributed three fighting ships to join the Japanese total of 34 fighting ships and seven Gunboats; the Germans in Tsingtao had four fighting ships and six Gunboats. Fierce storms delayed Kamio's operations but by 18th September he was also landing men on the south of the Shantung Peninsula in Lao Shan Bay, in the German sphere of influence. On the previous day troops from the Lung Kow landings had cut the railway line out of Tsingtao, isolating the port. The Germans did not oppose the Lao Shan Bay landings, preferring to keep their troops in their own defence lines.

Barnardiston and all of his small force except the 36th Sikhs started landing at Lao Shan Bay on 23rd September. The Japanese were methodically advancing to a carefully prepared plan and were moving their siege artillery into positions from where they could engage the German forts in the inner defence lines; the German outer defence line was captured before the British expedition came into action. Kamio wanted to keep an eye on the British force to ensure that it complied with his plans and so Barnardiston's men were allocated a sector on the centre-right of the Japanese assault line. After a fortnight spent in moving forward and siting the British field ambulance and the supply depots, on 10th October the South Wales Borderers occupied 550 metres of front-line trenches. Meanwhile, Regimental Headquarters and half of the 36th Sikhs were still in Tientsin awaiting orders to move.

The arrival of the 36th Sikhs

At last Lieutenant Colonel Edward Langford Sullivan, commanding the 36th Sikhs, was ordered to embark his 450 Sepoys on *S.S. Kwanping* on 19th October. The regiment disembarked at Lao Shan Bay on 21st October but were delayed there for over 24 hours by orders to unload and stack freight from the *Kwanping*. This delay was unfortunate because a typhoon burst over the Shantung Peninsula that night, flooding the area and making movement on the muddy tracks very difficult. But on the 26th October the regiment had arrived at Litsun where immediately one double-company moved into the trenches to relieve a South Wales Borderers' double company, whilst the other double-company and the machine gun section went into reserve two kilometres to the rear. Four days later the reserves were pushed forward another 800 metres but this put them next to a Japanese artillery battery. Gunther Pluschow in his Taube aircraft soon spotted the battery and the area was subjected to sporadic but effective German artillery fire.

Meanwhile the British soldiers and sepoys were suffering in their thin cotton summer uniforms, as rain kept pounding down and cold winds kept blowing. The ground that the men occupied was intersected by small ravines, which soon became watercourses; the sides of the ravines often collapsed burying equipment, ammunition and weapons under layers of thick mud. Apart from using artillery and occasional machine gun fire the German troops stayed on the defensive, only once moving forward to counter-attack.

The Japanese siege gunners were ready on 31st October and a heavy bombardment of the first enemy inner defensive line began that night. Meanwhile at sea, the Japanese and British ships added to the bombardment with their firepower, or else engaged targets of opportunity that were observed. The allied naval gunners hit the Tsingtao dockyards and fuel storage tanks, causing thick smoke to arise over the port. After expending their ammunition the Germans in the first inner defensive line covertly withdrew, allowing the Japanese infantry to seize the empty positions without a fight.

The allied line moved forward but the German artillery fire became more accurate, and on 4th November the 36th Sikhs lost two sepoys killed and two officers wounded. One of the Sikhs killed had his head blown off by a shell that hit his two-man bivouac, but his companion in the bivouac was unscathed. During the following night as working parties prepared an attack start-line along a river bank the German gunners again engaged them, killing eight and wounding 24 of the South Wales Borderers and wounding a few Sikhs. Five Welsh soldiers received Distinguished Conduct Medals for gallantry displayed on this night as frantic efforts were made in the darkness to return enemy fire and to retrieve wounded men.

The final assault on the second and last German inner defensive line was planned for the 7th November and during the preceding night British officers' patrols ascertained that the German redoubts facing them were manned effectively, as the German defenders fired at the patrols. However the Japanese had their own agenda and elsewhere along the attack line they were making substantial gains that did not involve the British. Suddenly during the morning of 7th November white flags were displayed by the Germans on Diederich's Hill signalling station and the other defensive posts that the Japanese had not yet taken. Kapitan Alfred Meyer-Waldeck had surrendered Tsingtao.

The Allied victory

Tsingtao town was quickly occupied by the Japanese and all surviving German combatants were incarcerated as prisoners of war. This had been an impressive Japanese victory. Many observers and commentators expressed the opinion that the Germans had given-in too readily. One German excuse was that ammunition stocks had been expended, but subsequent Allied inspection teams found that this was not the case. Certainly the lack of aggressive action by the Germans as the Allied attackers advanced showed that the defence lacked fighting spirit. The Germans knew the ground and could have successfully ambushed Allied sub-units even though they could not have halted the advance. Perhaps Alfred Meyer-Waldeck knew in his heart that his was a hopeless task, and so after withstanding several weeks of siege he limited the loss of German life for the future good of his nation. Just before the surrender Meyer-Waldeck had ordered Gunther Pluschow to fly away into China with despatches for Berlin.

The Japanese had lost 236 men killed and 1,282 wounded; the British, 12 killed and 53 wounded. The German defenders suffered 199 dead and 504 wounded whilst over 90 German prisoners of war subsequently died in captivity in Japan, where their treatment was humane. The two dead men of the 36th Sikhs were No. 2806 Sepoy Udham Singh and No. 2819 Lance Naik Bishn Singh; both are commemorated on the Sai Wan (China) Memorial in Hong Kong.

Awards to the 36th Sikhs

Companion of the Order of Saint Michael

Lieutenant Colonel E.L. Sullivan, 36th Sikhs.

Companion of the Order of Saint George (CMG)

Lieutenant Colonel E.L. Sullivan, 36th Sikhs.

Mentions in Despatches

The following officers and men were mentioned in Brigadier General Barnardiston's despatches, and this list shows some of the senior regimental personalities of the 36th Sikhs who participated in the Tsingtao Expedition:

- Lieutenant-Colonel E. L. Sullivan.
- Major E. F. Knox.
- Captain A. D. Martin.
- Captain J. Gray (Staff officer).
- Lieutenant and Adjutant S. des Voeux.
- Subadar Gurmukh Singh, I.O.M.
- Jemadar Sundar Singh.
- Jemadar Jaimal Singh.
- No. 1707 Havildar Massa Singh.
- No. 2711 Lance-Naik Bhagat Singh.
- No. 2757 Lance-Naik Harman Singh.
- No. 2829 Lance-Naik Hari Singh.
- No. 3126 Sepoy Fakir Singh.
- No. 3785 Sepoy Ram Singh.
- No. 3782 Sepoy Bant Singh.

Observers were unanimous in the opinion that all ranks of the 36th Sikhs got on very well with the Japanese, who respected both the Sikhs' military professionalism and their positive attitude towards hard work in extremely unpleasant conditions. Sadly this familiarity and mutual respect was not a feature of the relationship between the South Wales Borderers and the Japanese.

The aftermath

The British had made a late entry into the Tsingtao campaign, and they were so under-resourced on the ground that they could not have operated without generous Japanese logistical support; the British presence had been a token one in a successfully planned and directed Japanese campaign.

The Japanese remained in Tsingtao until December 1922 when, after strong international pressure, the territory reverted to Chinese control – but the Japanese were back in occupation again in 1938. The South Wales Borderers sailed away to fight the Turks at Gallipoli. The 36th Sikhs returned to garrison Tientsin before the regiment was also sent to fight the Turks but in Mesopotamia. After the Great War the South Wales Borderers and the 11th Sikh Regiment, the successor regiment to the 36th Sikhs, were both awarded the exclusive battle honour; TSINGTAO.

The Suez Canal 1914-15

Great Britain and France declared war against Turkey on 5th November 1914. At that time Egypt was theoretically still a province of the Turkish Empire but for practical purposes the country had been occupied and controlled by Britain since 1882. Egypt's strategic importance lay in its possession of the Suez Canal, a waterway regarded with good reason by the Germans as the jugular vein of the British Empire. Britain needed to keep the Canal open to facilitate the transport of troops and mounts from India and Australasia. Also commercial shipping needed the Canal open in order to speedily move the military equipment, food and commodities that originated in British colonies and Dominions in the Far East and which were required in Europe. Germany needed to close the Canal. Indian Army infantry battalions were to play a vital role in the forthcoming struggle.

The Allied declaration of war resulted in the Sultan of the Ottoman Empire obtaining from the Islamic clergy in Constantinople a proclamation of a Holy War against the Allies. The Sultan himself, as Khalif of his Empire, proclaimed a Jihad (religious war) on all those who were militarily confronting Turkey or her allies. The Khedive (Viceroy of Egypt appointed by Turkey), Abbas Hilmi, had been in Turkey since August 1914; he was actively and openly pro-Turk and he stayed in Turkey where he was used politically by the Central Powers. The British response was to proclaim Egypt to be a British Protectorate on 18th December 1914. Khedive Abbas Hilmi was deposed and his uncle, Prince Hussein Kamal Pasha, elevated to the Egyptian throne with the new title of Sultan. The British Consul-General, Lord Kitchener, (the real power behind the Egyptian throne) was in England in August 1914 and he remained there to become Secretary of State for War. He was replaced in Egypt in January 1915 by Sir Henry M'Mahon who held the new title of High Commissioner. In an attempt to reduce tensions in Egypt where the vast majority of the population was Muslim and where nationalist agitation and hostility to Britain were on the increase, the Egyptians were told that they would not be pressed into fighting the Turks.

The British defence of Egypt

The British peace-time Regular Army garrison in Egypt had consisted of one cavalry regiment, four infantry battalions, one horse and one mountain artillery batteries and an engineer field company plus supporting services. In August 1914, these troops were needed in France. The primary task of the Egyptian Army, which contained many British officers, was the defence of and maintenance of security within the Sudan, and just one field artillery battery, one garrison company and three infantry battalions were located in Egypt when war broke out. They should not have been involved in operations against Turkish troops but British demands of expediency were soon to alter that arrangement.

The Indian Army now took over the first-line defence of the Suez Canal, supported by Allied warships. The Lahore (3rd Indian) and Meerut (7th Indian) Divisions passed through the waterway towards France leaving the 9th (Sirhind) Brigade temporarily detached to man the Canal defences. This allowed the British Regular Army garrison in Egypt to also move to France. The Lucknow Brigade was then dispatched from India to relieve the Sirhind Brigade allowing the latter to move on and re-join the Lahore Division. The Egyptian theatre was also allocated an Imperial Service cavalry brigade and composite infantry brigade and the Bikaner Camel Corps (all provided by Indian Princely states), eight Indian Army battalions, and then three all-Indian Army brigades. These troops were organized into two Divisions, the 10th and 11th, and eventually were titled 'Indian Expeditionary Force E'.

One other British formation had been mobilized in England and sent to Egypt. This was the Territorial Army East Lancashire Division which needed intensive training to reach operational fitness. Newly-raised and mobilised units from the Australian and New Zealand Corps (ANZACs) were also heading for Egypt for war training before deployment to France. The British rather complacently considered the Sinai Desert east of the canal to also be a defence because it was mostly water-less, and to make things even more difficult for any Turkish movement westwards from Palestine a detachment of Egyptian Coastguards destroyed the wells at Nekhl, 70 miles east of Suez.

Turkish and German preparations

However there was one man in Palestine who considered that the Sinai Desert was more of a logistical challenge than an obstacle. He was Oberst Freiherr Kress von Kressenstein, a German officer attached to the Turkish Army. Kress had previously reconnoitered into the Desert of Sinai, and after hostilities were declared he headed a German team of six staff officers attached to the Turkish VIII Corps at Damascus.

When a decision was made to attack the Suez Canal Kress became the chief planner of this Turkish operation. In Damascus Djemal Pasha, the energetic Commander of the Turkish Fourth Army, and his German Army Chief of Staff, Oberst von Frankenberg und Proschlitz, organized an expeditionary force of around 23,000 men, nine field batteries of artillery plus a 15-centimeter howitzer battery. The majority of the men to be used in the initial attacks on the Canal came from the Syrian territories of the Ottoman Empire but the force reserve was the 10th Division composed of Turks. Regular cavalry and camel-mounted troops supplemented the Bedouin irregulars that were raised for the operation. Djemal Pasha was hoping to provoke a revolt within Egypt against the British occupiers. Kress was probably more realistic in wanting (he later claimed) to hold the west bank of the waterway for two or three days whilst ships were sunk to cause a serious blockage. Kress' team purchased camels and loaded 5,000 of them with water carriers, prepared roads and brushwood tracks through the Sinai for the artillery, and equipped the two engineer battalions with pontoons.

Meanwhile in northern Sinai the first confrontation between the Turkish and British armies had occurred at Bir El Nuss. On 20th November 1915, a 22-man strong patrol from the Bikaner Camel Corps fought with a group of 200 Bedouins and Turks, losing one Indian officer and twelve men killed and three men wounded. The British patrol commander, Captain A.J.H. Chope, 2nd Gurkha Rifles, returned with an enemy bullet lodged in his saddle and claimed to have inflicted 60 casualties on the enemy. An Indian Order of Merit 2nd Class was awarded to No. 1534 Sepoy Ali Khan and an Indian Distinguished Service Medal to No. 115 Sepoy Faiz Ali Khan. Unfortunately during this patrol several Sudanese members of the Egyptian Coastguard who were acting as guides for Chope allowed themselves to be captured. These men then served as guides for the Turks.

By mid-January 1915 the General Officer Commanding Canal Defences, Major General A. Wilson, had allocated his troops into three sectors. The units in each sector were:

Sector I (Southern) Port Tewfik to Geneffe.

30th Brigade.

24th Punjabis. 76th Punjabis. 126th Baluchis. 2/7th Gurkha Rifles.1 squadron Imperial Service Cavalry. 1 Company Bikaner Camel Corps. A half-company of Sappers and Miners. 1 Territorial Battery Royal Field Artillery. 1 Indian Field Ambulance.

Sector II. (Central) Deversoir to El Ferdan (inclusive).

22nd Brigade (less 3rd Brahmans).

62nd Punjabis. 92nd Punjabis. 2/10th Gurkha Rifles.

28th Frontier Force Brigade.

51st Sikhs. 53rd Sikhs. 65th Punjabis. 1/5th Gurkha Rifles. 1 squadron Imperial Service Cavalry. Bikaner Camel Corps (less 3 and ½ companies). The Machine Gun section of the Egyptian Camel Corps. 1 Territorial Brigade Royal Field Artillery. 1 Battery Indian Mountain Artillery. 2 Field Ambulances.

Sector III.(Northern) El Ferdan (exclusive) to Port Said.

29th Brigade.

14th Sikhs. 69th Punjabis. 89th Punjabis. 1/6th Gurkha Rifles. 3rd Brahmans from 22nd Brigade. A half company of Sappers and Miners. 1 squadron Imperial Service Cavalry. 2 companys Bikaner Camel Corps. 2 Territorial Batteries Royal Field Artillery. 26th Battery Indian Mountain Artillery. An Armoured Train with a half company of Indian infantry. An Indian Field Ambulance. A Territorial Royal Army Medical Corps detachment.

Other Indian Army and Imperial Service troops secured the Advanced Ordnance Depot at Zagazig, the railway, the Sweet Water Canal and also formed a General Reserve at Moascar (The Imperial Service Cavalrymen were the Mysore and Hyderabad Lancers, whilst the Rulers of Alwar, Gwalior and Patiala provided the infantry).Territorial, Indian, Australian and Egyptian sappers, pioneers and military works personnel were given engineering tasks to strengthen the Canal defences, which included a few strongly-defended posts on the east bank. British and French planes flew reconnaissance missions whilst British and French warships entered or stood by to enter the Canal to provide fire support wherever required. As the British prepared their defences the Turks advanced in three columns across the Sinai Desert, encouraged by their German mentors.

Initial contacts and British reactions

From the 18th January 1915 onwards, Allied aircraft began reporting the progress of the Turkish advance and two brigades of British Territorial field artillery were deployed forward into prepared positions west of the Canal. On 22nd January the enemy skirmished with British covering forces east of Kantara leading to the 33rd Punjabis and the 4th Gwalior Infantry, both from 32 Brigade, being deployed forward into that sector. The New Zealand Infantry Brigade also moved forward and detrained at Kubri and Ismailiah.

Five days later, the Turkish southern column attacked the British Baluchistan and El Kubri posts on the east side of the Canal in Sector I. Both attacks were easily beaten off without loss and appeared to be diversionary. The following day attacks were mounted on the Kantara outposts but without conviction. In the belief that Sector II would see the decisive confrontation, 2nd Rajputs from 31st Brigade was sent to reinforce Serapeum. The large Turkish central column was observed in the vicinity of Jebel Habeita and the 5th Battery, Egyptian Artillery was deployed to Toussom. On 1st February troops from the enemy central column advanced northeast towards the Ismailia Ferry post. The British outer screen engaged these troops but the Turks did not press forward and dug themselves in at about three kilometres distance from the British main positions.

Crossing the Canal

A decisive Turkish move was made at 0330 hours on 3rd February when several pontoons and rafts were launched 1,500 metres south of Toussom. Heavy rifle and machine gun fire from the 62nd Punjabis supported by excellent gunnery from the 5th Battery, Egyptian Artillery, decimated the attackers. But at least two pontoons reached the west bank. The Turks who had crossed the Canal could make no headway against determined British counter-attacks and the survivors hid along the edge of the Canal. This action was not without British loss as the Turkish covering fire was effective, Mulazzim Awaal Effendi Helmi of the 5th Battery, Egyptian Artillery being killed whilst gallantly fighting his gun under heavy fire at short range. Lieutenant R.A. Fitzgibbon, 128th Pioneers, who commanded the protection party for the Egyptian battery died of wounds after counter-attacking Turks on the west bank. Two other smaller Turkish landings on the west bank were made nearby but neither progressed far, as Indian troops either killed or captured the enemy who survived the crossing. Whilst this action took place the enemy northern column unsuccessfully attacked the Kantara outposts, losing many men.

As dawn broke the British saw that nearly all of the Turks on the west bank had been neutralized but that was not the case on the east bank, where an enemy attack was being launched against the Toussoum post. Turks were occupying trenches around the post and the 92nd Punjabis, supported by naval gunfire and enfilade machine gun fire, successfully cleared this ground during a nine-hour fight. Seven Turkish officers and 280 other ranks were killed or captured. The 2nd Rajputs mopped up the Turkish survivors sheltering along the west bank.

Serapeum post, south of Toussoum, was also under attack. Two companies of 2/10th Gurkhas and six platoons of 2nd Rajputs crossed the Canal by ferry where they were joined by two companies of 92nd Punjabis from a post on the east bank. This force advanced north up the Canal edge clearing a surprising number of Turks out of broken ground until the enemy 74th Regiment of the 25th Division advanced towards Serapeum. Heavy firing now started and Captain R.T. Arundel, 2nd Rajputs, was killed whilst moving his men along the canal bank. But with the aid of fire support from two French warships the small British force halted the Turkish regiment about one kilometer away from the Canal.

As the unused pontoons lying on the east bank needed destroying, a Royal Navy torpedo boat moved along the canal using its 3-pounder gun to fire two rounds into each pontoon. When the boat commander decided to land in order to use gun cotton against any pontoons out of sight over the Canal bank, he almost walked into a manned Turkish trench. During the scramble back aboard the boat the commander and another officer were wounded.

Further north, the Turkish 68th Regiment of the 23rd Division advanced against Ismailiah ferry post but the attack halted 750 metres from the British wire. Whilst the enemy infantry attacks had not prevailed, the Turkish artillery fire was effective and the armed Indian ship *Hardinge* had to quickly move after receiving hits from a 15-centimetre howitzer battery. The French Requin finally silenced the enemy howitzers. The Turkish southern column made no further aggressive moves. During the night of 3rd March Australian infantry was moved up to support Sector II. This Sector received sniping during the hours of darkness.

As daylight crept across the desert on 4th February, the British in Sector II observed that the main body of Turks had withdrawn but scattered groups of enemy remained near the east bank. Captain L.F.A. Cochran, 92nd Punjabis, was in a post on the east bank and was ordered to use two companies to clear the enemy stragglers. Whilst attempting to do this Captain Cochran was killed. A company from each of the 27th Punjabis, 62nd Punjabis and the 128th Pioneers were now sent across the Canal and after an action lasting an hour, 298 of the enemy surrendered, 52 of them being seriously wounded. Amongst the 59 enemy dead was the body of Hauptmann von den Hagen, the German staff officer who had supervised the operation to cross the Canal.

Conclusion

All three Turkish columns now withdrew eastwards across Sinai. The British failed to mount a pursuit, citing lack of training especially amongst the cavalry, and so the Turkish guns and gunners and the mass of infantry lived to fight another day. Allied aviators did drop some bombs on the withdrawing enemy. The battle was hailed as a British defensive success, which it was, and a Turkish defeat, which it only partially was as the bulk of the enemy forces withdrew in good order along their well-constructed desert tracks. British casualties numbered 163 (ten of them being naval) and Turkish casualties were estimated at over 2,000.

Had Djemel Pasha's dream of an Egyptian uprising actually happened then the British would have been pressed to both maintain internal security throughout Egypt and the Sudan and to defend the complete length of the Canal. The Indian Army had fought professionally to hold the Canal and Indian and Egyptian Muslim troops had shown no collective desire to be associated with the Turkish Holy War.

The Hong Kong - Singapore Mountain Battery in Egypt, Sinai and Palestine 1915 – 1918

The Hong Kong-Singapore Royal Garrison Artillery

In 1847 the British authorities in Hong Kong began using Indians as gun lascars, or general workers, because the climatic conditions were unsuitable for white soldiers, and also because Indians were much more economical to employ and to administer. The practice spread throughout the British possessions in the Far East and by 1908 all the gunners were Sikhs or Muslims recruited from the Punjab. The quality of recruit was excellent as the pay was higher than that offered by the Indian Army, and also there was prestige involved in manning field or larger guns that were not used by Indian Army units. In that year a British Army Imperial[20] unit named The Hong Kong-Singapore Battalion Royal Garrison Artillery was formed with three companies in Hong Kong and one company each in Singapore and Mauritius. The gunners were focused towards coastal defence duties but some of them had been employed as machine and mountain gunners during operations in China in 1900 and 1901. After that conflict[21] ended permission was requested to maintain a mountain battery in Hong Kong, but London dismissed the idea. Eleven years later action was taken and the 24th Hazara Mountain Battery, Frontier Force, Indian Army, arrived in Hong Kong in 1912. When that battery departed in 1914 it left behind a trained company of mountain gunners, No. 1 Company, in the Hong Kong-Singapore battalion.

After war had commenced in 1914 the commander of No. 1 Company requested an overseas operational deployment for his sub-unit. This was

---
20 Paid for and directed from London.
21 Known as the Boxer Rebellion or Uprising, or the Yihetuan Movement.

granted in September 1915 when the War Office requested a four 10-pounder gun[22] battery be deployed to Egypt; the number of guns required was then increased to six. No. 1 Company was the nucleus of this new battery but drafts were allotted from No. 4 Company in Mauritius and No. 5 Company in Singapore; there was keen competition throughout the battalion to be selected for this deployment. The battery strength was: 3 British officers, 3 Indian officers, 205 Rank and File and a few British non-commissioned-officer (NCO) specialists. Initially mules were the pack animals. The battery embarked at Hong Kong on 8th November 1915, called in at Singapore to collect the draft from that station, and disembarked at Suez; the draft from Mauritius joined in Moascar near Ismailia where the battery was attached to the Imperial Service Cavalry Brigade. Initially the Right and Centre Sections were employed along the line of the Suez Canal.

The Senussi invasion of the Egyptian Western Desert

The first threat that the Hong Kong-Singapore gunners faced did not come from the east[23] but from the west, where Turks and Germans had incited the Senussi to invade western Egypt from Libya[24]. Fighting had started in December 1915 and the Hong Kong-Singapore Mountain Battery was deployed to Sidi Barrani on 7th March 1916. However by now the Senussi along the coast had lost too many men and too much ground and they were dispirited. The battery joined in the British advance towards the Libyan border but did not fight although the experience of operating in the desert on long marches was excellent preparation for the battlefields that lay ahead. In April most of the British Western Frontier Force moved back towards the Canal, but a small detachment including a section of the battery remained for a time to garrison Sollum.

---

22 The breech-loading 10-pounder mountain gun had been hurriedly introduced in 1903 after the failure of the 2.5-inch muzzle-loading mountain gun during the South Africa war. The new gun weighed 183 kilograms and the barrel was jointed for easy animal-packing. The caliber was 2.75-inches and the length of the assembled gun was 1.94 metres. Shrapnel ammunition and star shell were issued; the range was 5,486 metres but the gun sights were only engraved to 3840 metres. The recoil was controlled by a 'check rope' round the trail.

23 For details of the initial Turkish attack on the Suez Canal refer to the article *Turks Across the Canal* in *Durbar* Volume 27, No. 1, Spring 2010.

24 For further details of the Senussi invasion refer to the article *The 15th Ludhiana Sikhs and the Senussi* in *Durbar* Volume 27, No. 2, Summer 2010.

Into action in the Eastern Desert

As 1916 developed the British commenced advancing over and occupying the coastal areas of the desert east of the Suez Canal. A railway was constructed and also a water pipeline, whilst wire netting stretched over the sand alongside the rail line provided a suitable road for both vehicles and marching men. British aeroplanes made reconnaissance flights, but had to be careful because of the superior performance of the German planes used by the enemy[25]. The Turks reacted to the British pressure, capturing a Yeomanry garrison at Qatiya in April whilst unsuccessfully attacking Romani in July; they then withdrew their main force eastwards to El Arish, leaving outposts at waterholes.

In an attempt to demonstrate British superiority in the northern Sinai Desert two small raids were mounted on isolated Turkish positions during the Autumn of 1916, and the Hong Kong-Singapore Mountain Battery was involved in both raids. On 17th August two Australian Light Horse brigades, three companies of Imperial Camel Corps, with two horse artillery batteries and one section of the Hong Kong-Singapore battery in support, attacked Bir (well) El Mazar on the track to El Arish. But the Turks were prepared and the British horse batteries were misled by a guide so the British commander, Major General Sir H.G. Chauvel KCMG CB, broke off the action and returned to base. Shortly afterwards the Turks withdrew their post from Bir El Mazar.

The second raid, on 15th October, was a more daunting proposition against Bir El Maghara, which was 80 kilometres south-east of Romani and surrounded by difficult ground. Major General A.G. Dallas CB CMG commanded two regiments of Australian Light Horse, the 1st City of London Yeomanry, 300 men of the Imperial Camel Corps and a section of the Hong Kong-Singapore battery. The British force deployed from Bir Bayud and made two night marches before attacking. An advanced enemy post was taken and 18 Turks captured, but the enemy main body was in a well-fortified position on the steep slopes of Jebel (mountain) El Maghara. After exchanging fire for a couple of hours General Dallas broke off the engagement and withdrew. Both Generals commanding these raids had been ordered not to become involved in heavy fighting with strong enemy positions, but the Hong Kong-Singapore gunners had come into action and

---

25 German planes from El Arish attacked Port Said on 1st September 1916.

had been able to test their drills and operational procedures. The Battery then moved to Abbasia where the mules were handed in and replaced by camels; each of the three sections receiving an animal strength of 3 horses, 73 riding camels and 47 pack camels.

The actions at El Maghdaba and Rafa

The next British objective along the coast was El Arish but as the Turks had a railhead at El Kossaima the British decided to also attack El Maghdaba in between El Arish and the railhead. On 19th December 1916 the Imperial Camel Brigade was formed from the Imperial Camel Corps. In the brigade were four battalions[26] of camel infantry, a machine gun company[27], an engineer troop, a field ambulance[28], a signal section and administrative and logistic elements; the gunners in the Brigade were the Indians of the Hong Kong-Singapore Mountain Battery. Each infantry battalion had a section equipped with three Lewis light machine guns. The Brigade Commander was Temporary Brigadier General C.L. Smith VC[29] MC, of the Duke of Cornwall's Light Infantry.

On 20th December the British occupied El Arish which had been abandoned by the enemy, and then advanced up the El Arish Wadi (valley) to attack Maghdaba three days later. The attack was commanded by General Chauvel who used most of his Australian & New Zealand Mounted Division and the Imperial Camel Brigade. The Turks manned five strong redoubts on dominating ground above both sides of the wadi and the British plan of attack engaged every redoubt and cut-off likely enemy retreat routes. The Turks held strong positions but a large number of their Arab soldiers fled from the battlefield during the action, lowering the morale of those that stayed to fight. After some tense moments throughout the day, especially as regards the very limited water supplies carried by the British troops, Chauvel's men seized all the enemy positions by 1630 hours, having lost 146 men and 51 horses killed or wounded. Turkish losses were 97 killed and 1,282 taken

---

26 The 1st, 3rd and 4th Battalions were composed of Australians and New Zealanders whilst the 2nd Battalion was recruited from British Yeomanry Regiments.

27 The machine gunners came from the Scottish Horse, the Lanarkshire Yeomanry and the Ayrshire Yeomanry.

28 Australian.

29 For details of the VC award please refer to the article: http://www.kaiserscross.com/188001/487401.html

prisoner. The Hong Kong-Singapore Mountain Battery had performed well, advancing as the battle developed from its initial gun position north of the wadi to come into action again in a second position south of the wadi.

The following four gallantry awards can be attributed to the Maghdaba action:

Distinguished Service Order to the Battery Commander, Major William Agnew Moore, Royal Garrison Artillery: *For conspicuous gallantry in action. He handled his battery during the action with marked skill, thereby clearing a redoubt which was checking the infantry advance.*

Imperial Distinguished Conduct Medal[30]. Three awards to Havildars:

- No. 712 Havildar Piran Ditta. *For conspicuous gallantry in action. He displayed great courage and determination throughout the engagement under very heavy fire. He has at all times set a fine example.*

- No. 722 Havildar Nawab Khan. *For conspicuous gallantry and devotion to duty. On two occasions he displayed great courage and coolness under heavy fire. He has at all times set a splendid example.*

- No. 1050 Havildar Fatteh Singh. *For conspicuous gallantry and devotion to duty. He displayed great coolness under fire, and set a fine example of determination on the night marches which the operations entailed.*

The occupation of El Arish allowed the Royal Navy to land supplies on the beaches there until the railway and water pipeline construction teams reached the town. The commander of the British Desert Column that was spearheading the British advance, Temporary Lieutenant General Sir P. Chetwode, Baronet, CB DSO, decided to personally lead an attack on Rafah on the Palestinian border. The Australian & New Zealand Mounted Division, the Imperial Camel Brigade and the 5th Mounted Brigade[31] were the attacking troops who advanced during the night of 8th-9th January 1917. Security was maintained until dawn when the inhabitants of Arab desert encampments

---

30 There was one other medal for military distinguished conduct, the African Distinguished Conduct Medal that was awarded specifically to troops in the West African Frontier Force and the King's African Rifles.

31 Comprised of the 1/1st of each of the Warwick, Gloucester and Worcester Yeomanry Regiments, the 16th Machine Gun Squadron and a Mounted Signal Troop. The Brigade Commander was Temporary Brigadier General E.A. Wiggin DSO.

saw the British advance and passed the information across the desert from camp to camp and to the enemy by verbal ululations.

The Turks, with a few German advisors, held strong fortified positions at Rafah on the western side of the border. The British surrounded the enemy posts and commenced attacking over very open ground at 0930 hours. Again water supply was a major distraction for the British, as the wheeled supply transport had been left 15 kilometres to the rear at Sheikh Zowaiid. The British attacks made little progress against effective enemy shrapnel and machine gun fire, and reconnaissance patrols reported that Turkish troops were advancing from the north-east to relieve Rafah. In the mid-afternoon General Chauvel sent his mounted New Zealanders to make a fresh attack on the key enemy position, the Reduit, and he was discussing the likely necessity of a withdrawal[32] by field telephone with General Chetwode when New Zealand bayonets were observed going in hard over the Reduit slopes. Turkish hands swiftly rose in surrender and the crisis was over. The other enemy positions then fell, the Imperial Camel Brigade taking its objectives in another bayonet charge; the British troops now accessed the water sources previously denied to them by enemy fire.

The British wounded[33] and the guns of a captured Turkish mountain battery were brought in and General Chetwode withdrew his exhausted force. However British air patrols the following morning reported that the enemy had not re-occupied Rafah so a return was made to the battlefield to recover the abandoned Turkish material[34] that had not already been removed by local Arab looters. Enemy prisoners taken at Rafah numbered 1,635[35] including the Turkish commander and eleven Germans. The British casualty total was 71 officers and men killed, and 414 officers and men wounded with 1 man missing; Rafah had proved to be a much tougher nut to crack than El

---

32 Besides the water shortage one British artillery battery had been withdrawn from the action as it had only 19 rounds remaining.

33 As an example of casualty evacuation at that time in desert conditions the Australian & New Zealand Mounted Division allotted to each field ambulance: 10 pairs of litters, 15 pairs of cacolets (stretchers slung on each side of a camel), 12 sand carts, 12 cycle stretchers, and 6 sledges. All were animal-drawn except the cycle stretchers, and each field ambulance could concurrently evacuate 92 patients. But soon, when the desert sands had been left behind, motor ambulances would appear.

34 The British seized 4 mountain guns, 4 machine guns, 578 rifles with considerable quantities of ammunition, 83 camels and 54 mules and horses.

35 These men had belonged to the 31st Regiment of the Turkish 3rd Division.

Maghdaba. After Rafah the battery replaced its old 10-pounder guns with six 2.75-inch guns[36].

The First Battle of Gaza

The British theatre commander, Lieutenant General Sir A.J. Murray KCB GCMG CVO DSO, was under instructions from London not to advance into Palestine and capture Jerusalem until the Autumn of 1917. However both he and General Chauvel wished to attack Gaza and destroy the enemy garrison there before the Turks withdrew it. Gaza was just over 30 kilometres distant from Rafah. The British commander of the Eastern Force, Temporary Lieutenant General Sir C.M. Dobell[37] KCB CMG DSO, was ordered to seize Gaza and its garrison by a *coup de main*; the resources with which he had to achieve this task were two mounted divisions, three infantry divisions and the Imperial Camel Brigade. However General Dobell had an inadequate number of both staff officers and artillery guns, and he had the normal problems associated with water and ammunition supplies that occurred when British forces advanced beyond their railhead[38].

A preliminary British objective was the occupation of the line of the Wadi El Ghazze, which was to be held to protect the advancement of the railroad, and this was achieved before first light on 26th March 1917. However dawn saw dense fog rolling up the wadi from the sea, reducing visibility to around 15 metres distance, causing confusion for a time amongst the advancing troops. The timetable in the battle plan was permanently disrupted as the scheduled hours for reconnaissance and the issuing of orders had been lost due to the fog, resulting in the loss of valuable hours of daylight for Dobell's formation commanders to deploy and attack. But the mounted troops pressed on, the fog started lifting at around 0800 hours, and by 1030 hours Gaza was enveloped. The Turkish general commanding the enemy 53rd Division was captured by Australian light horsemen during this envelopment, but the general's division was behind him and it continued marching towards Gaza.

---

36 These 2.75-inch guns were 10-pounders without trunnions, recoiling through a cradle after firing to the extent allowed by the piston of a hydraulic buffer, and forced back to the firing position by the energy of springs compressed during the recoil.

37 Charles Macpherson Dobell was of Canadian extraction and had been the British commander during the successful Allied invasion of German Kamerun in West Africa.

38 Some batteries had to deploy some of their gun numbers on ammunition column duties.

By noon General Chetwode's mounted troops were well forward but he became concerned at the slow deployment of the British marching infantry divisions. This concern was compounded by information from a prisoner that the Gaza garrison was not just two battalions as the British had believed, but that six battalions were holding the town; reconnaissance patrols reported that Turkish reinforcements were on their way. However the battle proceeded at its own pace, and by nightfall the enemy positions at Ali Muntar immediately south-east of the town had been taken despite some fierce resistance. Gaza was surrounded but Turkish reinforcements were closing-in from the north-east.

Unfortunately the British chain of command across the battlefield, its reporting systems, its battle procedures and its required liaison between formation commanders were all not functioning effectively, and the senior British commanders became pessimistic because of the paucity of corroborated information. British intelligence officers back in Sinai possessed the Turkish cypher key and they intercepted and translated most enemy messages speedily, but the British telegraph system then failed to quickly forward them to General Dobell. Lack of water for the horses weighed heavily on the minds of senior officers, as did the fear of Turkish reinforcement arriving. Despite significant gains by the infantry and the mounted troops a decision was made to withdraw back across the Wadi El Ghazze if Gaza had not been seized by last light, and although hindsight shows that much of the ground taken did not have to be surrendered, the British troops left the battlefield during 27th March. The British force had lost 523 officers and men killed, 2,932 wounded and 512 missing. The enemy casualty figure totalled 2,447 Turks, Germans and Austro-Hungarians killed, wounded and missing.

Unfortunately in his report to London the British theatre commander, who had been following events from a train on the new Eastern Desert railway line, down-played the various difficulties that had overwhelmed the British command and control system, and predicted that a swift second attempt would unhesitatingly take Gaza. This resulted in a change of attitude in London and General Murray was authorized to advance on and capture Jerusalem, but sadly his Egyptian Expeditionary Force was not either ready or competent to undertake such a task.

During the First Battle of Gaza the Hong Kong-Singapore gunners had been involved in some fierce fighting as the Imperial Camel Brigade fought the rearguard actions on 27th March that allowed other formations to safely withdraw across the Wadi El Ghazze.

The Second Battle of Gaza

A three-week pause occurred whilst the British prepared for a second attack on Gaza; during this breathing-space the Turks positioned good units forward of and to the east of Gaza, resulting in 18,000 men being ready to meet the next British move. The British Eastern Desert rail line was extended to a railhead just behind Wadi El Ghazze and more artillery was deployed forward, however there was insufficient ammunition available although 4,000 gas shells were distributed to some of the British artillery units. Again British air reconnaissance was subject to interdiction by superior German planes[39] but successful aerial photography resulted in a new partially contoured map being produced for British commanders. Off the coast the French navy positioned ships to provide fire support, as this part of the Mediterranean coastline was in the French naval zone.

General Dobell did not attempt to turn the enemy inland flank, presumably because of perceived water-supply restrictions, and he rejected the view of some of his infantry commanders who wanted to punch powerfully up the coastline, as he saw no influential employment for his mounted troops in that tactic. On 17th April the British force of two mounted and three infantry divisions advanced to locations from where it could launch frontal attacks. On 18th April the attacking troops halted whilst the British artillery and the French navy bombarded Turkish positions, using gas[40] to try to neutralize enemy gun lines. On the 19th the attacks went in but it was immediately obvious that the previous day's bombardments had done very little to disrupt the Turkish artillery or to cow the Turkish defenders of strong points. British attacks were repulsed or only made ground at a high cost in casualties.

In this battle the Imperial Camel Brigade was attached to, and attacking on the right flank of, the British 54th Division. The Brigade objective was a redoubt 1.5 kilometres north-west of Khirbet (ruins) Sihan. A British tank[41]

---

39 German pilots were flying Halberstadts against the British BE2's and Martinsydes.

40 The first use of gas in this theatre.

41 A few tanks, formerly used for training, were sent out from Britain and arrived in time for this action; it was found that if the traditional grease was not used on the tracks then the tanks could move through and on sand.

supported the assault on the redoubt but it was hit repeatedly and burst into flames. Then infantrymen got into the redoubt, now nick-named 'Tank Redoubt', but most of them were killed by enemy fire or counter attacks. Other infantrymen of the Brigade crossed the Gaza-Beersheba road and temporarily established themselves on two hummocks nick-named 'Jack' and 'Jill'; the mountain battery provided close fire support throughout these actions and took casualties. Lieutenant Ben Fletcher Chapman of the battery was killed in action whilst acting as a Forward Observation Officer; Gunners 1704 Kishn Singh and 1745 Saudagar Singh were also killed and several others were wounded.

By now the British ammunition shortage was being felt and effective Turkish counter-attacks were being delivered including a spirited cavalry attack on the Desert Column operating on the British right flank. It was obvious to the British divisional commanders that there was no chance of a success on the battlefield and that more casualties would be taken for little gain if the fighting went on next day. From Khan Yunis in the rear the theatre commander, General Murray, wanted the ground that had been taken to be held and General Dobell ordered his troops to dig-in where they were. The Second Battle of Gaza ended at this point, the British having lost 509 men killed, 4,259 wounded and 1,576 missing; the Imperial Camel Brigade had taken 345 casualties. Three British tanks were lost out of the eight deployed and 2,129 British animals were casualties. The triumphant Turkish defenders had lost 402 men killed, 1,364 wounded and 247 missing, but they had ensured that the British Eastern Force was not in a fit state to take Jerusalem.

On 21st April General Murray moved quickly to focus the blame elsewhere, dismissing General Dobell on health grounds and sending him back to England; General Chetwode was appointed as the new commander of the Eastern Force. But on 11th June General Murray himself was ordered to return to England and he was replaced as Theatre Commander by General Sir. E.H.H. Allenby.

Beersheba to Jerusalem

General Allenby, a cavalry expert, re-vitalized the British force after its misfortunes at Gaza, and he created a new Desert Mounted Corps under Lieutenant General Chauvel that included the Imperial Camel Corps. Allenby decided to prize the Turks out of Gaza by first taking Beersheba in the desert on the enemy eastern flank. The Desert Mounted Corps took Beersheba in a charge on 31st October 1917 but the Imperial Camel Corps was on detached duty further to the west and the Hong Kong-Singapore Mountain Battery was not involved in the fighting. A third attack on Gaza was then successfully launched on 6th November; after a heavy British bombardment the Turks slipped away in the night leaving behind only a few worn-out guns.

The next British objective was Jerusalem. During this operation the Hong Kong-Singapore Mountain Battery was attached to the Australian Mounted Division as the ground to be crossed was too rough for the division's wheeled artillery and transport. The ground was also rough for camels. When on 21st November the East Riding Yeomanry from 22nd Brigade was ordered to advance on Ram Allah Hill, a section of the battery was attached in support; the ground was rocky, boulder strewn, often precipitous and was slippery from regular rainfall. The Official History contains an eye-witness account of the Hong Kong-Singapore gunners in action:

> *The section attached to the 22nd Brigade by sheer determination got their little gun as forward as El Muntar[42]. Their camels' feet were bleeding, and as they progressed by the narrow wadi beds it was not an uncommon sight to see them practically lifting their animals laden with ammunition over high boulders and rock which obstructed the path. They started dauntless and remained undaunted . . . Even when they were actually in action, each time they fired their gun a cloud of black smoke gave away their position, and they were replied to by batteries which they could not reach with shells that came over them like coveys of partridges.. . . Yet, despite the fact that on account of range they could really do little damage, they continued to invite destruction all through the afternoon.[43]*

This particular operation was aborted but the battery remained up in the hills; however it was doubtless cheered-up by the sight and companionship of Indian Army units who were now reinforcing the British troops in Palestine. On 1st December a Turkish attack penetrated the line north-east of El Burj held by the 8th Australian Light Horse. The situation was saved by a fierce Australian defence, the rapid arrival of aggressive reinforcements and the steady fire of the Hong Kong-Singapore gunners. Seven days later the successful British attack on Jerusalem commenced, the battery proving its worth up in the hills with its ability to closely follow the infantry and

---

42 1.5 kilometres north of Beitunye and 2.5 kilometres from Ram Allah from which Turkish batteries were engaging them over open sights

43 Footnote at page 200 of the second volume of the Official history.

the mounted troops – a decisive factor that the wheeled batteries could not emulate.

Three more awards of the Imperial Distinguished Conduct Medal can be attributed to the Jerusalem area actions:

- No. 762 Havildar Sultan Mohamed: *For conspicuous gallantry and devotion to duty. When his section was subjected to very heavy shell fire, which eventually made it necessary to withdraw the guns, his gallantry, fine example, and devotion to duty were most marked.*

- No. 1081 Havildar Piran Ditta: *For conspicuous gallantry and devotion to duty. He showed great coolness and determination when an ammunition convoy of which he was in charge came under heavy shellfire during an action. His cheerfulness and good example have been an inspiration to his section on several occasions.*

- No. 1213 Havildar Chajja Singh: *For conspicuous gallantry and devotion to duty. When his section was forced to retire over very difficult country and during a period which became increasingly critical owing to enemy pressure, his gallantry, coolness, and devotion to duty proved of inestimable value during this withdrawal.*

The final year in Palestine

On 5th January 1918 the battery rejoined the Imperial Camel Brigade at Rafa where a period of rest and refurbishment was programmed. All equipment was thoroughly overhauled; saddles were taken to pieces and the pads re-stuffed and fitted to suit the backs of the camels, whilst all leather work was renewed as necessary and oiled, dubbined and polished. Camels were inspected by veterinary specialists and the guns were meticulously stripped, cleaned, inspected and serviced. Casualty replacements joined the battery.

In March the Imperial Camel Brigade moved north and entered a region full of significance to the Christian infantry soldiers who were familiar with biblical tales. On the 23rd of that month Jericho was reached, the Jordan Valley crossed, and a point less than a kilometer from the Dead Sea reached. Gunfire from ahead signaled where fighting was taking place and dead Turks, stripped of every piece of clothing by the local inhabitants, lay beside the tracks. As the hills on the east side of the Jordan Valley were climbed the wheeled artillery started to turn back to find other routes, but the battery camels maintained their pace with the infantry.

The author[44] of *The Australian Imperial Force in Sinai and Palestine, 1914–1918* **later wrote:**

> *Immediately after leaving the foothills, General Smith was obliged to dismount his force, and all night the men of the three Battalions (and of course the battery) dragged their camels up the mountain-side. The men hauled and urged, the camels slipped and fell, but still fought steadily on. The Brigade straggled in single file almost from the valley to the Plateau, winding its fantastic course along crooked and flooded wadi beds, and treading narrow ledges round the sides of hills. In peace time such a feat would have been deemed impossible by any Eastern master of caravanning; but under the brutal lash of war the Brigade went surely up to the tableland.*

The purpose behind this trek was for one battalion to demolish a portion of the Hedjaz railway south of Amman whilst the remainder of the brigade took part in a raid designed to seize the city. Several kilometres of rail track were disrupted by the demolition battalion blowing culverts but the attacking force soon had its hands full with fierce Turkish resistance; the Hong Kong-Singapore battery was the only artillery unit firing in support. The Imperial Camel Brigade advanced to within 230 metres of the enemy trenches defending Amman but was then held up by heavy machine gun fire. British reinforcements were sent but also so were fresh Turkish troops, and enemy aircraft successfully bombed the British logistical tail. In the final attack on 30th March British troops penetrated the trenches around Amman but the defensive fire from the Citadel fortress made the captured positions untenable, and the British were forced to withdraw in appalling weather conditions back down into the Jordan Valley.

As General Allenby's force fought northwards camel country was left behind and in June 1918 the infantry battalions in the Imperial Camel Brigade were re-mounted on horses as mounted light infantry units. What happened to the Hong Kong-Singapore Mountain Battery is not clear, but it is probable that it was re-issued with pack mules for the guns and horse-drawn wagons for the ammunition and stores.

The final mention of the Hong Kong-Singapore Mountain Battery in the Official History is made during an account of the fierce fighting for Megiddo

---

44 Sir H.S. Gullett.

on 21st September 1918. The battery fired in close support of the 1st Royal Irish and the 38th Dogras, Indian Army, as those battalions drove back Turks holding positions 50 kilometres south of the Sea of Galilea. Megiddo was the final victory for General Allenby as he successfully concluded the Palestinian Campaign. As usual since its arrival in the theatre, the Hong Kong-Singapore Mountain Battery was up with the infantry and in the thick of the fighting.

Another Imperial Distinguished Conduct Medal was awarded to a British specialist with the battery for the Megiddo action:

No. RGA/13318 Serjeant (Assistant in Gunnery) M.J. Muldowny: *He has done invaluable work with the battery since its formation. He behaved with conspicuous coolness and gallantry during the operations from the 19th to the 22nd September, 1918, and on one occasion when the battery wagon lines came under considerable hostile shell fire he was conspicuous in superintending the removal of the animals.*

And two further similar awards were made to Havildars, the respective actions could have occurred from the First Battle of Gaza onwards:

- No. 1178 Havildar Kishen Singh: *For conspicuous gallantry and devotion to duty. When the officer of his section was wounded, he took his place, and though subsequently slightly wounded himself, performed the duties thoroughly and capably. By his cheerfulness and efficiency he was a fine example to the men of his section, and greatly contributed to the success of the action.*

- Havildar Rur Singh. *For conspicuous gallantry and devotion to duty, cheerfulness and never failing keenness throughout active operations. On one occasion when the battery was compelled to withdraw under heavy fire his coolness and total disregard of personal danger was worthy of the highest praise.*

General Allenby's troops rode on to capture Damascus and Aleppo, but by 2nd November 1918 the Turkish Government had accepted surrender terms and ceased fighting, as the surrender of Bulgaria had broken the communications link between Germany and Turkey.

On the 5th November an announcement in the London Gazette stated: *The KING has been pleased to approve of the Hong Kong-Singapore Battalion, Royal Garrison Artillery, being in future designated "Hong Kong-Singapore Royal Garrison Artillery."*

The weary but triumphant Punjabi Gunners handed in their surplus Palestine equipment and were shipped back to a garrison routine with their batteries in Hong Kong and Singapore[45]. Every other soldier who had seen them in action, and especially their British, Australian and New Zealand colleagues in the Imperial Camel Corps, had regarded them with respect as professional gunners who fought their guns well forward and who put rounds on the target, whatever the personal risks.

Other Awards

In addition to the Distinguished Service Order and the nine Imperial Distinguished Service Medals already described, these other awards were made to battery members:

Military Cross

Jemadar (Acting Subadar) Iman Din Khan: *For conspicuous gallantry and devotion to duty. On two occasions he displayed great coolness and courage under heavy fire. He has at all times set a fine example to his men.*

Jemadar (Acting Subadar) Alim Sher; Lieutenant (Acting Captain) Francis Lisney Skilton, Royal Garrison Artillery; Temporary Lieutenant Leonard Benjamin Tyler, Royal Garrison Artillery. (No citations published.)

Military Medal

No. 918 Gunner Ghulam Mohamed; No. 1642 Gunner Nihal Singh; No. 1624 Acting Naik Labh Singh; No. 1422 Acting Naik Ghulam Hussain; No. 1390 Naik Tika Khan.

Serbian Silver Medal for Bravery

No. 699 Gunner Karam Din.

Mentions in Despatches

- Major William Agnew Moore, Royal Garrison Artillery.

---

45 In 1915 the Hong Kong-Shanghai gunners serving in Singapore had helped in suppressing the mutiny of the 5th Light Infantry, Indian Army, in Singapore.

- No. 15682 Company Quarter Master Serjeant H.H. Waldren, Royal Garrison Artillery.

- Jemadar (Acting Subadar) Iman Din Khan.

- No.1050 Havildar Fatteh Singh.

- No. 699 Gunner (Acting Naik) Karam Din.

- No. 722 Havildar Nawab Khan.

- No. 1081 Havildar Piran Ditta.

- No. 1255 Naik Rahmahtullah.

- No. 1159 Havildar Rur Singh.

- No. 1828 Havildar Sher Muhammed.

- No. 1390 Naik Tika Khan.

Indian Distinguished Service Medal

As a British Imperial unit members of the Hong Kong-Singapore Mountain Battery, Royal Garrison Artillery, were not eligible for awards specific to the Indian Army. Despite this fact two recipients of the Indian Distinguished Service Medal have been found, and the reasons for the award of this medal are a matter for conjecture:

No. 1623 RGA Gunner (Acting Naik) Jinder Singh and Senior Sub Assistant Surgeon Chaudri Maula Baksh.

Commemorations

These ten names are inscribed on the Heliopolis (Port Tewfik) Memorial in Egypt:

No. 1728 Gunner Bhagel Singh; No. 1756 Gunner Bur Singh; No. 1789 Gunner Harnam Singh; No. 1501 Lance Naik Khalas Khan; No. 1740 Gunner Kishn Singh; No. 1817 Gunner Muhammad Zaman; No. 1290 Naik Muzaffar Khan; No. 1745 Gunner Saudagar Singh; No. 1705 Gunner Sultan Ahmad; and Jemadar Wasawa Singh.

These two British Royal Garrison Artillery soldiers attached to the battery lie buried in Kantara War Memorial Cemetery, Egypt:

- No. 69539 Saddler Donald Gillies and No. 9850 Gunner (Wheeler) V.A. Sykes.

- Second Lieutenant Ben Fletcher Chapman is buried in Gaza War Cemetery in Palestine.

The Imperial Camel Corps Memorial in London

On 22nd July 1921 a memorial to the Imperial Camel Corps was unveiled on the Thames Embankment in London. On the front of the base is the sentiment: *To the Glorious and Immortal Memory of the Officers, N.C.O's and Men of the Imperial Camel Corps – British, Australian, New Zealand, Indian – who fell in action or died of wounds and disease in Egypt, Sinai, and Palestine, 1916, 1917, 1918.*

The East Persia Cordon and the Sarhad Operations 1915 – 1917

The East Persia Cordon

Before the Great War commenced Britain had involved itself in Persia in an attempt to create a compliant and neutral buffer-state that would help to protect India's western borders, and Indian Army troops were stationed in Persia at posts along the telegraph lines that ran beside the Gulf coast. However Britain's most public political gesture towards Persia had been made in 1907 when a convention was agreed with Imperial Russia that delineated respective spheres of interest in Persia. Although Persia was a weakly-governed state its people were proud of their heritage and identity, and many Persians felt deeply affronted by the Anglo-Russian Convention.

Also there was an important reason why Britain had an interest specifically in South-Eastern Persia, and that involved the weapons trade between Arab towns across the Gulf, such as Muscat in Oman, and India's North-West Frontier. On the Frontier British and Indian Army units were discovering that their tribal opponents now possessed rifles that were as accurate as they themselves used. Whereas previously picqueting had only involved temporarily holding flanking high ground within musket or jezail-range of a marching column, now picquets had to be deployed at much greater distances from the column. Consequently picqueting took more time to perform, more troops had to be used and the planning and execution could be intricate; modern rifles in the hands of tribal dissidents were dramatically changing the nature of frontier warfare.

In attempts to stop the flow of arms from across the Gulf being landed on Indian or Persian coastlines before being transported on camels into Afghanistan and onwards to the Frontier, the Indian Army had made some deployments. Along the coastline battalions had operated both in Baluchistan and across the border in Persia, and other battalions had operated further inland near the Baluchistan-Afghanistan border. Regiments at Quetta took it in turn to send detachments to Robat, a desolate post near the point where the border-lines of Persia, Afghanistan and Baluchistan met. In pre-Great War days the railway from Quetta terminated at Nushki which was 600 kilometres east of Robat, and troops bound for Robat had to then march by night for a month across a hot desert. Few good water holes existed on this route and large camel trains carrying water had to accompany the troops.

In July 1915 the 19th Punjabis was providing the Robat detachment that was billeted at Kacha, 67 kilometres east of Robat. The 19th Punjabis was a Class Company Regiment with 4 companies of Jat Sikhs, 2 companies of Punjabi Mussalmans and 2 companies of Pathans[46]. Lieutenant-Colonel G.A. Dale commanded at Kacha, and his detachment consisted of two Sikh companies, one Punjabi Mussulman company and the Afridi company. Also at Kacha were the 19th Punjabis' machine gun section (two guns) and the machine gun section of the 12th Pioneers (The Khelat-i-Ghilzal Regiment). Meanwhile back in Quetta the other half of the 19th Punjabis was busily recruiting and providing trained drafts of men for overseas theatres.

Germany had placed several agents in Persia before the war, disguising their activities by appointing them as consuls or setting them up as traders. Once war started these agents operated openly and often successfully against British interests, and both local tribesmen and elements of the Persian Gendarmerie were exhorted and paid to attack Indian Army posts. When Turkey allied itself with Germany direct routes into Persia from across the Turkish and Mesopotamian borders were opened, and Germany used these routes to send missions to Afghanistan. Germany's hope was that both Persia and Afghanistan would join the Central Powers and attack India across its western borders, tying-up hundreds of thousands of Indian troops in India and fomenting revolt against British rule on the sub-continent. By July 1915 Britain and Russia had heard of five different German parties moving across Persia towards Afghanistan. Colonel Dale was ordered to intercept and capture or destroy any German parties that he could apprehend in the Sistan region of Persia, which lay north of Robat. Cavalry support was to be

---

46 One Pathan company was all-Afridi and the other was partly Muhammadazi and partly Yusufzai including trans-border Dush Khel from Southern Dir.

provided by headquarters and two squadrons of the 28th Light Cavalry, plus that regiment's machine gun section.

The 28th Light Cavalry was a Class Squadron Regiment stationed in Quetta, consisting of 1 squadron Madras and Dekhani Mussalmans, 1 squadron Punjabi Mussalmans (Awans), 1 squadron Rathore Rajputs and 1 squadron Jats from Hoshiarpur District. Colonel J.M. Wikeley, the Commandant, led the two squadrons[47] going to Robat and his orders were to proceed by train to Nushki without horses, and there to take over both riding and baggage camels. After marching for five weeks the sowars met up with the jawans at Kacha, and the whole force moved across the Persian border into Sistan. The British section of the East Persia Cordon had commenced its duties. In the north the Russians were assuming responsibility for cordoning their section of the Afghan-Persian border.

Sistan, Birjand and death in the desert

Sistan was a very fertile region that had been claimed by both Afghanistan and Persia, but Britain acting as an international arbiter had awarded most of the region to Persia. Because of its water courses and crops Sistan offered a useful route into Afghanistan for the Germans, as the desert routes to the north or south involved many hardships and dangers. The Punjabis left detachments at Kacha and Robat and marched 140 kilometres to Nasratabad, the capital of Sistan Province. After leaving another detachment there Colonel Dale made a long march north of 350 kilometres to Birjand where he established his headquarters. A short distance further north at Sedeh Village contact was made with Cossack cavalry at the southern end of the Russian cordon. A telegraph line ran northwards from Robat up to Meshed near the Russian border, and this provided an efficient means of communications between military posts.

By mid-1915 the upper echelons of the Indian Army regarded Trans-Frontier Pathans with distrust. The homes of these Pathans were in Afghanistan and once there they were beyond the control of the Indian Army. The Central Powers, through Turkey, used religious propaganda to urge Muslims in Indian Army units not to wage war against the Caliphate. Some Pathan sepoys, recruited from a prisoner of war camp in Germany, were escorting Germans through Persia to Afghanistan. Also Afridi sepoys

---

47 'C' Squadron of Rajputs and 'D' Squadron of Jats.

had deserted to the enemy both in France and Mesopotamia, so it was decided in Delhi to muster-out Afridis for the duration of the war. Delhi ordered the return of the 19th Punjabis' Afridi company to Quetta although that company had performed well on operations so far; Colonel Dale wished to disarm the men first to remove temptation, but Delhi ordered the retention of weapons.

The Afridi company was ordered to escort convoys from Kacha to Nushki and then to entrain for Quetta. The first of these convoy escorts was 39 men strong under a Colour Havildar, and doubtless he and his jawans discussed the respective merits of going home immediately with a modern rifle and ammunition or being discharged perhaps ungenerously at Quetta. Avarice won and on the third march from Kacha the 39 Afridis broke away from the convoy near Amalaf and marched towards the Helmand River, 100 kilometres to the north. But before reaching the river a harsh, sun-scorched waterless salt-pan, the Gaud-i-Zirreh, had to be crossed. Local Chagai Camel Levies were sent to track the deserters down, and eventually 37 bodies and all the rifles were found. The Afridis had exhausted themselves and died in the old bed of the Helmand River. The corpses were contorted and hands were thrust into holes that had been scooped out in failed attempts to find drinkable water.

The bodies of the Colour Havildar and the bugler were missing, as they had staggered onwards for a few kilometres to find the fresh water in the Helmand River; years later these two men were recognised in their native Tirah, perhaps living with vivid memories of their narrow escape from death. After this incident the remainder of the Afridis were disarmed and they marched back loyally with the next convoy to Quetta where they were discharged from military service. In September a double-company of Sikhs and Punjabi Mussulmans from the Punjabis' Depot joined Colonel Dale's command and was deployed to Dehan-i-Baghi, a small telegraph station 140 kilometres west of Robat on the desert trade route from Kirman in central Persia.

The 28th Light Cavalry enters Persia

After a rest halt at Kacha, Headquarters and 'C' Squadron, 28th Light Cavalry, garrisoned Nasratabad whilst 'D' Squadron joined Colonel Dale at Birjand. In November 'A' Squadron (Punjabi Mussulmans) arrived at Nasratabad with 400 horses, which permitted all three squadrons and the Machine Gun

Section to be mounted on horses again. One interesting mission that 'D' Squadron completed was to escort 300 Shia Hazara tribesmen from Quain, north of Birjand, down to Seistan. The Hazaras had been recruited by the British Consul-General in Meshed[48], and they were destined for service in the Seistan Levy Corps. Also in November 'B' Squadron (Dekhani Mussulmans) came out from Quetta escorting a section (2 guns) of 10-pounder screw-guns of the 25th Mountain Battery; later another section of guns from the battery arrived in Seistan. At the end of 1915 'A' Squadron was at Birjand with a detachment at Seddeh; 'D' Squadron had 2 troops at Neh, 1 troop at Bandan and 1 troop at Nasratabad; 'C' Squadron was at Nasratabad alongside Regimental Headquarters; and 'B' Squadron was also at Nasratabad with a detachment at Kacha.

In early January 1916 'D' Squadron at Neh received information from a local intelligence agent that three Germans with a group of hostile Bakhtiari tribesmen were at Deh Salim to the west. Water pools near Deh Salim were picquetted and the village was occupied, the enemy having already moved out. However the villagers volunteered the information that a second enemy group containing Austrian machine gunners was believed to be approaching from the west; 'D' Squadron prepared a defensive position at Deh Salim. Patrols searched for the three Germans and found them in a good defensive position in nearby foothills, and fire was exchanged until dusk. After dark the sentries on the southern edge of the village saw a man approaching and Acting Lance Daffadar Munshi leapt out and captured him. The prisoner was a German named Winkleman who was looking for water; his group had first tried but failed to penetrate the Russian cordon to the north, and had then tried again against the British cordon. Winkleman had stayed behind to cover the withdrawal of his comrades who managed to reach Kirman, further west in Persia. Acting Lance Daffadar Munshi was later mentioned in despatches.

Fighting the Sarhad Baluchis

Running down the Persian side of the border with Baluchistan was a hilly desert area inhabited by fierce Baluchi tribes, known as the Dahmanis, who supplemented an agricultural existence by regularly raiding westwards into Persia, seizing herds of livestock and female villagers, whom they enslaved. This area was known as the Sarhad and it was targeted by the Germans who

---

48 Hazaras in Afghanistan tended to be discriminated against, but many lived in Persia where they could practice their Shia Islamic religion alongside fellow-Shia Persians.

incited and paid the tribesmen to attack the British camel supply convoys marching westwards from the Nushki railhead. The British had to rapidly solve this problem as without regular supply convoys the East Persia Cordon could not be maintained. The railway was extended westwards from Nushki and a road suitable for motor vehicles was made alongside it, units from Quetta sent detachments to guard the road and railheads as they progressed

A Colonel was sent from Rawalpindi to deal with the raiding problem, and in a few years' time – because of a notorious shooting incident in Amritsar - his name would be widely known throughout the British Empire; he was Colonel Reginald Edward Harry Dyer. In early March 1916 Colonel Dyer drove in a car, the first one seen in the area, to Robat and with the help of his chief intelligence officer, Major C.R.H. Landon, 35th Scinde Horse, he quickly assessed the situation. In the Sarhad there was one friendly tribe - the Rekis, and three hostile ones - the Gamshadzais in the east, the Yarmuhammadzais in the centre and the Ismailzais on the west. To produce a fighting force Dyer could only thin-out the various detachments of Punjabis and Light Cavalry in their chain of posts running up to Birjand, as the East Persia Cordon had to continue patrolling against German infiltrators whilst he dealt with the Sarhad Baluchis.

For the next eight months Dyer, assisted by his Brigade Major Captain M. Saunders, 36th Sikhs, energetically marched his small force against his opponents, often bluffing them as to his exact strength. He preferred to negotiate but sometimes combat was unavoidable. In April a fight occurred against a strong Ismailzai lashkar (fighting force) near Dahan-i-Bagh. Captain A.D. Bennett, 19th Punjabis, with 80 Sikhs and Punjabi Mussulmans suddenly saw the Izmailzais and engaged them. After fighting all day under a very hot sun the tribesmen made a sword charge which was interrupted by a sandstorm that allowed both sides to withdraw. The Punjabis lost 10 men and 2nd Lieutenant W.H. Chalmers killed, and 20 more wounded. The Izmailzais had captured the Punjabi transport camels but they did not get far with them, as next day a mounted force of Seistan Levies and Light Cavalry surprised the enemy who were cooking a meal. As the fight developed Subadar Mehdi Khan brought up the Punjabis and closed-off the enemy escape route. As the Izmailis broke out across the plain in front of them the cavalry charged, killing over 30 tribesmen and recovering the lost transport camels plus 2,000 of the tribesmens' sheep. Captain Bennett later received a Military Cross.

But Dyers' men did not always win their fights and once when the cavalry and the Punjabis were escorting bound Yarmuhammadzai prisoners most of the prisoners managed to escape at night after releasing their bindings. The fugitives then ran the 100 kilometres to and from their homes to collect weapons, positioned themselves in the Laramba Pass ahead of the escort party and ambushed it, releasing the two remaining important prisoners. The escort party lost several men killed and others badly wounded, including two British cavalry officers; Duffadar Sheikh Haidar, 28th Light Cavalry, was a tower of strength during this fight and he was afterwards promoted to Jemadar. Reinforcements arrived when 300 men of the 106th Hazara Pioneers joined Dyer in July; these men had been working on the road from Dushki but they came to fight in their infantry role.

The fight for the Gusht defile

In late July Dyer led a moveable column out from Khwash with the aim of isolating Baluchi flocks, herds and families that were reported to be concentrated in the Morpeish Hills; the families and livestock were the raiders' Achilles heel, and by isolating them Dyer could force the tribes to come to terms. The column consisted of the 300 Hazara Pioneers, two troops of cavalry, two mountain guns and two machine guns. When in the foothills Dyer used a troop of cavalry to simulate the march of the column in a false direction, whilst he marched towards his target. Seeing the many camp fires that the sowars had lit the enemy was deceived and moved out to attack the supposed British force. Dyer got his column into the hills, seizing Gusht Fort which surrendered to him, and picqueting Gusht Pass. The enemy were now on the wrong side of the pass and they soon responded fiercely. A renowned Gamadshai chief, Halil Khan, arrived to take command of the attack on the British. Interestingly Halil Khan did not deploy his own Gamshadzais but only used the Yarmuhammadzais that were already surrounding Dyer.

Three days of heavy fighting for the mouth of the Gusht Pass followed, during which the Hazaras were heavily involved. Captain L.E. Lane of the Pioneers was later awarded the Military Cross. Dyer's column was forced back, carrying its wounded, and every man was involved in holding the perimeter against ever-bolder enemy attacks. The section of mountain guns under Captain J.W. English, Royal Artillery, provided invaluable fire support at critical times. This involuntary withdrawal allowed the Baluchis to dig up and hideously mutilate several Pioneer bodies that had been buried after the first day's fighting. But then a Pioneer fired at a tribesman looking over a sangar wall, the shot deflected off the sangar and blew the back of the tribesman's head off, and Halil Khan was dead. The death demoralised the Baluchis, as they had also lost 80 other men killed for no material gain; within an hour the Baluchis had withdrawn. Over the next two days and despite the severe water problems, Dyer's cavalry located and rounded up the enemy flocks of sheep, meeting with only long-range sniping from the herdsmen. The climate was the real enemy now as three of the sowars' horses died of heat-stroke. Dyer now had only the Gamshadzais to subdue and he quickly marched eastwards and seized the two strong forts at Jalk; without Halil Khan to stiffen their resolve the Gamshadzais declined to fight.

As the Gusht fighting commenced an isolated group of around 30 raiders were reported to be at a waterhole near Khwash. On 29th July 2nd Lieutenant A.B. Duncan, 28th Light Cavalry, was sent out with 6 sowars and 15 Punjabis. At the sight of the cavalry the Baluchis scattered and took cover in clumps of bush; Duncan made three charges through the area, being badly wounded on the second charge, along with three of his men. When the Punjabis came up the area was secured but Duncan and two of his men died of wounds before they could receive medical attention.

After the intense fighting at Gusht the Baluchis considered their situation and requested from Dyer that they be offered terms to submit to British authority, and this was mutually agreed. In order to keep the Baluchis out of German hands a new British irregular unit, the Sarhadi Levies, was formed and former raiders were recruited into it. Although the Sarhad was Persian territory the exigencies of war and a weak Persian central government permitted Britain to act in the Sarhad as though it was British territory.

Gun-running continued because of the massive profits associated with it, and in September 1916 news was received of a party of gun-runners making for the Afghan border. Lieutenant B.W. Wahl, 28th Light Cavalry, took out a party of sowars and Punjabis and met up with the gun-runners at the Shorab waterhole. The cavalry charged and although Wahl and Lance Daffadar Mohammed Abdulla were killed, the enemy was quickly dispersed, leaving behind on the ground 5 men dead and 400 rifles and 60,000 rounds. In March 1917 at the same water hole a party of sowars and Punjabis under Captain J.A.C. Kreyer, 28th Light Cavalry, was to have a similar success, capturing 447 rifles, 23,600 rounds of ammunition and 20 pack camels.

By October 1916 Dyer, now a Brigadier-General, had contracted medical problems after several months of hard but successful campaigning in one of the harshest theatres of the war, and he returned to India. Brigadier-General C.O.O. Tanner relieved Dyer. With the Baluchis now subdued half of the 28th Light Cavalry moved back to Quetta. The 19th Punjabis was reorganized with the jawans being Punjabi Mussulmans and Jat Sikhs, with the exception of one platoon that was recruited from the Pathan Yousafzai tribe. The attached machine gun section from the 12th Pioneers (The Khelat-i-Ghilzal Regiment) was incorporated into the battalion, giving the Punjabis 4 machine guns for future operations. Drafts arrived from the Punjabis' Depot that was now at Hyderabad, Sind, and Temporary Lieutenant-Colonel D.E. Knollys arrived to take command of the Battalion. Duties on the East Persia Cordon continued into 1917 as did operations against gun-runners, but soon the effect of the Russian Revolution was to lead to a collapse in Russian participation on the Cordon whilst a new German threat appeared in the Caucasus. Although they could not have guessed it in early 1917, both the 28th Light Cavalry and the 19th Punjabis were destined to be eventually fighting Bolshevik forces across the Russian border in Transcaspia.

Awards for operations in Sistan

Companion of the Order of the Bath (CB)

Temporary Brigadier-General Reginald Edward Henry Dyer, Indian Army.

Companion of the Order of Saint Michael and Saint George (CMG)

Lieutenant-Colonel George Arthur Dale, 19th Punjabis.

Companion of the Distinguished Service Order (DSO)

Captain (Temporary Major) Macan Saunders, 36th Sikhs.

Military Cross (MC)

Captain Alexander Dumaresque Bennet, 19th Punjabis.

Captain Lionel Edward Lang, 106th Hazara Pioneers.

Indian Distinguished Service Medal (IDSM)

Jemadar Haider Khan, 25th Mountain Battery. (He appears to have been attached to the 25th Mountain Battery from the 34th (Reserve) Mountain Battery.)

Subadar Muhammad Hassan; 774 Colour Havildar Kalbi Hassan; and 862 Lance-Naik Abdul Hakim, all of the 2nd Battalion the 12th Pioneers (The Kelat-i-Ghilzai Regiment).(These three men were probably in the machine gun section that was attached to the 19th Punjabis, and later absorbed into it.)

Subadars Rulla Singh and Ghulam Muhammad; 372 Havildar Sher Ahmed Khan; and 1455 Bugler Kishen Singh, all of the 19th Punjabis.

Subadars Ali Dost and Ali Juma; and 1533 Naik Ali Nazar, all of the 106th Hazara Pioneers.

Jemadar Radho, Chagai Levy Corps; Risaldar Edoo Khan, Sarhadi Levy Corps; Jemadars Bairat Ali and Juma Jalal, both of the Sistan Levy Corps.

Indian Meritorious Service Medal

Dafadars 1830 Shaitan Singh, 1961 Nur Khan, 2101 Ujagar Khan; Lance-Dafadars 2210 Boor Singh, 1892 Sultan Singh and 2354 Tek Chand, all of the 28th Light Cavalry.

Driver Havildars 1056 Sikander Khan, 1180 Ghulab Khan and Gunner Havildars 2622 Karam Dad and 113 Khan Bahadur, all of the 25th Mountain Battery.

Colour Havildars 4673 Rajwali, 4151 Gopal Singh; Havildars 4969 Narinjan Singh, 4751 Santa Singh; Naiks 4404 Nur Ahmad, 1159 Nadir Khan; Naik (Ward Orderly) 1312 Ujagar Singh; Sepoys 552 Dul Singh and 1487 Ganga Singh, all of the 19th Punjabis.

Havildars 808 Gharib Dad, 541 Saiyid Raza; Naiks 1302 Khuda Baksh, 237 Ghulam Ali; Lance Naik 116 Ali Akbar; Sepoys 2166 Mausam and 2686 Najaf, all of the 106th Hazara Pioneers.

1st Class Sub-Assistant Surgeons 884 Jawal Singh, 1072 Saiyed Ahmad, and 3rd Grade Civil Sub-Assistant Surgeon 491 Shrikrishna Raghunath Ingle, all of the Indian Subordinate Medical Department.

3rd Class Veterinary Assistant Inder Singh of the Indian Veterinary Department.

1395 Naik Shakar Khan and 2922 Sowar Hussain Gulmir, both of the Sistan Levy Corps.

Indian Military Transport units in Macedonia 1916 – 1918

The Macedonian Campaign

Between October 1915 and September 1918 the Allies engaged Bulgarian, German and Turkish forces in an area of Macedonia north of the Greek port of Salonika in the eastern Mediterranean Sea. The Allied effort was promoted by France and the initial aim was to rescue the Serbian Army that was being driven southwards by the Central Powers. The intervention initially failed as after a brief campaign in severe winter conditions Bulgarian troops drove the Anglo-French force back towards the Mediterranean coast. Britain then advised withdrawing from the theatre but France, Russia and Italy disagreed so Salonika was prepared for defence and another inland advance was made in 1916.

Russian and Italian troops entered the theatre, as did a reconstituted Serbian Army, and the town of Monastir fell to Franco-Serbian troops in November 1916. Despite aggressive action little else was gained by the Allies for the next two years as the Bulgarians held the vital ground on the mountain tops inland. In 1917 Greece joined the Allies and Greek troops fought in Macedonia in 1918. Finally an Allied offensive in September 1918 led to a Serbian break-through west of the River Vardar; the enemy forces crumbled and Bulgaria surrendered to the Allies on 30th September 1918.

Britain regarded Macedonia as an unnecessary 'Sideshow' but at its height the British force in the theatre comprised six divisions organised into two corps. Although you have to search hard in the British Official History of the campaign to find the word 'Indian', transport units from both the Indian Army and Indian Imperial State Forces were active in the theatre from January 1916 to the conclusion of hostilities, and their details follow.

3rd (Cavalry Brigade) Mule Corps

The unit was mobilised as a draught sub-division at Dalhousie, Punjab, on 20th October 1915. Captain G.H. Wilkinson, Supply and Transport Corps, Indian Army, was appointed as the Officer Commanding the Corps. 22nd Mule Corps at Ambala transferred 100 mule carts, personnel and animals into the unit. The unit strength was 1 British officer; 1 Indian officer; 4 British senior ranks; 557 Indian ranks; 15 riding ponies; 864 mules; and 400 carts. The Corps concentrated at Lahore and departed in late October on three trains for Karachi where it loaded men, animals, carts, gear, tentage and stores on the transports *Taroba* and *Umeta*. The transports departed from Kiamari Docks on 2nd November and arrived at Suez twelve days later where the Corps disembarked and entrained for Ismailia. After working for two weeks on station duties at Ismailia, Suez, Port Said and Tel-el-Kebir the Corps received orders to embark for Salonika. The transports *Haverford* and *Karoo* carried the Corps and departed from Alexandria on 27th December arriving at Salonika Port on 1st January 1916. Disembarkation was completed the following day and the Corps moved into a camp on Monastir Road; 200 carts were immediately employed on duties and the camp came under an enemy air attack on 6th January, fortunately the bombs landed 200 metres north of the camp. Hostilities had commenced for the 3rd (Cavalry Brigade) Mule Corps and in early February the soldiers observed an enemy Zeppelin air-ship that bombed Salonika.

31st Mule Corps

On Mudros Island on 28th December 1915 Captain A.E.E. Sargent MC, Supply and Transport Corps, Indian Army, was appointed Commandant of the 31st Mule Corps and ordered to form four troops each containing 108 mules and 50 carts for service in Salonika. British troops had almost completed their withdrawal from Gallipoli and several Indian mule units were on the island which was a main base. To make up the Corps to eight troops, Imperial Service units from the princely states of Bharatpur and Indore were attached to the Corps for operations, however the Imperial Service troops remained under the command of their respective commandants for internal administration. Lieutenant G.B. Roger, Indian Army Reserve of Officers, was posted as a junior officer in the Corps. The enhanced Corps embarked at Mudros on 8th January 1916 and disembarked at Salonika four days later, losing two mules drowned during the disembarkation. Operational deployments commenced on the 14th January.

Bharatpur Imperial Service Transport Corps

The unit had first served in France and then at Suvla Bay, Gallipoli, where it used pack mules to resupply the trenches of the British 10th Division, losing 110 mules to enemy shell fire. After evacuation to Mudros it was reconstituted into two troops for service in Salonika. Lieutenant Colonel Kishen Singh was the Commandant and Major J.H. Watson, 13th Duke of Connaught's Lancers (Watson's Horse), was the Indian Army Special Service Officer (SSO) who was there to offer advice when the Commandant requested it. The unit strength was 172 all ranks, 9 horses and 216 mules. The Bharatpurs moved to Salonika attached to 31st Mule Corps, disembarking from the transport *S.S. Haverford* and moving into Kalamaria Camp on 12th January 1916. Two weeks later pack mule deliveries commenced from Kalamaria Camp to Hortachoi. In early February 100 carts were received and cart transport operations commenced.

Indore Imperial Service Transport Corps

The Indore Corps had served alongside the Bharatpurs in France and at Suvla Bay, and it was also reconstituted on Mudros Island in late December 1915. Major Lutf Ali Khan was Commandant and the SSO was Major Nawab Mohamed Akbar Khan. On strength were 5 Indian officers, 132 Indian ranks, 12 artificers, 23 followers, 14 riding ponies and 216 mules. During the embarkation from Mudros Driver Onkar argued with Daffadar Sirdar Ali Khan and wounded him; Onkar later received a sentence of five years rigorous imprisonment and was returned to India. After moving to Salonika with 31st Mule Corps the Indore Corps spent ten days in Kalamaria Camp and then marched as a pack mule unit to Hortachoi. On 22nd January the Corps moved to Aivasil and commenced supporting the 27th Division. In February the Indore Corps also received 100 carts and began cart transport duties.

The duties of the Mule Corps units

The Mule Corps units were designated as Army Troops and were deployed by the British Salonika Force headquarters both in the British sector and sometimes in support of Allied troops in other sectors. The transport duties were carried out in rear areas but attacks by enemy aircraft and Zeppelin air ships were a major risk. The carts were in constant use moving rations, forage, baggage, ammunition, coal and other supplies forward to divisional locations. Occasionally road stone was the cargo as engineers constructed more all-weather roads running inland. A lighter load sometimes was charcoal.

The British members of 3rd (Cavalry Brigade) Mule Corps were often used to run courses on pack-mule handling for divisional personnel who then used their own pack-mules within their divisional areas. After battles with the Bulgarians the return loads of many of the carts were wounded Allied soldiers. Often a Mule Corps would have camps in two or three different locations, dependant on the taskings received for the Corps; unit quartermasters, veterinary assistants, farriers, carpenters, artificers, saddlers, shoeing smiths, medical dressers, tailors, cooks, barbers and sweepers manned the camps. Hutted camps were erected in base areas but in forward locations the camps were tented.

When a mule was sick or wounded and could not be satisfactorily treated by the Veterinary Officer or Assistant in the unit it was sent to a Veterinary hospital for treatment and convalescence. When Corps needed fresh mules to replace casualties these were drawn from Remount units; however war diaries show that the number of remounts needed was low because of the excellent care and grooming that the Indian mule units practised. Because of forage shortages, off-duty mules were allowed to graze freely in safe areas. Unit artificers and saddlers maintained and repaired the carts and equipment.

As the campaign progressed the British set up agricultural units in Macedonia to grow produce for food supplies, and mule teams were employed on ploughing with both Punjabi ploughs made within the Corps and Greek iron ploughs bought locally. The Mule Corps ran its own vegetable gardens and produced substantial amounts of crops.

The men and their recreation

Whilst the Indian State Forces units were usually reinforced with drafts from their princely states, the Indian Army Mule Companies received drafts that included many different castes. The 31st Mule Corps war diary for 25th June 1917 records the following castes or types as being on strength: Christian, Parsi, Pathan, Punjabi Musulman, Madrasi Musulman, Tamil, Telegu, Sikh, Mahratta, Gurkha, Brahman, Rajput, Hindustani Musulman and Sweeper.

Hardly any instances of serious disciplinary action are recorded in the war diaries, and two weeks imprisonment in a local military jail is the severest sentence recorded.

Hardly any home leave was granted because there were never enough men on the ground to keep all the carts running, which was the military priority. That led to the men becoming exhausted as the work was strenuous, and this contributed to higher sickness rates. By late 1918 the 3rd (Cavalry Brigade) Mule Corps war diary is noting that: "The question of leave for both British and Indians during the three years and three months during which the unit has been on Active Service has been very unsatisfactory, one British officer and one serjeant and less than 100 Indian other ranks only have as yet proceeded on leave, and this entirely owing to reinforcements not being available to make up the requisite number of men to work the 400 carts of this unit."

A telling entry in the same war diary after the Armistice comments: "The type of reinforcement being received from India is very unsatisfactory, physique poor, weak and not up to the hard work and climatic conditions of Macedonia. In many cases, on the line of march, they were too weak to be able to saddle up their animals, which work had to be done for them by the older hands. They are received from India absolutely untrained."

Civilian charitable organisations such as the Young Men's Christian Association organised secular recreational facilities such as film shows and units established canteens or relaxation areas in base areas. The Imperial War Museum has archived some interesting photographs of the Mule Corps men at sports meetings showing athletic events and displays plus mule-back wrestling and tug-of-war matches. However a popular off-duty activity for the sepoys must have been to wander the ancient streets of Salonika, observing the cultures and customs of the polyglot community that lived there.

The medical situation on the Macedonian Front

Macedonia was not a healthy theatre for British soldiers. Winters that could be brutally cold were followed by summers that were very hot and debilitating. The low plains occupied by many British soldiers contained several malarial swamps. Troops that moved from Gallipoli to Macedonia were already weakened by the insanitary field conditions that they had endured on the peninsula, and many of those soldiers soon suffered from dysentery and other enteric diseases in Macedonia. If mosquito nets were not used to sleep under then malaria could strike quickly, and sometimes also Sand Fly Fever; over 160,000 cases of malaria were recorded. Poor sanitation discipline could lead to Black Water Fever. However once the scale of the problem was realised the British went to great lengths to ensure that Hygiene and Sanitation standards were maintained, nevertheless the British force suffered over half a million non-combat casualties during the campaign. In 1918 the world-wide influenza epidemic struck Macedonia and caused casualties.

No. 137 Indian Field Ambulance was deployed to Salonika along with the Mule Corps, and unit Sub-Assistant Surgeons would refer casualties that could not be treated in the units to that Field Ambulance. If the casualty needed hospitalisation he was sent to a British Army hospital in Salonika from where serious cases would be shipped to Egypt or India.

Monastir Road Indian Cemetery and Indian Memorial, Salonika, Greece

From 1916 deaths of Indian soldiers occurred in Macedonia, mainly from disease or other medical reasons. An Indian cemetery was located on Monastir Road, Salonika, the southern plot was used for burials and the northern plot for the over 200 cremations that took place. A Memorial in the northern half commemorates the deaths of those with no known graves. A total of 358 Indian soldiers are commemorated by the Commonwealth War Graves Commission in a well-maintained little cemetery.

Of the listed casualties 58 are Mule Corps, 10 are Bharatpur Imperial Service Transport Corps and 7 are Indore Imperial Service Transport Corps.

One hundred and ten men are from the Royal Horse and Field Artillery, Indian Army, as from 1918 that regiment provided drivers for the ammunition columns of the British horse-drawn artillery in Macedonia. The remaining commemorations are mainly for sepoys whose units were employed after the Armistice in the British Army of the Black Sea.

An Indian in the Bulgarian Flying Corps

The war diary for 3rd (Cavalry Brigade) Mule Corps records an interesting event. No. 622 Driver Santa Singh had been reported missing on 16th August 1917 and he reported back for duty on 10th November of the same year.

Santa Singh had followed a mule that he believed belonged to his unit but he was captured by Bulgarian troops and kept in a prisoner of war camp near Fort Rupel for about five weeks. Then he was employed as a cook and orderly for Captain Kishen Singh of the Bulgarian Flying Corps, and Kishen Singh related his story to his new orderly. Kishen Singh was born in Calcutta and had two brothers working on the railways in Lahore. Kishen became a tramway driver in Bombay but then took work afloat as a lascar and later as a cleaner in the engine rooms of ships. In 1912 he sailed for Europe in a French vessel and landed at Salonika where he married a Macedonian lady and settled down in Rupel Pass. When Bulgaria entered the war Kishen Singh joined the Bulgarian Army. After five weeks working as an orderly Santa Singh found an opportunity to escape and made his way across country to the British lines. Nothing more was heard of Kishen Singh.

Further deployment

In 1919, when shipping space was secured, the Indian State Forces units returned to India, both Corps serving in the Third Afghan War. Unfortunately Major Lutf Ali Khan, Commandant of the Indore Transport Corps, was killed in an air crash near Salonika in April 1919 just before his unit embarked. Major Gopal Puri took over as Commandant. The Indian Army units, although tired out and receiving untrained reinforcements of poor quality, were redeployed into the Army of the Black Sea, 3rd (Cavalry Brigade) Mule Corps being shipped to the Georgian port of Batum in the south-east of the Black Sea.

Although in Macedonia the British built roads for motor transport and railways for the movement of large numbers of men and stores, the mule-cart units were in great demand from January 1916 to the Armistice and beyond. The Mule Corps were flexible and reliable assets for the logisticians, needing no petrol or coal to power them. The sepoys were used to living in basic conditions in hostile climates and their administrative requirements were minimal. The mules did not need spare parts nor skilled mechanics to repair them. The artificers and saddlers in the mule-cart units were adept at keeping the carts and equipment in excellent working order, and the veterinary staff, shoe-smiths and drivers understood their mules and took great care of them. It is unfortunate that the contribution of the Indian Mule Corps to the Macedonian Campaign is not more widely recognised.

It is appropriate to end by quoting Major Wilkinson's closing comment in the war diary of the 3rd (Cavalry Brigade) Mule Corps as it prepared to embark for Batum:

> *"In spite of these adverse conditions and the fact that nearly all the original transport drivers left in the unit have had no leave whatever since embarking at Karachi on 2nd November 1915, they are and have all along been behaving like 'TRUMPS', there is no other word to describe their work."*

Awards made to members of Indian Mule Corps and Supply and Transport units serving in Macedonia

Companion of the Distinguished Service Order (DSO)

Majors A.E.E. Sargent MC and G.H. Wilkinson, both Supply and Transport Corps, Indian Army.

Companion of the Indian Empire (CIE)

Lieutenant Colonel (Sirdar) Kishen Singh, Bharatpur Imperial Service Transport Corps.

Order of British India (OBI)

Major Lutf Ali Khan (Bahadur); Captain Santuji Bapuji; Lieutenant Colonel Gopal Puri, all of the Indore Imperial Service Transport Corps.

Indian Distinguished Service Medal

Jemadar Muhammad Ismail and No. 216 Daffadar Fazal Elahi, both Supply and Transport Corps, Indian Army.

Meritorious Service Medal

Sergeant F. Rowell, Supply and Transport Corps, Indian Army.

Indian Meritorious Service Medal

MULE CORPS awards: No. 438 Saddler Allah Ditta; 3rd Grade Veterinary Assistants No. 1604 Hari Singh and No. 1246 Mir Zaman; Kot Dafadars No. 288 Nazir Ahmad, No. 508 Ali Murid and No. 1170 Muhammad Kasim; No. 501 Quartermaster Daffadar Roshan Khan; Lance Naiks No. 861 Saif Ali, No. 980 Ghulam Muhammad, No. 1205 Muhammad Qasim and No. 1338 Abdul Jaheel; Drivers No. 1383 Mohmin Shah and No. 1234 Phinoo.

BHARATPUR IMPERIAL SERVICE TRANSPORT CORPS awards: No. 907 Kot Daffadar Bashir Ahmed; No. 855 Lance Daffadar Sukkha; No. 671 Driver Chand Khan.

INDORE IMPERIAL SERVICE TRANSPORT CORPS awards: Kot Daffadars No. 18 Alladin, No. 18 Aladin Khan, and No. 9 Bane Singh; No. 14 Farrier Major Nabi Baksh.

Croix de Guerre (French)

Lieutenant Colonel (Commandant) Sardar Kishen Singh, Sirdar Bahadur, CIE, Bharatpur Imperial Service Transport Corps.

Mention in Dispatches

MULE CORPS: Major A.E.E. Sargent DSO MC; No. 1338 Lance Naik Abdul Jaheel; No. 1253 Lance Naik Michael; No. 1383 Driver Mohmin Shah; No. 501 Quartermaster Daffadar Roshan Khan; No. 938 Lance Naik Samander.

BHARATPUR IMPERIAL SERVICE TRANSPORT CORPS: No. 688 Daffadar Ganpat Singh; No. 671 Driver Chand Khan; No. 855 Lance Daffadar Surkha.

INDORE IMPERIAL SERVICE TRANSPORT CORPS: Risalder Wali Mahomed Khan; Veterinary Surgeon Moladad Khan; No. 20Quartermaster Daffadar Abdul Latif; No. 9 Kot Daffadar Bane Singh; No. 14 Farrier Major Nabi Baksh.

SUPPLY AND TRANSPORT CORPS: Staff Serjeant (Local Sub-Conductor) H. Cooper; No. 508 Kot Daffadar Ali Marid; No. 474 Driver Fazal Khan; No. 1408 Kot Daffadar Khul Ahmed.

Recommended Background Reading:

Major H.M. Alexander DSO: *On Two Fronts. Being the Adventures of an Indian Mule Corps in France and Gallipoli*. Download at: http://www.archive.org/stream/ontwofrontsbeing00alexrich#page/n7/mode/2up

The website of the Salonika Campaign Society may also be of interest: http://www.salonikacampaignsociety.org.uk/index.php/campaign/76-campaign

The 25th Cavalry (Frontier Force) in German and Portugese East Africa September 1917 – February 1918

From the North-west Frontier to tropical Africa

In mid-1917 the 25th Cavalry (Frontier Force) was warned-off to move to East Africa for a short operational tour. The 25th was a Class Squadron Regiment with a squadron each of Sikhs, Dogras, and Punjabi Mussalmans plus a squadron split between Hindustani Mussalmans and Pathans. The war diary for the East Africa theatre is very short on detail but it can be deduced that the Commanding Officer was Brevet Lieutenant Colonel G.A.R. Watts and the Second in Command was Major P.W. Burrowes.

The Regiment had spent the first three years of the Great War on the North-West Frontier, and at Miramshah in the Tochi Valley it was part of the Bannu Column that decisively defeated a large Khostwal Lashkar on 26th March 1915. The Regiment had secured the British right flank and had so roughly handled its adversaries that the tribesmen fled the battlefield without first recovering their casualties, an unusual act. For gallantry displayed in that action the **Indian Distinguished Service Medal** had been awarded to Jemadar Sher Ali and to No. 3843 Acting Lance Dafadar Sundar Singh; both men also received a **Mention in Despatches** as did the then Commanding Officer, Lieutenant Colonel G.M. Baldwin DSO.

The situation in East Africa in late 1917

In East Africa in late 1917 British and Belgian troops had pushed the local German army named the Schutztruppe back towards the south-eastern corner of German East Africa. The British held all the ports on the Indian Ocean seaboard and the Germans, under their very talented and energetic commander, General Paul von Lettow-Vorbeck, were operating inland in three dispersed groups near Kilwa, Mahenge and Lindi.

General von Lettow-Vorbeck was a professional and experienced field soldier who concentrated on administrative detail before committing his troops, a mixture of Germans, Austro-Hungarians and Africans, into battle. He fought a war of attrition against the Belgians and British, holding good defensive positions whilst he beat off Allied attacks, and then withdrawing to other previously-prepared positions. On his withdrawal routes he positioned food and supply dumps so that his troops were retreating on interior lines of communication whilst the Allies were forever extending their own lines of communication as they followed him.

The Allied theatre commander, the South African General Jacob Louis van Deventer, a horseman himself, saw the need for a cavalry regiment that was capable of operating behind enemy lines to locate and destroy the German supply dumps before they could be used. The one South African mounted regiment in German East Africa was becoming worn out, and so the 25th Cavalry (Frontier Force) was despatched from India to join the East African Expeditionary Force.

An introduction to tropical Africa

The 25th Cavalry arrived in German East Africa in September 1917 without its own horses, but on arrival it was issued with 600 excellent South African horses and the same number of supply mules. However the Regiment was told that before the end of the year tsetse-fly would have killed all the horses, and so the next three months must be spent in literally working mounts to death in order to inflict the maximum punishment on the enemy in the shortest space of time. For the sowars this was a contradiction to their usual practice of preserving their mounts by all possible means.

A British East Africa settler, Captain N.J.M. Barry, East Africa Mounted Rifles, joined the Regiment as the Transport Officer. Lieutenant N.S. Bruce, Royal Army Medical Corps Special Reserve, also joined as a Medical Officer. A team of five Intelligence Officers and their African Scouts were attached to the Regiment under the command of Major Clifford Hill DSO, East African Mounted Rifles.

The cavalrymen had to quickly adjust to operating in the unmapped African bush where visibility could be as much as 200 metres or less than 10 metres. The German African soldiers, known as Askari, were ferocious bayonet fighters in thick bush but they were unused to facing a mounted enemy and when they did then they became agitated and often fired wildly. On several occasions the leading troop of a patrol rode into an enemy ambush and whilst some mounts were hit it was rare to see a sowar receive a bullet wound.

In the bush carnivorous animals and snakes lay in waiting whilst mosquitos preyed on unprotected human skin and often inflicted malaria on the men. Apart from the intense heat during daylight hours, one of the biggest problems on bush operations was the locating of suitable water sources; sometimes dry river beds had to be excavated before water could be found for both mounts and men, and when running water was found then crocodiles could lie in wait for unwary horses and their riders. The horses suffered, often being watered only once a day and sometimes only every 36 hours.

The normal formation used on bush patrols was single file; when the Regiment advanced an advance guard led, flanking guards moved on each side of the transport mules, and a rear guard moved behind the transport, constantly checking if an enemy patrol was following the move. On making contact with the enemy all troops dismounted, half the sowars seized the reins of all the horses and the other half engaged the enemy on foot. The priority then was to protect the horses from coming under effective enemy fire. At night the Regiment deployed in a square, with the horses being protected in the centre. However it soon became apparent that the best defence at night was to never occupy the same location twice.

Operating around the Mhumbira water holes

In early October the Regiment was deployed from Kilwa to move behind enemy lines. A 50-kilometre night march was made on a very dark night but the Intelligence staff navigated successfully to the Mhumbira water holes that were well to the rear of the Germans opposing the British at Kilwa. For the next nine days the Regiment searched for enemy supply dumps, and often these dumps were pointed out to the Intelligence staff by local villagers. A total of 2,000 man-pack loads of grain, meat and tobacco were found and destroyed, whilst the Regiment covered over 300 kilometres of ground on patrols. The dumps were usually guarded by two or three enemy Askari with occasionally a German being present whose task it was to hunt for bush meat to be sent up the line to the troops facing the British near Kilwa. The enemy guards usually took to the bush when the sowars appeared but five or six of them were killed or captured. No doubt the local villager informants were allowed to pillage the dumps before fires were lit to destroy the food and tobacco.

At one dump 300 wives of the German Askari were captured, "a fine buxom-looking lot, though with more beef than beauty". A small guard of doubtless happy sowars escorted the ladies back to the British lines. This capture was regarded as important as the Germans maintained morale amongst their Askari by allowing wives to accompany columns on the move. This first raid was judged to have been a success as when the enemy companies around Kilwa withdrew they had to march through Mhumbira without the opportunity to replenish supplies.

The fight at the Lukuledi Mission

By early October the enemy troops from the Kilwa area had crossed the Mbemkuru River and were preparing to withdraw through Nangamo, Ruponda, Lukuledi and Masasi; a German garrison was located at the Lukuledi Mission station. The German force from Mahenge commanded by Captain Theodor Tafel was to the north of them and therefore General von Lettow-Vorbeck had positioned food dumps at Ruponda and the garrison at Lukuledi Mission to assist Tafel's men. Meanwhile the German General was preparing for a decisive battle with the British forces advancing from Lindi.

In mid-October the 25th Cavalry joined the British No. 1 Column that was commanded by Brevet Lieutenant Colonel G.M. Orr, 11th King Edward's Own Lancers (Probyn's Horse). No. 1 Column advanced to Ruponda and discovered a major German depot with not only supply dumps but also workshops for repairing weapons and refurbishing equipment. This depot was destroyed after the Column had removed what it needed for its own use. During these operations the cavalry patrolled the surrounding area, having sporadic contacts with groups of enemy; one patrol located a main enemy hospital and captured the staff and patients.

On the 20th October Headquarters 25th Cavalry and 'A' (Captain H.V. Yule), and 'D' squadrons plus the two Regimental machine guns established a camp near the camp of No. 1 Column north of Lukuledi Mission. Because of the need for water for the mounts and supply mules the cavalry often camped by itself near a good water source rather than with the main Column camp. On the previous day two battalions in the Column, the Gold Coast Regiment and the 1st Battalion 3rd King's African Rifles, had attacked the German garrison at the Mission. The Gold Coast Regiment had suffered heavily by attacking down a forward slope in daylight, but the King's African Rifles had approached through bush from the west and this move caused the Germans to withdraw during the night.

At dawn the following day the 25th Cavalry advanced from Lukuledi Mission towards Masasi to reconnoitre the area, and the King's African Rifles followed in support. However the advance guard had hardly moved beyond the Mission church when it encountered machine gun fire from a strong enemy column advancing towards it. General von Lettow-Vorbeck had fought the Lindi-based British units to a standstill over the previous two days and now he was coming to re-capture Lukuledi Mission. The cavalry dismounted and took up a defensive line level with the church and the King's African Rifles occupied the old Mission compound.

The cavalry was ordered to hold the British right (west) flank and the two squadrons moved into an area of brick fields where there was some cover for the horses, and defended that flank for the remainder of the day and ensuing night. Here the two machine guns were very useful as although the Germans could often not be seen because of thick bush, the machine guns easily penetrated the bush to cause enemy casualties. Fortunately the Germans threw all their weight against the old Mission compound and the King's African Rifles fought the heaviest battle of their war against repeated enemy attacks. Finally as dusk fell the Germans withdrew.

However the cavalry camp had fared far worse, as at 0830 hours on the 21st October an enemy force under Major Georg Kraut, one of the best German field commanders, attacked the camp. Column Headquarters sent two armoured cars to assist the 40 cavalry defenders, several of whom were non-combatants, but Captain Barry was soon killed and the enemy Askari swarmed over the lines, killing animals and looting and destroying the baggage. Two British officers and three sowars managed to escape to the Column camp but the other defenders were all killed, wounded or captured.

On the 22nd October the Regiment recovered what it could of its transport and marched back to Ruponda where 'C' Squadron (Captain J. Nethersole MC), who had been on a separate local reconnaissance mission, joined it. A few days were then spent in re-organising and re-equipping and during this time 'B' Squadron (Captain C.H. Trehane) re-joined after a detached reconnaissance mission with No. 2 Column. Although the Regimental war diary does not list the casualties lost at Lukuledi, the Commonwealth War Graves Commission figures show that 22 members of the 25th Cavalry died during October 1917; this figure does not include African non-combatants such as cart drivers and labourers.

Patrolling around the Makonde Plateau

On 1st November 1917 the 25th Cavalry formed a mounted column with the only other mounted regiment in the theatre, the 10th South African Horse. The South African Colonel J.H. Breytenbach commanded the column. During November the column patrolled around the lower slopes of the Makonde Plateau in an attempt to prevent the German Schutztruppe from concentrating on the plateau. Detachments patrolled south to the Rovuma River which was the boundary between German territory to the north and Portuguese East Africa to the south. By this time tsetse-fly had killed many of the horses and well over half of the Regiment was dismounted.

But General von Lettow-Vorbeck succeeded in concentrating two-thirds of his army on the Makonde Plateau. There he ruthlessly removed the sick, wounded and faint-at-heart, leaving them to surrender to the British; he also abandoned his prisoners-of-war. With a new slimmed-down Schutztruppe of 1,500 men he crossed the Rovuma River and immediately began successfully raiding Portuguese forts and trading centres to obtain supplies, weapons and ammunition. With bolts of cloth seized from trading centres food was bought from local villagers; this endeared the Germans to the villagers as under Portuguese rule food was requisitioned from them without compensation. This consideration shown to the local villagers ensured that the Germans received good information about Allied movements in Portuguese East Africa during the next ten months of operations.

One success that the British could claim at the end of 1917 was that Tafel and his men reached the Rovuma River but as they were without rations and had no knowledge of where their General had taken his Schutztruppe, they surrendered.

Patrolling into Portuguese East Africa

From early December onwards the 25th Cavalry sent patrols into Portuguese East Africa to reconnoitre enemy positions and to record geographical data. Prominent leaders of these patrols were Captains J. Nethersole MC, L. Gall MC and W.K. Fraser-Tytler. The Medical Officer Captain N.S. Bruce usually accompanied these patrols. Later Nethersole received a **Bar** to his **Military Cross** and Fraser-Tytler and Bruce were awarded **Military Crosses**.

At this time the 10th South African Horse was repatriated and it gave its remaining horses to the 25th Cavalry. Remounts were also issued and the Regiment was able to get its dismounted men back into the saddle. The patrolling in Portuguese East Africa did not result in any contacts with the enemy but two patrols each covered over 300 kilometres of country, making useful topographical observations. The Intelligence Officers accompanying the patrols were able to identify from discussions with villagers where many of the Schutztruppe units and formations were located. Even negative information was important, as knowing where the enemy was not could be as useful as knowing where he was.

The return to India

In January 1918 the rains fell and the Rovuma River rose. All British troops south of the river were recalled back to German East Africa. The 25th Cavalry (Frontier Force) re-grouped and rode its way slowly back through the rain to Lindi harbour. After handing in horses and mules the Regiment, after four hard and often unpleasant months of campaigning, embarked on His Majesty's Transport *Salamis* on 1st February 1918 and returned to India.

Commemorations

These 26 men of the Regiment were killed or died of wounds or disease whilst in East Africa and they are commemorated in Dar Es Salaam, Tanzania, on the British and Indian Memorial and on a screen wall in the War Cemetery:

Jemadar Bachhitar; 3074 Kot Daffadar Tara Singh; 3381 Daffadar Khazan Singh; 3303 Daffadar Labh Singh; 3744 Daffadar Muhammad Akbar; 3371 Daffadar Muhammad Aman; 3870 Lance Daffadar Kishn Singh; 3193 Lance Daffadar Kehr Singh; 3553 Lance Daffadar Nand Singh; 4451 Sowar Alli Muhammad; 4157 Sowar Bahadur Khan; 4593 Sowar Banaras Khan;

4143 Sowar Banta Singh; 4639 Sowar Bir Singh; 4938 Fateh Mehdi; 4255 Sowar Jamit Singh; 4402 Sowar Jiwa Ram; 4313 Sowar Musahib Khan; 3808 Sowar Rahnat Khan; 4425 Sowar Sant Ram; 4271 Sowar Sher Singh; 3874 Sowar Teja Singh; 3794 Sowar Yusuf Khan; Followers Pal Singh, Ghasita and Kirpa.

Captain Nathanial James Merriman Barry, East African Mounted Rifles attached to the 25th Cavalry (Frontier Force) is buried in Dar Es Salaam War Cemetery, Tanzania.

Awards made to the 25th Cavalry (Frontier Force) for service in the Great War East Africa Campaign

Bar to the Military Cross:

Captain John Nethersole MC.

Military Cross:

Captain William Kerr Fraser-Tytler.

Captain Norman Stewart Bruce, Royal Army Medical Corps Special Reserve, attached to the 25th Cavalry (Frontier Force).

Indian Distinguished Service Medal:

No. 3236 Dafadar Ibrahim Khan; No. 4122 Sowar Janak Singh; No. 3612 Acting Lance Dafadar Pahlwan Khan; No. 3616 Dafadar Sehju Ram; No. 3936 Lance Dafadar Sohan Singh; and No. 3204 Kot Dafadar Suba Singh.

Mention in Despatches:

Brevet Lieutenant Colonel G.A.R. Watts; Major P.W. Burrowes; No. 3423 Lance Dafadar Abdul Samad; No. 3087 Lance Dafadar Assa Singh; No. 3302 Lance Dafadar Bishan Singh; No. 3536 Dafadar Fateh Muhammad; No. 4520 Sowar Gul Sher Khan; No. 3642 Dafadar Lachman Singh; No. 3137 Dafadar Mal Singh; Ressaidar Sher Ali Khan IDSM; and Risaldar Thakur Chand.

Operations in Transcaspia 1918 – 1919
Sowars, Sepoys and Guides fight the Bolsheviks

The Central Powers in the Caucasus in 1918

Prior to 1918 Germany and Turkey had despatched missions to Afghanistan from Baghdad that travelled through Persia. To counter these attempts by the Central Powers to influence Afghanistan to join the Jihad or Holy War against the Allies, Britain and Imperial Russia had established the East Persia Cordon. This cordon ran from Baluchistan in the south up to the Russian border in the north, and was mostly on Persian soil, just west of the Persia-Afghanistan border. The Cordon worked reasonably effectively as a barrier until the Russian Revolution in 1917 led to the dispersal of the Russian cavalry who secured the northern stretch of the Cordon; these Cossacks decided to go home. Britain then used units of the Indian Army to secure the whole length of the Cordon.

In March 1917 British forces in Mesopotamia seized Baghdad, forcing the Turks further northwards, and denying them their previous entry route into Persia. However the Turks still had an Anatolian border with Persia but far more importantly the collapse of Imperial Russian rule in the Caucasus led to a new route being opened for the Central Powers to use. Starting at Batum on the eastern shore of the Black Sea a railway led to Baku, an important oil-producing city and port in Azerbaijan on the western shore of the Caspian Sea. Across the Caspian Sea was Krasnovodsk, a very important export port for Turkestan cotton; from Krasnovodsk the Central Asian Railway led to Tashkent and then joined the Siberian and Trans-Aral Railway lines.

Germany took advantage of its Bresk-Livotsk treaty with revolutionary Russia to infiltrate purchasing agents as far as Orenburg, north of the Caspian and Aral Seas, whilst in the Caucasus German troops moved from

Batum to Tiflis ostensibly to support the breakaway state of Georgia that did not wish to remain in revolutionary Russia. The German mission in Orenburg travelled down to Baku and made arrangements to purchase Azerbaijani oil and Turkestani cotton; both commodities were desperately needed by Germany and now they could be transported westwards through the Caucasus or the Ural mountains by pipeline or rail. The cotton could be shipped from Krasnovodsk to Baku or to Astrakhan at the north-west of the Caspian where Bolshevik revolutionaries ruled. The cotton was a vital component for the German factories that produced ammunition and explosives.

Meanwhile the Turks had political ambitions of their own. Knowing that it had probably lost its Arab possessions for ever, Turkey attempted to expand its influence eastwards into the Turkic regions of Central Asia, and the apparent disintegration of the former Russian Empire provided an opportunity for action. For a time Turks and Germans worked against each other but in the end Turkey infiltrated troops across the eastern end of its Caucasian border and into Azerbaijan where they advanced on Baku. In Azerbaijan Bolshevik revolutionaries at first prevailed but the Azerbaijanis as a whole wanted to be independent and they resisted the Turkish advance.

The threat to British interests and DUNSTERFORCE

Britain saw that both Germany and Turkey could now move through the Caucasus, cross the Caspian Sea, and enter Afghanistan through its northern border; a railway branch-line ran from Merv on the Central Asian Railway to Kushka on the Afghan border where a massive arsenal of former Imperial Russian weapons and ammunition was located. Afghanistan could be pushed into a confrontation with British India that might inflame anti-colonial and religious passion in the sub-continent. The validity of this threat was demonstrated in 1919 when Afghanistan, under a new ruler, did attack India. But the important British aim in early 1918 was to stop the Central Powers from using the Russian railway system to send oil and cotton to Europe.

Britain deployed a small mission into Georgia that was expanded in January 1918 into a training mission of 200 officers and 200 senior ranks, mostly selected from Canadian, Australian, New Zealand and South African units. This unit was named DUNSTERFORCE after its commander Major General Lionel Charles Dunsterville CB, Indian Army. There were no British brigades or divisions available for use in the Caucasus, and it was hoped that Dunsterville's men could recruit and train Caucasian units that would keep German and Turkish hands off the Baku oil and Transcaspian cotton. DUNSTERFORCE entered Persia from Baghdad and was very successful at stopping Turkish advances through northern Persia. Dunsterville and a small force got to Baku and defended it from Turkish attack. However the British theatre commander in Mesopotamia, Lieutenant General W.R. Marshall KCB, denied Dunsterville reinforcements and Baku had to be evacuated by the British in mid-September 1918[49]. The Turks seized the port and the adjacent oilfields.

The response from India – the Malleson Mission

A second British Mission was sent into the region from India. Major General Wilfrid Malleson, Indian Army, moved from Quetta up the East Persia Cordon and arrived in Meshed in north-eastern Persia in July 1918. At that time the only troops available for the General's use were those serving on the Cordon, and the most effective of those were the 28th Light Cavalry and the 1st Battalion 19th Punjabis (1/19th Punjabis).General Malleson, like Dunsterville, was a linguist and he had others attached to his staff. The tasks of the Malleson Mission, known as MALMISS, were to closely observe events in Transcaspia, to rebuff enemy agents attempting to enter Afghanistan or Baluchistan from the west, to report on Afghan political developments in Herat, and to deny the Turks use of the Central Asian Railway should they seize Baku. This last task became more significant when the Turks did seize Baku in mid-September 1918.

MALMISS was resupplied by a new rail line pushed through northern Baluchistan from Quetta that was to terminate just inside the Persian border. From there a good but long motorable road was being constructed northwards to Meshed. Basically MALMISS was 'out on a limb' and would have to solve its own problems as there could be no quick response from India to requests for support. General Malleson was not a sound field commander, having been sent home by General Smuts from the East Africa campaign as a failed brigade commander, but he was an experienced intelligence staff officer and

---

49 A fuller story of DUNSTERFORCE and its achievements in Persia can be seen at: http://www.westernfrontassociation.com/great-war-on-land/other-war-theatres/3305-dunsterforce-part-1.html

at the time of his appointment Army Headquarters in Delhi had not foreseen that combat operations would occur in Transcaspia.

General Malleson quickly deployed intelligence agents across both the Afghan and Transcaspian borders and used their information to build up an accurate picture of what was happening in both regions. The Bolsheviks held a firm base in Tashkent, but in Transcaspia the Russian railway workers and the local Turcoman tribesmen had rejected the high-handed actions of the Bolsheviks and had formed their own provisional government based on the socialist ideals of Menshevism. Thus there was in Transcaspia a Menshevik government fighting against Bolshevik attacks down the railway line from Tashkent. The Menshevik government was based in Ashkhabad and it controlled the Central Asian Railway from Krasnovodsk to Bairam Ali, east of Merv, where the spearhead of the Bolshevik forces was operating.

The fighting was done along the railway line and both sides used improvised armoured trains; operations in the Kara Kum desert on either side of the line were not feasible because of the lack of water. The Menshevik soldiers were Russian ex-officers manning the armoured trains, field guns and a cavalry squadron, some Armenian and Turcoman infantry, and 500 local Turcoman cavalrymen. Colonel Oraz Sirdar, a Turcoman officer of the former Tsarist army, was the Menshevik commander. Sadly he could not discipline his Turcoman cavalry who were unreliable and motivated by self-interest and loot.

The Bolshevik army in Tashkent contained many German and Austro-Hungarian former prisoners of war[50] who had been kept in camps in Central Asia until the Russian Revolution, when they were told that they could go home if they first fought their way through the Mensheviks, as an Austro-Hungarian Mission was waiting in Tiflis to repatriate them. These Germans and Austro-Hungarians provided the professional element that the Bolshevik forces needed. Other men drafted into the Bolshevik army were former Imperial Russian soldiers, railway men and Russians living locally. The Bolsheviks were not short of weapons as they had seized the arsenal at Kushka. As the fighting developed both sides could generally get one military aircraft into the air each day for reconnaissance duties; the Mensheviks flew a Henri-Farman biplane until it crashed whilst the Bolsheviks flew a Morane-Saulnier monoplane plus a Henri-Farman.

---

50 A Swedish Red Cross report stated that there were 29,000 Germans and 26,000 Austro-Hungarian former prisoners still living in camps in Central Asia.

Malleson's agents reported that the Mensheviks in Ashkhabad wanted assistance from MALMISS and Captain Reginald Teague-Jones[51], Indian Army Reserve of Officers, was despatched to be a MALMISS liaison officer in Ashkabad. Sub-units of the 28th Light Cavalry and the 1/19th Punjabis were moved up to the Persian-Transcaspian border area, and on 8th August 1918 Delhi authorised Malleson to provide limited military and financial assistance to the Transcaspian government. As MALMISS only had the finance to cover its own needs there could be no immediate cash contributions to the Menshevik government treasury, but two days later a rifle company and a machine gun section from the Punjabis crossed into Transcaspia and occupied Artik, a station on the Central Asian Railway. From there the machine gun section under Lieutenant W.F. Gipps was sent forward to Bairam Ali accompanied by Major W.H. Bingham[52], 1/69th Punjabis, as a liaison officer.

British hostilities with the Bolsheviks commence

On 15th August the Bolsheviks attacked Bairam Ali, advancing on both flanks. The Menshevik Armenian infantry dispersed and leaped on trains to ride back 100 kilometres to Dushak. But the Menshevik No. 1 Armoured Train, manned by Russians and supported by the Punjabi machine gunners under Havildars Imam Din and Nand Singh, stood its ground until nightfall when it withdrew to Tejend. The Bolsheviks were held at Tejend the next day by a combination of firepower and track demolition, then No. 1 Train steamed back to Dushak. Havildar Nand Singh and one sepoy had been wounded and the whole machine gun section was exhausted and affected by fever, so it was withdrawn to the Persian border.

The actions at Kaakha

The Menshevik high command decided to withdraw and make a stand at Kaakha, so the armoured trains moved back. The arrangement made between MALMISS and the Transcaspian government permitted British troops to come under Menshevik tactical command, but the senior British

---

51 Captain Reginald Teague-Jones became a notorious figure as far as the Bolsheviks were concerned as they believed that he was implicated in the murder of 26 Bolshevik Commissars from Baku who were shot by the Mensheviks east of Krasnovodsk; he was later appointed to be a Member of the Order of the British Empire (MBE).

52 Major William Henry Bingham was later appointed to be an Officer of the Order of the British Empire (OBE).

officer present could request discussion of any order that was judged to be inappropriate in the prevailing circumstances. As it was now apparent that British support had to be in greater strength to be of any use at all, No. 2 Company 1/19th Punjabis, under Captain G.E.F. Shute, also moved to Kaakha. The remainder of the Punjabis concentrated at Artik.

The first Bolshevik attack on Kaakha on 26th August petered out without Captain Shute's company having to move out of its reserve position. However the situation was serious, as the Bolsheviks had come forward with several trains full of troops, and Lieutenant Colonel D.E. Knollys, the Punjabi commanding officer, advanced the remainder of his battalion to Kaakha. Colonel Knollys was not impressed with the Menshevik appreciation of and use of ground and he did not allow his battalion to be distributed in penny packets around the battlefield. The Menshevik Russian gunners and crew of No. 1 Train fought well as usual, and with Punjabi fire support held back the Bolsheviks. This train crew included a Russian lady, the widow of a Tsarist officer who had been killed by the Bolsheviks. However the Turcoman cavalry did not attempt to interfere with the main enemy attack that entered Kaakha Village. Meanwhile the Punjabis were using their Lewis light machine guns for the first time in action, and Sepoy Natha Singh had an excellent shoot from the roof of a hut before he was wounded by enemy machine gun fire[53].

As the enemy advanced through the village the Punjabi Quartermaster, Lieutenant F.W. Stewart, organised a detail of administrative sepoys and followers and blocked the enemy advance. This defensive action allowed Colonel Knollys to launch his No. 1 Company in a flank attack on the enemy advance; the Pathans and Punjabi Mussulmans of No. 1 Company wielded their bayonets with vigour and drove the Bolsheviks back into the village where a two-hour long fight succeeded in ejecting the enemy out of Kaakha and capturing four of their machine guns. During the fighting the Turcoman cavalry were totally ineffective. Lieutenant Francis William Stewart, 1/19th Punjabis, was awarded a **Military Cross**:

> *For conspicuous gallantry and devotion to duty when the enemy got round the flank and rear of camp. He collected all available odd men, and by prompt dispositions and gallant leading held off the enemy until reinforcements arrived, thereby averting complete disaster. Although wounded he continued fighting, and throughout showed great pluck and tenacity.*

---

53 No.1367 Sepoy Natha Singh, 19th Punjabis, was later Mentioned in Despatches.

The Punjabis had won the day for the Mensheviks but at a cost, as 4 sepoys were dead and 15 wounded. Captain Teague-Jones and Lieutenant Stewart were wounded, and a liaison officer, Captain K.H.W. Ward, King's Royal Rifle Corps, later died of wounds. Medical support was provided by a section of a Combined Field Ambulance under Captain J.A. Sinton VC[54] assisted by Lieutenant M. Nawaz, both of the Indian Medical Service. The Bolsheviks appeared to have taken up to 40 casualties, most of them wounded. Several sepoys had been shot from behind as during the fighting in the village it was extremely difficult to recognize which Russian troops were Bolsheviks and which were Mensheviks as the uniforms were similar, and the Bolsheviks had taken advantage of this to operate in the Punjabi rear.

On the following day a company of the 1/4th Hampshire Regiment (120 rifles) arrived at Kaakha having been sent across the Caspian Sea from Enzeli in northern Persia to Krasnovodsk, and then onwards by rail into Transcaspia. On 5th September a section (two guns) of 18-pounder field guns from 44th Battery, Royal Field Artillery, also arrived from Enzeli via Krasnovodsk. MALMISS had been authorized to raise a local levy from the Hazara Shiite population around Meshed, and 50 of these levies were sent to Kaakha. The Menshevik military situation was considerably improved. This was largely due to DUNSTERFORCE having seized much of the shipping on the Caspian Sea to place it under the command of Commodore D.T. Norris CB[55], Royal Navy, who mounted guns on most of his new fleet. With the Royal Navy controlling the southern Caspian waters the sea route from Enzeli to Krasnovodsk was secure.

The Bolsheviks attacked again at Kaakha on 11th September and used ten field guns to support their infantry, however the British 18-pounders broke up the attack so accurately that the enemy withdrew. Once again the Turcoman cavalry declined to ride down the withdrawing enemy. Seven days later the final Bolshevik attack on Kaakha was launched, this time supported by 15 guns, but again shrapnel fired by the British and Menshevik gunners deterred the enemy infantry from assaulting the British and Transcaspian defensive positions, and the Bolsheviks withdrew. On this occasion an enemy

---

54 John Alexander Sinton was awarded the Victoria Cross with the citation: 21 January 1916. At Orah Ruins, Mesopotamia, he remained on duty and tended to the wounded under very heavy fire. Even after he was shot through both arms and through the side, he refused to go to hospital. In three previous actions, he had displayed the utmost bravery.

55 Commodore David Thomas Norris, Royal Navy, was later appointed a Companion of the Most Distinguished Order of Saint Michael and Saint George (CMG).

cavalry unit got behind the Kaakha position and ripped up railway track, tore down signal cables and burned a wooden bridge before withdrawing. Yet again the Turcoman cavalry declined to participate. But a sound cavalry force was on the way as on 21st September 'C' and 'D' squadrons of the 28th Light Cavalry from Meshed, under Major J.A.C. Kreyer, joined Colonel Knollys at Kaakha.

The Battle of Dushak

The Menshevik Headquarters ordered an advance against the Bolsheviks and plans were made for an attack on Dushak. Reconnaissance patrols from the 28th Light Cavalry went out and two in particular, commanded by Lance Duffadars Ganga Singh and Tek Chand[56], had contacts with the enemy and came back with useful information. The Menshevik advance was in two columns that left Kaakha on 9th October 1918. The left column consisted of the Punjabi Nos. 2 and 3 Companies and both sections of machine guns, the British field guns escorted by the 50 Hazara levies, four Russian-manned guns and around 800 Turcoman and Armenian infantry. The right column was composed of the two Indian cavalry squadrons; the Turcoman cavalry was tasked independently with getting behind the enemy position and cutting the railway line to prevent the withdrawal of the Bolshevik trains. The Punjabi No. 1 Company and the Hampshires remained in reserve at Kaakha and at the British railhead of Arman Sagad.

After four days of marching and waiting that was confused by various orders and counter-orders from the Menshevik Headquarters, the left column approached Dushak just before first light on 14th October, but two Punjabi patrols fired at each other in the darkness and the enemy was alerted. Unfortunately in the ensuing disorder several machine and Lewis gun mules broke away from their handlers and their loads were not recovered until later. Nevertheless the left column attacked Dushak Station at dawn, trying to capitalise on what advantage of surprise still remained. The start line was 1.5 kilometres distant from the Station and the ground to be covered was very open, being a flat plain with vegetation growing to a height of 60 centimetres. One or two nullahs crossed the plain and these soon attracted many of the Turcoman and Armenian infantrymen.

---

56 Both Lance Duffadars were Mentioned in Despatches.

The British and Menshevik guns came into action efficiently in the open but the Bolshevik guns were also well manned and fired over open sights at the advancing sepoys, using percussion shrapnel and grape shot; the Punjabi casualty figure quickly rose. By now the Menshevik infantry had gone to ground and the Punjabis were fighting forward alone in short rushes, using their machine gun sections and Lewis gunners to cover the flanks. As soon as a charge could be made the Punjabis concentrated fire on the enemy machine guns and went in with the bayonet, quickly over-running 6 enemy field guns and 16 machine guns. No. 440 Havildar Imam Din, 1/19th Punjabis, was awarded an **Indian Order of Merit (2nd Class):** *When in charge of a machine gun, brought into action under very heavy gun and rifle fire, he successfully silenced one of the enemy's guns. When finally severely wounded and unable to move, he refused all assistance and ordered his gun back into safety. He had previously done exceedingly well on with his gun on 11th August[57] on which occasion he commanded the section in the absence of his officer.*

Having reached the Station the Punjabi advance continued into the railway yards beyond. At this time the officer commanding No. 1 Company, Lieutenant James Eliot Stephen, and Subadar Mehdi Khan, both of the 1/19th Punjabis, were killed in action. Officer casualties quickly mounted, Lieutenant Gipps being hit in the leg and Captain G.E.F. Shute in the shoulder; both were in No. 2 Company. Undaunted Subadar Bal Singh took over as company commander and was awarded an **Indian Order of Merit (2nd Class):** *In an attack on the enemy he led his platoon with great dash and bravery under very heavy machine gun fire. He took command of the company when the British Officer had been wounded and by his coolness and power of command, ensured the retirement being conducted in an orderly manner.*

During the fighting in the station yard and village that lay beyond Captain G. Pigot, commanding No. 3 Company, was wounded in the throat and evacuated; Subadar Major Isa Singh took over command of the two Punjabi companies, and he was later admitted to **The Order of British India** (OBI). Captains George Eric FitzGerald Shute and Geoffrey Pigot, both 19th Punjabis, and Lieutenant Mohamed Nawaz, Indian Medical Service, were all awarded **Military Crosses.**

Indian Orders of Merit (2nd Class) were awarded to No. 2532 Sepoy Dalel Singh: *He carried messages throughout the day for his company commander*

---

57 This must refer to the first action at Kaakha on 15th August 1918.

regardless of personal safety and finally delivered an important message after being severely wounded. And to No. 1352 Lance Naik Muhammad Akbar, 19th Punjabis: *He showed great bravery and initiative when in command of a Lewis gun on the 14th October 1918. He climbed onto the roof of a house with his gun, 40 yards in advance of all other troops and in spite of heavy fire and his exposed position, kept up a concentrated fire on the enemy. Later, from the same position, he fired on one of the enemy's trains and forced it to retire.*

When the two 28th Light Infantry squadrons in the right column heard the heavy firing at Dushak a decision was made to proceed there mounted to support the Punjabis. An enemy armoured train opened fire on the sowars but fortunately most shells were High Explosive and not shrapnel. The squadrons were ordered into 'half squadron column' at 100 metres interval and they galloped to the station; on the way they met scattered groups of hostile Bolsheviks and killed around 60 of them, mostly with the lance. Unfortunately during one of these skirmishes Jemadar Basanta Ram was killed in action.

One of the last shells fired in the battle by the British 18-pounder guns detonated three enemy railway ammunition trucks in a siding; the ensuing explosion flattened the surrounding area and killed many Bolsheviks. Sadly an enemy waggon load of horses was burned to death in the fire that followed the explosion. However the Bolsheviks were reluctant to withdraw as some of their armoured trains were trapped on the railway line west of Dushak station. Bolshevik reinforcements arrived by train from Tejend and Merv, proving that the Turcoman cavalry had not cut the line to the east, and the Menshevik commander ordered a withdrawal. At this time the two 28th Light Cavalry squadrons were east of the station with the British guns and Hazara Levies, and the Punjabis were re-grouping west of the station with the Menshevik guns and the remaining 40 Russian and Armenian infantry who had not by now disappeared from the battlefield. The Turcoman cavalrymen were out of sight on their way home, laden with loot from Dushak station and village, and from damaged or wrecked Bolshevik trains.

The dismounted cavalry covered the Menshevik withdrawal; the Bolsheviks quickly got machine guns into action and hit around 30 of the cavalry mounts that were being led to the rear. By now the Bolshevik artillerymen were shaken and although they engaged the withdrawing sowars they did not inflict casualties. After withdrawing to the Menshevik railhead at

Arman Sagad the infantry and gunners were railed back to Kaakha whilst the cavalry marched, arriving there at dawn on 15th October.

During the fighting at Dushak the 28th Light Cavalry lost 1 Indian officer and 7 sowars killed, 12 sowars wounded and 60 horses killed and wounded. The 1/19th Punjabis lost 1 British and 1 Indian officer and 45 sepoys killed, 3 British officers, 1 Indian officer and 135 sepoys wounded. The Hazara Levies lost 5 sepoys missing believed killed. The withdrawal from Dushak in the face of an enemy counter-attack was initially a disappointment to those who fought there, however the Bolsheviks had been so shaken by their experiences and the loss of over 500 men that soon they withdrew eastwards all the way to Merv. The Mensheviks, thanks to the courage and audacity of their Russian crew on No. 1 Armoured Train, quickly advanced and established a new railhead east of Tejend. This move was followed by a joint force of 28th Light Cavalry and Turcoman cavalry demonstrating their ability to appear to the east of Merv, causing the Bolsheviks to withdraw even further to the east of Bairam Ali.

The Punjabis were re-grouping and training up key personnel to replace casualties; the only British officers left were Colonel Knollys and the Adjutant, Captain R.F.G. Adams[58]; Indian officers commanded the companies. The Hampshire company garrisoned Merv and the 28th Light Cavalry accompanied the Menshevik armoured trains now located east of Bairam Ali. The occupation of Tejend and Merv was critical for the Menshevik government, as the agricultural land around those two oases provided the food that was needed in Ashkhabad.

A winter lull

The Bolshevik withdrawal from Dushak allowed the sepoys and sowars on 18th October to recover and bury or cremate the bodies of their comrades who had fallen on the battlefield. At the end of that month Turkey signed an armistice and ceased fighting, followed by Austria-Hungary and Germany. This soon made the politicians in London and Delhi question the future of MALMISS, and whilst this subject was debated General Malleson was ordered not to take any further offensive action against the Tashkent Bolsheviks without receiving prior authority, but his force could fight defensively. In late 1918 the various White Russian armies that were fighting against Bolshevism

---

58 Captain R.F.G. Adams was later Mentioned in Despatches.

appeared to be reasonably competent, and it was hoped that the White Russians would contain and destroy the Reds.

From Mesopotamia General Marshall, who had previously overseen the fall of Baku to the Turks by refusing reinforcements to the DUNSTERFORCE units fighting around that city, had to send British troops back to Baku to enforce the armistice terms on the Turks there, to maintain law and order, and to secure the oilfields. The British control of Baku port allowed the White Russians to send units of Caucasian Daghestan Cossack cavalry across the Caspian to reinforce the Ashkhabad Mensheviks. As the Ashkhabad government was perpetually facing dissent from within the Transcaspian population these Cossacks were retained in Ashkhabad for a time as an internal security force, but as the Daghestanis' favourite pastimes were to gallop madly around town and loot the bazaars they were soon sent to the Bairam Ali front. Rifle companies from the 9th Battalion The Royal Warwickshire Regiment moved into barracks in Krasnovodsk and Ashkhabad for security duties.

The British Army of the Black Sea, under General Sir G.F. Milne KCB, KCMG, DSO, the former British commander in Salonika, extended its garrisoning of the Caucasus and took control of the railway that ran from Batum to Baku. This led to the handing over of MALMISS from Delhi to London, resulting in the Line of Communication for MALMISS being through the Caucasus and over the Caspian. As this route used ships and railways this was in fact a more efficient arrangement than the previous overland camel-convoy and motor route up the East Persia Cordon, or the alternative Persian route from Krasnovodsk to Enzeli and then overland to Baghdad.

Winter in Transcaspia brought heavy snowfalls and freezing temperatures and initially both sides concentrated more on survival than on fighting. MALMISS propaganda aimed at the German and Austro-Hungarian former prisoners of war fighting for the Bolsheviks offered repatriation to them if they crossed over to the Menshevik lines. This worked well for a time with up to 20 men per night crossing over until the Menshevik Turcoman cavalry realised what was happening; the Turcomans then intercepted the ex-prisoners of war in the desert and murdered them for their clothing. This stopped the flow of enemy troops seeking repatriation to Europe.

General Malleson had asked Delhi for a Brigadier General to be sent to command the British troops in action in Transcaspia, as Colonel Knollys who had been doing that job as well as commanding his battalion was over-tasked. Lieutenant Colonel (Temporary Brigadier General) G.A.H. Beatty DSO & Bar[59], 9th Hodson's Horse, was selected and he travelled up the East Persia Cordon to arrive at Meshed on 9th November. He was accompanied by a small brigade headquarters and his principal staff officer was Major J.P. Thompson[60], 35th Scinde Horse. For a few weeks Malleson retained Beatty in Meshed whilst various conferences and debates took place, but in early January 1919 General Beatty crossed the border and took up his command appointment at Bairam Ali.

The appearance of the Guides' patrol

In January Captain L.V.S. Blacker and 16 men of the Queen's Own Corps of Guides (Lumsden's) appeared at the Menshevik railhead at Bairam Ali. On 7th February 1918 this mounted patrol had moved from Kashmir through Gilgit, Hunza and then Kashgar in Chinese Turkestan; from there permission was eventually granted to visit Tashkent in Russian Turkestan. The patrol was escorting Sir George Macartney who was on a diplomatic mission to learn what he could of the political situation in Bolshevik-governed Tashkent. Then, moving on a reconnaissance mission, Blacker and his men went back through the Kunlun mountains and the Muztagh Pass to Yarkand and on to Merv. The patrol contained specialist linguists, topographic scouts, weapons specialists, a signaller and a carrier pigeon expert, a first-aid man and veterinarian. Three Hazara men of this patrol actually owned land at Merv, obtained by their families in Tsarist times

Whilst at Bairam Ali the Guides trained the soldiers of the Menshevik army in basic military skills, familiarising them with the Lee-Metford rifles that MALMISS was supplying to the Ashkabad government. Following up a suggestion from the Menshevik military commander Oraz Sirdar, MALMISS decided to send a 100-camel convoy of weapons and ammunition to the Emir of Bokhara who wished to remain independent of Bolshevik, Menshevik or any other kind of rule. Two Guides' non-commissioned officers, Awal

---

59 Temporary Brigadier General Guy Archibald Hastings Beatty was later appointed a Companion of the Most Distinguished Order of Saint Michael and Saint George (CMG).

60 Major John Pickering Thompson was later appointed to be an Officer of the Order of the British Empire (OBE).

Nur and Karbali Muhammad, took the convoy around the Bolshevik lines to Bokhara, where the Emir decorated them with the **Star of Bokhara** and gave them temporary officer appointments in his army whilst they trained the Bokharan soldiers on the new weapons. The journey had been dangerous and on one occasion a Bolshevik patrol was dispersed with rifle fire. In recognition of their achievements No. 156 Company Quartermaster Havildar Awal Nur was later awarded an **Indian Order of Merit (2nd Class)** and Temporary Lance Dafadar Karbali Muhammad received an **Indian Distinguished Service Medal**.

The battle of Annenkovo

In January 1919 the front was on the Central Asia Railway north-east of Merv near Annenkovo which lay 50 kilometres forward from Bairam Ali. The Mensheviks were dispirited with the British decision not to advance as it was thought that the Bolshevik forces would easily fold and that a Menshevik bridgehead could be captured at Charjui on the east bank of the Oxus River. Such a move would improve the Menshevik position in Transcaspia considerably. To strengthen Menshevik resolve a half-squadron of the 28th Light Cavalry and a company (150 rifles) of the 1/19th Punjabis were stationed at the front at Annenkovo. These British troops were relieved every eight days or so from Bairam Ali where there were a squadron of 28th Light Cavalry, the Battalion Headquarters and two companies of the 1/19th Punjabis and the two British 18-pounder guns.

On 16th January the Bolsheviks achieved total surprise by attacking with 4,000 infantry, 8 guns and several squadrons of cavalry. Thick fog covered the ground at daybreak and the Menshevik cavalry patrols reported nothing unusual. The first intimation of trouble came at 0850 hours when the sepoys and sowars at the front heard the railway line being blown to the south-west, signalling that the enemy was behind them. Menshevik cavalry patrols then reported that the railway and telegraph lines were cut and that four squadrons of Bolshevik cavalry had been observed about five kilometres to the north-west. A prisoner was taken who stated that the enemy intended to attack from the north.

The sowars not out on patrol positioned themselves to fight with the armoured trains against enemy advancing from the east whilst Captain G. Pigot MC, 19th Punjabis, now recovered from his throat wound and in command of No. 3 Company, deployed his men to face the attack from the north. A decisive factor that was going to save the day for the Indian troops was that the enemy did not prevent the Menshevik train repair crew from repairing the blown track, and the Punjabis' No. 1 Company under Major J.G.P. Drummond was equipped and standing by to routinely relieve No. 3 Company at the front.

The Menshevik Turcoman and Armenian infantry advanced north to find the enemy who soon outflanked them, causing a rapid retreat. Thick mist still hugged the ground making it difficult to recognise friend from foe. Captain Pigot sent two platoons under Lieutenant L.S. Ingle, Indian Army Reserve of Officers attached to 1/19th Punjabis, to extend the left flank of the Menshevik infantry. This was achieved and the Mensheviks briefly halted until enemy machine gunners infiltrated in the mist causing the Mensheviks to withdraw again. Pigot sent another platoon forward and Louis Sobaux Ingle used it effectively, being awarded a **Military Cross**: *For conspicuous gallantry on Bahram Ali Front on 16th January, 1919. He showed marked ability in handling three platoons with which he was opposing the enemy's attack. He continually led his platoon forward under heavy fire, though the enemy were enveloping his flank, to restore order on the right. His cool courage inspired his men during a critical period, and he kept his company commander informed of the situation.*

Two Indian officers of the 19th Punjabis were later awarded the **Indian Order of Merit (2nd Class),** one being a posthumous award. Subadar Aziz Ullah's citation was: *This Indian officer showed conspicuous gallantry and ability in the leading of his platoon when out of touch with his company commander on the 16th January 1919. He also behaved with conspicuous bravery on two former occasions.* The citation for Subadar Hukam Singh read: *This Indian officer led his platoon into action on 19th January 1919[61] with the greatest gallantry and inspired all his men by his fearlessness. He was killed while encouraging and leading his men.*

The fighting continued throughout the day but at 1500 hours the situation changed when the train carrying No. 1 Company chugged into the fight. Sepoys de-trained at high speed, and after a quick briefing from Pigot, Drummond led three platoons of Pathans forward northwards to halt the Bolshevik advance. The enemy outflanked them so Drummond sent Lieutenant Cuvelier with No. 4 Platoon out wide, and a well-sited Lewis gun prevented the enemy from reaching the railway line. Captain (Acting Major) James Geoffrey Powys Drummond, 1/19th Punjabis, later received

---

61 The action was on the 16th January 1919.

a **Military Cross**: *For conspicuous gallantry on Bahram Ali Front on 16th January, 1919. When sent to reinforce our troops, who were being heavily shelled, he detrained his company under heavy fire, and promptly led them forward, though neither our own troops nor the enemy could be located owing to a thick mist. His prompt action and bold initiative and leading resulted in the enemy being driven off with heavy losses.*

Captain Pigot had to deal with an attack from the east. The sowars, using a Hotchkiss gun, had supported the armoured trains in stopping the enemy moving down the railway line towards them, but at 1730 hours a strong enemy attack was put in using new troops. Pigot ran down the line with his company headquarters and remaining platoon just as the Bolsheviks were reaching the Menshevik armoured trains. A group of seven Russians from a train counter-attacked the enemy with the bayonet closely followed by Pigot's Punjabi Mussulmans who drove the enemy out of the railway cutting and into the desert. Geoffrey Pigot received a **Bar to his Military Cross**: *For gallantry in action on Bahram Ali front on 16th January, 1919. By his prompt action and able disposition of the advanced British troops, of which he was in command, he enabled an attack by the enemy in overwhelming numbers to be held off till reinforcements arrived. His coolness and decision throughout the action inspired confidence in all ranks.*

Throughout the battle Nos. 1 and 3 Companies had not been able to see each other due to the mist, but by advancing towards the sound of the guns and reacting rapidly to enemy sightings the company officers had been able to decisively blunt the enemy attacks. The Bolsheviks, who held the advantages of surprise and superior numbers throughout the action, could have stayed and probably won the fight, and if they had captured the Menshevik armoured trains the Transcaspian forces would have been emasculated. But perhaps becoming disillusioned by both the thick mist that hampered visibility and battlefield control, and by the arrival of Drummond's company, the Bolsheviks broke contact and withdrew at 1800 hours. Bolshevik casualties were estimated at 600 from the fighting and 500 from frostbite due to the bitterly cold night approach and withdrawal marches. After the action nearly 200 enemy bodies were found around the battlefield, including those of two females; all the corpses had been stripped of clothing by the Turcomans.

The Mensheviks had suffered around 70 casualties and the 1/19th Punjabis lost Subadar Hukam Singh and 7 sepoys killed, 2 sepoys died of wounds and 36 were wounded. One other posthumous **Indian Order of Merit (2nd Class)** was awarded to No. 989 Havildar Farid Khan, 1/19th Punjabis: *For conspicuous gallantry on the 16th January 1919 in pressing forward at the* head of his section under very heavy fire. His total disregard of danger on this and former occasions was of the greatest assistance to his platoon commander and an example to his men. This non-commissioned officer was killed in action.* Subedar Nihal Singh and several sepoys received the **Indian Distinguished Service Medal**.

Cavalry Actions

After the Annenkovo battle General Beatty introduced a new defence plan of wired-in mutually supporting picquet positions manned by sepoys. The sowars were heavily tasked with cavalry patrols, having to count the number of Bolshevik trains at the front each night as well as observing possible enemy approach routes. The enemy was not going to be allowed to launch another surprise attack.

Although the sepoys did not know it, 1/19th Punjabis had fought its last action in Transcaspia; but this was not the case for the 28th Light Cavalry. Whilst leading a nine-man patrol in January 1919 No. 1621 Lance Duffadar Bhola Ram of 'D' Squadron, 28th Light Cavalry, found himself cut off by about 25 Bolsheviks. Bhola Ram ordered a charge, and spearing two enemy his patrol broke through the Bolshevik ranks. Bhola Ram later received an **Indian Distinguished Service Medal** and a **Russian Cross of St. George (2nd Class)**[62].

A more serious engagement took place later in early March when No. 2249 Lance Duffadar Manawar Khan of 'A' Squadron, 28th Light Cavalry, found his 13-man patrol surrounded by around 150 enemy cavalry who appeared from behind large sand hills. Manawar Khan ordered his Punjabi Mussulmans to close ranks and charge through the enemy, which they did cutting down 22 Bolsheviks in the process. Manowar Khan received the only **Indian Order of Merit (2nd Class)** awarded to his regiment during the Great War: *For conspicuous gallantry and dash on the 2nd March 1919; when in command of a patrol of 13 men he was surrounded by about 150 of the enemy's cavalry, he without hesitation led his patrol to the charge and broke through the enemy's ranks, spearing all opposed to them. Later when pursued by the enemy he himself halted, took up a position and opened rapid fire on the enemy, shooting 3 of them and checking the pursuit, thereby saving the lives of the remainder of the patrol with him.*

---

62 These two medals were auctioned by Dix, Noonan and Webb on 19th September 2003. The Russian medal was officially numbered 35 313.

No. 2311 Trumpeter Murad Ali killed two enemy with his sword and a third with his revolver as he galloped away; he later received an **Indian Distinguished Service Medal** as did another member of the patrol, No. 2452 Acting Lance Duffadar Fazal Khan. All members of the patrol were awarded the **Russian Cross of St. George** in a variety of classes; the regimental history states that the medal ribbons were received but that the medals were not.

The patrol was scattered and trickled back to the Menshevik railhead over the following 24 hours, except for three sowars who were missing. These three lost their mounts in the fighting and were taken prisoner by the Bolsheviks, who deserve credit for this act considering the losses that they had themselves suffered. The three sowars were incarcerated in a camp at Vyerni, about 800 kilometres north-east of Tashkent. Two men, No.2391 Acting Lance Dafadar Lall Khan and No. 2663 Sowar (Shoeing Smith) Muhammad Yar Khan, escaped separately. Both men used their initiative in getting themselves back to their regiment, Lal Khan travelled on train and foot through Tashkent, Bokhara and Ashkabad to Meshed whilst Muhammad Yar Khan walked from Vyerni to Kashgar in China, where the British Consul-General forwarded him through Gilgit to Srinagar. Both men also received the **Indian Distinguished Service Medal**. The third man, No. 2479 Sowar Gulfaraz Khan, was known to be alive when the other two escaped, but he was never seen again.

British intervention in Transcaspia ends

In late January 1919 General Milne, Commander of the Army of the Black Sea, travelled to Transcaspia and after discussions with General Malleson he visited Annenkovo to see the front and congratulate the Punjabis, 28th Light Cavalry and British gunners on their prowess on the battlefield. However General Milne was not happy to have part of his command extended so far eastwards into Central Asia with what were by now redundant objectives. On his return to Constantinople he advised London that British and Indian troops should be withdrawn from Transcaspia, and this was agreed. The Transcaspian government was understandably not happy with this news, and even unhappier were the Turcomans who expected to get a rough deal from whatever Russian administration came to power. The White Russian General Denikin sent troops, guns and aircraft across the Caspian Sea and these units took over the front from the Punjabis, Light Cavalry and British gunners. A considerable quantity of military supplies was left by MALMISS for the use of the Transcaspian government.

By 1st April 1919 the British units in Transcaspia had been evacuated to or through Krasnovodsk whilst the Indian Army units, including Captain Blacker's Guides patrol, crossed the Persian border to Meshed where they were employed on security duties along the East Persia Cordon necessitated by the 3rd Afghan War. As the White Russian armies in Russia faltered and lost ground the Tashkent Bolsheviks were able to receive 'Red Army' Russian military reinforcements and in May they captured Annenkovo and Merv, in June they took Tejend, in July Kaakha and Ashkabad fell to them, and following the British evacuation of Krasnovodsk that port was in Bolshevik hands in January 1920. The Turkic and other local inhabitants of Central Asia were subjected to a re-colonisation from Russia, but one with ruthless socialist ideals rather than Imperial objectives; seventy years were to pass before Transcaspia re-emerged as an independent nation titled Turkmenistan, with its capital city being Ashgabat.

Gallantry awards made to Indian Army units for the Transcaspia operations

Distinguished Service Order

- Major William George Broughton Ischia Hawley, 28th Light Cavalry.
- Major (Acting Lieutenant Colonel) Denis Erskine Knollys, 1/19th Punjabis.
- Major John Arthur Claude Kreyer, 28th Light Cavalry.

Bar to the Military Cross

- Lieutenant (Acting Captain) Geoffrey Pigot, 1/19th Punjabis.

Military Cross

- Captain (Acting Major) James Geoffrey Powys Drummond, 1/19th Punjabis.
- Lieutenant Louis Sobaux Ingle, Indian Army Reserve of Officers attached to 1/19th Punjabis.
- Lieutenant Mohamad Nawaz, Indian Medical Service.

- Lieutenant (Acting Captain) Geoffrey Pigot, 1/19th Punjabis.

- Captain George Eric FitzGerald Shute, 1/19th Punjabis.

- Lieutenant Francis William Stewart, Indian Army Reserve of Officers attached to 1/19th Punjabis.

Order of British India (2nd Class)

- Subadar Major and Honorary Lieutenant Isar Singh (Bahadur), 1/19th Punjabis.

Indian Order of Merit (2nd Class)

- **28th Light Cavalry:** 2249 Lance Dafadar Manawar Khan.

- **19th Punjabis:** Subadar Bal Singh; 2352 Sepoy Dalel Singh; 440 Havildar Imam Din; 1352 Lance Naik Muhammed Akbar; Subadar Aziz Ullah; Subadar Hukam Singh; Havildar Farid Khan.

- **2nd Battalion Queen Victoria's Own Corps of Guides (Frontier Force) (Lumsden's Infantry):** 156 Company Quartermaster Havildar Awal Nur.

Indian Distinguished Service Medal

- **28th Light Cavalry:** Risaldar Sawant Singh; Ressaidar Sher Singh;

- 2180 Dafadar Rajoo Singh; 2264 Lance Dafadar Munshi; 1550 Acting Lance Dafadar Dhanpat; 1997 Acting Lance Dafadar Jaman Singh; 2527 Acting Lance Dafadar Kishore Singh; 2502 Sowar Harnath Singh;

- 1621 Dafadar Bola Ram; 2452 Acting Lance Dafadar Fazal Khan; 2311 Trumpeter Murad Ali; 2391 Acting Lance Dafadar Lall Khan;No. 2663 Sowar (Shoeing smith) Muhammad Yar Khan

- **19th Punjabis:** Jemadar Nihal Singh; 623 Havildar Mustamir; 92 Havildar Asa Singh; 528 Havildar Tora Khan; 533 Naik Jowala Singh; 1156 Naik Karam Singh; 348 Naik Sher Singh; 954 Lance Naik Gurdit Singh; 939 Lance Naik Sohan Singh; 767 Lance Naik Gian Singh; 1440 Lance Naik Gulab Khan; 1397 Lance Naik Shah Sowar; 465 Lance Naik Asa Singh; 2933 Sepoy Surjan Singh; 1372

Sepoy Udham Singh; 2495 Sepoy Charag Din; 1725 Sepoy Karim Shah.

- **Queen Victoria's Own Corps of Guides (Frontier Force) Cavalry:** Temporary Lance Dafadar Karbali Muhammad.

Russian Cross of St. George (2nd Class)

- **28th Light Cavalry:** 2249 Lance Duffadar Manowar Khan; 1621 Duffadar Bhola Ram.

Russian Cross of St. George (3rd Class)

- **28th Light Cavalry:** 2311 Trooper Murad Ali.

Russian Cross of St. George (4th Class)

- **28th Light Cavalry:** Sowars 2447 Nadir Khan; 2479 Gulfaraz Khan; 2494 Shaikh Abdulla; 2623 Mohammed Yar Khan; 2722 Taib Khan; 2764 Fateh Khan; 2809 Shabaz Khan; 2823 Mehar Khan; 2826 Ghulam Muhammad Khan; 2813 Fazal Ilahi Khan.

Bokharan Decorations

The regimental history of the 28th Light Cavalry lists Captain J.A.C. Kreyer as receiving the Star of Bokhara (1st Class).

The same history lists the following recipients of the Bokharan Star: 1911 Duffadar Quader Khan; 1874 Farrier Abdul Karim; 1894 Sowar Shaikh Fayaz; 1984 Duffadar Raot Singh; 1640 Sowar Nar Singh; 2642 Sowar Kishore Singh; 2228 Duffadar Batna; 3336 Sowar Dalipa; 2420 Sowar Basanta.

Blacker's *On Secret Patrol in High Asia* names 156 Company Quartermaster Havildar Awal Nur and Temporary Lance Dafadar Karbali Muhammad, both of the Guides, as receiving the Star of Bokhara.

Battle Honour

The 28th Light Cavalry and the 1/19th Punjabis were awarded the unique Battle Honour "**MERV**".

Fighting The Tangistanis
Bushire, Persia, July – September 1915

Persia and German Influence

When the Great War started, Persia was a weakly-governed country because effective power lay in the hands of regional administrators and their war-lord allies. The Persian Army provided colour on ceremonial occasions but did not fare well when fighting the many bandits and war-lords within the country. The Persian Gendarmerie, the equivalent of an armed national police force that also collected revenue, was controlled by Swedish officers on contract appointments, and many of these Swedes supported Germany and Kaiser Wilhelm's ambitions. Dotted around Persia in strategic locations were German political and intelligence agents who generally operated under the guise of businessmen. Once hostilities between the Great Powers commenced these German agents used gold, weapons and ammunition to create alliances with Persian tribes who were prepared to attack British interests.

By agreement with the Persian government in Tehran, Britain maintained a string of posts along the telegraph line that followed the Persian Gulf northern coastline; these posts were garrisoned by detachments from units of the Indian Army. British ambitions were to preserve the integrity of Persia as an independent but compliant state whilst using it as a buffer to protect India. German long-term ambitions were to use Persia as a neutral route to Afghanistan from where, hopefully, India could be de-stabilised by Ghadarite Indian revolutionaries. Once Turkey became a German ally Jihad, or Holy War, was declared from Constantinople and the Germans used Turkish religious and social influence to inflame susceptible Persians against the British presence in their Muslim country. The hope was that Persia would ally itself with the Central Powers.

But there was one other powerful nation in the region who wished Persia to remain neutral, and also to be compliant – Britain's ally Imperial Russia who was Persia's northern neighbour. In 1907 Britain had signed an agreement with Russia termed the Anglo-Russian Convention. This agreement partitioned Persia into two spheres of influence and a neutral sphere. The British sphere of influence lay in the south-east (see map of Persia), the Russian sphere was the northern half of Persia, and the neutral sphere stretched across the country. Whilst both Britain and Russia argued that their Convention was designed to strengthen the integrity and independence of Persia, the Persians saw Russia's move as being a prelude to partition. Britain's apparent aim was to secure India from Russian territorial advances, as had occurred in Central Asia, but whatever the real British reason, the Convention was deeply unpopular amongst Persians who thenceforth regarded Britain with suspicion or enmity.

Once the Great War started Persian territory in the Russian sphere of influence was invaded by the Turks, and then fought over by Russian and Turkish armies. In July 1915, after considerable political activity, Britain and Russia intervened militarily in eastern Persia including in the neutral sphere, by creating the East Persia Cordon. Indian Army troops entered south-eastern Persia whilst Russian troops entered from across their border east of the Caspian Sea. The two allied forces linked up and attempted to prevent infiltration by the Central Powers through Persia into Afghanistan.

Bushire in mid-1915

Bushire was a Persian island on the north Gulf coast, but unless there were abnormally high tides it could always be accessed by an expanse of sand called the Mashileh that acted as a causeway to the mainland. As Bushire was the principal Persian port, a British political Residency and a telegraph station were located there, along with a garrison consisting of a double-company from an Indian infantry regiment. The tribal area of Tangistan was located south-east of Bushire and the Tangistanis were a ferocious and predatory people. Inflaming these tribesmen against the British was Doctor Listermann, the German consul in Bushire who had received instructions from his Legation in Tehran to cut the British telegraph cable. Listermann incited Rais Ali, the tribal Chief of Dilwar, 40 kilometres south of Bushire and also on the coast, to attack the British Residency. Rais Ali had an axe to grind as the Royal Navy had destroyed many of Dilwar's fishing and cargo vessels in 1913 during a dispute over piracy.

The British, being aware of Listerman's activities because of information supplied by friendly Khans or tribal chiefs, sent warships to Bushire and Dilwar, and prepared to land troops bound for Basra, Mesopotamia at Bushire. Parallel political activity persuaded the local Persian Governor that the German Consul's activities were un-neutral, and the Tehran government was informed that Britain would arrest any other European who provoked anti-British activities. These measures led to a lessening of tension. However in May 1915 the Persian Governor of Bushire, aware of a village chieftain's plot to attack the British residency and needing support because his own gendarmes were defecting, asked for British help. In the resulting action on 7th May about 200 rifles of the 96th Berar Infantry under Major C.E.H. Wintle engaged and defeated the insurgents in their village, killing, wounding or capturing 28 of them at a cost of three sepoy casualties. The Bushire garrison was then increased to half-battalion size.

Then a German equivalent of Lawrence of Arabia appeared, he was Wilhelm Wassmuss, a former Bushire Consul who had spent three months during 1913 in Shiraz, the important city north-east of Bushire. Wassmuss' activities in Persia were to occupy many British troops for the remainder of the Great War. Wassmuss had been tasked by Berlin with crossing Persia and entering Afghanistan, along with two German companions, Niedermayer and Hentig. The latter two reached Kabul in September 1915, but Wassmuss was apprehended by tribes on the British pay-roll. He escaped and made his way down to Shiraz where he spread the word that Kaiser Wilhelm had converted to Islam and had visited Mecca. Many in Shiraz, especially the Gendarmerie and its Swedish officers there, warmed to Wassmuss' inflammatory speeches against the British presence in Bushire.

The action at Bushire 12th – 13th July 1915

In 1915 Ramadhan, the Muslim month of day-time fasting, was expected to commence on 15th July. Wassmuss urged the Dilwar Tangistanis to attack Bushire and kill all the British there before Ramadhan started, and some of them obliged him. A two-pronged insurgent attack was planned from the south and from the east. On 12th July a report reached Major H.E. Oliphant, 96th Berar Infantry and commander of the British outposts, that enemy tribesmen had been observed in nullas (dry water-courses) three kilometres south of the outpost line.

Oliphant was not inclined to believe the report but he rode out on reconnaissance with the Assistant Political Officer, Captain G.J.L. Ranking, Indian Political Department; accompanying the two officers were five mounted sowars of the Residency escort and 27 rifles of the 96th Berar Infantry. Unfortunately Oliphant's mounted party rode too far ahead of its supporting riflemen and was surprised by the insurgents; Oliphant and Ranking were killed and three sowars were killed or wounded. Oliphant died in a gallant attempt to save Ranking. As dusk fell that evening the insurgents attacked the outposts but were repulsed. Another attack early next day was also defeated and the Tangistanis then disappeared. The enemy plan had miscarried because the southern group had been observed before the eastern group had concentrated to attack. Major Edward Havelock Oliphant was later posthumously Mentioned in Despatches.

The British attack on Dilwar, 13th–15th August 1915

Britain complained to Persia about the attack on Bushire and demanded reparations; until these were paid Britain determined to occupy Bushire and to attack Dilwar to punish the insurgents. Naval craft, a squadron from the 16th Cavalry and the entire 11th Rajputs were sent to Bushire, along with two captured Turkish guns, only one of which was later found to be serviceable. Meanwhile the Germans in Bushire were believed to have slipped away to Shiraz; soon afterwards the Khans astride the Shiraz road blocked it and cut the telegraph wires running inland.

On 10th August 1915 a British expedition left Bushire to carry out punitive measures against Dilwar. The ships involved were:

- *HMS Juno* (Captain D. St. A. Wake) – 11 x 6-inch, 8 x 12-pounder and 1 x 3-pounder guns.

- *HMS Pyramus* – 8 x 4-inch and 8 x 3-pounder guns.

- *HMIMS Lawrence* – 4 x 4-inch and 4 x 6-pounder guns.

- *HMIMS Dalhousie* – 6 x 6-pounder guns.

The designated landing party, under Commander Viscount Kelburn, Royal Navy (*HMS Pyramus*), consisted of:

- Captain G. Carpenter, Royal Marine Light Infantry (RMLI), with 50 NCOs and marines and from *HMS Juno*.

- 9 marines from *HMS Pyramus*.

- 11 Petty Officers and seamen from *HMS Juno* manning machine guns.

- A demolition party of 1 Warrant Officer and 20 men from *HMS Juno*.

- 4 signallers from *HMS Juno*.

- 1 Medical Officer and 10 stretcher bearers from *HMS Juno*.

- 24 Seedie Boys (locally enlisted stokers) acting as ammunition and machine gun carriers.

- Major Wintle with one British officer and 280 sepoys of the 96th Berar Infantry.

- 5 machine guns.

Because of unfavourable weather, landings could not commence until 11th August, and then conditions were still difficult. An inshore current took the boats 1,600 metres away from the planned landing site, and the steamboats had to slip the tow-ropes 350 metres from the beach. Whilst the boats were being hauled ashore the Tangistanis fired their rifles from trenches, *Juno*'s pinnacle losing four men killed and seven wounded. *HMS Juno* bombarded the foreshore at a range of about 7,250 metres with her 6-inch guns, but the fire had little effect on the enemy.

However once marines landed the tribesmen hastily withdrew about two kilometres inland. A base was established and entrenched near the beach, reconnaissance patrols went out, and stores and the balance of the landing party were brought ashore. Major Wintle took command. This was an extremely difficult time of the year for infantry operations because of the severely hot climatic conditions.

The village to be destroyed was New Dilwar and its large fort, but it was not marked on the British maps. Major Wintle decided to advance 2,000 metres to a palm grove known to be occupied by the Tangistanis that lay in front of the village of Old Dilwar; from the grove he hoped to be able to sight New Dilwar. The British silent advance began at 0330 hours on 14th August, led by the marines and a company of sepoys without any machine guns. The palm grove was rushed quietly without use of covering fire and its inhabitants sprinted away into the darkness. As day broke New Dilwar could be observed 1,300 metres away to the north-east across a plain; the fort had walls 10 metres high with a large tower above the gateway, and a strong garrison was present. The enemy strength was estimated at up to 400 riflemen, and the Tangistanis opened fire on the British and moved forward into Old Dilwar.

Major Wintle did not wish to make a potentially costly day-time assault so he kept his men occupied in the palm grove by entrenching a position and in cutting down the palm trees as part of the punitive measures. Also he requested *HMS Juno* to shell Old Dilwar. Due to an error, a salvo of lyddite shells landed in the palm grove, wounding some men and confusing and demoralising others. As he could not halt the shelling quickly Wintle ordered an immediate withdrawal to the base camp. The Tangistanis saw an opportunity and attacked the retreating British, causing a number of casualties before base camp was reached. During the rapid and energetic withdrawal several of Wintle's men became heat-stroke casualties, some of them failing to recover. The remainder of that day was spent on reconnaissance and on effective direction of naval fire against Old and New Dilwar.

Having re-grouped and issued orders for a plan of attack Wintle led his men back towards New Dilwar at 0330 hours on 15th August. Marching on a compass bearing, Old Dilwar was reached without opposition and a company of sepoys stayed there to secure the further advance of the assault group. As the attackers moved through the half-light of dawn towards the fort a British revolver was fired by accident. Wintle ordered the demolition party to run forward and breach the wall, which it successfully did, allowing the fort to be immediately rushed and occupied. Most of the fort garrison was in the partly-demolished palm grove to the south as the Tangistanis had expected the British to occupy that location again. Hearing the explosion from the fort the tribesmen advanced on New Dilwar but many of them were cut down in the open ground where the machine gunners could see them. It was obvious that the enemy had received reinforcements from other villages as around 200 more tribesmen were present.

Once in the fort the British destroyed it and New Dilwar. Wintle then commanded a fighting withdrawal back through the sepoy company at Old Dilwar and then all the way back to the beach. Naval guns and the machine guns covered this withdrawal which was completed with the loss of only six men wounded. Re-embarkation back on to the ships was completed that night and the expedition returned to Bushire. The landing party and their boat crews had taken 55 casualties from fighting, most of these occurring during and after the erroneous shelling of the palm grove, and 11 casualties from heatstroke. The Tangistanis were believed to have lost a considerable number of men.

Gallantry awards for the Dilwar Expedition were:

Distinguished Service Order

- Commander Patrick James Boyle, Viscount Kelburn, Royal Navy.
- Captain Shirley East Apthorp, 96th Berar Infantry, Indian Army- *For conspicuous gallantry. During a retirement, when it was found that two wounded men had been left behind, he immediately volunteered with a private to return some 300 yards to their rescue in face of a heavy fire from the advancing enemy. A serjeant and private were guarding the wounded men, and between them all they brought them back into safety.*

Distinguished Service Cross

- Captain George Carpenter, Royal Marine Light Infantry.
- Lieutenant Edward Albert Singeisen, Royal Naval Reserve.
- Acting Boatswain Thomas Tierney, Royal Navy.
- The citation for these three men read: *For services during landing operations in the Persian Gulf in August, 1915.*

Distinguished Service Medal

- Private Frederick William Rayner (Plymouth 11072), Royal Marine Light Infantry.

- Private Arthur Ramsey (Chatham 19271), Royal Marine Light Infantry.

- Private G. Yates (Plymouth), Royal Marine Light Infantry.

These men received the Distinguished Service Medal for their services in the operations in the Gulf, and it is likely that these awards were earned at Dilwar.

Indian Order of Merit (2nd Class)

Citations are not available but they doubtless relate to Captain Apthorp's DSO incident above.

- Subadar Dharam Singh, 96th Berar Infantry (posthumous as he died of wounds).

- No. 1356 Sepoy Surjan, 96th Berar Infantry.

- No. 6694 Dooly Bearer Hussain Khan, No 6 Army Bearer Corps.

Mention in Despatches

- Captain S.E. Apthorn DSO, 96th Berar Infantry.

- Major C.E.H. Wintle, 96th Berar Infantry.

- Subadar Dharam Singh, 96th Berar Infantry.

- No. 1336 Sepoy Surjan, 96th Berar Infantry

- No. 6694 Dooly Bearer Hussain Khan, No 6 Army Bearer Corps.

The Tangistani attack on Bushire on 9th September 1915

During July and August tribesmen regularly infiltrated through the British outposts around Bushire and mounted four serious raids, causing eleven casualties. The Tangistanis killed or captured around 40 horses and mules and only suffered minor casualties themselves. The British troops had become passive and defensively-minded. On 20th August an attempt by 300 sepoys to close with an enemy force of up to 100 raiders failed due to inadequate tactical direction, and 13 sepoys became casualties. However the squadron of 16th Cavalry had more success in closing with the Tangistanis and inflicting casualties on them.

The **Indian Distinguished Service Medal** was awarded for gallantry displayed on 20th August 1915 to:

- No 1724 Acting Lance Daffadar Kirpa Singh and No 2003 Sowar Atma Singh, both of the 16th Cavalry.

On that day Brigadier General H.T. Brooking CB arrived at Bushire from Mesopotamia, having been sent by the theatre commander General Sir J.E. Nixon. Brooking took over command in Bushire and brought with him his 33 Brigade staff officers, 50 men of the 2/7th Gurkhas to specialise in ambushing enemy raiding parties, two more Turkish guns and two field searchlights. He also had authority to call on the warships for a landing party if required.

General Brooking reorganised the defence, having searchlights sweep the approaches by night where the Gurkhas laid ambushes; also an outpost reserve of two rifle companies with four guns and four machine guns was established at Imamzadeh. Machine gun parties from HMS *Juno* and *Pyramus* stood by to assist, and *Juno*'s guns were practised onto laying onto any part of Bushire Island. The navy patrolled the creeks and shallow water east of Bushire town.

Captain R.S. Rothwell, Royal Artillery, had arrived in Bushire on the 3rd of July along with one Havildar one Naik and two gunners who were trained gun-layers, from 23rd (Peshawar) Mountain Battery; this battery was located near Basra in Mesopotamia. The 16th Rajputs and the 96th Berar Infantry each supplied two gun teams that were trained by Rothwell and his men. The gunners received a total of four captured Turkish guns from Basra; two were field guns firing shrapnel and two were 7-pounder light guns firing a segment-shell. The powder charges for the field guns generated great heat on ignition, and part of the improvised gun equipment consisted of heavy pieces of hard wood with which the breech-blocks had to be beaten open after firing. Rothwell got all the guns into action and through trial and error taught the infantry gunners how to adjust the fuzes that were marked in Turkish numerals, and how to operate with improvised range tables that compensated for the gun sights being marked in metres. Mobility was added by Indian pattern Army Transport carts each drawn by a pair of mules; the carts acted as limbers with the guns being attached in rear. The only real drawbacks were that because of the breech-block problem the field guns could only fire one round each every two minutes, whilst the segment-shells were ineffective on the soft Mashileh sand. Nevertheless the four gun teams, nicknamed the 'Royal Bushire Artillery', were soon to prove their worth in action.

On 3rd September Tangistanis attacked the Bushire outposts but were driven back; amongst the enemy dead was Rais Ali, the hostile Khan of Dilwar. Five days later Captain Carpenter RMLI was ashore at Bushire with a party for machine gun training; he had with him 35 officers and men from *HMS Pyramus* plus the Royal Marine detachment from that ship – one sergeant, one corporal and seven privates. Carpenter's party had three machine guns with it, and their presence was fortuitous.

The 9th August was an extremely hot day at Bushire. General Brooking was out and at about 0630 hours – the most pleasant part of the day – when a patrol near Imamzadeh reported observing about 20 of the enemy in the low broken ground that lay on the edge of the Mashileh south of Zangina. There were several palm groves and water holes here and a sizeable enemy force had gathered to attack Bushire; the firing had already started as the south-eastern British outposts, manned by the Rajputs, engaged the Tangistanis. Brooking immediately issued orders to deploy troops to defensive tasks including fire missions for the guns, and he also prepared a counter-attack. The Gurkhas, who had been out all night on ambush duties, were initially held in reserve.

Carpenter's naval party was ordered to move to Zangina to occupy a position where the machine guns could fire down the cliffs onto tribesmen attacking across the Mashileh. On reaching the position it could be seen that the situation was serious and the 16th Rajputs were hard-pressed to hold their outposts. Carpenter deployed his three machine guns under heavy fire coming from tribesmen only 300 metres distant, but his right hand gun had no hard cover to fire from. Lieutenant Commander T.S.L. Dorman and Yeoman of Signals F.S. Wood volunteered to man the exposed gun but Wood was soon mortally wounded and Dorman was ordered to fall back; the gun was left in position as its approaches were covered by one of the other guns that was mounted in a tower. For the next two hours, the two functioning naval machine guns held a gap in the defences that the enemy tried to infiltrate through. On the left a small detachment under Sergeant J. Wall engaged attackers at 200 metres range and prevented enemy movement on that flank. Sergeant John Wall, RMLI (Plymouth) later received a **Distinguished Service Medal**; Lieutenant Commander Thomas Stephen Lewis Dorman, Royal Navy, later received a **Distinguished Service Order** with the citation-

For his gallant conduct at Reshire on the 9th September, 1915, when he volunteered and endeavoured to bring a machine-gun into action, exposed to a heavy fire from the enemy, at about 300 yards range. A Yeoman of Signals who accompanied Lieutenant Commander Dorman was mortally wounded.

Meanwhile the four machine guns of the 11th Rajputs were also heavily engaged, two of them also at Zangina and the other two south of Outpost 4 (Point B on the Bushire map) where the enemy were attacking from the palm groves on the Mashileh. Lieutenant Edmund Cyril Staples, 11th Rajputs, was later awarded a **Military Cross** -*He was in command of Brigade machine guns, and, although wounded himself and with only one wounded man to help him, he continued to work one of the guns at close range and under heavy fire for about an hour until the action closed. At the end he was working the gun alone as the man helping him was a second time wounded.*

No. 1829 Sepoy Ram Kishor Singh, 11th Rajputs, received the **Indian Order of Merit (2nd Class)** - *For very conspicuous gallantry and coolness at Bushire on the 9th September 1915, when although wounded and the only man left, he nobly assisted Lieutenant Staples in working one of the machine guns under heavy fire. He was twice wounded.*

The British counter-attack

General Brooking ordered a counter-attack to commence at around 1030 hours. Lieutenant Colonel H.P. Lane steadily attacked with his 96th Berar Infantry from Point B causing the enemy to break and run back across the Mashileh; about 600 tribesmen could be counted. For his performance during this fighting No. 2331 Sepoy Mehar Singh, 96th Berar Infantry, received the **Indian Order of Merit (2nd Class)**-*For very conspicuous gallantry and coolness at Bushire on the 9th September 1915, in continuing to fight after being twice wounded. He afterwards received three more wounds and only then did he fall out.*

Then Major William Herbert Pennington, 12th Cavalry, commanding the squadron of 16th Cavalry and positioned on the Mashileh east of Point B, was ordered to close in on the enemy. The squadron advanced on foot through a mirage-like heat haze until the enemy was suddenly seen at close range, and fire was opened. Immediately, the order to mount and charge was given and the squadron charged straight into the mass of the withdrawing enemy. Very savage fighting followed in which the squadron lost a third of its strength, Major Pennington, 2nd Lieutenant Leslie Irvine Lumsden

Thornton, Indian Army Reserve of Officers (IARO), two Indian officers and 11 rank and file being killed or dying of wounds whilst 10 rank and file were wounded.

The two Indian officer fatalities both received a posthumous **Indian Order of Merit (2nd Class)**, the citation for Jemadar Gopal Singh, 16th Cavalry, read - *For very conspicuous gallantry and coolness in action at Bushire on the 9th September 1915, in courageously supporting the lead of his superior officers into the midst of the enemy where he was killed. This charge thoroughly disorganised the enemy.*

The citation for Risaldar Prem Singh, 16th Cavalry, read - *For very conspicuous gallantry and coolness in action at Bushire on the 9th September 1915, in courageously leading his troop into the middle of some 400 of the enemy where he was killed. He also set a gallant example under heavy fire at Barjisiyah, (Mesopotamia) on the 14th April 1915.*

Two of the rank and file of the squadron, both being men of the 27th Light Cavalry attached to the 16th Cavalry, later received the **Indian Distinguished Service Medal** for gallantry displayed during this action:

- No. 1016 Acting Lance Daffadar Ram Lal.

- No. 1612 Sowar Khazan Singh.

Three men of the 39th Mule Corps, No. 799 Driver Johdia, No. 589 Naik (Acting Kot Dafadar) Din Muhammad and No. 498 Kot Dafadar Ahmad Khan, also received the **Indian Meritorious Service Medal (IMSM)** for the manner in which they performed their duties during the Bushire fighting on 9th September 1915. Their work doubtless involved bringing mule-loads of ammunition and water forward into outposts subject to heavy fire from nearby enemy groups. No. 4293 Lance-Naik Rati Ram, 96th Berar Infantry, also received the IMSM.

After the charge by the cavalry into the ranks of the enemy the squadron needed time to reorganise its troops and evacuate casualties. This gave the Tangistanis a breathing space to break contact with the pursuing infantry although the British guns continued to inflict casualties. Soon the fleet-footed tribesmen were across the Mashileh and hidden in the broken ground on the mainland; they had left 43 dead, 14 wounded and 4 unwounded prisoners behind on the sand, but they were believed to have taken many wounded men with them. Besides the 25 British cavalry casualties there were 5 in the naval detachment, 34 in the 11th Rajputs and 22 in the 96th Berar Infantry, 2nd Lieutenant R.W. Robinson of the latter regiment dying of wounds. However the Tangistanis had been defeated without having captured one British outpost, and brave men though they were, they did not mount further attacks on Bushire. On 13th September, General Brooking, his task of defending Bushire successfully completed, left for Mesopotamia and handed over to Colonel S.M. Edwardes DSO, Indian Army.

Mentions in Despatches for the defence of Bushire on 9th September 1915.

16th Cavalry

- Major W.H. Pennington, 12th Cavalry attached 16th Cavalry
- 2nd Lieutenant L.I.L. Thornton, Indian Army Reserve of Officers attached to 16th Cavalry.
- Rissaldar Prem Singh
- Jemadar Gopal Singh

23rd Mountain Battery

- Major R.S. Rothwell, Royal Artillery

11th Rajputs

- Lieutenant E.C. Staples
- No. 1829 Sepoy Ram Kishor Singh

96th Berar Infantry

- Lieutenant Colonel H.P. Lane
- Captain L.D. Rollo
- No. 2331 Sepoy Mehar Singh
- No. 2762 Sepoy Nadir
- No 2766. Sepoy Maula Baksh

Staff, etc

- Temporary Major General H.T. Brooking CB
- Captain G.H. Plinston, 11th Rajputs
- Lieutenant H.P. Radley, 72nd Punjabis attached 33rd (Divisional Signal) Company
- Captain W.E. Wilson-Johnston, 36th Sikhs
- No. 8119 Rifleman H. Ball, 3rd Battalion, The King's Royal Rifle Corps.

The British dead are buried in the Tehran War Cemetery or named on the Tehran Memorial, Iran or on the Basra Memorial, Iraq.

(Grateful acknowledgement is expressed to Cliff Parrett, a leading researcher of Indian Army gallantry awards and the editor of *Durbar*, the Journal of the Indian Military Historical Society, for the research he provided for this article, as three awards previously overlooked by the major compilers can now be recognised, and others can be assigned to the correct theatre.)

The Gurkha Action at Tor, Sinai
The 2/7th Gurkhas in action on 12th February 1915

The Sinai Peninsula in 1915

On 3rd February a well-organised Turkish force with German advisors attacked the Suez Canal after marching across the Sinai Peninsula. A few Turks crossed the canal but they were quickly killed or captured by the British canal defenders, who were predominantly from the Indian Army. Two days later the surviving Turks withdrew in good order, and apart from air sorties the British failed to interfere with the withdrawal.[63]

However the canal was not the only Turkish objective in Sinai. Much further south on Sinai's Red Sea coast was the small port of Tor. This was a quarantine station for pilgrims travelling inland to the Convent of Saint Catherine that lay at the foot of the Mount of Moses. If the Turks seized Tor then they could float mines into the Red Sea to attack and disrupt Allied shipping sailing in and out of the Suez Canal.

The British had seized the Turkish territory of Egypt in 1882 and that theoretically included Sinai; however the peninsula had basically been ignored apart from small British garrisons at El Arish on the Mediterranean coast and at Nakl, mid-way across the peninsula due east from the town of Suez. The status of Tor was not defined, both sides assuming that the town was theirs. The British forces in Sinai were Arab camel-mounted or dismounted policemen, and when Britain abandoned the Sinai ahead of the Turkish advance to the canal, most of these police went over to the Turkish side, as did many of the Sinai tribes.

---

63 An account of the battle was published in *Durbar* Volume 27, No. 1 under the title: 'Turks Across the Canal'.

Parker Pasha

One British officer serving in the Egyptian Army knew the Sinai exceptionally well, he was Lieutenant Colonel Alfred Chevallier Parker, known as Parker Pasha. He was very well-connected, being a nephew of Lord Kitchener, and he had served for several years in Nakhl, commanding the garrison and organising an intelligence network amongst local tribesmen. After that he worked in the Intelligence Department in Cairo; in early 1915 he held the appointment of Governor of Sinai, reporting to the Director of Intelligence.

In February 1915, Tor was garrisoned by 150 men of the 2nd Egyptian Battalion commanded by Captain C.E. Barlow. Reports of nearby Turkish troops accompanied by Germans reached Barlow, and he passed these on to Parker, also stating that he could not trust his own troops to attack the enemy. On 7th February Parker arrived at Tor aboard HMS *Minerva* to investigate. He found a worsening situation in the town; the local police had looted shops and deserted and the enemy force outside the town was suborning the townsfolk and the Egyptian garrison to join the Turkish cause or to at least surrender. Curfews and access control measures were difficult to implement because monks from the convent and desert tribesmen from the interior were constantly moving in and out of the town.

Parker telegraphed this message to the Director of Intelligence in Cairo, Colonel Gilbert Clayton:

> *In my opinion the present situation contains very dangerous elements, which can be obviated in two ways:*
>
> a) *the entire abandonment of Tor and the withdrawal of the garrison*
>
> b) *the sending of a sufficiently strong party of Gurkhas or British to ensure the destruction of the enemy.*
>
> *The first would entail an incalculable loss of prestige among Egyptians and Muhammadans who know Tor as a pilgrim station, as well as among Russians who regard the Convent and its environs as a holy place.*

Parker added:

> *Unless reinforcements reach enemy, a double company of Gurkhas should be sufficient. The arrival of the ship or the disembarkation of men should be by night to avoid the possibility of alarming the enemy.*

It was the proximity of the Convent that swayed Cairo headquarters to act. Parker had discovered from monks in his intelligence network that the Turkish camp was at the rear of Jabal Hammam, among the hills of Saidna Musa (our Lord Moses), in the Wadi of Al Sidd. The British government did not want to publicly appear unconcerned about the fate of the Convent of Saint Catherine. Parker returned across the Red Sea to join a British operation that was being mounted against the enemy force outside Tor.

The voyage

The commanding officer of the 2nd Battalion of the 7th Gurkha Rifles, Lieutenant Colonel C.L. Haldane, was ordered to embark half his battalion at Suez in HMS *Minerva* on 10th February. His mission was to punish a party of the enemy that was harassing the Tor garrison. Haldane selected Numbers 2 and 3 Companies and his Machine Gun Section for the operation; the British officers who sailed with the half-battalion were Captain C. Macdonald, Captain H. Exham, Captain N.M. Wilson and 2nd Lieutenant A. Mills. Captain A.S. Alexander of the Indian Medical Service also boarded *Minerva* with a Section of the 135th Indian Field Ambulance. Colonel Parker was also aboard with Major A.T.S. Dickinson, Brigade Major of 30th Infantry Brigade.

HMS *Minerva* left Suez at noon on 11th February and steamed the 200 kilometres to Tor in 10 hours. The sea at Tor was rough and it was decided to leave the machine guns on board; also a plan to covertly land north of the town was abandoned and the troops were rowed directly into Tor harbour. All ranks were ashore by 0100 hours 12th February, where they met up with the 150 Egyptian soldiers of the garrison.

The approach march

Speed was now vital in order to achieve surprise. Haldane's column, augmented by the Egyptian troops, commenced marching at 0130 hours, although some of the Gurkhas were so sea-sick that they had to stay behind in Tor. Parker had enlisted the support of the one local leader who had stayed loyal to the British, Shaikh Mudakhil Suleiman, and Mudakhil's son Zaidan led the column with Parker on the 13 kilometre circuitous approach march through the desert.

Parker, Zaidan and 12 scouts led, followed by No 2 Company and then No 3 Company, the 150 Egyptians, the Section of Field Ambulance and finally a Gurkha section as the rearguard. At 0530 hours the range of rocky hills was approached where the enemy camp had been reported, and Captain Exham moved off with his No 2 Company to the right. No 3 Company under Captain Wilson then formed up as the centre of the force with 1,450 Egyptians moving to the left. Haldane's HQ party with 50 Egyptians formed a reserve 750 metres to the rear, with the medical staff behind them.

The advance to contact

At 0600 hours the advance began and after 900 metres No 3 Company found the camp and quickly encircled it. Enemy sentries must have alerted the camp as although some ammunition was found weapons were not, and had probably been quickly buried. Prisoners taken, who came from the recalcitrant tribes in the region who had sided with the Turks, were handed over to the Egyptians in the Reserve.

As No 3 Company moved forward from the camp, which had been sited by a small village, enemy rifle fire started coming down on No 2 Company from the rocky high ground ahead. This firing then spread along the front of the British force from spurs, ridges and sangars. Both Gurkha companies now commenced a slower and more methodical tactical advance, often encountering Arab adversaries who would fight to the death. Meanwhile, the Egyptian infantry turned the Arabs' right flank and positioned a group in the enemy rear.

As the morning progressed Nos 2 and 3 Companies joined up in the hills and worked together to eliminate the trapped enemy; it appears that few if any prisoners were taken now. By noon the remaining enemy groups had been isolated and destroyed and Colonel Haldane ordered the concentration of his troops, who were now widely scattered.

Captain Exham had found another enemy camp in the hills and he returned there with a party of Egyptian soldiers who destroyed the camp and drove in the enemy camels and goats that were there. Captain Macdonald with a party of Gurkhas under Jemadar Jamansing Gurung searched the village whilst Egyptian troops cordoned it off.

The withdrawal

Colonel Haldane then ordered a withdrawal to Tor. The Egyptians formed the Advance Guard, Captain Macdonald commanded a Right Flank Guard and Subadar Pahalsing Karki commanded the Rear Guard. Tor was reached at 1600 hours and the prisoners, 20 camels and various arms that had been seized were handed over to a Royal Marine detachment that was garrisoning the town. HMS *Minerva* was signalled with a message stating that success had been achieved, 60 enemy had been killed, 108 prisoners including 6 wounded taken, and 5,123 rounds expended. One of the prisoners was a Turkish major. Haldane's losses had been one Gurkha killed and another wounded. A later visit to the battlefield by the Egyptian garrison found that in fact 78 Arab bodies were lying there.

A military funeral and the return to Suez

Upon hearing that there was a fatal casualty, the *Minerva*'s Captain indicated his intention of holding a military funeral ashore. Thus a solitary Gurkha was buried whilst a Royal Navy Guard of Honour paraded and a Royal Marine party fired a salute. Wearing swords, the naval Captain and three or four of his officers attended the funeral alongside the Gurkha officers, both as a mark of respect to the battalion and in recognition of the exemplary behaviour of the Gurkhas when they were on board and when they were in action. All British ships in the harbour flew their flags at half mast and a Royal Navy wreath was placed over the grave by men of HMS *Minerva*.

Colonel Haldane boarded his men at 1720 hours and *Minerva* departed at 2230 hours. The Captain dined in the wardroom and toasted the 2/7th Gurkha Rifles, Colonel Haldane responded and expressed great satisfaction at the kindness and consideration shown to his Gurkhas whilst on board HMS *Minerva*.

On the return journey the ship arrived at 0600 hours, 13th February, at Abu Senima further up the Sinai coast, where it was seen that the local manganese mine had been attacked by saboteurs. The report of Germans in the area had not been inaccurate, as two Hungarian demolition officers were operating in the Sinai under the direction of the Turks and their German advisors.

Eight hours later the Gurkhas landed back at Suez, and before leaving the ship in lighters Subadar Pahalsing Karki gave three cheers for HMS *Minerva*, which was responded to by the Captain piping all hands on deck, lining the side of the ship, and giving three cheers for the 2/7th Gurkha Rifles. The Gurkhas then returned to take over their old post at El Shatt.

Recognition

The action at Tor had been a classic example of an intelligence-led military operation. Lieutenant Colonels Alfred Chevallier Parker and Charles Levenax Haldane were Mentioned in Despatches. Later that year Colonel Haldane received a CMG – Companionship of the Most Distinguished Order of Saint Michael and Saint George and he was promoted; during the following year he was awarded the Order of the Nile 4th Grade. None of Colonel Haldane's subordinates received awards for gallantry displayed in the action at Tor, on the basis of: *'No names were submitted owing to the fact that where all did well it was impossible to differentiate'.*

However one Gurkha Naik (Corporal) who had been reduced to the ranks by order of the Brigade Commander for slackness on patrol in letting deserters pass him, was reinstated in his rank and place of seniority because of the good work of himself and his detachment at Tor.

ATONEMENT
The 5th Light Infantry in German Kamerun - August 1915 to February 1916

The 5th Light Infantry and the Singapore Mutiny

In 1915 the 5th Light Infantry, known as the Loyal 5th, was a Class Regiment composed of 8 companies organised into two wings; the Indian strength was 818 all ranks. One wing was composed of Hindustani Mussulmans and the other contained Mussalman Rajputs (Ranghars); the regimental centre was located at Benares. In February 1915 the regiment was stationed in Singapore and was about to embark for Hong Kong, but for security reasons the destination was not publicised.[64] The unit had command problems and a break-down in communications appears to have occurred between the British officers and their sepoys, as the latter thought that they were being sent to fight against the Turks, their fellow Muslims. Ghadarite[65] and religious agitators incited the men, probably aided by German prisoners from the light cruiser *SMS Emden*[66] who were being guarded in Singapore by the sepoys.

On 15th February the Ranghar wing mutinied and went on a rampage in Singapore, murdering over 30 British soldiers and civilians, including an officer's wife. Sailors from British, French and Japanese vessels were landed with machine guns to assist the Singapore Volunteer Rifles in quelling the mutiny, and the Sultan of Johore provided 150 of his own troops. A

---

64 German intelligence agents based in the neighbouring Dutch colonies were active in Singapore and British ships were at risk in the adjacent seas.

65 Indian revolutionaries wishing to liberate India from British rule. A useful explanation is given in *Haj to Utopia* by Maia Ramnath (University of California Press, 2011).

66 A ship of the Imperial German Navy that raided locations in the Indian Ocean before being beached and captured in the Cocos Islands.

detachment of 36th Sikhs was also in Singapore but without ammunition; the Sikhs remained loyal and one man, 2187 Havildar Nand Singh, received the Indian Distinguished Service Medal for gallantry displayed during the mutiny.

Although caught totally unawares the British administration responded quickly and vigorously. At dawn the next day, after eighty of the 5th Light Infantry sepoys had crossed the lines to declare their loyalty, a hastily improvised British force determinedly attacked the mutineers in Alexandra Barracks. The attack was led by a North-West Frontier veteran, Colonel Charles Brownlow, Royal Garrison Artillery. The barracks were seized without loss as most of the defenders occupied an adjacent ridge; however the mutiny was running out of steam now and the participants dispersed to surrender or flee across the Johore Straits. Within a week 46 of the fleeing sepoys had been killed or drowned and 422 had been rounded up; the remainder were being pursued through the Johore swamps. Fresh British troops and Dyak head-hunters from Borneo arrived to continue the hunt.

Two hundred and two men were tried by summary general courts-martial, 37 mutineers were executed and ten others had their death sentences commuted whilst 89 men were imprisoned for varying terms up to transportation for life. Fewer than a dozen mutineers are believed to have escaped. Retribution was vengeful and British volunteers queued up to join firing parties that were inadequately trained or briefed, resulting in messy executions[67].

In one of his books Lieutenant General Sir George MacMunn stated: *A senior officer was deputed from India with considerable powers to investigate, and ere long the remnant of the unit was brought back to India, to be drafted-out and reformed with better material. Its record marked it for early disappearance when reductions in the Indian Army took place after the World War.*

But the General was less than generous with the reality. A re-formed 5th Light Infantry with Ahirs[68] replacing Ranghars was despatched to West Africa to serve in the German Kamerun (now Cameroon) – the only Indian Army unit to serve in that theatre during the Great War. When that campaign was successfully concluded the regiment sailed for German East Africa (now Tanzania) where it took part in heavy fighting, suffering many casualties including losing its commanding officer on the battlefield.

---
67 The numbers quoted come from *Fidelity & Honour* by General S.L. Menezes.
68 An Indian ethnic group whose main and traditional occupation is cow-herding.

German Kamerun

On the outbreak of war Germany held two possessions in West Africa. Small Togo was quickly over-run by British and French troops but the invasion of the much larger Kamerun involved sixteen months of fighting by British, French and Belgian soldiers and seamen. The German defence force in Kamerun was named the Schutztruppe and it consisted of companies of local African Askari supported by some artillery pieces and a larger number of machine guns. Allied forces were nearly all African units such as the Nigerian, Sierra Leonian and Gold Coast battalions of the West African Frontier Force and their French and Belgian equivalents; some European artillery and logistical units supported the infantry. The Allies advanced using the railways constructed by the Germans and also up navigable rivers in naval craft. As well as Germans the Allied soldiers had to contend with dense forests and bush, heavy rainfall, jigger fleas that burrowed under toe nails, and the prevalent tropical diseases. Re-supply was a major concern involving thousands of porters from adjacent Allied territories; by contrast the enemy withdrew on interior lines of communication in an organised and disciplined manner.

The 5th Light Infantry, organised into three double-companies and commanded by Lieutenant Colonel W.L. Cotton, landed at Duala, Kamerun, on 11th August 1915 from *H.T. Bamora*. The regimental strength was seven British and twelve Indian officers, 546 rank and file, three Sub-Assistant Surgeons and forty-five Followers. At this point in the campaign Allied columns were threatening the Kamerun inland administrative centre, Yaunde, but the Germans were maintaining resistance as they received supplies across the River Campo from neutral Spanish Muni (now Equatorial Guinea), an enclave in German territory. Colonel Cotton was ordered to disperse his command and the distribution on 30th August 1915 was:

- NKONGSAMBA 155 rifles - Capt. J.W.H.D. Tyndall, Lt. E.M. Malone

- CAMPO AREA 173 rifles and 2 machine guns - Capt. W.D. Hall, 2-Lt. Collins, IARO

- LINE OF COMMUNICATION 218 rifles - Colonel Cotton. This double-coy provided working parties to construct blockhouses and defences, and to guard trains and railway bridges. An example of the latter was the guard of forty rifles under Captain W.G. Strover that secured Kake bridge.

During August four more British officers: Major C.S. Stooks; Lieutenant C.E. Boulton; Captain C.S. Thane; and Lieutenant R. Thorburn arrived to join the Regiment. The latter two were both from the Indian Army Reserve of Officers. Captain R.V. Morrison, Lieutenant W.C. Gray and Lieutenant S.A.B. Paymaster, all of the Indian Medical Service, served for differing periods as Medical Officers with the Regiment.

The Campo column

Captain Hall and his men of C and D Companies boarded *HT Lagos* and after an overnight journey disembarked at Dipikar on the River Campo on 15th August. The situation in this area was not good as one week earlier the enemy had repulsed a British attack on its supply base at Njabesan. After re-organising and receiving 10 days' rations and porters to carry them, the sepoys joined a column consisting of a company of the Gold Coast Battalion and a Nigerian mountain gun; the gun and its first-line ammunition were transported on the heads of dedicated gun porters. This column was commanded by the Gold Coasters' Commandant, Lieutenant Colonel R.A. de B. Rose, who commanded in the Campo area. He had deployed another column inland whilst his column moved up the Kamerun bank of the River Campo. Rose's column marched for four days along a narrow bush track until it was about 5 kilometres east of the junction of the Bongola and Campo Rivers. A base camp was made and the sepoys patrolled towards a ferry crossing used by the Germans. The tropical rain poured down.

On 28th August, after using Berthon Boats[69] (also carried by porters) to cross rivers and often spending some time moving in waist-deep water there was a contact with an enemy sentry at a crossing point near Nguambang. The enemy force appeared to be local irregulars and it quickly retired after receiving 65 rounds from the leading sepoys. The column advanced to Nkweiteng but then Colonel Rose withdrew as planned because most of his African troops needed to rest and re-group before the general advance on Yaounde. After initially finding conditions alien to them the sepoys had settled down and performed well. However the shortcomings of the supply situation had been experienced as the Indians had not eaten fresh hot food or meat for 10

---

69 A British-designed collapsible and man-packable light boat.

days, and much of the vegetables and atta received had been condemned as rotten because of inadequate packaging against the constant rain. On 11th September Captain Hall and his men were withdrawn to Douala.

The Bare Column

During August and September the remainder of the 5th Light Infantry had been acclimatising and performing routine patrolling and security duties on the Northern Railway that ran from Duala to Nkongsamba. In early October the regiment discontinued the double-company system and used a six single-company organisation.

Colonel Cotton was instructed by the theatre commander, Lieutenant General Sir C.M. Dobell, to march northwards with a column on 12th October from Bare, north-east of Nkongsamba, to Chang; the aim of the column's move was to draw off German forces that were resisting a British advance from across the border with Nigeria. Colonel Cotton had under command three of his own companies, two companies of the West African Regiment[70], and one section of the Sierra Leone mountain battery. In total this amounted to 500 rifles, four machine guns, two 2.95-inch mountain guns and 800 porters[71]. The column was to hold the enemy in Chang or draw him southwards, but was not to risk a major confrontation that it might not win.

After two days of marching a brisk contact was made on the bank of the Mwu River; the enemy dispersed and the sepoys re-constructed the partially destroyed bridge. Once across a patrol under Captain Thane had another fleeting contact; 468 rounds were expended that day. On the following day, 15th October, Major Stooks was leading the advance when he was engaged whilst crossing the Nkam River. Fortunately suitable high ground was nearby and the regimental machine gunners came into action, forcing the enemy out of his trenches on the far bank. Another destroyed bridge was re-built and a bridgehead stockade containing Havildar Imamuddin and 12 men was left on the far bank. The stockade was fired at twice during the following night.

After a West African Regiment company had been engaged whilst reconnoitring Fongwang Colonel Cotton halted his column at Mbo for a

---

70 An Imperial unit recruited in Sierra Leone and paid for and deployed by Britain. (The West African Frontier Force units were paid for and deployed by their respective territories.)

71 The 5th Light Infantry had, as an Indian Army unit, been allocated a higher scale of porters than had the African units.

couple of days, resuming his advance towards Chang on 21st October. Major Stooks took the lead with D and E Companies and soon met opposition, No 2954 Sepoy Mohamdoo being wounded and No 2686 Sepoy Hakim Ali Khan being mortally wounded. Fiercer opposition was encountered on 24th October when the vanguard commanded by Captain Hall advanced into the line of fire of enemy machine guns at a road block. The British machine guns and mountain artillery responded but an attempted outflanking movement was thwarted by the unfordable Merua River.

The enemy had anticipated this British move and a heavy fire was placed on the column from the far bank of the Merua. Sepoys No 2371 Fazal Ali Khan and 1829 Akbar Khan were killed; Captain Morrison, Indian Medical Service, was wounded in the foot and five sepoys – 2135 Umrao Ali Khan, 2846 Keri, 2113 Sajawal Khan, 2568 Nanha and 3022 Sepoy Fazal Ali Khan – were also wounded. During this action the machine gunners had fired 2,579 rounds and the riflemen had expended 2,488 rounds. The West African Regiment had taken 24 casualties including a British officer killed. Colonel Cotton then pulled the column back and occupied a road junction controlling access to Chang, this was named Junction Camp.

Extensive patrolling took place and the route already marched was stockaded and garrisoned to protect re-supply columns. On 5th November the column advanced and seized Chang the following day, the enemy firing one volley before withdrawing. The column then performed a flag-raising ceremony in Chang.

Ten days later, having received sufficient supplies, the Bare Column advanced on Fumban. Several days of skirmishes with a withdrawing enemy followed until the Nun River was reached on 23rd November, and a three-day camp was made. Every day of marching further away from Bare meant that a larger number of porters was needed, not just to re-supply the column but also to re-supply the porters who consumed supplies themselves.

Contact had been made with a British column from Nigeria on 21st November and now the two columns advanced on Fumban. The swamps adjacent to the Nun River presented many problems to the porters, particularly those carrying the mountain guns, but the river bank was reached and grass rafts made to float the troops and equipment across. Envoys from Fumban arrived with more rafts; the Fumban ruler requested a speedy

British occupation as the Germans were busily hanging any local Chiefs and Headmen whose loyalties were suspect.

Fumban was occupied on 2nd December just as an enemy column was reported to be approaching from the west. The British deployed in ambush in long grass on the enemy approach route but surprise was not achieved; although the British charged with the bayonet the enemy troops were faster on their feet and they disappeared rapidly, discarding ammunition and equipment as they went. Fumban was a large walled city whose outer circular defences of mound and ditch, around 50 kilometres in length, enclosed large cultivated areas as well as the city itself.[72] The surrounding area was patrolled and an enemy post to the north was captured by the West African Regiment.

By now Colonel Cotton's mission had been achieved as the British columns from Nigeria had arrived, and in this area of Kamerun the local chiefs were declaring for the British. On 21st December General Dobell ordered Colonel Cotton to garrison Fumban, Bagam, Chang, Bana and the Northern Railway whilst the African units in the column were re-deployed to the advance on Yaounde.

The end of the campaign in German Kamerun

Whilst the Bare Column had been marching the other half of 5th Light Infantry had been performing Line of Communication duties on and around the Northern Railway, as well as sending personnel forward as required to join the Bare Column.

Now the campaign in German Kamerun was quickly terminated. General Dobell advanced directly on Yaounde, seizing it from weak enemy opposition on 1st January 1916. The remnants of the Schutztruppe crossed the Campo region into Spanish Muni where they were interned. The only remaining German garrison in Kamerun, at Mora in the north of the territory, capitulated on 18th February 1916.

In that month the 5th Light Infantry embarked for a voyage around Africa to German East Africa, where the regiment was welcomed and immediately deployed against another German Schutztruppe. The brief period of operations in German Kamerun had seen, after some nervousness

---

72 A very informative and entertaining account of the crossing of the Nun River and the occupation of Fumban is available on the link to *From a Diary in the Cameroons* by Major C.S. Stooks DSO, listed below in SOURCES.

due to inexperience, the regiment weld itself together into a sound fighting unit. Atonement for Singapore had been satisfactorily achieved.

Indian officers of the 5th Light Infantry who served in German Kamerun

- A Company: Subadar Major Wahid Ali Khan; Jemadar Abdul Aziz Khan.

- B Company: Subedar Hansraj; Jemadar Rahmat Khan.

- C Company: Subedar Suleman Khan; Jemadar Anwar.

- D Company: Subedar Bahadur; Jemadar Mohammad Hussein Khan.

- E Company: Subedar Sharfud Din Khan; Jemadar Ghafoor Khan.

- F Company: Subedar Aziz Ud Din; Jemadar Ghulam Haider Khan.

- Sub-Assistant Surgeons: Sumar Bhaig, Shambunath, R.S. Bell and J.C. Aseerwatham (all 2nd Class), Karim Baksh and V.S. Gaikwad (both 3rd Class).

A nominal roll of 5th Light Infantry Indian personnel who served in German Kamerun can be found at the end of the unit war diary.

Awards of the Indian Distinguished Service Medal (IDSM):

Five soldiers were awarded the IDSM for service in West Africa: Jemadar Rahmat Khan; 1973 Colour Havildar Ajmeri; 1975 Sepoy Munsab Khan; 2126 Sepoy Faiz Muhammad Khan; and 2728 Lance Naik (then Sepoy) Mazhar Khan.

Mentions in Despatches for West Africa:

Lieutenant Colonel W.L. Cotton; Subadar Major Wahid Ali Khan; Jemadar Rahmat Khan; 1973 Colour Havildar Ajmeri; 2128 Colour Havildar Gharfur Khan; 1915 Sepoy Munsab Khan; 2126 Sepoy Faiz Mahomed Khan; 2725 Sepoy Mazhan Khan.

Sepoys of the 5th Light Infantry who died in German Kamerun:

- Commemorated on the British & Indian Memorial, Nairobi, Kenya: 1829 Akbar Khan.

- Commemorated on the Delhi Memorial (India Gate), India:2371 Fazal Ali Khan and 2686 Hakim Ali Khan.

Attached personnel from No. 5 Company, Army Bearer Corps, Mhow, who served in German Kamerun:

11025 Ghauribardar Bhoti Ram; 5202 Ghauribardur Anandi; 5607 Ghauribardur Ghariba; 5153 Dhooly Bearer Binda; 5191 Dhooly Bearer Rupa; 5216 Dhooly Bearer Ajudhia.

A grateful Frenchwoman greets Indian troops on the Champs Elysee, Paris 1916
Source: Rana Chhina

Indian Cavalry, France, 1915
Source: Rana Chhina

A regiment of the Indian Army arrive in France, 1914
Source: Rana Chhina

German East Africa - A column of Indian troops marching south through the heat and dust of a tropical jungle, 1916.
Source: Andrew Kerr

Exhausted sepoys of an Indian regiment on the march take a welcome break beneath makeshift shelters made by hanging their turbans on poles. The photograph shows the typical flat terrain devoid of natural cover, over which the armies fought during the advance on Baghdad.
Source: USI

Indian troops repelling a night attack by the Ottoman Forces on Toussum in Egypt. An attempt to cross the canal was made on the night of 2/3 February 1915 but was successfully repulsed. No further attempts were made thereafter.
Source: USI

The SMS *Emden* steams away from Madras after shelling the port on the night of 22-23 September 1914.
Source: USI

Christmas greeting card showing the various nationalities deployed as a part of the force in Salonika, December 1916.
Source: USI

Sketch showing Naik Sher Singh and Havildar Teja Singh of the 23rd Sikh Pioneers in action at Shimberberris, Somaliland.
Source: USI

Indian soldiers at the Corn Exchange hospital, Brighton, 1915.
Source: USI

A charge by Indian cavalry in Mespotamia.
Source: USI

Two sepoys of the Indian Army advancing ahead of their comrades to attack the turks on the West Bank of the Suez Canal.
Source: USI

A sepoy protecting a badly wounded comrade during the operations on the Persian Gulf, January 1915.
Source: USI

Wounded Indian soldiers recuperating in Cairo are photographed on the roof of the hospital in the citadel from where they could obtain a fine view of the town and surrounding countryside.
Source: USI.

A British Artillery position in Macedonia (refer chapter 8)
Source: Harry Fecitt

Monastir Road Indian Cemetery and Memorial, Salonika (refer chapter 8)
Source: Harry Fecitt

Marri Nawab signs terms with General Hardy (refer chapter 24)
Source: Royal Geographical Society

Marri Nawab with retainers (refer chapter 24)
Source: Royal Geographical Society

The interior of Fort Gumbaz (refer chapter 24)
Source: Royal Geographical Society

The Jirgah deciding Marri & Khetrani guilt for the uprising (refer chapter 24)
Source: Royal Geographical Society

The 5th Light Infantry in East Africa
March 1916 – January 1918

Initial deployment

On 14th March 1916 the 5th Light Infantry (5LI) arrived in Mombasa Harbour, British East Africa (BEA), from German Kamerun in West Africa. The regiment immediately transhipped and next day sailed down the BEA coast and landed at Gazi, north of the border with German East Africa (GEA). The commanding officer was Lieutenant Colonel W.L. Cotton and with him were 8 British officers, 12 Indian officers, 508 Rank & File, 3 Sub-Assistant Surgeons and 4 machine guns. Half the regiment garrisoned Msambweni Fort and the other half marched to join the garrison at Mwele Mdogo Fort. Reports were received of German intrusions into the border area and patrolling commenced; the first skirmish with the German Schutztruppe occurred on 9th April when a patrol under Lieutenant C.E. Boulton exchanged shots on the River Ramisi.

Skirmishes continued throughout April and May, often accompanied by heavy and incessant monsoon rain. On 22nd May a patrol under 2nd Lieutenant R. Thorburn had a serious contact with an enemy patrol resulting in one non-commissioned officer and three sepoys being killed whilst another sepoy was wounded. The German patrol encountered had been around 70 men strong with one machine gun; two of the enemy had been killed and, to judge from the discarded field dressings found later, about ten of them had been wounded. During the contact No. 2579 Sepoy Rahimdad Khan displayed gallantry in removing the wounded man from the battlefield whilst under enemy fire, and he later received an **Indian Distinguished Service Medal** and the **Russian Medal of Saint George, 4th Class.**

Lieutenant William Henry Wood of the East African Intelligence Department was a prominent figure in the 5LI area of operations, often working with 5LI patrols. With his local scouts he captured several enemy prisoners that were sent back to Mombasa by regimental headquarters; Lieutenant Wood later received a **Military Cross**. In June a detachment from 5LI under 2nd Lieutenant L.D. Modgett was sent north to take over the garrison duties on Kasigau Mountain from the Jind Imperial Service Infantry.

Operations in German East Africa

In early July 1916 the anticipated order to move into GEA was received and 5LI moved down the coast by boat, accompanied by two companies from the 101st Grenadiers. An enemy position in Manza Bay, north of Tanga, was encountered on 5th July. The enemy force of 8 Europeans and 60 Askari fought a delaying action, using a machine gun effectively. The British advance guard was commanded by Captain Charles Sumner Stooks, 5LI, and he was badly wounded along with a sepoy and two African machine gun carriers; two other sepoys and a machine gun carrier were killed, whilst the bodies of eight enemy Askari were counted.

Captain Stooks later received a **Distinguished Service Order** with the citation: *For conspicuous gallantry in action. He showed marked courage and skill in commanding the advanced guard under machine gun and heavy rifle fire. He was severely wounded.* Subadar Aziz-ud-din-Khan was awarded an **Indian Distinguished Service Medal**. After some skirmishing Tanga was occupied by 5LI and the Grenadiers on the 7th July. This was an important achievement as now a very useful GEA port was in British hands.

During July the regiment extended its influence around Tanga by patrolling, encountering light German resistance and sniping. More garrisons were put in place on key features, including at Pangani, the next harbour down the coast. But the health of the sepoys had suffered badly in the malarial coastal zone and around half of the regiment was always sick with continuous fevers. At the end of July 5LI was shipped back up the coast to Mombasa excepting the Pangani garrison which comprised 2nd Lieutenant Modgett and his two Indian officers and 50 men from Kasigau plus 50 more sepoys.

Back into German East Africa by train

The regiment entrained at Mombasa on 3rd August 1916 and experienced a two-day journey by rail up to Voi, westwards on the new military line to Taveta, across the GEA border to Kahe and then down the repaired German Usambara line to Korogwe which was located 75 kilometres west of Tanga. The regiment then marched through Handeni and southwards to Morogoro on the German Central Railway line, arriving there on 8th October. Many sepoys were still ill with fevers and parties of them were being invalided back to India by the medical authorities.

The 5th Light Infantry was tasked with Lines of Communication security duties until mid-February 1917 when it marched to Dar Es Salaam and was shipped southwards to Lindi. Now under the command of Lieutenant Colonel Arthur Lucius Wilford who had been awarded a **Distinguished Service Order** in February, the sepoys patrolled extensively from Lindi and often had contacts with enemy foraging parties. In May 1917 a rifle company under Captain E.M. Malone was shipped to Dar Es Salaam and then up around the Horn of Africa to join the garrison in British Somaliland. To add to the medical risks prevalent in the theatre, cases of cerebral spinal meningitis occurred amongst the regiment's transport porters and then amongst the sepoys.

British offensive operations out of Lindi increased and during May and June Colonel Wilford took out columns of his men to work with battalions of the King's African Rifles, a trench mortar detachment from the West India Regiment, the locally-recruited Arab Rifles, and a section of guns from the 27th (Bengal) Mountain Battery. An unsuccessful attack was made on the enemy position at Schaeffer's Farm on 19th May, Jemadar Muhammad Baksh and 3 sepoys being killed whilst 7 others were wounded.

The reverse at Lutende

On 22nd June 1917 5LI occupied a post at Naitiwi, 30 kilometres west of Lindi. Brigade Headquarters in Lindi requested confirmation of an intelligence report that the enemy was holding a position a few kilometres away at Lutende. Patrols made by the regiment and its attached Intelligence Scouts confirmed that a force of 5 Germans and 80 Askari was at Lutende. Colonel Wilford decided to act on his own initiative and attack, but he was not aware of the number of other enemy units that were camped in the vicinity.

At 2200 hours on 29th June Colonel Wilford set out with 4 other British officers including the Medical Officer and an Intelligence Agent, 6 Indian officers, 143 sepoys, 3 machine guns and 8 African Intelligence Department scouts. The enemy post at Lutende was approached quietly and successfully rushed at 0630 hours on 30th June; 3 Germans were captured along with a food depot and stocks of ammunition. The remainder of the enemy force, the 30th Field Company, was dispersed and pursued through the bush for about 750 metres.

5LI concentrated again in the enemy location, formed a perimeter and began making improvised stretchers to carry away the sepoys who had been wounded in the attack. But other German units had heard the fighting and the 3rd, 4th, 9th and 13th Field Companies quickly arrived on the scene and surrounded 5LI. Intense fire was directed into the British perimeter, mortally wounding Colonel Wilford, badly wounding the Medical Officer, Captain H. Stokes, Royal Army Medical Corps, disabling a machine gun and hitting more sepoys. Several enemy bayonet charges were beaten back by counter-charges mounted by British and Indian officers.

Great gallantry and powers of leadership were displayed by these officers and their havildars and naiks. Jemadar Munshi Khan, 18th Infantry attached to 5LI, won a posthumous **Indian Order of Merit, 2nd Class**, as did No. 2505 Havildar Habib-ur-Rahman Khan, 5LI, but he survived; sadly the citations cannot be located. A similar award was later made to Subadar Wahid Ali Khan, 5LI: *For conspicuous gallantry in action on the 30th June 1917. He commanded his platoon with great gallantry and skill against a superior enemy force at close range. Though exposed to very heavy rifle and machine-gun fire he beat off numerous enemy attacks and counter-charged them. Throughout the action he displayed great courage and devotion to duty. He was wounded.*

Lieutenant Robert Thorburn, 5LI, was awarded a **Military Cross** as was Captain William Draper Hall, 5LI, who took over command when Colonel Wilford was hit. When the ammunition carried by the sepoys was expended Captain Hall led a breakout, and his citation read: *When in action against superior enemy forces at close range his commanding officer became a casualty and he took over command. He led frequent bayonet charges with great gallantry under very heavy rifle and machine gun fire, and eventually succeeded in extricating the remnant of* his force from an exceedingly difficult situation. His courage and resource under extremely trying circumstances were worthy of the highest praise.

The survivors of the breakout, 55 officers and men with one machine gun, reached their base at Naitiwi, but they had left behind Colonel Wilford and Captain Stokes, 3 Indian officers and 17 sepoys confirmed killed, 35 wounded sepoys and 45 missing sepoys who were believed to have been killed. The porters had also suffered as 2 machine gun porters and a stretcher bearer had been killed, 6 machine gun porters had been wounded and 24 were missing, along with a stretcher bearer. Two machine guns and 72 rifles had been lost. It was finally established that 46 sepoys had been killed on 30th June 1917, and 3 more, presumably mortally wounded, died during July. The Indian officers killed in the action were Jemadars Munshi Khan IOM, Khan Muhammad Khan and Subadar Nabi Baksh. The Germans reported their casualties as 2 Europeans and 7 Askari killed and 6 Europeans and 20 Askari wounded.

On the following day the Germans returned the dying Colonel Wilford under a flag of truce, along with the severely wounded Subedar Major. Major L.P. Ball temporarily assumed command of the regiment which stayed in the field patrolling for three weeks before going into Lindi to rest for a few days.

The final months in German East Africa

The regiment was back in the field on 31st July manning posts at Naitiwi Ngapa and Mingoyo, and constantly patrolling. On 19th August a patrol had a contact at Lutembe Lake and the patrol commander became a casualty. Sepoy No. 3291 Abdul Khan, 5LI, took command and received an **Indian Order of Merit, 2nd Class**: *For conspicuous gallantry in an encounter with an enemy patrol on the 19th August 1917. After the non-commissioned officer in charge had been wounded, he took command of his patrol and successfully charged and drove off the enemy. He acted with great coolness.* On his return to base Abdul Khan was promoted Lance Naik.

Major J.W.H.D. Tyndall took over command of the regiment on 10th September and Major Hall MC was attached to the Bharatpur Imperial Service Infantry. Patrolling and the manning of posts continued until early October when the regiment was deployed to be Lindi Force Column Reserve. This new employment saw the regiment split up into protection details for all the British artillery units around Lindi. 5LI was not deployed in the major battle at Mahiwa in mid-October, but Major Hall MC was there and was wounded whilst with the Bharatpurs whilst his orderly was killed. After that savage confrontation 5LI worked operationally with the Nigerian troops that had come in a brigade from West Africa.

In November the regiment was employed for a short time on road building as the British moved supplies forward to push the Schutztruppe out of German East Africa and across the Rovuma River into Portuguese East Africa. On 1st December the order was received for 5LI to march to Lindi and embark for Dar Es Salaam prior to being hopefully repatriated to India; Dar Es Salaam was reached one week later.

But not all news was good news. On 13th December another order was received to post 200 sepoys plus the required numbers of British and Indian officers to Somaliland to relieve the 73rd Carnatic Infantry; Regimental Headquarters and the balance of the regiment was to proceed to India. On 30th December the Somaliland contingent embarked led by Major (Acting Lieutenant Colonel) Tyndall with two British and 4 Indian officers. Major Ball took over command of the regiment which was now four Indian officers and 139 sepoys who were all medically unfit; this party then instead of going directly to India was tasked to sail to Suez escorting captured German prisoners of war. Finally at the end of January 1918 Major Ball and his unfit men sailed for India from Suez.

Somaliland and the end of a regiment

Somaliland was a cruel posting for men whose physical health had been severely debilitated by more than two years of active campaigning in tropical West and East Africa, and 56 sepoys did not survive Somaliland's savage and unforgiving climate; their names can be seen on the Berbera Memorial in Hargeisa War Cemetery. Some men were deployed across the sea in Aden, and four of them died there. In East Africa 124 sepoys are commemorated on the Nairobi and Dar Es Salaam British and Indian Memorials. But despite this sacrifice the 5th Light Infantry was not destined to survive the 1922 re-organization of the Indian Army, and in that year the regiment ceased to exist.

Awards to the 5th Light Infantry for service in East Africa not previously mentioned

Distinguished Service Order – Major Lionel Plomer Ball.

Indian Distinguished Service Medal – No. 2351 Lance Naik Rustam Khan; No. 2506 Havildar Ghulam Nabi Khan; No. 2517 Havildar Maula Baksh; No. 3094 Temporary Lance Naik Karam Illahi Khan; No. 1985 Naik Maru Khan; Jemadar Sikhdar; No. 2636 Sepoy (Acting Naik) Ishmael Khan (this last name appears in East Africa General Routine Orders dated 10th June 1917 but not in medal reference books).

Indian Meritorious Service Medal - No. 2799 Havildar Ahmad Din; No. 2433 Havildar Manzur Ahmad; No. 2308 Lance Naik Zafar Ali Khan; No. 3129 Sepoy Dullah; No.1826 Lance Naik Ismail Khan; No. 2122 Sepoy Rahman Khan; No. 2062 Lance Naik Allah Din; No. 2358 Lance Naik Ashraf Khan; No. 1982 Sepoy Kamdar Khan; No. 2829 Lance Naik Bashir Ahmad Khan; No. 1938 Havildar Sazewar Khan; No. 2863 Havildar Dost Muhammad; and No 3178 Naik Muhammad Akbar.

Lake Victoria, German East Africa
6th December 1915

In December 1915, Britain and Belgium were making plans to invade German East Africa (GEA, now Tanzania). British troops would advance from Uganda, British East Africa (BEA, now Kenya), Nyasaland (Malawi) and Northern Rhodesia (Zambia) whilst their ally advanced from the Belgian Congo (Democratic Republic of the Congo).

In order to occupy German attention, the Belgians requested that the British make diversionary moves on the western side of Lake Victoria. The British consented and planned two operations, a crossing of the Kagera River south of the Ugandan border with GEA, and the temporary occupation of the Lubembe peninsula south of Bukoba in GEA. This peninsula forms the south side of Kemondo Bay. A company of the 98th Infantry was chosen for the latter operation, and it was to be transported and supported with gunfire by the Royal Navy Lake Flotilla.

The Lake Flotilla

During 1914 and 1915, the British had secured control of Lake Victoria by arming the civilian passenger and goods vessels that steamed their way between Kisumu in BEA and ports in Uganda. Royal Navy sailors were sent up by train from Mombasa on the Indian Ocean coast to supplement the local African crews, along with a variety of weapons that were fitted to the decks of the steamers. Selected European civilian officers on the vessels were commissioned into the Royal Naval Volunteer Reserve.

Three steamers were tasked with supporting the 98th Infantry's occupation of the Lubembe peninsula:

HMS Winifred – a twin-screw 600-tons passenger ferry armed with one 4-inch gun, one 12-pounder gun and one machine gun.

HMS Nyanza – a single-screw 1000-tons cargo vessel armed with one 4-inch gun, one 6-pounder gun and one machine gun.

HMS Kavirondo – a tugboat armed with one 12-pounder gun, one 3-pounder gun and a machine gun.

The 98th Infantry

The 98th Infantry had been despatched to East Africa as part of Indian Expeditionary Force "B" which initially landed at Tanga in GEA in November 1914. The 98th was a Class Company Regiment, 25% of the sepoys were Ahirs from the Eastern Punjab and the remainder were equal numbers of Rajputs and Hindustani Musulmans. Although holding the Battle Honour China 1900, the regiment had on that campaign not moved beyond Hong Kong, and it had not seen active service since that date. Machine guns were not issued to the 98th until just before embarkation for East Africa.

At Tanga the 98th Infantry did not flee as others did, but when ordered to advance it chose to lie down and not become closely engaged with the enemy, and thus the Regiment was regarded as being unreliable. After the evacuation from Tanga the 98th was employed on guarding the Uganda Railway, and then was deployed to north-western BEA and the Lake Victoria region. There the Commanding Officer, Lieutenant Colonel Colin Campbell Renton, shot himself on the 2nd September 1915; the unit war diary described the fatality as an accident that occurred whilst hunting game. Lieutenant Colonel D.R. Adye was appointed as the new Commanding Officer. During 1915 the 98th appears to have regained confidence in itself as detachments fought minor skirmishes with German troops.

In December 1915, the 98th Infantry had "E" Company commanded by Lieutenant D.R. Montford located at Kisumu. "E" Company worked with the Lake Flotilla and provided detachments for vessels, and this company was chosen to occupy the Lubembe peninsula for two or three days to divert enemy troops away from the Belgian Congolese border area. Overall command of this operation was in the hands of the Senior Naval Officer (SNO) who was aboard HMS *Nyanza*.

Enemy troops on the western shore of Lake Victoria

The Germans operated from a base at Bukoba just to the north of Kemondo Bay. From Bukoba enemy troops under Major Willibald von Stuemer were deployed northwards on the Kagera River line where British troops from Uganda confronted them. In June 1915, a British force had successfully raided Bukoba, overcome limited opposition, destroyed a large communications tower, and then sailed away again. It was assumed that a similar but much smaller operation could be carried out at Lubembe where it was believed that only a small German detachment was located. However the British military planners had not obtained sound intelligence reports on enemy troop dispositions near Lubembe. Nor had they considered that Willibald von Stuemer might have learned something from the Bukoba raid, and that his troops might be better prepared to deal with a British landing in his area.

The landing

On 2nd December *Nyanza*, *Winifred* and *Kavirondo* left Kisumu. The first two vessels were loaded with two officers and nearly 100 sepoys of "E" Company 98th Infantry, plus 100 porters who were tasked with carrying stores and ammunition off the landing beach. A Royal Navy landing party with two .450-inch machine guns accompanied the sepoys. The vessels lay off the Ugandan shore at Sango Bay for two nights and then steamed south, passing Bukoba and Lubembe in an attempted deception plan that may not have succeeded. They then took cover behind the uninhabited Bukerebe Island.

At dawn on 6th December the ships entered Kemondo Bay and approached the chosen landing beach on the north side of Lubembe Point. There are three main features on the Lubembe peninsula which had been named Hills A, B, and C, the latter being the highest. The plan was to seize Hill B, bombard Hill C and seize it, and to dig in on the summit of Hill C for two or three days. An orderly evacuation would then take place, as it was believed that the Germans would be too weak to interfere with the British plan.

The naval guns bombarded trenches that were seen above the beach, and also a redoubt that was observed further along the shore of the bay. At 0645 hours the troops were moved to the beach in six ships' boats that were towed by a motor launch.

Enemy rifle fire wounded two sepoys in the boats. From the shore Lieutenant A.J. St Leger-Hansard led a section of sepoys up Hill B, but he was opposed by two platoons of enemy riflemen firing from a knoll on the slopes of the hill. Four sepoys were hit by German rifle fire before Hill B was secure. The German reservist Lieutenant Koller was defending Kenondo Bay with 50 Askari, and he fiercely resisted the British landing. Perhaps his men were alert because of the previous day's sighting of the British steamers.

Lieutenant Montford then wheeled right with the remainder of his company and advanced on Hill C. The ground was a mixture of banana plantation and rocky bush, but the Company Commander and his men gained the summit and occupied it. However Montford had been wounded, along with eleven sepoys. Montford's wound was a shot through the thigh, but he refused to be evacuated and used a stick as a support. His presence on the battlefield was later to be a crucial factor in averting disaster.

The naval machine gunners left their carriages behind and quickly moved their weapons up on both flanks of Hill C just as a German counter-attack developed. The concerted fire of the two .450-inch guns deterred the enemy Askari who retired into thick bush on the hill's lower slopes. This attack had got to within 200 metres of the sepoys' hastily-dug trenches. Naval gunfire was then concentrated on enemy riflemen firing from the redoubt; whilst this was happening gangs of porters cut a path from Hill B to Hill C. Tools, greatcoats, sepoys' personal kits and ammunition reserves were landed on the beach. Winifred moved to the south side of the peninsula where she hoped to suppress enemy movement along that flank.

The withdrawal

But by now more of Koller's men were moving forward to disappear into the bush below Hill C. The naval gunfire could not be relied upon to stop an enemy attack that the gunners could not see until it had been launched. Meanwhile enemy snipers were wounding more men, including Lieutenant St Leger-Hansard. At 1100 hours Montford signalled his feeling of insecurity to the SNO. He felt that he could stay on the hill but that future evacuation might be extremely dangerous.

The SNO decided that the forceful German reaction signified that the mission had been achieved, albeit in a much shorter time than had been anticipated. The order for evacuation was given and stores, personal kits and porters were embarked in an orderly fashion.

A further 200 or more enemy troops were then seen marching down the road from Bukoba to Kemondo Bay. This was a detachment of 120 Askari from the Bukoba garrison under Captain Louis von Brandis, accompanied by a group of Ruga Ruga irregular Askari. The *Kavirondo* was the only vessel carrying shrapnel ammunition and she was tasked to engage these troops. The German arrivals were observed understandably rushing into the bush to seek cover from the shrapnel. Half of "E" Company then withdrew from Hill C to Hill B. One .450-inch gun was embarked whilst the other maintained a position above the beach, however German guns then came into action. A 4.7-centimetre enemy gun engaged the .450-inch machine gun until a 4-inch lyddite shell from Nyanza scored a hit on the German gun position. Then a 6-centimetre gun came into action from above the redoubt, and the enemy small-arms fire increased in volume. "E" Company continued its tactical withdrawal back to the beach. An enemy machine gun opened up from the shoreline but fortunately the landing cove was in dead ground to the German gunner, and could not be observed by him.

Evacuating the infantry and naval machine gunners

Winifred had been ordered back to the north side of the peninsula and she was protecting the evacuation from the beach. Three of the ships' boats were with Winifred, having evacuated the porters and stores, whilst three more boats were on the beach. These latter three boats were loaded with the infantry and naval machine gunners and were waiting for the motor launch to return and take them in tow. At that point the motor launch broke down.

The two wounded infantry officers, the naval machine gun officer and the Beach Master, plus the three sailors of the machine gun crew, split themselves amongst the three boats and started rowing to the safety of the ships. As soon as they rounded the rocks along the shore the German fire intensified. The first boat got to the *Winifred* with two men killed and four wounded. The second boat got to safety with unrecorded casualties, but the third boat had her oarsmen hit and started to drift.

The *Winifred* and *Kavirondo* approached to within 200 metres of the shore to provide fire support whilst the *Nyanza* fired from deeper water. An enemy 6-centimetre shell struck *Winifred* wounding several men. Lieutenant Robert Aslin, Royal Naval Reserve and HMS *Hyacinth*, was mortally wounded by a bullet as he attempted to throw a line from *Kavirondo* to the third boat. Finally *Winifred* got a line to the drifting boat and then at 1600 hours she towed all six of the ships' boats out of the bay, two of them by this time being submerged.

A close run thing

The SNO had made the correct decision at the right moment and "E" Company and its supporting personnel had got away in the nick of time. The naval gun fire had proved to be decisive in limiting German fire and movement until all the British troops were evacuated. *Winifred* had borne the brunt of the enemy fire and she was chipped by enemy bullets from stem to stern.

The British diversion plan had worked for a few hours but at a cost. The 98th Infantry had lost four men killed, two officers and 29 men wounded and one man wounded and taken prisoner. It is likely that at least one wounded man died later. Two naval machine gunners were wounded as well as the casualties that occurred amongst the crews of the vessels.

The German account of the fight states that one Askari and one porter were killed and that three Askari, two Ruga Ruga and one German reservist, Chief Pharmacist Held, were wounded. The British reaction to the operation appears to be one of embarrassment covered by fabrication, as an entry in the Nairobi Headquarters War Diary claimed that the Germans had suffered severe casualties. The British Official History claims that "the affair was magnified by the enemy into a German victory". The unofficial Royal Navy account claimed that the Germans took over 100 casualties including six Germans killed. Whilst enemy casualty figures may have been understated the Germans had won decisively on the battlefield, forcing a British evacuation 48 hours before it had been anticipated.

Robert Aslin lies buried in Entebbe European Cemetery, Uganda. The dead sepoys lie in unmarked graves in the African bush and are commemorated on the Nairobi British and Indian Memorial, Kenya. The German dead also lie somewhere in the African bush and they are commemorated by a memorial adjacent to the Commonwealth War Graves Commission cemetery at Moshi in Tanzania.

In the Spring of 1916, the 98th Infantry and the Lake Flotilla worked together during the clearing of the enemy from Lake Victoria and in the advance south towards the GEA Central Railway. During the advance sailors from the Flotilla dismounted some of their guns and placed them on wheeled carriages.

The 15th Ludhiana Sikhs and the Senussi
The Egyptian Western Desert, November 1915 to February 1916

Introduction

In 1914, the 15th Ludhiana Sikhs went to fight in France with the 3rd Lahore Division, but in late 1915 the Regiment was posted to Egypt where it operated against a much more traditional and tribal enemy.

Working from eastern Libya, Sayed Ahmed, known as the Senussi, was the leader of a sect of devout Muslims. His men had been fighting the Italian occupiers of Libya with considerable success. They were trained and assisted by a group of Turkish military officers led by Nuri Bey, half-brother of the Turkish War Minister, Enver Pasha. During 1915 German submarines began supporting the Turkish effort with the Senussi's army by transporting Turks and weapons to Eastern Libya and attacking shipping along the Egyptian coast. The Senussi was at first reluctant to fight Britain, but in the end Nuri Bey persuaded him to join the Turkish Holy War and to invade Egypt. The Allied reverses at Gallipoli doubtless influenced the Senussi's thoughts and actions.

In early November 1915, a German submarine sank the British ships Tara and Moorina off the western Egyptian coast, and the British survivors of these attacks were handed over by the submarine to the Senussi who arranged their captivity. The Senussi's troops then harassed and fired upon the British outposts at Sollum and Sidi el Barrani. British Headquarters in Cairo decided that a withdrawal was necessary, and all British troops west of Matruh were ordered to move to that location. At Sollum, the most westerly British post, the withdrawal was effected rather too hastily, as the Egyptian

Army garrison of the fort was left behind. During the withdrawal, many Egyptian Coastguards deserted to the Senussi with their weapons and camels. The Senussi's followers now occupied and pillaged all the abandoned British locations.

The First action at Wadi Senab

On the 20th November 1915, the British formed the Western Frontier Force (WFF). The commander was Major-General A. Wallace and he assembled his force at Matruh. A light railway moved the men and mounts from Alexandria to Dabaa, and from there the men marched or were shipped the seventy-five miles to Matruh.

The WFF contained an infantry brigade composed of three partially-trained British battalions, the 6th Royal Scots and the 2/7th and 2/8th Middlesex, plus the 15th Sikhs. The other main component of the WFF was the cavalry brigade consisting of three composite British Yeomanry regiments and a composite regiment of Australian Light Horse. Brigadier-General the Earl of Lucan commanded the infantry, and Brigadier-General J.D.T. Tyndale-Biscoe commanded the cavalry. The 15th Sikhs was the only regular major unit. The one artillery battery, the Notts Battery Royal Horse Artillery, was to perform very well in the forthcoming actions.

By the 3rd December the British garrison at Matruh numbered 1,400 men. New arrivals included 'A' Battery, Honourable Artillery Company, two 4-inch guns manned by Royal Marines, two aircraft of the 17th Squadron, Royal Flying Corps, and a six-car detachment from the Royal Naval Armoured Car Division. Meanwhile, over 2,000 of the Senussi's men were believed to be moving south and west of Matruh.

On the 11th December, General Wallace sent out a column to disperse a group of enemy reported to be at Duwwar Hussein, sixteen miles west of Matruh. Lieutenant-Colonel J.L.R. Gordon, 15th Sikhs, was appointed Column Commander. The column consisted of the 15th Sikhs, less two companies, the 2nd Composite Yeomanry Regiment, a section of guns of the Notts Battery and a detachment of armoured cars. Lieutenant-Colonel Gordon took his infantry along a track that followed the telegraph line westwards to Sollum, while the cavalry, guns and armoured cars used a road to the south-west, known as the Khedivial Motor Road, which also led to Sollum.

The mounted column departed at 07.00 hrs on 11th December, but the cavalry moved so quickly that the scouts could not keep sufficiently ahead of the main body. Around 300 enemy were waiting to the north of the road in the Wadi (valley) Senab, and they successfully ambushed the cavalry. Attempts made to turn the enemy's right flank were driven back by heavy fire, and a stalemate existed until a squadron of Australian Light Horse arrived from Matruh in the afternoon. Then, using artillery support, the cavalry forced the enemy group out of its position. Eighty dead and seven prisoners were left behind by the Senussi troops. British losses were sixteen killed and seventeen wounded. During this action Lieutenant-Colonel Gordon continued along his track and established a firm base at the Umm Er Rakham wells. The cavalry joined him here during the night.

As the cavalry mounts were now exhausted, the 12th December was spent in resting and in rounding up nearby enemy stock. The 6th Royal Scots, less two companies, joined Gordon during the night of the 12th, as did a convoy of stores. On the following morning at 08.30 hrs, Gordon marched west to Wadi Hasheifat planning to turn south up the wadi towards Duwwar Hussein. As the track was expected to be unfit for heavy wheels, the sixty 1st Line Transport pack mules of the 15th Sikhs were loaded with reserve ammunition and extra water for the column. One company of the 15th Sikhs was left to guard the camp.

As the British column approached the Wadi Hasheifat from the east, the cavalry was forward and dispersed, No. 2 Company of the 15th Sikhs was the advanced guard, and two platoons of the Royal Scots formed the left flank guard. Lieutenant-Colonel Gordon heard heavy firing on his left and observed his left flank guard running very swiftly towards the shore, pursued by an equal number of uniformed and well-drilled soldiers who used formations and cover as they followed up the fleeing Royal Scots. The British soldiers were making no attempt to engage the enemy, who were troops of the Muhafizia, the Senussi's regular army trained by the Turks. The Sikhs' two machine guns came into action to halt the enemy advance.

Many more of the enemy now appeared and Lieutenant-Colonel Gordon decided to fight on the edge of the plateau that rose from the coastal plain. The Royal Scots were ordered to move forward and to the left, and the cavalry were brought back to man the right of the line; however the cavalry took some time to reorganize, and the Royal Scots appeared unwilling to advance. This left the advanced guard, which had occupied some mounds, in an exposed position and Gordon ordered it to withdraw towards the headquarters. The 15th Sikhs' company commander, Captain C.F.W. Hughes, replied that he could not comply with the order unless he abandoned his wounded, and that he was therefore obliged to hold his ground. The enemy increased the pressure around 10.00 hrs by bringing 4-inch guns into action and by effectively deploying machine guns.

Lieutenant-Colonel Gordon radioed back to the camp at Umm Rakham ordering forward all reinforcements that could be spared, and the machine gun section of the Royal Scots and seventy-five men of the Australian Service Corps, armed with rifles, were sent forward. As these reinforcements approached the main body, an enemy machine gun engaged them. This induced the Royal Scots machine gun section to break and run for cover with their guns into the sand dunes on the beach, but the Australians stayed and fought well. Finally two squadrons of Australian Light Horse came forward from Matruh and escorted two Royal Horse Artillery field guns onto the beach where they engaged the Senussi's warriors. Also HMS Clematis, a newly-built submarine trawler mounting two 4-inch guns, appeared offshore and fired at the enemy positions. A lucky British shell exploded amongst one of the largest groups of enemy, scattering it, and that was the turning-point of the action. The enemy began to withdraw, and as his machine guns ceased firing the Royal Scots advanced to their nominated objective. The 15th Sikhs advanced guard regrouped and evacuated its four dead and nineteen wounded.

Knowing he could not achieve a decisive result and aware of the fatigue felt by men and mounts, Lieut.-Colonel Gordon withdrew his men to their camp and on the next day the column returned to Matruh. British casualties amounted to nine killed and fifty-six wounded whilst enemy casualties were around 100 killed and wounded. The Official History comments:

'The enemy had been driven off, but had been able to retire unmolested, and must be given credit for the surprise and the vigour of his attack. Had the standard of training and the experience of the whole column been equal to those of the 15th Sikhs, the Senussi might have been heavily defeated.'

The action around the Wadi Majid

Bad weather now prevented operations for ten days and during this time the 1st Battalion, New Zealand Rifle Brigade arrived to join the WFF. Meanwhile

British aerial reconnaissance reported that the enemy was concentrating 900 Muhafizia in three battalions, plus four mountain guns and two machine guns, six miles south-west of Matruh where Jebel (mountain) Medwa dominated the road to Sollum. General Wallace hoped to surprise the enemy force, and at 05.00 hrs on 25th December two columns moved out from Matruh.

The southern composite cavalry column under Brigadier Tyndale-Biscoe detoured on a southern loop through Wadi Toweiwa, attempting to position itself to prevent an enemy withdrawal. The infantry column, comprising the 15th Sikhs, 1st N.Z. Rifle Brigade and 2/8th Middlesex, plus supporting arms, advanced down the Sollum road. General Wallace's headquarters followed the infantry column. The only effective signaling sub-unit in the force was the 15th Sikhs signals platoon. Lieut.-Colonel Gordon, who had asked to command his battalion rather than do a job that General Wallace could easily manage, was ordered to command the infantry column. Major G. Pennefather-Evans commanded the 15th Sikhs. As dawn broke, an enemy outpost spotted the British advance and gave the alarm by lighting a huge bonfire.

Observing that Jebel Medwa was not occupied, Gordon sent one of the two 15th Sikh companies forming the advanced guard to seize the Jebel, and this was achieved without opposition. At around 08.00 hrs an enemy mountain gun began to shell the road from a ridge west of Jebel Medwa where the enemy battalions were forming up. This caused the 15th Sikhs to open out into artillery (i.e. dispersed) formation, astride of but well clear of the road. With Lieut.-Colonel Gordon using his telescope and acting as an observer, the Notts Battery engaged and silenced the enemy gun from a range of 2,000 yards, whilst shells from HMS Clematis also fell on the enemy-occupied ridge from a range of 10,000 yards.

Lieut-Colonel Gordon requested General Wallace to relieve the Sikh company on Jebel Medwa, and a company of the Middlesex did this. The 15th Sikhs now advanced on the enemy ridge on a frontage of 200 yards, with the 1st New Zealand Rifles following. Companies of New Zealanders were placed as guards on each flank as the Sikhs moved briskly across an open plateau. The advance was halted 800 yards from the enemy to allow the cavalry to appear and take up position. As the cavalry did not appear, the advance continued but now with both New Zealand companies on the right flank. As the British troops moved onto the ridge the enemy broke and fled, some of them hiding in caves and gullies where they were shot or bayoneted.

The whole of the ridge was secured by 10.00 hrs. Gordon now brought the guns forward onto the plateau where they fired into the retreating enemy. Regrettably the cavalry was not in position to complete the destruction of the Muhafizia battalions.

The southern column had first been delayed by moving its guns over difficult terrain, and then had been engaged at around 08.00 hours by enemy camelry and horsed cavalry who had anticipated the British cavalry move. Although machine gun fire finally dispersed the enemy, this contact disrupted the column's advance. At 15.00 hrs the cavalry column appeared but by then the battle was nearly over. The enemy had retreated into Wadi Majid followed by the Sikhs and New Zealanders. The enemy camp in the wadi was set alight and the Muhafizia rearguard, demoralized but still fighting effectively, was driven onto the beach. Some of the enemy feigned death or wounds, but then opened fire at close range. This so enraged the Sikhs that any of these men taken alive were thrown into the burning tents.

The light was fading and at 17.00 hrs Colonel Gordon broke off the infantry pursuit, ordering the battalions to bivouac on Jebel Medwa. The mounted troops returned to Matruh that night, followed by the infantry early the next morning, 26th December. British losses had been thirteen killed and fifty-one wounded. The Senussi's force lost between 300 and 400 dead, and eighty prisoners were taken.

The action at Halazin

The 15th Sikhs were now involved in two minor operations as a result of aerial observation of enemy encampments. On the 28th December a column marched out to Bir Gerawla, twelve miles south-east of Matruh, and on 12th January 1916 another column marched to Jebel Howeimil, thirty-five miles in a similar direction and fifteen miles south of the coast at Baqqush. In both cases the camps were found to be deserted and were burned down. Livestock in the immediate vicinities was seized.

On 19th January an aeroplane located the main enemy camp at Halazin, twenty-two miles south-west of Matruh. Over 300 tents were observed, one of them belonging to the Senussi himself. General Wallace left Matruh at 04.00 hrs on 22nd January with an infantry and a mounted column. A South African battalion now joined the WFF. The right-hand infantry column was commanded by Lieut.-Colonel Gordon and the left-hand mounted column by

Brigadier Tyndale-Biscoe. The force bivouacked in bad weather at Bir Shola, just over half way to Halazin. On the 23rd, Gordon's column advanced on a compass bearing directly towards the enemy whilst the mounted column echeloned to the left front of the infantry. Motor transport experienced extreme difficulty on the sodden ground, and the armoured cars returned to Matruh.

By 09.25 hrs the cavalry were in action against parties of the Senussi's men and Brigadier Biscoe requested the infantry to attack whilst the cavalry manoevred against the enemy's right flank. At 10.00 hrs the 15th Sikhs advanced with No. 1 Company leading, No.2 Company 200 yards behind, and No.3 and No. 4 Company 300 yards further to the rear. Each company echeloned its platoons to the left. Support was provided by the 2nd South African Infantry, the 1st New Zealand rifles and the covering fire of four guns of the Notts Battery. The enemy displayed considerable skill in withdrawing to prepared defences and made good use of mountain guns and machine guns, causing attrition amongst the British troops. Seeing that his right flank was being aggressively turned by parties of the enemy, Gordon reinforced that flank, first with two companies of South Africans, then with a company of New Zealanders with machine guns, and finally by a company of Royal Scots.

Meanwhile, on the British force's left flank the cavalry was also outflanked and receiving effective enemy machine gun and artillery fire. Despite receiving reserves, the mounted troops were gradually driven in. Two companies of New Zealanders were sent to stabilize the left flank, which they did, and the remaining New Zealand company advanced on the left of the Sikhs. The shape of the British advance now resembled a horse shoe with the Sikhs in the centre of the curve. The British infantry did not flinch, despite the open ground it crossed and the punishment it took. By 14.45 hrs the Sikhs, New Zealanders and South Africans were through the enemy camp and into the entrenchments.

The enemy defenders broke and retreated into the desert, abandoning their position. The British cavalry mounts needed water and were not in a condition to pursue, so again the Senussi's men escaped. The British had lost one British officer and twenty men killed, ten British and three Indian officers and 278 other ranks wounded. The 15th Sikhs suffered eighteen men killed and two British and three Indian officers and 115 men wounded. The Senussi escaped, but he had lost around 200 men killed, including Turkish troops, and up to 500 wounded. General Wallace camped two miles to the east, and the non-walking or riding wounded had to be carried through the wet ground on stretchers. The British force took two days to complete its withdrawal to Matruh.

Jemadar Basant Singh, 15th Sikhs, received the Indian Order of Merit for gallantry at Halazin, the only I.O.M. granted for this action. In addition, eight other ranks of the 15th Sikhs were awarded the Indian Distinguished Service Medal. These awards were promulgated in GO 1531 of 14th September 1917.

Conclusion.

The Senussi and his followers continued to present a security threat in the Western Desert for a further twelve months. But the participation of the 15th Sikhs in the campaign was over, as the regiment now received orders to proceed to India. The 15th Sikhs had borne the brunt of the fighting so far, and had provided the backbone for a very untrained, inexperienced and under-staffed Western Frontier Force. The regiment had acquitted itself with distinction, and for its services in this theatre it received the honour 'Egypt 1915-17.' As a result of the post-war reforms of the Indian Army, it became the 2nd Battalion, 11th Sikh Regiment.

The 40th Pathans in action in East Africa January 1916 to February 1918

Arrival in East Africa

When the Great War started the 40th Pathans was stationed in Hong Kong, but in February 1915 it embarked for France where it fought for over eight months, suffering many casualties. In mid-December 1915 the regiment embarked again but this time the final destination was East Africa[73]. The commanding officer was Lieutenant Colonel J.W. Mitchell, 124th Duchess of Connaught's Own Baluchistan Infantry attached to 40th Pathans. The recruitment of trans-Frontier Pathans had ceased and the composition of the regiment was:

- No.1 Double Company – one company contained the remnants of the original 'A', 'B', 'G' and 'H' Pathan companies and the other company contained Punjabi Muhammadans.

- Nos. 2 and 3 Double Companies were composed of Muhammadan drafts from other regiments.

- No. 4 Double Company contained the Dogras of 40th Pathans.

On landing in East Africa the regiment included individuals and drafts from 12 other regiments. As the regiment arrived at Mombasa a local British unit, the Arab Rifles, was ambushed with heavy casualties down the coastline near the border with German East Africa. No. 1 Company under Major H.A. Carter VC, 101st Grenadiers attached to 40th Pathans, immediately marched to Mwele Mdogo, a defensive position near the border. No. 3 Double

---

73 It is probable that a decision was made not to send this predominantly Muslim regiment to fight the Turks in Mesopotamia. Seven Orakzai Pathans and three Punjabis had deserted to the enemy in France on 4th October 1915.

Company, commanded by Captain G.S. Douglas, 18th Infantry attached to 40th Pathans, followed. Sadly at Mwele Mdogo early on the morning of 13th January 1916 Major Herbert Augustine Carter VC was found dead outside his tent with a bullet wound in the head[74]. Regimental headquarters and No. 2 Double Company also moved to Mwele Mdogo where extensive patrolling took place. Detachments from the regiment occupied posts on Kasigao mountain and Samburu station on the Uganda Railway, and these deployments were effective until the end of March.

During this initial period in British East Africa drafts from other regiments except linked battalions were withdrawn and the 40th Pathans was re-constituted with drafts from the Depot at Fategarh. Double Companies were changed into a single company establishment that read:

- No. 1 Company – Pathans and Punjabis of the 40th.

- No. 2 Company – Punjabis of the 40th.

- No. 3 Company – Dogras of the 40th.

- No. 4 Company – Punjabis of the 33rd and 46th Punjabis (the two linked battalions).

The advance into German East Africa

During March 1916 British forces in British East Africa advanced into German East Africa under the command of the South African General Jan Smuts. The 40th Pathans moved across the border at Taveta on 9th April and then camped near Moshi on the lower slopes of Mount Kilimanjaro until the seasonal rains ended a month later. During this period a large draft arrived partly from the Depot in India and partly from Mesopotamia. The men from the Depot were absorbed into the existing companies but the men from Mesopotamia were trans-frontier Pathans from the 20th and 26th Punjabis and they were formed into No. 5 Company. Also during this month the African climate with its accompanying diseases started to take a toll with many men going sick with fevers such as malaria. Jigger fleas were encountered that wormed their way under toe-nails unless the feet had been rubbed with kerosene oil; bad cases of jigger fleas needed the amputation of toes.

---

74 For more information on this incident refer to: http://www.kaiserscross.com/188001/465701.html

The regiment had brought four machine guns from France and two more were issued in BEA. They were distributed one to each company with one in reserve; the carriers were cheerful African Kavirondo tribesmen from the region near Lake Victoria whose bravery in carrying the guns and ammunition into and out of battle was to result in many Kavirondo casualties.

As part of the 2nd East African Brigade the 40th Pathans marched down the line of the German Usambara Railway, first coming into contact with the enemy at Mombo on 9th June 1916. However the German Schutztruppe, as the local army was named, had no intention of standing and fighting and it sprang ambushes before withdrawing, leaving behind demolished bridges and ripped-up railway track. Although by the end of June the regiment had only suffered a handful of battle casualties from enemy machine gun and artillery fire, it had lost 475 men to sickness and disease during the brief advance; the regimental strength was now 250 sepoys. The sick men that were not invalided to India slowly trickled back to the regiment from hospital, but many of them quickly relapsed and needed evacuating again. Men were not the only casualties of disease and when following the routes of the South African mounted formations the tracks were littered with the decomposing carcases of horses and mules that had succumbed to the bites of tsetse flies.

The 40th Pathans was employed on Lines of Communication security duties south and east of Handeni until late August when it marched into Bagamoyo, north of Dar Es Salaam, which had been captured by the Royal Navy and Royal Marines. Just over 1,000 men were by now on the strength of the regiment in East Africa but over half of those were sick in hospital. Captain E.H.V. Hodge, Indian Medical Service, was hospitalised himself and Captain H.S. Golam-Hossain, Indian Medical Service, was posted in as the replacement Regimental Medical Officer. Prior to Captain Haji arriving No. 914 2nd Class Sub Assistant Surgeon Arjan Dass Gossain, Indian Subordinate Medical Department, had been acting as Regimental Medical Officer; Arjan Dass Gossain was to be rewarded for his efforts by the award of an **Indian Order of Merit, 2nd Class**, in 1917. Colonel Mitchell was evacuated with prolonged dysentery and Major H.S. Tyndall, 40th Pathans, temporarily assumed command of the regiment.

The advance on Dar Es Salaam

On 31st August the 40th Pathans marched out of Bagamoyo on an independent mission connected with the capture of Dar Es Salaam; three other British columns also marched out with differing tasks. The Pathans were to march south-west through Mbawa to Ruwu station on the German Central Railway. If the adjacent bridge over the Kingani River was intact then the regiment was to guard it, but if the bridge was blown the Pathans were to loop eastwards and occupy Pugu Hill west of Dar Es Salaam. Accompanying the Pathans column were two British intelligence officers with African Scouts, and the Bishop of Zanzibar with a Labour Corps of Zanzibaris who carried the column's supplies.

The Pathans had a small contact at Mbawa during which Subedar Najibullah, 46th Punjabis attached to 40th Pathans, and one sepoy were wounded. At Ruvu on 1st September the railway bridge was seen to be completely destroyed. Quickly moving south to Msenga two Germans and a few askari from the 3rd Schutzen Company were captured. Major H.R. Lawrence, Indian Political Department attached to 40th Pathans, was sent with the Dogra company and two machine guns to attack Kola, which was taken after a sharp fight, Jemadar Mainu being slightly wounded. Twelve Germans were captured and one killed. With the remainder of the regiment Major Tyndall captured nine Germans, a few Askari and about 2,000 porter loads of rations, clothing and supplies in a large depot at Kasinga. Major Lawrence made a night march through the bush to join the regiment at Kasinga. On 5th September the 40th Pathans marched into Dar Es Salaam, the town having been surrendered by the Germans the previous day.

Awards made for Tyndall's very successful operations west of Dar Es Salaam were the **Distinguished Service Order** to Major Henry Stewart Tyndall, and the **Military Cross** to the acting regimental adjutant, Temporary 2nd Lieutenant Reginald Trelawny Thornton, Indian Army Reserve of Officers attached to 40th Pathans. Reginald Thornton's citation read: *For conspicuous gallantry in action. He displayed great coolness and initiative when heavy machine-gun fire was opened on his regiment, which was acting as advance guard. He rendered valuable service during the coast operations.* No. 4079 Sepoy Chamel Singh was awarded an **Indian Distinguished Service Medal** for saving Major Lawrence's life during the Kola Fighting. Chamel Singh was also mentioned in Despatches and he received the Russian Medal of Saint George, 3rd Class. Another recipient of the **Indian Distinguished Service Medal** at this time was No. 2718 Sepoy Mohammed Gafar Khan.

Operations on the southern German East Africa coast

The operational tempo now increased for the 40th Pathans. After seizing, Dar Es Salaam the British decided to occupy all other ports south of that city up to the border with Portuguese East Africa, now Mozambique. Since the start of the war two disguised German blockade-running ships had arrived in German East Africa with weapons including howitzers, ammunition, military supplies and artillerymen; now points of access along the southern coastline were to be denied to German shipping.

On 11th September a force of around 1,100 men embarked at Dar Es Salaam; the commander for land operations was Major Henry Tyndall and his force comprised:

- The 40th Pathans.
- a composite battalion (detachments of 129th Baluchis & 5th Light Infantry).
- 200 Zanzibar and Mafia Rifles.
- 200 Royal Marines with 2 Hotchkiss guns.
- 60 sailors.
- A total of 12 machine guns, a pack-radio and teams of local porters.

On 13th September the force made an unopposed landing at Mikindani, leaving 3 officers and 117 men of the Baluchis, plus 3 naval machine guns, there as a garrison. The remainder of the force marched up the coast to Sudi Bay, where the most recent blockade runner had landed its cargo. Sudi was also occupied without opposition on 15th September. Two of the Baluch companies were left there whilst the remainder of the force re-embarked by boats, transferred to trawlers, and was then taken to the transports that had to lie some way off the shallow shore. Sailing north the 40th Pathans was landed at Lindi on 17th September. A detachment of 5th Light Infantry was landed further north at Kiswere the next day[75].

At Lindi 40 mines were discovered on the beaches and safely dealt with whilst the navy dredged 3 modern sea mines out of the harbour. In Lindi

---

75 The most important port south of Dar Es Salaam, Kilwa Kisiwani, had been occupied by the 2nd West India Regiment on 7th September. This had a deep-water anchorage.

with Henry Tyndall and his Pathans were marines and their Hotchkiss guns, two naval machine guns with their crews and two Intelligence Officers. A defensive perimeter was constructed around Lindi town. But there were Germans in the area. They had not contested the landings because of the firepower superiority provided by the Royal Navy, but nevertheless they intended to keep the British garrisons close to the coastline.

Colonel Mitchell had been released from hospital and it was decided to maintain the Pathans' Battalion HQ at Dar Es Salaam, so transfers of administrative staff were made back there, leaving Henry Tyndall with 7 British officers, 4 Indian officers and 234 rank and file as detachment commander at Lindi. He quickly decided on offensive action and obtained naval gunfire barrages against reported enemy positions to the west. On 27th September Tyndall took 100 rifles and 4 machine guns, supported by porters carrying water, and marched 25 kilometres west to the reported enemy location. His advance came across enemy observation points with telephone lines and then he came near the German hand-powered trolley line that ran from Lindi port to service agricultural plantations inland.

At noon he was opposed by a strong Schutztruppe detachment in concealed trenches that fired at 300 yards range when the Pathans crossed an open sandy clearing. The porters fled discarding their loads of water in the bush. Fortunately the shooting of the enemy Askari was very poor. The German ambush had caught the Pathans in a poor position but they maintained their firing line for three hours. Later Subadar Jan Gul, 26th Punjabis attached 40th Pathans, was awarded an **Indian Order of Merit, 2nd Class:** *For conspicuous gallantry and courageous example in leading his men across the open up to 300 yards from the enemy's position and maintaining them there for three hours under very heavy fire.*

4799 Naik Punna Khan also received an **Indian Order of Merit, 2nd Class:** *For conspicuous gallantry in action on 27th September 1916. He maintained his machine gun for three hours under very heavy frontal machine gun and rifle fire 300 yards from the enemy's position. During this time the enemy brought up another machine gun on his right flank in order to enfilade our line, but Naik Punna Khan silenced this machine gun every time it opened fire, until he was wounded.*

The Germans sent reinforcements up the trolley line and Tyndall had to withdraw. At this point an enemy counter-attack of 20 Askari led by a German sergeant captured a machine gun, killing or wounding and capturing most of the crew. Things started to go badly wrong for the Pathans but 2nd Lieutenant Dennis George Whigham-Teasdale, Indian Army Reserve of Officers attached to 40th Pathans, saved the day and earned a **Military Cross**: *For conspicuous gallantry and devotion to duty. He handled a machine gun with great skill, and thereby enabled the rearguard to withdraw at a critical time from a difficult situation.* No. 4699 Sepoy Aijal, 40th Pathans, rushed an enemy Askari who emptied his magazine at him, but Ajjal was unwounded and he captured the Askari, earning an **Indian Meritorious Service Medal** for this deed.

Tyndall withdrew his force and marched back to Lindi, having lost 4212 Sepoy Sher Ali killed, and having been himself wounded along with 11 other men. One sepoy with a broken leg, Naik Sanam Gul, was brought in under a flag of truce by the Germans[76]. It was believed that the German casualties were 10 Askari and 4 Europeans killed, including the Sergeant who captured the machine gun.

Operations near Kilwa

On 30th September 1916 the 40th Pathans concentrated on the coast at Kilwa. Here an issue of clothing was made and eagerly received as many sepoys had been without boots for several weeks and others were wearing captured German uniforms; logistics was never a subject that General Smuts devoted time towards and neither was the administration of African and Indian troops. An intense patrolling programme was initiated, Subedar Mehrab Din capturing a German and an Askari and shooting a prowling lioness. Captain Eric Conway Irwin, 20th Punjabis attached to 40th Pathans, raided an enemy post at Samanga and was awarded a **Military Cross**: *For conspicuous gallantry and devotion to duty when in command of a patrol. He carried out a successful raid on a strong hostile position and accounted for twelve of the enemy.*

In early December a British outpost at Kibata was besieged and attacked by a strong German force that included heavy artillery[77]. The 40th Pathans and the Gold Coast Regiment marched up to Kitambe to threaten the enemy's right flank. The Gold Coasters advanced and soon were involved in serious fighting, losing two British officers killed with seven others wounded and 30 soldiers killed and 86 wounded. The Pathans were in

---

76 The Germans often returned wounded prisoners to the British, thereby passing over the logistical burden and the casualty evacuation problems.

77 For further details of the Kibata action see: http://www.kaiserscross.com/188001/447622.html

support, occupying picquets on vital ground until the Gold Coast Regiment withdrew; the Pathans then occupied Gold Coast Hill as it had been named, and defended it until 22nd December when a withdrawal was ordered. Whilst on this operation the 40th Pathans had two machine gun porters killed and two others wounded, and 15 sepoys and Subedar Najibullah, 46th Punjabis attached to 40th Pathans, also wounded; however an average of 10 men per day had been evacuated with malaria. On 29th December 1916 Colonel Mitchell was posted to command a battalion of his own regiment and Major Tyndall was appointed to command the 40th Pathans.

The Pathans remained in the vicinity of Kitambe for a couple of months, working closely with the Calcutta Volunteer Battery of 12-pounder guns and the 22nd Derajat Mountain Battery. However the supply system failed leaving the sepoys on half-rations during this time; regimental game-hunting parties scoured the area but without much success, although Subedars Gul Zaman and Mehrab Din did sometimes bring meat home.

In late February the regiment was ordered to concentrate at Kitambe and as Captain Irwin's company left its post at Kiyombo the enemy made a surprise attack. The porters disappeared into the bush and shed their loads and the sepoys jumped back into their trenches to fight off four attacks. Jemadar Sher Ahmad, 26th Punjabis attached to 40th Pathans, was awarded an **Indian Order of Merit, 2nd Class**: *For gallantry and devotion to duty in the field*. Havildar Mir Dast, 26th Punjabis attached to 40th Pathans, was shot through the liver but crawled off into the bush. The enemy took him prisoner but he escaped and continued crawling through the bush for several days until he made contact with the regiment. For this extraordinary feat he was awarded an **Indian Distinguished Service Medal**.

At Kitambe full rations were issued and the men could rest. A draft of two Indian officers and 170 sepoys was sent from the 46th Punjabis in India, however before the draft reached the Pathans 50 sepoys had been hospitalised with fever. This draft had not been issued with rifle oil since landing in East Africa, and on arrival at Kitambe many of the rifle barrels were corroded because of the heavy rain and consequent mud. On 28th March 1917 2nd Lieutenant John Francis Gardener, 40th Pathans, died at Kibata hospital of enteric fever after a long illness. At that time the 40th Pathans was down to only three fit British officers.

The fight at Rumbo

By April 1917 German detachments were threatening Kilwa from the southwest and a British entrenched camp was established at Rumbo with a forward post on the Ngaura River; the 40th Pathans garrisoned Rumbo. Henry Tyndall was ordered to take out a force to attack and halt a German move towards Kilwa. His available troops were:

- the 40th Pathans with 3 machine guns, less 100 men left to hold Rumbo camp.

- 2 mountain guns of the Gold Coast Regiment Artillery Battery, with an escort of 30 men from 'A' Company Gold Coast Regiment.

- 140 Askari of Nos 1 and 3 Companies of 2/2nd King's African Rifles with 2 machine guns.

- A Royal Navy Lewis Gun detachment.

- The 22nd (Derajat) Mountain Battery, Indian Army, which remained at Rumbo camp.

The Royal Navy detachment had previously manned a 12-pounder gun during the Kibata fighting, but the gun produced so much smoke after firing that German gunners had been able to easily identify its location and return fire. The gun was withdrawn to the coast but the detachment was issued with Lewis Guns and tasked with supporting infantry operations.

Tyndall only had two other British officers in the 40th Pathans at that time, and he appointed one of them, 2nd Lieutenant J.T.G. Humphreys, to be his staff officer in a Column Headquarters that he decided to form. Humphreys had recently joined the regiment and had not yet learned to speak to the sepoys in an Indian dialect. Unfortunately but perhaps understandably Tyndall did not appoint an officer to command his porters who carried reserve ammunition and supplies for the column. Facing the British were over 300 German Askari and 4 machine guns of the 11th and 17th Field Companies under Captain von Lieberman and Lieutenant Bueschel. The Germans occupied high ground that rose away from the southern bank of the Ngaura River.

Tyndall's force left Rumbo at 0700 hours on 18th April and waded across the Ngaura which at that time was knee-deep. However rain began to fall and the river began to rise. The single-file track being followed passed through high elephant grass for over a kilometre and a half and the ground on either side was covered in dense bush. No 3 Company of Dogras was the Pathan advance guard and at 0945 hours it drove back an enemy piquet on the track, and from then on the Germans laid increasingly heavy fire down on the British troops. The Gold Coast Regiment 2.95-inch guns came into action. The Pathans advanced Nos 2 and 4 companies on either side of No 3 Company but forward movement became impossible as enemy machine guns dominated the ground ahead.

The 2/2nd King's African Rifles detachment under Major W.T. Gregg was detailed to outflank the 17th Field Company position on a spur on the left of the track whilst the 40th Pathans confronted the enemy on and near the track. However von Lieberman held his ground against the King's African Rifles whilst Bueschel mounted fierce flank attacks against the Pathans' advance. The Pathan veterans remaining in the unit held their positions but lost two machine guns, both of the weapons having their crews shot down. The Havildars commanding the gun teams, 3214 Bachitru (Dogras) and 3570 Haider Ali (Pathans) were both killed. The advance guard commander, Subedar Mainu, was also killed and confusion reigned amongst the sepoys due to lack of sufficient leaders in the platoons and companies. The forward companies were severely shaken. Tyndall and Humphreys issued and despatched orders to companies but they were not heeded. Tyndall himself moved around the battlefield but found that the sepoys did not know what to do because of the absence of known leaders giving them orders that they could obey.

One order sent to the King's African Rifles detachment was to re-capture the two lost Pathan machine guns. Gregg crossed the track to try to find out what was going on and saw that Major Robert Naismyth MacPherson, 40th Pathans, the only British officer with the Pathan rifle companies, had been shot dead with a bullet through his heart. He had been killed whilst trying to rally his men. Gregg was unable to recapture the lost machine guns as his Askari were heavily involved with fighting the 17th Field Company.

Meanwhile the Gold Coast Regiment gunners were firing at likely enemy locations ahead of the advance, but their shells were bursting short of the intended targets as they impacted on tree branches that were in the way. The

Battery Commander, Captain J.G. Foley, believed that only the Pathans were to his front. Then his Battery Trumpeter approached to inform him that the men seen ahead in the bush were in fact German Askari who had infiltrated forward. Foley did not believe this until the trumpeter fired at one of the men and the bush came alive with enemy returning fire. Foley quickly issued orders to take the guns out of action and transport them back across the river whilst two teams of Gold Coast riflemen alternately charged the enemy, now only 20 metres away, and then leap-frogged back to the river. This tactic kept the enemy from over-running the guns. The withdrawal of the guns was supported by 50 King's African Rifles Askari and by 70 sepoys under Subedar Sher Ahmad IOM (26th Punjabis attached to 40th Pathans).

Tyndall rallied the men that he could locate in the dense bush and fought a defensive action to protect the withdrawal of the guns. Fortunately most of the German Askari was firing high due to the higher ground that they were occupying. When the guns were across the river the Punjabi company of the 40th Pathans was ordered to be rearguard. The company commander, Subedar Ghulam Ali, fought a hectic but sound withdrawal action for which he later received a **Military Cross** with the citation: *For conspicuous gallantry and devotion to duty. He conducted the withdrawal of a rearguard with exceptional gallantry and skill. He set a magnificent example to his men.*

Fortunately for the Pathans a tree had fallen across the river and by clinging on to it a hazardous crossing could be made, but the remaining Pathan machine gun was lost in the turbulent water. Many loads of ammunition and stores were also lost in the river as panic set in amongst the porters. Casualty evacuation across the river became extremely difficult and hazardous. As the retreating British troops neared Rumbo Camp they heard the 2.75-inch guns of the 22nd (Derajat) Mountain Battery firing over their heads to deter the German pursuit. The mountain gunners had established an Observation Post in a tall tree, but the observers up aloft had to endure the ferocious stings of a colony of red ants that had been disturbed.

In the Rumbo battle the 40th Pathans lost 1 British officer, 1 Indian officer and 25 sepoys killed; 1 Indian officer and 34 sepoys wounded, and 35 sepoys missing. Most of the missing men were wounded and captured, and were later recovered by British forces from enemy bush hospitals as the Germans withdrew southwards. Three Kavirondo machine gun porters were killed and 6 wounded. The other units lost totals of 10 killed, 30 wounded and nine men missing.

During the following afternoon the Germans handed over several badly wounded British prisoners under a flag of truce. The Germans intimated that they had taken around 30 casualties during the previous day's fighting. Henry Stewart Tyndall received a **French Croix de Guerre**, as did Major W.T. Gregg of the King's African Rifles. Two recipients of the **Indian Distinguished Service Medal** around this time were Lance Naiks No. 1016 Alam Khan and No. 1570 Gul Haider, both 20th Duke of Cambridge's Own Infantry (Brownlow's Punjabis) attached to 40th Pathans.

Lines of Communication duties and the Narungombe battle

In May 1917 the medical services declared that the 40th Pathans was 60% unfit and the unit was placed on Lines of Communication security duties. However because of active enemy patrols around Kilwa many sepoys were sent out on patrol even when unfit. Just after morning 'stand to' had been stood down on 25th May around 90 enemy troops crawled up under cover of ground mist and attacked a Pathans post at Mitole. The sepoys fought back but Jemadar Shiraz, IDSM[78] and three sepoys were killed and three others were wounded. The Germans left 10 dead on the position and were observed carrying away 15 other men. Captain Roland Richardson, 55th Coke's Rifles (Frontier Force) attached to 40th Pathans, was awarded a **Military Cross** for his gallant defence of the post, and No. 3952 Naik Sahib Shah was awarded an **Indian Distinguished Service Medal**.

In July 1917 the 40th Pathans under Major E.C. Irwin MC was placed in No. 3 Column that was commanded by Lieutenant Colonel A.J. Taylor DSO, 8th South African Infantry. Colonel Tyndall was on leave in South Africa. The column also contained the 3/3rd King's African Rifles, two companies of the 8th South African Infantry, and a section of a Stokes Mortar battery. Two other British columns were in the field and the objective was to capture the important water holes at Narungombe.

On 19th July the three British columns attacked strong German defences at Narungombe. The 40th Pathans had recently received many new and only partially trained recruits from India and it was placed in reserve in No. 3 Column which was on the left flank of the British attack. However the Germans chose to vigorously counter-attack on this flank. During the fighting a gap developed between the King's African Rifles and one of the

---

78 Jemadar Shiraz had received his Indian Distinguished Service Medal in France in 1915 when he was No. 3372 Colour Havildar Shiraz.

South African companies, and Colonel Taylor ordered Major Irwin to fill the gap. The Pathans found themselves in a large hollow that was commanded by an enemy machine gun. The situation was not helped by the hasty withdrawal without notice of the South African company, and the enemy quickly sited another machine gun on the opposite side of the hollow. The German units opposing the 40th Pathans were Nos. 10, 11 and 17 Field Companies.

Major Irwin and 2nd Lieutenant Humphreys were soon killed and Lieutenant N.O. Burne, 40th Pathans, was mortally wounded. Captains Richardson and Gulam-Hossain were wounded. Haji Suleiman Gulam-Hossain, Indian Medical Service, continued to treat the wounded whilst he was himself wounded and under enemy fire, and for this gallant action he was awarded the **Military Cross**. With all the British officers killed or wounded Subadar Gul Zaman, 40th Pathans, rallied the young sepoys and led them out of the hollow and onto a location ordered by Colonel Taylor where the Pathans dug themselves in. Gul Zaman received an **Indian Order of Merit, 2nd Class**: *For conspicuous gallantry, great coolness and energy under fire on the 19th July 1917. When all the British officers had become casualties, he rallied his men and took them out of action. He is an excellent hard-working officer and has done hard work throughout the war.* Apart from those casualties already mentioned Jemadar Darjodhan and 11 men were killed and 25 sepoys were wounded at Narungombe. The Germans withdrew from their trenches during the night.

The final months in East Africa

Colonel Tyndall returned from leave to resume command and the 40th Pathans was deployed to man ten posts on the Lines of Communication with the Regimental Headquarters being located at Ssingino. Regular patrolling continued and on 4th September a patrol consisting of one non-commissioned officer and nine men was badly ambushed; three men were killed and the remaining seven were missing. Batches of the new recruits were sent back to Ssingino for training in bush warfare.

The Pathans came into contact with the Nigerian soldiers of the West African Frontier Force and Askari from the Belgian Congo, now the Democratic Republic of Congo, who had moved into southern German East Africa as the last of the Schutztruppe moved south towards Portuguese territory. By the end of 1917 the German theatre commander, General Paul von Lettow-Vorbeck, had moved a drastically slimmed-down force of his best men into Portuguese East Africa where he continued to operate.

The decision had been taken in 1917 to repatriate both British Army and Indian Army fighting units from East Africa because of the wastage of those units due to tropical diseases. New battalions of the King's African Rifles took their place and moved into Portuguese East Africa after the Schutztruppe. Colonel Tyndal was admitted to hospital and invalided to England on 11th November. Lieutenant Colonel A.I.R. Glasford CMG DSO, 46th Punjabis, was appointed to command the 40th Pathans on 12th November.

The regiment embarked at Dar Es Salaam on the Bibby Line S.S. *Warwickshire* on 7th February 1918, disembarking at Karachi and reaching Fatehgarh on 24th February. The 40th Pathans had fought a tough war; apart from those who were killed in action or who died in hospital, 1,167 all ranks had been invalided from East Africa.

Awards of the Indian Meritorious Service Medal

The following 18 men of the 40th Pathans received the Indian Meritorious Service Medal for service in East Africa:

Jemadar Gandki; 3484 Havildar Kambar Ali; 3242 Havildar Basant Singh; 4908 Sepoy Chur Singh; 3409 Havildar Piru; 4715 Sepoy Mira Khan; 4713 Lance Naik toti; 2962 Havildar Sultan Khan; 3328 Havildar Ansu; 4495 Naik Latif; 4156 Havildar Tek Chand; 4180 Lance Naik Nathu; 4689 Sepoy Ambu; 4699 Sepoy Aijal; 4897 Sepoy Maibullah; Jemadar Hazarat Nur; 3897 Lance Naik Sundar; 4779 Sepoy Lakhia.

The following 8 men received the medal for service whilst attached to the 40th Pathans in East Africa:

1980 Lance Naik Faqir Muhammad, 2683 Sepoy Fazal Khan, 2625 Sepoy Maula Dad, 2118 Naik Nawab Khan, 2371 Sepoy Fazal Din, all of the 46th Punjabis.630 Sepoy Nurdad Khan and 710 Havildar Said Akbar of the 20th Duke of Cambridge's Own Infantry (Brownlow's Punjabis).2557 Havildar Sohna Singh of the 124th Duchess of Connaught's Own Baluchistan Infantry.

Indian Army Units in Action
March to mid-June 1916

East Africa in March 1916

In February 1916 the South African General Jan Smuts arrived in British East Africa, now Kenya, with thousands of recently enlisted but inadequately trained and poorly disciplined South African mounted and infantry units. Smuts was determined to quickly knock the Schutztruppe, or German East Africa military force, out of the war. Thereafter, the German territory, presently divided into Tanzania, Ruanda and Burundi could be occupied by the Allies. Invasions of German East Africa were planned in the south from Northern Rhodesia and Nyasaland, now named respectively Zambia and Malawi; in the north-west and west from Uganda and the Belgian Congo, now named the Democratic Republic of Congo; and most importantly from British East Africa to the north.

Facing all these attacks was the experienced and professional German commander Colonel Paul von Lettow-Vorbeck with sixty companies of infantry organised into nineteen abteilungen (formations), each named after its respective commander. The core of the Schutztruppe was its African infantry field companies supported by units of European reservists and former civilian rifle club members. Each company usually had two or more machine guns. German artillery ranged from light revolver-cannon to 4.1-inch naval guns salvaged from the cruiser Konigsberg that had been sunk in the Rufiji River delta. Von Lettow realised that his best contribution towards Germany's war effort would be to attract as many Allied units as he could to oppose him in East Africa. It would also commit a considerable amount of scarce Allied shipping to supporting the British effort in the theatre.

As the East African campaign progressed, administrative planning was to become more important than actual combat. Von Lettow's staff approached this aspect with professional efficiency. After fighting short actions to cause British attrition, the Schutztruppe withdrew, using prepared interior lines of communication where supply dumps were in place and where thousands of African civilians could be mobilised for porterage and the digging of new defensive positions. In comparison, the ex-guerrilla leader Jan Smuts knew far more about politicking than about commanding three divisions of troops, and he rejected administrative advice from the few British professional staff officers that he employed.

Smuts was fixated on knocking von Lettow out of the war within six months, and he refused any discussion on aspects of logistics such as resupply, casualty treatment and evacuation, and transport. This last subject was critical because of the lack of good roads in German East Africa and the scarcity of British motor vehicles. Hundreds of thousands of overworked African porters were dragooned into carrying supplies for both sides, but the British never managed to raise sufficient numbers and the men themselves contributed to even more supply problems because they also had to be regularly fed. A favourite marching song of the porters was:

We are the porters carrying the food for the porters / carrying the food for the porters / (repeated appropriately) / carrying foods for the porters carrying the ammunition.

Several Indian Army units, including Imperial Service and Volunteer units, had been in East Africa since September 1914 when Indian Expeditionary Force 'C' under Brigadier-General J.M. 'Jimmie' Stewart, C.B., A.D.C., appeared in the theatre. Many more had arrived two months later with Indian Expeditionary Force 'B' under Major-General A.E. Aitken, and others were individually arriving in 1916 as they were re-deployed from France and Egypt. The South Africans held inflexible racial attitudes and most of them regarded sepoys as having the same standing as 'coolies' or labourers. Some Indian Army battalions had proved to be inadequately trained, prepared and led for offensive operations, and they had been relegated to duties on the lines of communication. Yet there were others who were actually fighting harder and more professionally than the South African troops. This article briefly describes the actions of the more aggressive Indian battalions between March and June 1916.

The fight for the Latema-Reata Nek

Before German East Africa could be invaded, a pass, or nek, through the Latema-Reata range of hills west of Taveta, had to be seized. The military railway from Voi, located on the Uganda Railway line from Mombasa to Lake Victoria, could then be pushed through the nek to join the existing German Usambara Railway that ran from Tanga on the Indian Ocean to Moshi, west of Taveta. General Smuts' plan was for the 2nd Division to attack the nek whilst the South African Mounted Brigade rode through the Mount Kilimanjaro foothills to attack Moshi. The 3rd South African Division would be held in reserve.

Three Indian Army units took part in the British attack on the nek on the 11th and 12th March 1916. The Cossipore Artillery Volunteers (known in East Africa as the Calcutta Volunteer Battery) and the Indian Volunteer Maxim Gun Company provided fire support. The third Indian unit was the 130th King George's Own Baluchis (Jacob's Rifles). The 130th Baluchis, a regiment with a previously outstanding record, experienced a bad start to the Great War. In Bombay, a Mahsud sepoy attacked the second-in-command, Major Norman Ruthven Anderson, with a bayonet. Major Anderson died of his wounds, and the regiment was posted to Burma, a backwater of the war. In Rangoon, the two Pathan companies mutinied and announced their refusal to fight their Turkish co-religionists. Around 200 men were court martialled; one Indian officer and one non-commissioned officer were executed, and the remainder were sentenced to various terms of hard labour.

A previous British commander in East Africa, General Richard Wapshare, had specifically requested that the regiment be posted to his theatre, and it had arrived in February 1915 – made up to War Establishment by the attachment of a double-company from the 46th Punjabis. The regiment had performed well in East Africa but had the misfortune to be part of two unsuccessful attacks at Mbuyuni and Salaita, both conceived and commanded by Brigadier-General Wilfrid Malleson, the commander of the 1st East African Brigade. At Salaita, where South African infantry broke and fled at the sight of attacking German Askari, the 130th Baluchis had fought a hard and isolated action, saving the situation for the South Africans. Now the regiment was to be used in yet another of Wilfrid Malleson's unimaginative frontal attacks.

At 1130hrs on 11th March, the 1st East African Brigade attacked the southern end of Latema ridge from the east. The 130th Baluchis attacked on the right with 3rd King's African Rifles to its left; the 2nd Rhodesia Regiment being retained in reserve. Three German field companies with two more in reserve defended the Latema-Reata position. The sepoys came under effective enemy fire when they were 900 metres from the nek, and the attack ground to a halt 550 metres further forward. The Baluchis were stopped not just by enemy light pom-pom guns and machine guns but also by many of their own artillery shrapnel shells that burst overhead. Around 1600hrs in the afternoon, Wilfrid Malleson reported sick with dysentery, General Michael J. Tighe, D.S.O., commanding the 2nd East African Division, took over the attack, and South African reinforcements began to arrive.

The Rhodesians were ordered forward to revitalise the attack at 1800hrs and they succeeded in getting men onto the Latema ridgeline. Then a decisive German counterattack pushed most of the Rhodesians off the hill. On the left the King's African Rifles lost their commanding officer; most of the British Askari were pushed back by an enemy attack from Reata. On the right the Baluchis repulsed a German attack, but the sepoys were now short of water and ammunition, and they fell back to seek replenishment. At midnight Tighe ordered the 5th and 7th South African Infantry to attack. Small elements of both battalions gained the ridgelines of Latema and Reata and stayed there, meeting up with isolated Rhodesians and K.A.R. Askari. But the bulk of the South Africans became confused in the darkness and withdrew. Furthermore, on his way back from the nek, the commanding officer of the 5th South African Infantry, who also commanded this latest attack, dissuaded the Baluchis from mounting a bayonet assault, which they had been ordered to do.

During the night the Germans quietly withdrew most of their defenders, because von Lettow feared being outflanked by the South African mounted troops that were advancing to the north. At dawn Tighe's patrols found a few isolated groups of British defenders still holding pockets on the ridgeline whilst the Germans could be observed withdrawing to the west. The battle was over. The Baluchis had lost Major George Newcombe and two sepoys killed. One sepoy dead from wounds, eleven were severely wounded and thirteen lightly wounded. One African machine gun porter was missing. A total of 40,000 rounds had been fired, 6,000 of them by the machine gun section. In papers written well after the event, one of the Baluchis' officers admitted that much of the night had been spent unwittingly exchanging fire with an isolated group of Rhodesians.

The advance of the 1st East African Division

General Smuts' plan envisaged the Germans withdrawing westwards through Arusha and down to the German Central Railway that ran from Dar Es Salaam on the coast to Lake Tanganyika. Consequently Brigadier-General Stewart, commanding the weak 1st East African Division, was ordered to advance from Longido, south of Nairobi, to cut the supposed enemy route to Arusha. Four Indian Army units were in 1st Division: the 27th (Bengal) Mountain Battery; the 29th Punjabis; the 129th Duke of Connaught's Own Baluchis; and the East African Squadron of the 17th Cavalry. The mountain gunners and Punjabis had arrived as part of Indian Expeditionary Force 'C' in August 1914 and by now were well used to the theatre conditions; whereas the Baluchis had recently arrived from France.

The only brigade in 1st Division was the 2nd East African Brigade commanded by Brigadier-General S.H. Sheppard, D.S.O., R.E., and the 29th Punjabis and 130th Baluchis in the brigade served alongside the 25th Royal Fusiliers (Frontiersmen), the South African Cape Corps and four companies of the 1st King's African Rifles from Nyasaland. The division was not involved in serious fighting during its march through the western foothills of Mount Kilimanjaro, and the Moshi to Arusha road was cut and blocked as ordered. The division then marched towards Moshi where, despite displaying an enormous Union Jack, it came under fire from South African troops who were busily looting the town.

General Smuts criticised the length of time that Stewart, an experienced North West Frontier soldier, had taken on his march through the western Kilimanjaro foothills. This was not entirely fair to Stewart, as a British reconnaissance plane flying from Mbuyuni had reported incorrectly that Stewart was not yet on the Moshi to Arusha road. Stewart was blamed for failing to trap the Germans before they reached Kahe to the south of Moshi, although that had never been his primary task. Stewart's real problem was that he had argued with Smuts, requesting an additional two days for his march from Longido; Jan Smuts did not like argumentative subordinates, especially when they were British generals.

Generals Stewart, Malleson and Tighe were now returned to the Indian Army for redeployment. 'Jimmie' Stewart ended the war commanding the British garrison in Aden. Stewart had been let down by the lack of aggression and speed displayed by the commander of his mounted troops, Lieutenant-Colonel F. Jollie, 28th Cavalry; Jollie was also returned to India. Wilfrid Malleson, who had left his brigade commander's post, ostensibly because of illness when the Latema-Reata attack ground to a halt, later re-surfaced with a promotion as commander of the British forces in Bolshevik Russian Transcaspia. Michael Tighe had been appointed to be Inspector of Infantry in India and Jan Smuts took pains to praise Tighe's service in the East African theatre.

28th (Lahore) Mountain Battery

Whilst the battle of Latema-Reata Nek was in progress, the 28th (Lahore) Battery had been marching with its six mule-packed 10-pounder screw guns in support of the South African Mounted Brigade commanded by Brigadier-General J.L. van Deventer. The battery had arrived in East Africa in November 1914 with Indian Expeditionary Force 'B'. It did not come into action as it advanced from Lake Chala to Mamba Mission and then down the Himo River, but many gunners were affected by malaria from the prevalent mosquitos.

Having secured Moshi, General Smuts discovered that the bulk of the Schutztruppe had not moved west but had withdrawn down the Usambara Railway. The 1st and 3rd Divisions were ordered to 'left wheel' and advance through thick bush towards Kahe Station, south of Moshi. The 28th Mountain Battery was in action on 17th March as it supported South African attacks on the mostly undefended hills of Unterer Himo, Kifumbu, Soko and Euphorbian. It also performed effective counter-battery fire against German guns deployed on Rasthaus Hill. Two days later the 3rd South African Brigade, with the 28th Mountain Battery in support, ran into the first serious opposition to the general advance. Abteilung Otto (9th and 24th Field Companies) was well dug in covering a cleared area two and a quarter kilometres south of Euphorbian Hill. The 12th South African Infantry led the advance and was suddenly punished by heavy enfilade fire. Around ten South Africans were killed and thirty more, including the commanding officer and his adjutant, were wounded before a withdrawal was organised under the effective covering fire of the mountain gunners. Lieutenant Edwin Arthur

Eden, East African Volunteer Artillery attached to the 28th Mountain Battery, received a Military Cross for gallantry displayed in this action. Lieutenant Eden and several of his gunners were amongst the wounded.

The night attack at Store

General Smuts now began to appreciate the difficulty of advancing formations of men through thick bush. He decided to concentrate his infantry on an advance directly towards the Ruwu River whilst he sent van Deventer's mounted brigade around to the west to deny the Germans a withdrawal route down the Usambara Railway and Pangani River valley. Sheppard's brigade marched through Masai Kraal to a location named Store, where the brigade entrenched. Reconnaissance was ordered and a patrol from the 129th Baluchis approached a river. No. 32 Lance-Naik Alim Khan, 127th Queen Mary's Own Baluch Light Infantry, attached to 129th Baluchis, scouted forward and walked into a five-man enemy picquet. Four of the enemy did not survive the Lance-Naik's marksmanship and the fifth man fled. For this action Alim Khan was admitted to the 2nd Class Indian Order of Merit with the general citation: 'For gallantry and devotion to duty in the field.' That day, 20th March, Sheppard had been appointed commander of the 1st Division in place of Stewart, but because of the uncertainty in the air about German intentions he remained with his old brigade headquarters.

During the evening of the same day, in an attempt to discover British locations and intentions, von Lettow ordered an attack on what he assumed was a light enemy screening force south of Store. The Germans attacked with several Field Companies and pushed the British screening outposts back until the entrenched 2nd East African Brigade was met. At that moment, around 2200hrs, a relief was being conducted in the trenches between the 29th Punjabis and 130th Baluchis, and many extra men were in the British firing line; also the ground forward of the trenches had been cleared of bush to a distance of 100 metres. The Germans mounted repeated attacks, as usual making good use of bugles for battlefield signalling, but the British position was not penetrated. After five determined attacks had been stopped by the rifles and machine guns of the Indian sepoys, the Germans withdrew at around 0100hrs on 21st March, taking their wounded and most of their dead with them. Von Lettow lost three company commanders that night, Lieutenants von Stosch and Freiherr Grote dying of wounds while Captain

Augar suffered a foot amputation. The 2nd East African Brigade's casualties numbered around thirty men and thirty animals.

Meanwhile, van Deventer's mounted brigade was taking advantage of the full moonlight to move from Moshi, halting before daybreak west of the Pangani River opposite Baumann Hill.

The battle around Kahe on 21st March

At dawn, the South African Horse failed to find crossings over the deep and fast-flowing Pangani and moved north towards the Kahe railway bridge, which a German demolition party blew before the horsemen arrived. Some intrepid South Africans swam the Pangani to seize the vital ground of Kahe Hill. The Germans now used two of their heaviest artillery pieces, the Konigsberg's salvaged 4.1-inch naval guns. One of the guns was mounted on a railway wagon and the other was hauled alternatively by oxen and large African labour gangs. They fired on Kahe Hill whilst German infantry attacked it, but the South African defenders held their ground. Van Deventer had left his two radio sets behind at Moshi and had no direct communications with Smuts. However a British plane flew over the battlefield, observing and assessing situations on the ground and dropping reports onto Smuts' headquarters. Sheppard had no contact with van Deventer at all.

East of the Pangani, Sheppard's 1st Division was advancing directly on the Ruwu River bridge which carried the main dirt road running south from Moshi. The division advanced with the attached 2nd South African Brigade on the right and the 2nd East African Brigade on the left. The battlefield was confined by the Defa River on the west and the Soko-Nassai River running in from the north-east to join the Defa. Both rivers were strongly running and housed aggressive crocodiles. The German main road running north to south down the battlefield was both the axis of advance and the boundary between the two brigades. Support was provided by South African 13-pounder field guns, British howitzers and the Indian Army's 27th (Bengal) Mountain Battery. Two armoured cars manned by men from the Machine Gun Corps (Motors) operated on the main road.

Unfortunately, Sheppard's reconnaissance patrols had failed to realize that the main German defensive position was not on the Ruwu River but on the Soko-Nassai river line which lay to the northwest of the Ruwu. Considering the dense bush and lack of good maps, this intelligence error was understandable, but it also came as a complete surprise to Sheppard. The Germans had a good field of fire and their many machine guns quickly caused attrition right across the British front. The German artillery observers were using prepared platforms in trees and they brought down accurate fire. Sheppard ordered his men to dig in whilst he attempted to outflank his enemy.

The British artillery observers could not at first see their fall of shot due to the dense bush, and so artillery fire was of little use to the infantry until mountain guns were brought forward into the firing line. The men of the 27th Mountain Battery fired 292 rounds, mostly over open sights whilst in full view of the enemy. The guns received continuous bullet strikes on the shields. For distinguished conduct in the field this day, Subadar Sher Baz was appointed to the Order of British India. Two non-commissioned officers received the Indian Distinguished Service Medal:

No. 702 Havildar Bhan Singh - At SOKO RIVER, 21st March 1916. As No. 1 of his gun in the infantry firing line, displayed great coolness and determination in the working of his gun under heavy fire, setting an excellent example to his men.

No. 1141 Lance Naik Sundar Singh - At SOKO RIVER, on 21st March 1916. Went forward as telephonist with the Battery Commander into the infantry firing line and did excellent work under heavy and accurate enemy gun and rifle fire, which he utterly disregarded, and kept the telephones working the whole day.

Sheppard ordered two companies of the 29th Punjabis to advance south-eastwards across the Soko-Nassai River. The Punjabi jawans achieved this objective but were then held up by effective enemy machine gun fire and the density of the bush. Lieutenant Harry George Rodney Bowes-Scott and nine sepoys were killed and machine gun officer Lieutenant G.S. Darby and sixty-five sepoys were wounded. No. 4 Company of the 129th Baluchis, under Captain H.J.D. O'Neill, was ordered to extend the line to the left and locate the German right flank. O'Neill did this but he and several of his men were wounded when their own machine gun jammed whilst they were charging an enemy gun. At 1700hrs that evening, the 29th Punjabis and 130th Baluchis east of the Soko-Nassai were withdrawn back across the river. Captain Henry Terence Skinner, 29th Punjabis, was later awarded the Distinguished Service Order.

On the right of the advance the South African Infantry was stopped and could not progress, but courageous individuals returned fire aggressively. On the main road, the armoured cars attracted heavy enemy fire and their commander was mortally wounded whilst firing from his gun turret.

Sadly, while 1st Division fought and bled before the Soko-Nassai River, the South African Horse to the west was busy looting Kahe station and village, which included the Kilimanjaro Hotel. Van Deventer declined to move south and block a German withdrawal. More than a few South African senior officers appeared to dislike risking their men's lives in direct confrontations, but preferred manoeuvring in order to force enemy withdrawals. This played into the hands of the astute and professional von Lettow, who did not wish to stand and fight for long. The Germans had very limited military manpower and other resources, but they did have the whole of German East Africa to withdraw into.

That evening, faced with the prospect of a move by van Deventer around his left flank, and having received a report suggesting that Kissangire to his rear was being threatened, von Lettow ordered his abteilung commanders to silently break contact and withdraw down the Usambara Railway. This they did with professional military efficiency whilst the 1st Division licked its wounds and the South African Horse slumbered. British dawn patrols found the Germans gone and an abandoned and destroyed Konigsberg 4.1-inch gun. It had been too heavy to drag away speedily.

Heavy rains set in

In the fighting on the 20th and 21st March, the British lost forty dead and 220 men wounded; thirteen sepoys had been killed, seventy-seven wounded, and three were missing. The German casualty figures between the 18th and 21st March probably totalled 200 men killed, wounded or missing. As very heavy rains set in, Smuts halted his advance on the Ruwu River and sent most of his troops back to higher ground near Moshi and Taveta. Further south, the Germans were back-loading stores down to the Central Railway that ran from Dar Es Salaam to Lake Tanganyika, and were digging extensive defensive positions.

The battle at Kahe was the best chance that the British had to destroy the Schutztruppe in 1916, and the chance was squandered. From now on debilitation through disease, climatic conditions and malnutrition caused by inadequate logistic support would shrink the British forces. During April, Brigadier-General Sheppard talked about the Soko-Nassai action with the commanding officer of the 2nd Battalion, The Loyal North Lancashire Regiment, Lieutenant-Colonel C.E.A. Jourdain, D.S.O. Jourdain's unit, which had arrived as part of the 27th Bangalore Brigade in Indian Expeditionary Force 'B', was the only regular British Army battalion in the theatre. Sheppard said that he now saw the need for infantry companies to have their own sections of machine guns always with them during fighting in thick bush, and that field guns were more useful when brought forward into the firing line than they were when firing without effective observation from the rear. He also saw a use for controlled rifle volley-firing when engaging a fleetingly-glimpsed enemy in thick bush. Sheppard also commented that 'General van Deventer lost a chance of defeating the Germans badly when near Kahe.' However, in his report, General Smuts dealt mildly with his old Boer War comrade's failure, and promoted him to command a new 2nd Division.

Major-General van Deventer and his mounted troops were despatched westwards on an epic trek through the mud to seize Kondoa Irangi. Indian Army units supporting this move were the 28th Mountain Battery and the Indian Volunteer Maxim Gun Company. A section of the mountain gunners often marched and fought alongside the machine gunners. Jacob Louis van Deventer was to end the war as the commander of the East African theatre.

Reorganisation of the 1st Division

In late May the rains eased sufficiently for General Smuts to continue his pursuit of the Schutztruppe down the west flank of the Pare Mountains. A major reorganisation had taken place and 1st Division was now commanded by Major-General A.R. Hoskins, a former Inspector-General of the King's African Rifles. The division now contained columns instead of brigades. Sheppard commanded the River Column, destined to follow the Pangani River, which included the 130th Baluchis, 2nd Kashmir Rifles (Imperial Service Troops), the 27th Mountain Battery less one section and the 17th Cavalry squadron. Brigadier-General J.A. Hannyngton, D.S.O., commanded the Centre Column which was to follow the track of the Usambara Railway. The Indian units under Hannyngton's command were the 40th Pathans recently arrived from France, the 129th Baluchis, and a half-battalion of the 3rd Kashmir Rifles (Imperial Service Troops). A third column, appropriately named Eastern Column, marched south from

Mbuyuni towards the Ngulu Gap in the Pare Mountains, and this column contained a section of 27th Mountain Battery that supported the 3rd King's African Rifles. The 29th Punjabis and the Calcutta Volunteer Battery were positioned as part of the Divisional Reserve.

The Kashmir Rifles, when attached to 1st East African Brigade, had been in action on 23rd March against a German blockhouse on the Ruwu River south of Taveta; the Calcutta Battery fired in support. After some further adventures, the Germans withdrew.

The fight at German Bridge

Centre Column advanced without serious opposition to Same, where it turned east to join up with Eastern Column and then advanced down the east side of the Pare Mountains as one unified column under Hannyngton. River Column slogged its way down the banks of the Pangani River, often having to hand-cut tracks for the mounts and supply wagons, until near Mikocheni the river swung east towards the mountains. Here was an uncompleted wooden bridge at a location quickly named German Bridge. Four enemy field companies were in the area and a defensive position had been sited. Heavy German artillery support came from a Konigsberg gun mounted on a railway truck.

On 30th May, Sheppard sent the 2nd Rhodesian Regiment in a frontal attack on the enemy position whilst 130th Baluchis and 27th Mountain Battery ascended partway up the mountainsides on the left flank to support the Rhodesians. The Germans fought but did not stay long, as Hannyngton's enhanced Centre Column was advancing on the other side of the mountains to cut them off. German Bridge was captured with a total British loss of eleven Rhodesian casualties.

The action at Mkalamo

On 1st June, River and Centre Columns met at Bwiko but had to halt for four days as the British advance had out-run its replenishment capability. Behind the leading battalions, railway track destroyed by the enemy was being repaired by the Indian Army's 25th and 26th Railway Companies (Sappers & Miners), and bridges and roads were constructed or repaired by the 61st King George's Own Pioneers and the Faridkot Sappers & Miners (Imperial Service Troops). Casualties, and sick men whose numbers increased dramatically each week due to disease and debilitation, were carried by the carts and trucks of the Indian Field Ambulances as far as the railheads prior to evacuation.

From Bwiko, Hannyngton's column advanced down the railway whilst Sheppard's again hacked its way down the Pangani River. From Mombo, southeast of Bwiko, a hand-powered trolley line ran southwest to Handeni, and the Germans were moving equipment and supplies down this line and onwards by porter towards the Central Railway. Aerial reconnaissance flown by 26th Squadron Royal Flying Corps reported an enemy defensive position at Mkalamo, where the trolley line crossed the Pangani. Improvised bombs were dropped onto this position.

Mkalamo was approached on 9th June. Lieutenant-Colonel P.H. Dyke commanded the advanced troops and his regiment, 130th Baluchis, was in the lead with the 29th Punjabis in support, the latter unit having been brought forward from Divisional Reserve. A company of the 61st Pioneers and a section of 27th Mountain Battery were also up with Dyke. The main body of the column was about four kilometres to the rear. The British were on the west bank of the river which at this point was fast-flowing, thirty metres wide and teeming with crocodiles that lay in wait for men, horses, mules and oxen. Abteilung Doring (Nos. 1, 3 and 16 Field Companies with a platoon of No. 5 Field Company) was entrenched in thick bush just west of the trolley line bridge.

Dyke had been advancing along the river bank but, at around 1130hrs, German gunners on hills to the east spotted him and engaged the column. To avoid this fire Dyke veered his advance away from the river into thicker bush. Here at around 1300hrs the two leading companies of the 130th Baluchis under the second in command, Major H.D. Moore, stumbled onto No. 3 Field Company's trenches and were engaged at close range. Moore tried to find an enemy flank but lost men quickly, including 2nd Lieutenants Roderick Spicer Russell Porter and Lawrence Benjamin Myers mortally wounded and machine gun officer Lieutenant Cousins severely wounded. But the Baluchis held their ground and beat back counter-attacks by Nos. 1 and 16 Field Companies.

Dyke tried to find an open enemy flank by sending forward four companies of 29th Punjabis on the right of the Baluchis and three companies on the left, one Punjabi company being retained as rearguard. To counter this, Doring extended his flanks. The Indian mountain guns came into action but the bush was so thick that targets could not be identified. The Baluchis were fighting fierce close-quarter actions and the Punjabis were trying to find the Baluchis' flanks and the enemy rear, but thick bush continued to impede both observation and movement as well as machine gun and rifle bullets, which were deflected or absorbed.

The column's main body now came up and Sheppard took command of the battle. However he did not take control, as his men were either fighting individual battles or trying to orientate themselves in the bush. No. 2 Company Kashmir Rifles was sent to reinforce the Punjabi left flank and it repulsed an enemy attack mounted by No. 3 Field Company, but not before German Askari had overrun the column medical aid post. As dusk fell the Germans pulled back and the British column dug itself in.

Doring had fought a useful action and during the night his abteilung made a clean break down the trolley line towards Handeni. The Baluchis had lost eleven men killed and twenty wounded, the other units involved lost a total of six killed and fourteen wounded. The low number of casualties was attributed to the enemy Askari firing high, as they usually did in thick bush. The Germans were thought to have lost thirty or more men killed, wounded and missing. For gallantry displayed both at Ruwu River and Mkalamo, Captain John Valentine MacDonald, M.D., Indian Medical Service, attached to 29th Punjabis, was awarded a Military Cross.

The long road ahead

On 18th June, after skirmishing down the trolley line, Sheppard's column entered Handeni unopposed, but his units and those in Hannyngton's column were losing many men daily to malaria and other diseases. General Smuts kept pushing his troops forward in the hope of achieving his knockout blow, but his opponent had the upper hand tactically and the Germans maintained this initiative until after the war in Europe had ended thirty months later.

Today the Kahe battlefield can be easily visited and all the major geographical points can be located. The rivers are now only trickles and not torrents, but crocodiles remain a hazard. The British buried or cremated their dead where they fell, but the Europeans were reinterred in the Commonwealth War Graves Commission's Moshi Cemetery. An adjacent German memorial, stark but atmospheric, commemorates European and African Askari dead of the Schutztruppe, whilst a stone memorial commemorates the dead Hindu,

Sikh and Moslem soldiers of the Indian Army. Sadly today metal parts in the cemetery, even from the Cross of Sacrifice, find their way into the yards of local Asian scrap metal merchants.

Kisangire and Kisiju
Operations North of the Rufiji River Delta, German East Africa
October and November 1916

The situation

By the end of September 1916 the British advance south of the Central Railway had stalled. The Allied theatre commander in East Africa, General J.C. Smuts, had failed to organize effective logistic support for his troops. General Northey's Rhodesia-Nyasaland Field Force was engaging the Germans in the south-west of German East Africa, and to the east the Royal Navy had seized all the German coastal ports on the Indian Ocean. But the German Schutztruppe, ably commanded by Colonel Paul von Lettow-Vorbeck, had no intention of surrendering and was determined to fight on. One of von Lettow's priorities was the harvesting of crops in the territory still under his control, and the area north of the Rufiji River Delta contained some rich farm land.

On 1st September the 40th Pathans, marching swiftly from Bagamoyo, had surprised a German detachment five kilometers east of Ruvu Station and routed it. This action secured the Central Railway for the Allies. The German detachment was from the 3rd Schutzen Kompagnie and consisted of about 50 Europeans and 100 Askari; the detachment commander was Lieutenant Baldamus. However the Germans had completely destroyed the main three-span railway bridge at Ruvu and had also destroyed 21 flood openings in a stretch of railway embankment. This damage compounded Smuts' problems as he was now depending on the railway line from Dar Es Salaam to bring supplies from the coast. Two weeks later the Indian Army 26th and 27th

(Railway) Companies, Sappers & Miners, were working to restore the line at Ruvu. Meanwhile Baldamus had marched his men 70 kilometres due south to Kisangire, which he garrisoned so that the agricultural land to the south could be protected.

The attack on Kisangire

Fearing that Baldamus might be tasked with operating against the Central Railway the British decided to attack Kisangire. Major General Natha Singh, the commander of the 240-man strong Jind Infantry, was ordered to march from Dar Es Salaam with his sepoys and his two machine guns. The Ruler of the Sikh Princely State of Jind had supplied the Jind Infantry to the war effort as part of the Indian Imperial Service Scheme. Major G.C. Denton, 12th Indian Pioneers (Kelat-i-Ghilzie Regiment), and two other British officers were attached to the unit. The Jind Infantry had been fighting in East Africa since 1914 and had gained a reputation for professionalism and bravery in action.

Already operating around Kisangire and observing Baldamus' movements were 40 Intelligence Scouts under the command of Lieutenant G.D. Howarth of the Intelligence Department. Howarth reported that the German post was in a building on top of a steep conical hill around which two lines of trenches had been dug. The easiest line of approach was from the west and south-west. Moving off before dawn on 9th October 1916 the Sikhs marched around the rear of the conical hill, and at 0930 hours they were ready to attack.

Nathan Singh placed three of his companies and the machine guns in the first line and kept his fourth company as a reserve in a second line. He had 183 sepoys deployed. The Sikhs worked through the bush towards the hill until enemy outposts engaged them and then they rushed forward and captured the first trench line. From there a bayonet attack was mounted that captured the inner trench line. But now problems arose because of the lack of artillery with the Jind troops. The building was engaged with machine gun and rifle fire but these rounds had no effect on the strong stone walls of the post. In retaliation the enemy shot down both Sikh machine gun crews.

Major Denton was mortally wounded and Captain P.N. Gurdon, 14th King George's Own Ferozepore Sikhs, was killed. 2238 Sepoy Sadha Singh displayed conspicuous gallantry for which he was awarded a posthumous Indian Order of Merit 2nd Class:

> *He proceeded forward under a hot fire along a communication trench and removed a number of dead bodies which were impeding the advance. He has since died of wounds.*

After losing a total of 13 men dead or mortally wounded, 27 others wounded, and 8 wounded and missing, Nathan Singh broke off the action. Now the intelligence officer Lieutenant George Dall Howarth took command of the situation for which he later received a Military Cross:

> *For conspicuous gallantry and devotion to duty. He assumed command and successfully withdrew an infantry regiment from a very difficult situation.*

The Jind Infantry withdrew to Maneromango and re-grouped. The German losses had been slight, except that Lieutenant Baldamus had been killed by one of the last shots fired during the action.

The British reinforce the area

General Smuts was concerned and ordered units into the area from two directions. From Dar Es Salaam a column of 300 recently-landed white South African reinforcement troops were marched to Maneromango under the command of Major R.H. Logan of the 2nd Bn The Loyal North Lancashire Regiment.

On 14th October the 1st Division on the River Mgeta dispatched the 57th Wilde's Rifles (Frontier Force), a section of two 10-pounder mountain guns from the 27th (Bengal) Mountain Battery and a section from an Indian Field Ambulance. The commanding officer of the 57th Wilde's Rifles, Lieutenant Colonel T.J. Willans, commanded this column which marched over 130 kilometres across densely-bushed un-mapped territory. Two sections of the King's African Rifles Mounted Infantry with Captain G.H.R. Hurst, a professional game hunter, were attached to the column to assist with navigation. Willans had to leave 50 of his sepoys behind as their boots had dropped to pieces and the supply system, heavily dependent on the labour of malnourished, under-strength and over-worked African porters, was incapable of bringing new boots forward.

Willans' column made two difficult crossings of the swift Ruvu River, the gunners and the column's porters having a particularly tough time as often deep potholes were encountered in the river bed whilst the men struggled across. Villagers approached the column on the 19th October to report that a German patrol was in the bush nearby. The King's African Rifles Mounted Infantry deployed into the area and captured the small patrol, which had become hopelessly lost. The two British columns met up at Msanga on 21st October and Colonel Willans took over command of all the troops. For his work with this column and for other unspecified duties, doubtless including intelligence activities, Captain George Henry Russell Hurst, East African Mounted Rifles, was later awarded a Military Cross.

Meanwhile von Lettow had ordered Abteilung Stemmerman to march north from Utete to hold the Kisangire area whilst the crops to the south were harvested. Stemmerman arrived at Kisangire the day after the Jind Infantry had withdrawn, and his 4 companies with several machine guns were now too strong a force for Willans to successfully attack. Both sides patrolled aggressively against each other.

On 1st November Willans sent a column under Major Logan to occupy Kongo, east of Msanga. Logan took with him 170 sepoys (two companies) of the 57th Wilde's Rifles with two machine guns, and 130 South African infantrymen. Stemmerman responded by occupying Lansi and raiding the British lines of communication back to Dar Es Salaam. But the Germans were not itching for a big fight, as their main task was to protect the harvesting to the south of Kisangire.

The Royal Navy intervenes on the coast

On the 25th October the Royal Navy seized Kwale Island and landed a garrison of 20 Intelligence Scouts and 50 Askari of the Zanzibar African Rifles. The latter unit was recruited from the islands of Zanzibar and Mafia and it worked closely with the navy, providing landing parties and coastal garrisons. In early November the scouts and Askari were transported to the mainland to seize and garrison Kisiju, and from there an intelligence operation was extended westwards through Kongo to Msanga. However this was too much of an intrusion for the Germans and on 24th November a detachment under Captain Liebermann re-captured Kisiju. The British garrison fled by boat back to Kwale Island under the covering fire of the British monitors *HMS Severn* and *HMS Mersey*. Meanwhile the headman of

Kisiju was executed by hanging, the standard German punishment for African leaders who collaborated with the enemy, and Kisiju was burned down. After firing a few field gun shells at the monitors Liebermann withdrew.

Patrolling contacts

Further inland Willans' sepoys were protecting their new line of communication overland to Dar Es Salaam. During one small action on 28th October Lieutenant R.L. Piper, out on patrol with 50 men, confronted a German patrol about 40 strong near Mkwata and dispersed it, inflicting several casualties and capturing several rifles. On the following day the body of the German commander was discovered in the bush where he had crawled to die of his wounds. Lieutenant Ronald Leslie Piper, 57th Wilde's Rifles, was later awarded a Military Cross.

In a similar incident on 30th October Captain E.K. Fowler MC with 2 Indian officers and 70 sepoys attacked an enemy position at Makuka. When it was realised that the enemy were in superior force with machine guns a skilful withdrawal action was fought with the loss of only one Sepoy killed. Four enemy Askari were killed during this action. Captain Fowler, 57th Wilde's Rifles, had gained his Military Cross in France and now he was awarded a Brevet Majority.

The Germans replied on 20th November when one of their patrols under Lieutenant Schreiner ambushed a 50-man South African detachment south of Kongo. Fourteen men of the South African party were killed or mortally wounded and 5 others were wounded. Ten days later a convoy party of 43 sepoys and 109 African porters marched from Msanga to Kongo. The convoy walked into a German ambush 3 kilometres before Kongo, and the porters dropped their loads and bolted. The convoy commander, Subadar Major Arsla Khan MC, rallied the sepoys to successfully protect the loads until support arrived from Kongo. All the loads were delivered. Subadar Major Arsla Khan, 57th Wilde's Rifles, who also had gained his Military Cross in France, was later appointed to be a member of the Order of British India 1st Class in recognition of his military performance in East Africa.

Conclusion

At the end of November 1916 the British forces under General Smuts, a former guerrilla leader turned professional politician, were still struggling to regain momentum in their advance. But rainfall, logistical inadequacy and above all else ruthless German military professionalism had thwarted the British plans. Smuts was so desperate to end the campaign in German East Africa that he had asked the War Office in London if using gas against the Schutztruppe was feasible. London's reply was that it was feasible on a frontage of 1,280 metres, but thankfully for East Africa and its inhabitants this idea was not pursued.

On the German side Colonel von Lettow-Vorbeck, a professional soldier with much operational experience, had made logistics his priority, and he had ensured that his Schutztruppe now stocked sufficient food supplies for the next few months. The unfortunate African villagers who were required to tend, harvest and then carry these supplies were, as usual in this campaign, the real losers.

The focus of military attention for both sides now moved south across the Rufiji River to Kibata north of Kilwa Kivinje.

THE 129th DUKE OF CONNAUGHT'S OWN BALUCHIS AT KIBATA, GERMAN EAST AFRICA
October 1916 to January 1917

The 129th Baluchis during 1914 and 1915

In 1914 the 129th Duke of Connaught's Own Baluchis was a Class Company Regiment comprised of 4 companies of North-West Frontier Pathans, 2 companies of Hill Baluchis and 2 companies of Punjabi Mussalmans. On 8th August 1914 the regiment mobilised as part of the Ferozepore Brigade of the 3rd (Lahore) Division and 16 days later embarked for France; Double Companies were formed for operational deployment. War Establishment was achieved by the posting-in of a Double Company of the 127th (Queen Mary's Own) Baluch Light Infantry.

The 129th Baluchis fought well and hard in Flanders, and on departure from Europe after 12 months' service in the trenches only 4 British and 5 Indian officers plus around 20 sepoys remained from the original contingent. The regiment embarked for East Africa, arriving at Mombasa, British East Africa (now Kenya) on 5th January 1916. With a strength of 13 British and 14 Indian officers and 740 sepoys the regiment joined the 2nd East African Brigade.

After a month of acclimatisation and theatre training the 129th Baluchis took part in the British 1st Division's advance from the north into German East Africa (now Tanzania). Sharp fighting was soon experienced on the night of 20th March 1916 when the German commander, Colonel Paul von Lettow-Vorbeck, ordered some of his Field Companies to attack the entrenched perimeter camp manned by the 2nd East African Brigade. The attack was successfully repulsed, the Baluchis recovering 3 enemy bugles from in front of the trenches; the bugle was an integral part of German battlefield communications.

Heavy seasonal rains now halted operations and the Baluchis started suffering losses from the biggest enemy in the theatre – the debilitating climate. Dysentery, malaria and other fevers laid men low, jigger-fleas burrowed under toe nails, and crocodiles, snakes and predators were encountered along river banks. When the rains ceased the sun overhead was harsh and relentless.

The British theatre commander, the South African General Jan Smuts, was a former guerrilla leader turned politician and not a professional soldier. He totally failed to organise an effective logistical support system for his troops who were dependent on rations and supplies carried on the heads of thousands of under-nourished, under-clothed and poorly administered local African porters. The result was that the British Indian, African and European soldiers regularly existed on half-rations, and often they received less than that. Although special ethnic rations for Indian troops were sent from India the British East African supply system was incapable of efficiently distributing them; the sepoys had to exist on whatever rations appeared and often the time allowed for food preparation and cooking was curtailed due to General Smuts' insistence on pressing on to defeat the enemy. Sadly this defeat never happened as the Schutztruppe, as the local German army was named, became adept at withdrawing before British encircling moves arrived.

The 129th Baluchis took part in the advance of its Brigade down the Pangani River and then southwards towards the German Central Railway. This railway line linked Dar Es Salaam on the Indian Ocean with Lake Tanganyika in the interior. The regiment halted at Handeni, north of the railway, from where it was despatched to Tanga on the coast. Here the Baluchis embarked for Bagamoyo, just north of Dar Es Salaam. On 31st August 1916 the march on Dar Es Salaam began, and after minor skirmishing en route the Baluchis led the way into the captured town on 5th September.

The enemy coastal towns in the south of German East Africa were now occupied but movement away from the coast was not made except at Kilwa. Here preparations were in hand to move a British force inland to block the withdrawal of the Schutztruppe units that were fighting along the Rufiji River. In late September the 129th Baluchis was landed at Kilwa.

The deployment to Kibata

Lieutenant Colonel H. Hulseberg DSO, (127th Baluchis attached to 129th Baluchis), commanding officer of 129th Baluchis, was ordered to lead a column consisting of his regiment and the 1st Battalion of the 2nd Regiment of the King's African Rifles (1/2 KAR) to Kibata. Kibata was located in the centre of a ring of hills lying three days march north-west of Kilwa. The Germans had built a substantial stone fort there, and General Smuts planned to seize the fort and surrounding area to prevent Colonel von Lettow-Vorbeck and his Schutztruppe from withdrawing southwards. However von Lettow was aware of how difficult the terrain was around Kibata and he initially welcomed his enemy's interest in the area, as he knew that the ground would suck-in more and more British troops to defend ridge lines and crests.

On 11th October, the second day of the advance, 1/2 KAR was leading the column just beyond the Matandu ford when contact was made with an entrenched enemy position at Kimbarambara. The KAR attacked, with support provided by 129th Baluchis, and the Germans retreated, leaving behind a dead Askari plus two other Askari and two Europeans who were captured. 1/2 KAR was a newly-formed battalion and this was its first action; one Askari was killed and another was wounded.

On the following day the Baluchis took the lead and fought a similar action at Nyambondo where the advance guard of veteran sepoys under Lieutenant V.G. Robert encountered a well-sited ambush. Robert's bush sense had caused him to order the sepoys out into attack formation just before the enemy opened fire. Subedar Mir Kambir Khan (127th Baluchis attached to 129th Baluchis) pushed his men forward into thick grass where the enemy charged them. Mir Kambir Khan ordered his men into the kneeling fire position and he himself killed one enemy European and wounded another. The sepoys' effective use of their rifles stopped the enemy attack and the Germans withdrew, leaving behind their brave but dead commander, Ober-Leutnant Steffans. One Baluchi, 872 Sepoy Khaim Khan, had been killed.

On 14th October Kibata was reached and the empty fort seized. The local German commander, Major Julius von Boemcken, had decided to secure the important German supply depot at Liwale to the south-west rather than defend Kibata fort. This fort had been initially designed as a base from which rebellious tribesmen armed with spears and bows could be subdued, and the

British were to find that the building could not be defended against modern artillery because a ring of higher ground surrounded the location.

The first German move against Kibata

After this successful seizure of Kibata Fort 1/2 KAR was left to garrison it whilst the Baluchis were withdrawn southwards to the Mitole area where they patrolled widely. A feature of this terrain was the large coconut plantations that often provided liquid for thirsty sepoys. In late October 1/2 KAR was ordered to leave two platoons and a machine gun at Kibata whilst the remainder of the battalion marched ten kilometres to Kitambi. This order was carried out on 28th October, but then the Germans saw an opportunity to inflict a defeat on the small British garrison, and sent 400 troops under Captain Hans Schulz to seize Kibata.

When news of the enemy move arrived at the British headquarters at Kilwa, a detachment of 100 sepoys of the 129th Baluchis relieved the main body of 1/2 KAR which was at Kitambi, allowing the KAR Askari to march quickly back across the hills to Kibata. After some heavy machine gun exchanges Schulz's troops were forced back from the area of the fort on 8th November, and 1/2 KAR dug itself in. The next morning British patrols discovered that the enemy had withdrawn; von Lettow realised that more companies had to be withdrawn from their Rufiji River positions to the north before a successful attack on Kibata could be mounted. Communications with Kilwa were established via signals posts on Red Hill to the south-east and on Ssongo Ssongo island off the coast. Lieutenant Colonel Hulseburg returned with his 129th Baluchis on 17th November and he took over command of Kibata from the commanding officer of 1/2 KAR, Major G.J. Giffard. Temporary Major H.V. Lewis MC assumed command of 129th Baluchis.

The German attacks start at Kibata

Lieutenant Colonel Hulseburg saw that Picquet Hill to the north-west of the fort was the vital ground, and the bush was stripped off the hill and two strong redoubts were constructed near the summit. The Baluchis garrisoned Kibata whilst 1/2 KAR patrolled and skirmished in the outlying region. Soon information was brought in that indicated an imminent German attack. Unconfirmed rumours amongst the local villagers suggested that heavy artillery was being dragged up the hills by German labour gangs; a

German 4-inch gun required a gang of 600 Africans to move the gun and its ammunition.

On 6th December enemy troops advanced on Kibata, driving in the KAR outposts on Ambush Hill and at Coconut Village. The Baluchis were manning the Picquet Hill redoubts and holding 100 sepoys as a reserve, along with a KAR company. On the next day at 0630 hours the KAR positions at Palm Village and Single Palm Village were attacked from the east, but these turned out to be diversions to occupy the defence whilst the main attack was mounted against Picquet Hill. Plain Hill and Big Hut Hill were being held by detachments of Baluchis, and on the former Jemadar Fateh Haider **IOM** was directing the fire of a machine gun. A shell hit the gun, killing Fateh Haider and wounding two sepoys.

The German guns then came into action against the two redoubts, obviously hoping to blast the Baluchi defenders off Picquet Hill. A 4.1-inch gun recovered from the sunken cruiser *Konigsberg*, a 4.1-inch howitzer and a lighter field gun targeted the redoubts all morning. The German artillery commander was naval Lieutenant Hans Apel from the *Konigsberg*'s crew. Enemy machine guns raked the British positions. More than 100 shells hit in or around No 2 Redoubt which was less than 40 metres by 20 metres in area, causing heavy loss to the Baluchis. Men were constantly being dug out of collapsed trenches – Major Lewis was buried once, Lieutenant C.W. Palin three times, and Lieutenant M.I.L. Smith was shot in the head. Five sepoys were killed. Major Lewis later wrote to his mother: *"An hour before dark, this developed into an intense bombardment, and except for the size of the shells, I never experienced such a hot one, even in France... We lost heavily in the redoubt... however our men stuck it like heroes, though there was little left of the trenches".*

During the afternoon the guns engaged targets elsewhere, but at 1730 hours they resumed bombarding Picquet Hill. Thirty minutes later enemy field companies attacked No 2 Redoubt but were repulsed by the sepoy defenders, the German Askari just failing to commit themselves totally to the attack. However one enemy company dug itself in on the western slope of Picquet Hill. This enemy position was named the Lodgement, and from there German machine gunners were able to put a water supply point below them out of reach of the British troops.

Lieutenant C.W. Palin was awarded a Military Cross with the citation: *For conspicuous gallantry and devotion to duty in defending a redoubt. Although three* times buried by falling parapets, he kept his men together under the most intense fire and maintained hold of his position.

44 Lance Naik Fateh Khan was awarded an Indian Distinguished Service Medal for gallantry on a night patrol on 7th December, with the citation: *When in command going close up to the enemy trenches and bringing back useful information in spite of the close-range fire he was subjected to*

A 1/2 KAR detachment under the command of Captain Alan Caldicott (10th Battalion The Loyal North Lancashire Regiment and 1/2 KAR) was sent up onto Picquet Hill to strengthen the defence during the attack. The Askari assisted materially with the defence but Captain Caldicott was shot dead. At last light the surviving Baluch defenders evacuated their wounded and withdrew to recover whilst the KAR took over the defence of Picquet Hill. "C" Company 1/2 KAR had planned to make a night attack against the Lodgement but this was called off when it was seen that the young Askari had been badly shaken by the intensity of the German artillery fire.

Next morning, 8th December, after intermittent shelling during the night the Germans attacked No 2 Redoubt from the Lodgement. Heavy rain fell onto the battlefield whilst effective enemy artillery and machine gun fire was delivered from Ambush Hill. The young KAR Askari wavered before responding to their fire orders and defending their positions. However some of the enemy got up to the redoubt's outer obstacles, and at the KAR's request 60 Baluchis under Captain C.S. Browning reinforced Picquet Hill, but before the sepoys arrived the Germans had been beaten back. Simultaneously the Germans attacked Plain Hill and Big Hut hill, attempting to prevent those locations from supporting the Picquet Hill defences. Meanwhile the enemy artillery pounded the fort, knocking chunks out of the walls.

The British defenders at Kibata now dug themselves in deeply, and a Western Front style of trench-warfare commenced. Meanwhile reinforcements were arriving.

Indian mountain artillery arrives

After a 58-kilometer forced march, completed in 34 hours of pouring rain and routed over a series of razor-backed ridges, reinforcements reached Kibata. The 2nd Battalion of the 2nd Regiment of the KAR (2/2 KAR) arrived at 0200 hours on the 9th December accompanied by a section of two guns of the 27th (Bengal) Mountain Battery. The 10-pounder guns, named "screw guns" because the barrel could be unscrewed into two pieces for ease of transport, and their ammunition came in on the backs of mules. The Indian gunners came into action on Village Hill and 2/2 KAR reinforced Picquet Hill with 60 Askari and a machine gun. The remainder of 2/2 KAR camped in between Mango Hill and the fort in what was named Happy Valley. However this was not an idyllic campsite as German artillery observers soon called down fire and the battalion made a hasty move to Fort Hill.

Lieutenant Colonel Filsell of 2/2 KAR took over command at Kibata and he ordered an attack on the Lodgement timed for 2200 hours on 9th December. Meanwhile the Indian mountain gunners fired shrapnel over the Lodgement. The attack was led by Captain C.S. Browning of the Baluchis who assaulted with his company of sepoys and two platoons of 1/2 KAR. The attackers ran through heavy enemy fire to the Lodgement defences where, although some sepoys entered the enemy trenches, Captain Browning was shot dead at point-blank range whilst on the enemy parapet. The German defenders were then reinforced from a feature to the west named the Hump, and they mounted a violent counter-attack, forcing the British troops to withdraw to No 2 Redoubt.

These two men later received an Indian Order of Merit 2nd Class with the citations:

Subadar Sarbiland (127th Baluch Light Infantry attached to 129th Baluchis): *For gallantry during the first night attack by us on the Lodgement. After the death of the British officer (Captain Browning), he maintained the attack for twenty minutes under the enemy's entanglement until casualties and want of ammunition compelled him to retire.*(Unit citation.)

659 Sepoy Munsib Dar: *For conspicuous gallantry in action on the 7th December 1916. He was continuously with his guns which were situated in the open under heavy shell and machine gun fire. He kept down the fire of two hostile guns and stopped their being employed against a redoubt. He has since died of his wounds.*(Gazetted citation.)

The German artillery continuously engaged all the British positions around Kibata on the 10th December, and on the following day a small field gun was covertly brought up to within 550 metres of No 1 Redoubt. When this gun opened fire it scored a direct hit on the position, killing a KAR officer and his machine gun team, and wounding several other Askari.

On 12th December German machine guns fired heavily on British positions east of the fort and onto the hospital. The Senior Medical Officer, Captain A.N. Dickson, Indian Medical Service and Medical Officer for 129th Baluchis, had to run into the open waving a Red Cross flag. Captain Dickson later received a Military Cross with the unit citation:

During the whole of this period this Medical Officer showed great devotion to duty. Though unwell himself, he frequently had to operate during intense fire, on one occasion the hospital coming under enemy's machine-gun fire. When Major Money, 129th Baluchis, was hit on PICQUET HILL, he at once moved out under rifle and machine-gun fire to the picquet to give what help he could. I have previously sent this Officer's name in for an honour. During most of the time he was Senior Medical Officer of the Post.

During the following day a 4.1-inch howitzer was used against No 1 Redoubt, but the damage caused was not serious. The mountain gunners replied when they could but the heavier German guns were well out of range of the 10-pounders.

The regular enemy artillery bombardments caused attrition and up to 12th December 129th Baluchis had lost 1 British officer, 1 Indian officer and 10 sepoys killed; 42 sepoys wounded and 7 sepoys missing. The Section 27th (Bengal) Mountain Battery had lost 5 gunners wounded and 10 mules killed. 'A' Section 139 Indian Field Ambulance had lost 1 sepoy and 2 porters wounded.

On 13th December the Baluch lost two experienced officers on Picquet Hill when Major C.A.G. Money (130th Baluchis attached to 129th Baluchis) was killed by machine gun fire and 4189 Colour Havildar Mohamed Sadin was hit and died of wounds. Mohamed Sadin received promotion to Jemadar on his death-bed in recognition of the services he had rendered to the regiment.

Very rudimentary medical support was provided by unit Medical Officers and "A" Section 139th Indian Field Ambulance. There was a complete lack of equipment, and bandages were so scarce that sometimes they were only changed weekly. Operations including amputations were carried out using a door as a table. Evacuation was extremely difficult and painful, and the opinion at Kibata was that it was better to be killed than to take a bad wound. Hunger was a factor affecting the morale and stability of the wounded, as supply convoys of porters and mules were arriving with ammunition as the priority loads, and so all ranks were on short rations during the fighting.

Trench warfare and further reinforcements

By now the Askari and sepoys in and around Kibata were well dug-in. The recent recruits became used to the shelling and they quickly adapted to trench warfare. The distance between British and German trenches varied from 70 metres to 370 metres. Trench periscopes were used and saps dug to cover movements towards the Lodgement. Snipers on both sides had telescopic sights, the Germans having the advantage because they occupied much of the higher ground. Heavy rain fell necessitating constant trench repairs and revetting, the rain and the mud making working conditions difficult.

After dark on 13 December Brigadier General H. de C. O'Grady (52nd Sikhs) arrived with his headquarters staff to take command at Kibata. The Loyal North Lancashire Machine Gun Company also arrived under the command of Major R.E. Berkeley, (Loyal North Lancashires). His eight .303-inch Maxim guns were deployed tactically in four sections each containing two guns; the company was also equipped with trench mortars. Major A.J.T. Farfan, Royal Garrison Artillery, marched in with another section of his 27th (Bengal) Mountain Battery. The defensive firepower at Kibata had been greatly increased. 1/2 KAR took over all positions on Picquet Hill on 14th December.

However German attention was now concentrated towards the south-west of Kibata where another British advance was forming up. The Gold Coast Regiment supported by the 40th Pathans mounted a determined attack on the German positions along the ridgeline west of Kibata. The Gold Coasters and Pathans took ground and then held it in fierce fighting that left a third of the British troops killed or wounded. Nearly 50% of the officers in these two units became casualties.

Capturing the Lodgement

Although the German infantry and some guns were heavily involved in fighting the Gold Coasters, artillery fire still hit the KAR and Baluchi positions at Kibata on 15th December. The Indian mountain gunners responded by bombarding the Lodgement whilst the Baluchis prepared a night attack, using Mills hand grenades for the first time in East Africa. At 2300 hours Major Lewis led his Baluchi assault team towards the Lodgement. The sky was dark but moonlight was expected to appear 15 minutes later.

Ten young barefoot Mahsud pioneer bombers carefully and quietly took the lead and threw their grenades into the Lodgement. Under this cover the other Baluchi troops tore out of the ground the sharpened bamboo stakes that protected the enemy trenches. Heavy British machine gun fire supported the attack and the mountain gunners put shrapnel above the Hump. With lanes made through the defences the bayonet attack then surged in. Enemy artillery responded by battering No 2 Redoubt and severely shaking the 1/2 KAR Askari defending it, but that was not going to stop the Baluchis who bayoneted the enemy soldiers that they found in the Lodgement trenches. The Germans fell back, leaving 11 men dead and 4 captured; the Baluchi casualties were 13 wounded, including 1 British and two Indian officers. The Lodgement was occupied by "A" Company 1/2 KAR and a section of Loyal North Lancashire machine guns.

Major H.V. Lewis, MC later received the **Distinguished Service Order** with a unit citation: *Arranged and commanded the bombing party on the night of 15/16 December 1916, against the enemy, who had secured a lodgement on an important tactical point on our picquet position. The seizure of the latter would have endangered our security in rear. The action was successful, the position taken. It was greatly due to this officer that the achievement was a success. He already possesses MC and one bar.*

Lieutenant W.S. Thatcher received a Military Cross with the citation:*For conspicuous gallantry and devotion to duty. He led a bombing party with great gallantry, driving the enemy out of his position and securing an important tactical position. He was wounded.*

Jemadar Ayub Khan IOM (124th Baluchis attached to 129th Baluchis) was awarded an Indian Order of Merit 1st Class with the unit citation: *Acted with great gallantry in a bomb attack against an enemy position on night of 15/16 December 1916. Wounded.*

The following five men received the Indian Order of Merit 2nd Class (unit citations are shown):

Subadar Muhammad Afzul (124th Baluchis attached 129th Baluchis): *Led his men with gallantry and greatly assisted 2nd Lieutenant W.S. Thatcher in a bomb attack. Slightly wounded.*

3151 Havildar Mirza Khan; 436 Sepoy Mirjan; 4656 Sepoy Abdullah Khan; 4469 Lance Naik Ghuljam Khan (the latter two being sepoys of 124th Baluchis attached 129th Baluchis) had similar citations: *Formed one of the party* in a bomb attack on an enemy position on night 15/16 December 1916. The attack was a success.

453 Naik Sahib Jan IOM received an Indian Distinguished Service Medal for the gallantry that he displayed during the successful attack.

Lieutenant Colonel H. Hulseberg received a Bar to his Distinguished Service Order.

Stalemate at Kibata

Now both sides maintained their positions in and around Kibata, but neither side was strong enough to successfully assault the other's main defences. The British kept the Union flag flying on Kibata fort and the German gunners tried to knock it down, succeeding on one occasion. Brigadier O'Grady and his Brigade Major, Major J.G. Cadell (45th Sikhs), climbed back up the walls under enemy fire and restored the flag. Later the Brigadier became a **Companion of the Order of the Indian Empire** (**CIE**) and the Brigade Major received a **Distinguished Service Order**. (The flag belonged to 1/2 KAR and that unit later presented it to 129th Baluchis *"as a small token of esteem that we feel for your magnificent regiment . . . it was the bravery and devotion of your regiment which saved the situation and kept the flag flying"* who displayed it in India in the regimental officers mess.)

Christmas Day saw a British BE 2C aeroplane of 26 Squadron, Royal Flying Corps, fly from its base at Kilwa to drop a large parcel of 6,000 cigarettes outside Kibata fort. The plane was piloted by Lieutenant The Honourable Bernard H.E. Howard, and his observer who dropped the parcel was the future author Lieutenant Leo Walmsley. After first assuming that the BE2C was bombing them by mistake the Kibata defenders were extremely cheered, as they had been out of cigarettes for a fortnight.

The 129th Baluchis had by now lost many officers and men to sickness and most of the regiment marched out of Kibata on Boxing Day 1916 to locations around Chumo, from where patrolling became the main activity. Another KAR battalion, the 1st Battalion of the 3rd Regiment (1/3 KAR), had marched in on 18th December and the three KAR battalions took over all infantry responsibilities at Kibata.

On 1st January 1917 the two 5-inch howitzers of the 14th Howitzer Battery arrived at Kibata. A massive labour effort had been put in to making a passable road over which the howitzers could be moved. A Royal Navy 12-pounder gun had been supporting the Kibata defences from Kitambi, but that gun created so much smoke when it fired that immediate German counter-battery fire was returned. The 12-pounder was moved back to the coast and the gun crew became a Royal Navy Lewis light machine gun detachment supporting infantry operations.

The German withdrawal from Kibata

At the beginning of January 1917 Colonel von Lettow-Vorbeck withdrew six of his nine companies from the Kibata area and moved them towards the Rufiji River. British intelligence scouts observed this and reported that the enemy was thinning-out around Kibata. On the 6th January Brigadier O'Grady's Headquarters ordered a general advance and 129th Baluchis marched back to Kibata to participate. Supported by the howitzers, mountain guns and Loyal North Lancashire machine guns the KAR units took Platform and Observation Hills and Palm Tree Village, followed by Ambush Hill, Cocunut Village and Kommando Berg Hill. The Baluchis stayed in reserve for these attacks, which succeeded without heavy fighting. The German priority now was to withdraw north to meet General Smuts' main body of British troops that was fighting for crossings over the Rufiji.

Following up the German withdrawal

As the Germans withdrew to Mwengei 129th Baluchis followed them up supported by two KAR companies and a section of the mountain battery. At Mwengei, from where the German heavy guns had been firing, a serious fight developed. The road was hilly and thickly bushed on either side, necessitating good picqueting drills which slowed the advance. As the Baluchis approached the location where the German 4.1-inch naval gun was being hauled away by African labour gangs, the withdrawing enemy formation, Abteilung Schulz, entrenched itself and fought.

At dawn on 12th January a patrol of 20 men under a havildar advanced into a machine gun ambush sprung by the enemy's 18 Field Company, and three guns opened fired at 150 metres range. Ten sepoys were killed and seven were wounded, the four survivors escaping into the bush. One of these survivors ran back to report the incident to Captain G.A. Phillips**VD** who was operating in the area with a larger patrol. Evacuation of the wounded lying in the road was requested but could not be performed in daylight;

after dark the new Regimental Medical Officer, Captain A.H. Brown, Indian Medical Service, courageously went out with stretcher bearers to bring the wounded in.

Captain Phillips sent a 12-man patrol up a steep and narrow ridge named Mbindia Hill that dominated the road, but this patrol was also machine gunned, losing two killed and four wounded. The German 18 and 30 Field Companies were well established in two lines of trenches, with four machine guns covering the British approaches. Progress could not be made that day, so Lieutenant Roberts with 50 rifles and a Loyal North Lancashire section of two machine guns were sent up to join Captain Phillips. The mountain gunners fired on the ridge and the German 4.1-inch gun retaliated by killing and wounding several of the African porters in the Baluchi transport column. A British aircraft was sent up to bomb the enemy, but as the draft Official History states:" *The aeroplane did not appear for several hours and then could effect nothing, having expended its bombs in error on some other hills far to the northward".*

The following morning, 13th January 1917, Brigadier O'Grady arrived with an additional gun of the 27th Mountain Battery. Captain Phillips was ordered to assault the enemy position on the ridge. He planned a two-phase afternoon attack and deployed 30 rifles with two machine guns onto a ridge east of the enemy's position, from where they could and did fire onto the German left flank and rear. Two other machine guns were positioned to be able to fire onto the first objective and then to be quickly switched onto the second objective whilst the first was being assaulted. At 1400 hours drenching rain fell chilling the sepoys. At 1430 hours the mountain guns fired onto the second objective, and at 1500 hours two mortars of the Loyal North Lancashires fired onto both objectives.

At 1505 hours No 1 Company under Lieutenant Thatcher and Jemadar Sikandar Khan attacked the first objective. The ridge was so narrow that file formation had to be used, slowing down movement. Two enemy machine guns came into action but the effective British covering fire interrupted the aim of the German gunners. After being pinned down 25 metres from the first trench line, Lieutenant Thatcher successfully assaulted it but was shot down with a serious wound. Jemadar Sikandar Khan pushed on with No 1 Company but ran into 'friendly' mortar fire as the range of the mortar bombs had been reached. Luckily for the sepoys at that moment a bomb exploded on the mortar line, stunning a Loyal North Lancashire mortar man, and the mortar fire was curtailed.

Major Lewis saw Lieutenant Thatcher fall and he immediately sent up Lieutenant Roberts to take over command. Reserves, mortars and a machine gun were moved forward to support the second phase but by now Lieutenant Robert's and Jemadar Sikandar Khan's men were unstoppable and they swept into the second line of trenches, killing or evicting the defenders whom they pursued along the ridge. Unfortunately the two machine guns that had been deployed to the east then jammed, as they had been heavily fired throughout the attack, and so the retreating Germans who were crowding the road got away without further losses. The mules of the mountain gunners were so debilitated by a diet of very poor forage at Kibata that they could not move quickly, and had to be frequently halted, so the screw-guns also could not be brought to bear on the retreating enemy.

The Baluchis had lost 2 men killed, and 1 British and 1 Indian officer and 12 sepoys wounded. This had been a very successful attack. The second position captured had been the firing location for the *Konigsberg* gun, which now could not be dragged swiftly enough away from the advancing British troops. Two days later scouts found the gun, abandoned and destroyed. The King's African Rifles now took up the pursuit of Abteilung Schulz. As the regimental history of the 129th Baluchis states: *"So ended the fighting that had begun on 6th December. By the time it was finished the regiment had lost about two-thirds of its original strength in fighting or in sickness, but it had lived up to its high reputation"*.

Lieutenant V.G. Robert received a Military Cross with the unit citation: *For gallantry during the attack on MBINDIA HILL. When 2/Lt W.S. Thatcher was wounded this officer carried on the attack and pursuit, and by his fine example led on the men against the enemy's hidden position in the bush, until all our objectives had been gained and the enemy put to rout.*

The following were Mentioned in Despatches for their gallantry, initiative or resourcefulness at Mwenge:

Captain G.A. Phillips VD; Captain R.S.P. MacIvor (Adjutant); Jemadar Sikandar Khan; 2630 Colour Havildar Alim Shah (124th Baluchis attached 129th Baluchis); 3659 Havildar Imam Din; 757 Sepoy Misri Khan; 225 Naik Mohamed Rahim (127th Baluchis attached 129th Baluchis); 290 Havildar Sardar Shah (Burma Military Police attached 129th Baluchis).

Conclusion

The Kibata fighting was a true all-arms effort, the sepoys of the 129th Baluchis often sharing defensive positions with the KAR Askariand attacking alongside them, whilst the Sikh mountain gunners, Indian medical personnel, British howitzer gunners, Loyal North Lancashire machine gunners, African porters and road labour gangs, and a volunteer Royal Flying Corps crew all provided necessary support.

Nobody won at Kibata. The Germans failed to take it, but General Smuts failed to trap his adversary, as the Germans side-stepped Kibata when they later withdrew south from the Rufiji. The Kibata fighting distracted the British away from the German crop-collection programme as perhaps Colonel von Lettow-Vorbeck hoped it would, and allowed Liwale to remain as an important Schutztruppe supply base when that location should have been seized by a British attack.

The long war of attrition in the disease-ridden heat, dust and swamps of the East African bush dragged on, but not for General Smuts who moved on to a far more pleasant post in London. The often half-starved and debilitated British sepoys, Askari and surviving European personnel tightened their belts, scraped the mud off their boots and followed the Schutztruppe's tactical withdrawals. A British gunner on the Rufiji, Sergeant Dan Fewster, wrote to his mother in Hull summing up the situation: *"Mosquitoes, tsetse fly and all other crawling insects are here by the million. At night the yelping and howling of wild beasts keeps us awake. We are having a bad time with fever. The gun can only be fired with help of two cooks and a servant"*.

Commemorations

Major Charles Arthur Gilbert Money and Captain Charles Stuart Browning were first buried at Kibata at night to avoid enemy artillery attention, then transferred to Kilwa Kivinje military cemetery, and later re-interred in the Commonwealth War Graves Commission Dar Es Salaam War Cemetery, Tanzania.

The Indian officers and their sepoys were buried where they fell and are commemorated on the British and Indian Memorial in Nairobi South Cemetery, Kenya.

The 22nd Derajat Mountain Battery (Frontier Force) in East Africa December 1916 to December 1918

Introduction

When war was declared in August 1914 the 22nd Derajat Mountain Battery was stationed in Burma, now Myanmar. The Battery was armed with six 10-pounder guns that were transported on mules. In January 1915 the two guns of No. 1 Section operated against dissident Kachin tribesmen in the Myitkyina area but returned to base at Maymyo, now Pyin Oo Lwin, a few weeks later. Routine duties and the sending of drafts to other units consumed the Battery's time until November 1916 when it was mobilised for service in German East Africa (GEA). The Battery was to stay in East Africa until the Armistice, and it was one of the very few Indian Army units that served operationally in Portuguese East Africa, now Mozambique.

Initial operations in German East Africa

The Battery sailed from Rangoon, now Yangon, on 1st December 1916 and disembarked at Kilwa Kissiwani in GEA on the 17th of that month. The composition of the unit was:

- British officers: Major S. Perry, Royal Artillery; Lieutenants J.P. Doyle, India Army Reserve of Officers, and H. Bastow, Royal Artillery; 2nd Lieutenant W. Hawes, Royal Artillery.

- Indian officers: Subedar Santa Singh; Jemadars Nur Hassan Khan and Jagat Singh.

- Sub-Assistant Surgeon: Mehdi Hassan Khan.

- Indian other ranks: 295.
- Public Followers: 18.
- Private Followers: 6.
- Ordnance mules: 164.
- Horses: 9.

Shortly after arrival a re-organisation took place to make the Battery a four-gun unit, with an Ammunition Column taking the place of the Centre Section. Initial deployments were around Kibata, inland from Kilwa, and the first shells were fired by the Right Section in a skirmish on 23rd-25th January 1918. Many mules quickly succumbed to Tsetse-fly bites and African porters were used to transport the guns and ammunition. Heavy rainfall destroyed the tracks impeding re-supply convoys, and rations received for both men and animals were totally inadequate. By the end of March all the mules were dead.

In April the Battery occupied Rumbo Camp and in May fired in support of the abortive attack made by the 40th Pathans on a nearby enemy force. During June 251 remount mules were received from South Africa and had to be trained for operations; also the Battery was re-organised back to being a six-gun unit.

The fights at Narungombe and Nanyati

In July 1917 the Battery was placed in No. 2 Column of a three-column British force that advanced south-west from Kilwa. The infantry units in the Column were the 7th South African Infantry and the 1st and 2nd Battalions of 3rd King's African Rifles (1/3KAR and 2/3KAR). The Germans were in strength occupying important water holes at Narungombe, and the British force deployed to attack the enemy positions on 19th July.

The fighting was intense, all three British columns attacking and making little headway. Many British casualties could not be evacuated because of their proximity to the enemy, and when the bush and scrub on the battlefield caught fire these wounded men were burned to death whilst the ammunition in their pouches exploded. The 1/3rd KAR saved the day by counter-charging an enemy attack, but the KAR lost 6 officers killed and 200 Askari dead or wounded. The Forward Observation Officer (FOO) for the Battery was Captain John Hugh Macdonald Stevenson, Royal Artillery, who held his ground when attacked until the bush fire forced him back to the battery; he later received a **Military Cross** whilst No. 1000 Lance Naik Payanda Khan who was with him received the **Indian Distinguished Service Medal**. The enemy later withdrew from Narungombe.

The Left Section of the Battery, under Major G.V. Dreyer, Royal Artillery, with Jemadar Nur Hassan Khan, was in action at Nanyati on 5th August along with 200 rifles of the 129th Duke of Connaught's Own Baluchis and 100 rifles of 1/3KAR. The Baluch attacked but could not force the Germans out of their well-sited trenches, despite effective fire from the Left Section directed by Major Dreyer who was up with the infantry. Then the enemy brought the fight to their opponents by counter-attacking from a flank and the Baluchis suffered badly, losing two British and two Indian officers, a Havildar Major, and nearly 20 sepoys, all killed. The KAR Askari then came forward from their reserve position and pushed the enemy back. As the wind was favourable for the British, a bush fire was lit that forced the Germans away from their trenches.

The final months in German East Africa

During September 1917 one 10-pounder gun, under Lieutenant J.P. Doyle, Indian Army Reserve of Officers, was temporarily attached to the 25th Cavalry (Frontier Force), to boost that regiment's firepower. The remainder of the Battery was in action on the 20th of the month at Ndessa Chini, where its accurate shrapnel fire prevented an enemy force from breaking through the British position. After making three desperate attempts the Germans were forced to withdraw and abandon their baggage. At the end of September the Battery was re-configured to operate with four 2.75-inch guns.

The Right Section under Major Dreyer, with 2nd Lieutenant R.W. Carrigan MC, Royal Artillery, Subadar Santa Singh and Jemadar Jagat Singh, was in action at Mtonone Chini in support of the KAR on 1st October. Things did not run smoothly as No. 2 gun jammed its range gear and could not fire, and Jemadar Jagat Singh was shot through the chest whilst talking to Major Dreyer. Robert William Carrigan was in the thick of the fighting as he was the FOO, and for his gallantry he was awarded a **Bar to his Military Cross**.

As the German theatre commander, General Paul von Lettow-Vorbeck, manoeuvred his Schutztruppe to fight withdrawal actions and move over the Rovuma River into Portuguese East Africa (PEA), the Battery marched and counter-marched through the dry bush of south-eastern GEA. The gunners did not fight in any decisive actions, but they suffered from debilitation and disease, and their mules suffered from lack of sufficient water and grain. The end of the year saw the battery at Kitunda, preparing to move into PEA.

Operations in Portuguese East Africa – the Medo battle

On 16th January 1918 Right Section was shipped down to Port Amelia, now Pemba, in PEA. Left Section remained at Kitunda in GEA until 31st March, training a newly arrived draft and converting to the new 3.7-inch howitzer. The Battery assembled again in PEA on 1st April.

For the first quarter of 1918 heavy rains prevented the movement of PAMFORCE, as the British force in Port Amelia was titled, but in April orders were received to advance westwards and two columns were formed. The first column, named ROSECOL after its commander, contained the Gold Coast Regiment (GCR), the Battery, the Ugandan 4th Battalion of the 4th Regiment of the King's African Rifles (4/4KAR), and a detachment from the KAR Mounted Infantry Company. Porters from the Sierra Leone Carrier Corps provided transport support. The other column in PAMFORCE was titled KARTUCOL and it contained the first two battalions of the 2nd Regiment of the King's African Rifles (1/2 and 2/2KAR).

Confronting any advance from Port Amelia was a German formation commanded by the Bavarian gunner Major Koehl, one of von Lettow's most able subordinates. Koehl's units were No 6 Schutzen Company and the 3rd, 11th, 13th, 14th and 17th Field Companies. These six companies each had at least two machine guns, and a captured Portuguese field gun was also deployed.

On 7th April the GCR led PAMFORCE westwards, meeting enemy snipers and ambushers who made good use of the thick bush on either side of the muddy road. Some of the enemy Askari wore captured GCR green caps and this created confusion during contacts. Four days later the force was established at Rock Camp, the GCR having lost 3 men killed and 7 wounded on the way. The immediate objective was the capture of Medo Boma, 10 kilometres to the west. On 12 April KARTUCOL was sent south of Chirimba Hill whilst 'B' Company GCR moved forward supported by two GCR Stokes guns (medium mortars) and the Mountain Battery. The enemy blocked the GCR advance very effectively with two companies and machine gun fire, although a small group of GCR men got to the summit of the hill and cleared an enemy observation post. A Battery FOO party accompanied this group and had to fight to hold its position. The Stokes guns, deployed about 45 metres behind the firing line, were now used very effectively, throwing bombs forward into the bush where enemy Askari were sited.

Around 1500 hours KARTUCOL walked into an enemy area ambush south of Chirimba Hill. Whilst this action was in progress Gunner Dyal Singh, a linesman with the Mountain Battery, trod on an improvised mine planted in the road. The mine was a 10.6 centimetre German naval shell. Both Dyall Singh's legs were blown off and he subsequently died. Lieutenant Colonel R.A. de B. Rose DSO, the column commander and the Commandant of the GCR, had been standing next to Dyal Singh and he had a fortunate escape, being drenched with blood but not wounded. The Battery, transported on its mules, had been firing in support of the GCR, and Subedar Santa Singh had been acting as Battery Commander because of sickness amongst the British officers. For gallantry displayed whilst calling fire down the FOO, Lieutenant Owen Gilbert Davies (Royal Artillery), was later awarded a **Military Cross**.

Koehl withdrew his men during the evening and next day PAMFORCE was on his trail. This was attritional fighting, the vanguard company always knowing that it was only a matter of time before an enemy ambush was sprung. The Germans defended water sources until the last minute, making the British troops expose themselves in attacks or else go thirsty. In the tropical climate a good water source just had to be seized before night fell, and the dense bush prevented the British from quickly putting in flank attacks. The rocky outcrops dotting the landscape ensured that the Schutztruppe could always observe PAMFORCE's approach.

The Koronje ambush

On 1st May 1918 at Koronje a party of Gold Coast soldiers was escorting the Mountain Gunners and their mule-loads through the bush when an enemy party attacked. Seven gunners and 11 mules were killed, with another 7 gunners and 8 mules being wounded; 5 mules were missing. Fitter Staff Sergeant E. Mason, Royal Garrison Artillery attached to 22nd Derajat Mountain Battery, was later awarded a **Distinguished Conduct Medal** with the citation: *On 1st May, 1918, at Koronje, Portuguese East Africa, when the battery* *was attacked on the line of march at short range by a field company with two machine guns, he, with two Indian non-commissioned officers, went out under heavy machine-gun fire and successfully brought in the breech of a howitzer which had been bucked off by its mule between the escort and the enemy. An act of great gallantry, as they were under fire from both sides, and the enemy was very close; but for these three men the breech might have been captured.* Naik Naryan Singh and Gunner Mahji Khan were mentioned in despatches. The remainder of May was spent in coming into action against ambushes mounted by the rearguard of the withdrawing German force.

The reduction of the Battery

Many gunners and drivers were now suffering from tropical diseases and ailments, and orders were received on 1st June for the Battery to return to GEA, less the Howitzer section which was required to stay in the field in PEA. The Battery marched back to Medo where Centre Section was reformed with all the fittest men in the Battery plus a 15% over-strength element, and it took over the two 3.7-inch howitzers. The remainder of the battery was shipped, with the 2.75-inch guns, from Port Amelia up to Dar Es Salaam where it was re-clothed and equipped and a new draft from India was trained in bush mountain gunnery warfare. The British officers remaining in PEA with Centre Section were Captain J.C. Bowering, Royal Artillery, plus Lieutenants D. Edwards, Royal Artillery, and W.N. Ogilvie, Indian Army Reserve of Officers.

Centre Section marched across northern PEA for the next three months as the Schutztruppe constantly withdrew and often turned back on its tracks and marched in the opposite direction. Centre Section left ROSECOL and joined KARTUCOL and then FITZCOL, a column of 3rd KAR troops. There were no serious military engagements for the Section, but it fired in support of its column vanguard's skirmishing. Hazardous river crossings were made, the guns going over on pontoons and the mules being swum across. On 8th October the Section was back at the Rovuma River, the frontier between GEA and PEA, and orders were received to cross the river and to march to Lindi; from there the Section was shipped to Dar Es Salaam where it re-joined the Battery. Repatriation was ordered and by 10th January 1919 the complete 22nd Derajat Mountain Battery was in barracks at Rawalpindi. A difficult job in the African bush had been performed well, and the casualty figures below reveal that the greatest danger, for mules as well as men, always came from the tropical environment and its diseases.

Casualties suffered in East Africa

British officers – 1 died of pneumonia and malaria (Lieutenant G.M. Helmsley, Royal Artillery); 2 wounded; and 7 invalided to India or England.

Indian officers – 1 wounded.

Non-commissioned officers and men – 9 killed in action; 57 died of disease; and 8 wounded.

Followers – 1 killed and 5 died of disease.

African porters – 2 killed and 3 wounded.

Invalided to India – 150 Gunners; 193 Drivers; and 8 Followers.

Mules – 11 killed in action and 948 died of disease and malnutrition.

Horses – 24 died of disease.

Awards to Indian personnel for service in East Africa

Order of British India, 2nd Class

Subedar Santa Singh.

Indian Distinguished Service Medal

Subedar Santa Singh; No. 352 1st Class Civil Sub-Assistant Surgeon Mehdi Hassan Khan, Indian Subordinate Medical Department attached to 22nd Derajat Mountain Battery; No. 773 Gunner Havildar Ghazan Khan; No. 917 Gunner Naik Aurangzeb; No. 1000 Lance Naik Payanda Khan; No. 1153 Driver Santokh Singh (28th Mountain Battery attached to 22nd).

Indian Meritorious Service Medal

No. 845 Naik Mansa Singh; No. 823 Naik Muhammad Baksh; No. 454 Driver Kanahiya Singh; and No. 821 Trumpeter Nur Muhammad.

Mention in Despatches

No. 828 Naik Narayan Singh; and No. 1013 Gunner (Acting Lance Naik) Majhi Khan.

Indian Army Battalions in the Battle of Ramadi, Mesopotamia, 27th-29th September 1917
Gurkhas, Garhwalis and Punjabis in Action

The First British attack on Ramadi

In mid-1917 the experienced and competent Lieutenant General Sir Frederick Stanley Maude was the British commander in Mesopotamia. His troops captured Baghdad on 11 March 1917 and Maude then methodically and soundly pushed the Turks up the Tigris towards Mosul and up the Euphrates towards Aleppo. He also sent a force up the Diyala River that runs through Bakuba and Kizil Robat to successfully liaise with allied Russian Cossack cavalry advancing from Persia, but the Russian strength was crumbling away because of the effects of the recent Russian revolution. One of Maude's concerns was that despite the British having sufficient cavalry to outflank and block the enemy's retreat, the Turks nearly always managed to successfully withdraw from British offensive operations.

British and Turkish movements in Mesopotamia had traditionally followed the banks of the Tigris and Euphrates Rivers. The rivers were used by both sides as waterways for military supply vessels and gunships, but more vitally as sources of drinking water for both men and mounts. In July 1917 General Maude decided to break from tradition and to move his men by motor transport through the desert away from the Euphrates in an attempt to encircle the Turks defending Ramadi, and thus destroy their force. This was the first serious attempt to use motorised infantry in the theatre. Previous attempts to encircle enemy posts using armoured cars alone had not been successful, and it was realised that lorry-borne infantry was needed to deliver the troops to suitable attack start lines that were well away from river banks. Then surprise could hopefully be achieved.

On 8th July the British moved against Ramadi, using 127 Ford vans to ferry infantry forward. The presumption of senior British officers was that the Turkish garrison would withdraw from the town rather than fight. But this was not the case. The British cavalry got to the west of Ramadi but the infantry, now on foot, were held up by a canal and enemy artillery fire. A dust storm blew in interfering with British communications and artillery observation. Casualties mounted and heat exhaustion added to the evacuations needed, the temperature taken that day in Baghdad being 160 degrees in the sun. Having lost 566 men as medical casualties, 321 of them to heat exhaustion, the British withdrew that night under cover of darkness to the river bank, totally incapable of further efforts. Some men had died of thirst or heat-stroke, and others went mad. The next day the British withdrew down the river, being harried by Arab horsemen who sniped and killed stragglers. A big lesson had been learned about taking offensive action during the summer months.

The second British attack on Ramadi

Two months later when the heat had lessened General Maude ordered another attack on Ramadi. The Turks expected an attack to come up the river bank and they had sited their defences accordingly. As a deception plan the British constructed a pontoon bridge across the Euphrates below Ramadi, and this led the enemy to believe that the next British advance would be along the north bank of the river. As yet the Turks had not appreciated how useful the British Ford vans could be, and it was the use of these vans to supply water to troops away from the river bank that gave the British a decided advantage.

The Turks in Ramadi had 3,500 infantrymen, 500 cavalrymen and 500 artillerymen with 10 guns. The British attacked with Major General Sir H.T. Brooking's 15th Division reinforced by the 6th Cavalry Brigade and the 50th Brigade Group; the British strength was around 15,000 men. The 12th and 42nd Infantry Brigades of 15th Division were to be used in the attack. Over 40 guns and howitzers were available. Support was provided by 'B' Flight 30th Squadron Royal Flying Corps, four armoured cars of the 13th Light Armoured Motor Battery, engineers, pioneers, three portable wireless stations and the Ford light vans.

In 42nd Infantry Brigade were the 1/5th, 2/5th and 2/6th Gurkhas, the 1/4th Dorsets, the 130th Machine Gun Company and the 448th Field Company Royal Engineers; the brigade commander was Brigadier General F.G. Lucas DSO, a former 5th Gurkha. 12th Infantry Brigade was commanded by Brigadier General F.P.S. Dunsford and it contained the 2/39th Gahrwal Rifles, 1/43rd Erinpura Regiment, 90th Punjabis, 1/5th Queens and the 128th Machine Gun Company.

On the night of 27th September 12th and 42nd Brigades moved forward from their assembly areas. The cavalry and armoured cars, using a dam that crossed the Euphrates Valley Canal, moved through the desert to cut the road to Aleppo west of Ramadi, digging in there to resist an enemy withdrawal. The infantry battalions also used the dam and seized unoccupied features as they advanced, coming under Turkish artillery fire once they had been observed. As soon as the British field batteries had also crossed the dam they came into action with artillery support. The howitzers fired from the area of First Knoll east of the canal. The divisional objective was to capture the Ramadi Ridge and the Azizya Ridge.

The 42nd Brigade attacks

The first opposed attack went in at 0600 hours on 28th September when 2/6th Gurkhas seized Mushaid Ridge and Mushaid Point; Turkish outposts withdrew quickly from those locations. Despite well-aimed enemy artillery fire only seven men were wounded because the Turks' inaccurate fuze settings caused their shells to burst too high, and the shrapnel lost much of its velocity before it struck the Gurkhas; some soldiers were knocked over but they were not seriously wounded by the shrapnel and this situation continued throughout the battle. The battalion consolidated its positions until 0930 hours when it was ordered to move to the dam across the Euphrates Valley Canal and to remain there. Meanwhile at 0930 hours 1/5th Gurkhas had advanced from the cover of Escape Hill onto Middle Hill which was taken with 'C' and 'D' Companies whilst 'A' and 'B' Companies remained as battalion reserve. Concurrently 2/5th Gurkhas advanced and seized Double Hill.

At 1300 hours the 1/5th and 2/5th Gurkhas were ordered to advance together on Ramadi Ridge with the 1/4th Dorsets in support. 2/6th Gurkhas remained behind as the Brigade reserve. 1/5th Gurkhas moved off at 1310 hours but 2/5th Gurkhas was heavily involved in fighting off hostile Arab irregular troops and did not move until 1400 hours, having lost Lieutenant J.F. Marindin and Jemadar Chintram Bura, both wounded. 1/4th Dorsets sent two companies to assist 2/5th Gurkhas and then advanced behind 1/5th Gurkhas.

The taking of Ramadi Ridge was described by an observer:

> *"This low, pebbly rise is perfectly smooth, a long and gentle gradient, a bare seventeen feet above plain level. It offered no cover of any kind, and our infantry became visible to the Turks a full two hundred yards before they reached the top of the rise. As soon as they came into view the enemy opened a concentrated rifle and machine gun fire on our front and from our right flank, while their guns, which were perfectly registered, opened intense enfilade fire from the batteries on our left. The Gurkhas and Dorsets hung on to the position."*

1/5th Gurkhas were on top of the ridge by 1335 hours but quickly took over 100 casualties. By 1415 hours two of the 1/4th Dorsets' companies had moved forward to fill in gaps on the ridge and had taken heavy casualties during this move. Shortly afterwards 2/5th Gurkhas arrived and extended the British line, followed by a third Dorset company. At 1600 hours the 2/6th Gurkhas came up and extended the line to the right from the ridge to the Euphrates Valley Canal.

All three Gurkha battalions were abreast on Ramadi Ridge and many acts of gallantry were recorded. A **Military Cross (MC)** was awarded to Subadar-Major Amar Singh Thapa, Sardar Bahadur, 2/5th Gurkha Rifles: *At a critical moment in the attack he showed the greatest determination and coolness in encouraging his men to dig themselves in, thus contributing largely to the maintenance of a difficult forward position. His complete disregard of danger was a fine example to all ranks.*

Lieutenant Kenneth John Macintosh, 1/5th Gurkhas, also received a **MC**: *Though wounded early in an attack he continued to command his company throughout the day. By his gallant bearing and fearlessness he encouraged his men to maintain the captured position.* Keith Macintosh had been wounded in the face on Middle Hill.

Major W.G. Harington DSO, the commanding officer of 2/5th Gurkhas, was mortally wounded and Captain Henry Augustus Wellesley MC, took over, earning a **Bar to his MC**: *He handled his battalion with the greatest* *coolness and determination, maintaining his position in close touch with the enemy until nightfall. By his fine personal example he encouraged all ranks*

The only **Indian Order of Merit (IOM), 2nd Class**, awarded to the 2/6th Gurkha Rifles for the Great War was presented to No. 1920 Rifleman Sukhbar Gurung: *After all the other men of his Lewis gun team had been killed or wounded, though wounded himself, he brought his gun up and kept it in action. He did not leave it until spare Lewis gunners relieved him.*

Four **IOMs, 2nd Class**, were awarded to the 1/5th Gurkhas. The citations of those to No. 4475 Havildar Jabarsing Thapa and No. 175 Rifleman Ramsing Gurung cannot be located, but No. 4683 Naik Anaram Thapa received his for: *As Hospital Naik he accompanied the medical officer and displayed marked courage, coolness and ability in attending to the wounded of all units for five hours in the open under continuous and heavy fire.* The citation for Subadar Dan Singh Gurung IDSM included: *When his company commander was wounded, he organised the company, dug forward trenches and showed a splendid example of cool courage under fire that was most inspiring to all around him.*

Jemadar Chint Ram Burathoki, 2/5th Gurkhas, received the only **IOM, 2nd Class**, awarded to his battalion at Ramadi: *Although wounded he assisted in organising the supply of ammunition to the advanced troops, refusing to report to the regimental aid post till the next morning. Throughout the operations he inspired all ranks by his magnificent courage. This officer has always displayed exceptional bravery.*

Admissions to the **Distinguished Service Order** were awarded to Major James Dunscomb Crowdy, 1/5th Gurkhas; Major (Acting Lieutenant Colonel) Brinsley Alexander McHenry Rice, 2/6th Gurkhas; Lieutenant (Acting Captain) Herbert Dryden Home Yorke Nepean. 1/5th Gurkhas: *He led his men under a withering fire to the capture of a ridge, and organised a strong defensive line on the position. Though wounded, he refused to leave his post for some hours. His fearless bearing was the greatest encouragement to his men;* and to Temporary Captain James Thornley Bowman MD, Royal Army Medical Corps attached 1/5th Gurkhas. *For conspicuous gallantry and devotion to duty. During an attack he attended to the wounded for five hours in the open under heavy fire. He showed the greatest coolness and courage throughout the day.*

Having dug-in on the forward slope of Ramadi Ridge 42nd Infantry Brigade had to hang-on until nightfall and endure fire from enemy machine guns only 750 metres away. The importance of well-trained junior leaders and Lewis light machine gunners, and of carrying parties constantly re-supplying ammunition to forward trenches can be appreciated in the citations of the following nine awards of the **Indian Distinguished Service Medal (IDSM)** to soldiers of 2/6th Gurkhas:

- No. 1061 Lance Naik Parmande Rana, 'A' Company. *For gallant conduct in the handling of his Lewis gun. He showed great bravery in getting his gun forward, under heavy machine gun fire, in an endeavour to silence it.*

- Jemadar Bagsing Gurung. *For the boldness and resourcefulness with which he organised and conducted an ammunition carrying party to the firing line under heavy fire. This officer set an excellent example.*

- No. 167 Naik Puranbahadur Gurung. 'A' Company. *By his utter contempt for danger under heavy fire, he set an excellent example to the men of his section. He continuously walked up and down the line controlling fire and encouraging his men during a critical half hour.*

- No. 76 Havildar Pahalsing Thapa. 'A' Company. *When his platoon commander was wounded he immediately assumed command of the platoon and directed it in offensive action with utmost coolness and skill. He supervised the men getting under cover, neglecting to dig himself in until the safety of his men was assured.*

- No. 464 Naik Ransing Thapa. 'A' Company. *For engaging in a duel with an entrenched enemy machine gun whilst his Lewis gun was in the open. By the coolness of his fire orders and the bold employment of his gun he very largely succeeded in subduing hostile fire.*

- No. 1540 Rifleman Parbir Pun. 'A' Company. *For employing his Lewis gun in a duel with a hostile machine gun, and by the accuracy and coolness of his fire so interfering with the enemy gun so as to render its fire ineffective. He was therefore the means of preserving many lives during the period his Lewis gun was in the open without cover.*

- No 1299 Naik Narbir Thapa. 'C' Company. *For the conspicuous gallantry which he showed in leading a carrying party up to the firing line under heavy machine gun fire. He showed utter contempt for danger.*

- No. 1444 Rifleman Mangalsing Gurung and No. 1741 Rifleman Manilal Rai. 'B' Company. *For bravery and devotion in working a Lewis gun under heavy and continuous fire. Repeated attempts were made by these two men to silence a machine gun, and both set an excellent example to the men near them.*

A **Mention in Despatches** was awarded to No. 537 Naik Dhanbahadur Gurung. 'C' Company, 2/6th Gurkhas: *For resourcefulness and gallantry when in charge of a party carrying ammunition to the firing line. Although under heavy shell and machine gun fire, he delivered the ammunition and brought his party back safely. He set an excellent and encouraging example to his men.*

12th Infantry Brigade's attacks on Aziziya Ridge, Shaikh Faraja Ridge and the Aziziya Bridge

The seizing and holding of Ramadi Ridge by 42nd Brigade pinned the Turkish troops in place and led to the recall of 1,000 enemy soldiers from the Aziziya Bridge area, where they were concentrating before attacking the cavalry brigade. Also 12th Brigade's attack on the southern part of Aziziya Ridge at 1445 hours succeeded with little interference from the Turks, who were bringing all their firepower down onto Ramadi Ridge. After last light the weary 42nd Brigade was withdrawn southwards to Middle Hill where it spent a quiet night. The Dorsets had lost 174 men killed or wounded and the 1/5th Gurkhas had taken 189 casualties. As well as losing Major Harington dead from wounds, the 2/5th Gurkhas had taken 98 casualties and the 2/6th Gurkhas took 85 casualties. Most wounds had been caused by high-bursting shrapnel or, more seriously, by machine gun bullets

The British cavalry commander, Brigadier General Pomeroy Holland-Pryor DSO MVO, believed that the Turks would have to withdraw from Ramadi along the river-bank road to ensure water supplies. He concentrated his defence across and around that road and also covered the western approach to the town in case enemy reinforcements were sent from Hit, the next enemy town upriver. At 0300 hours next morning, 29 September, the Turks made a strong attempt to break through the cavalry positions under cover of gunfire support from vessels on the river. The cavalry used twelve Vickers and 48 Hotchkiss guns, plus all available rifles, to successfully beat back enemy attacks that lasted until first light. Meanwhile the cavalry brigade's field battery engaged and neutralised the enemy gun boats.

The Turks now had only one escape route and that was to cross the Aziziya Bridge and get into the hills to the west. At 0635 hours on 29th September the 2/39th Garhwhalis and the 90th Punjabis from 12th Brigade advanced from Aziziya Ridge to take the bridge and the Shaikh Faraja Ridge. They met resistance and 1/5th Queens came up to join them. Ramadi was the Garhwalis first action in Mesopotamia and they made a magnificent charge, joined by some Punjabis and Queens, to take Aziziya Bridge in the face of three enemy guns firing shrapnel directly at them. The charge succeeded, the bridge and guns were captured, and white flags of surrender soon appeared from the remaining Turkish defensive positions in and around Ramadi. The Garhwalis had taken 166 casualties and the Punjabis 182, but the battle was now decisively won.

The attack mounted by 12th Infantry Brigade had involved some fierce fighting as can be seen by the awards made. A **Military Cross** was awarded to Subadar Dhirat Sing Pundir, 2/39th Garhwal Rifles: *His platoon throughout two days' operations was the most heavily engaged. He was posted on the right of the line, and came under severe enfilade fire. He displayed great courage, coolness and ability while directing the fire of his men, until a bullet broke his leg.*

Five **Indian Orders of Merit, 2nd Class**, were awarded to Garhwalis:

- Subadar Balbahadur Sing Gusain, Posthumous. *His company was in the front line of the assaulting waves and came under heavy enfilade fire. He displayed remarkable coolness and the success gained was largely due to his magnificent work. This gallant officer was dangerously wounded in the thigh during the attack and subsequently succumbed to his injuries.*

- Subadar Bhir Sing Dann IDSM. *He received a bullet wound through the point of his left shoulder but never left the firing line, though from the nature of the wound he would have been quite justified in doing so. His general conduct throughout and his gallant behaviour when wounded reflects the greatest credit on him. His work under fire and in trying and exhausting conditions was of the greatest value.*

- Subadar Tilok Sing Saubtiyal. *Although wounded in the head in the afternoon he refused to leave his platoon and continued to command it in action throughout that day and the next, though by that time his wound was giving him considerable pain. He took up reinforcements and ammunition under fire to our* advanced troops and showed himself to be an able and courageous officer. He only went to hospital when ordered to do so by the medical officer.

- No. 932 Naik Jitar Singh Negi and No. 1528 Naik Luthi Singh Rawat. *For their initiative and dash on 29th September 1917 following the assault on the Shaikh Faraja Ridge. In operations along a nearby canal, the two Naiks crossed the dry bed of the canal to the western bank and brought two Lewis guns into action, with which they knocked out all the Turkish gunners at 400 yards.*

The senior officer leading the attack on 29th September, Captain Alan Patrick Rodgerson, 2/39th Garwhalis, was admitted to the **Distinguished Service Order**: *He led the assaulting companies, on his own initiative, to the capture of a bridge under heavy fire, thereby cutting off the enemy's retreat. Though severely wounded, he refused to go back till he had reported on the situation, and sent in information, which was of the greatest value. His conduct throughout was worthy of the highest* praise.

At one point in the battle on 28th September the Punjabis had been pushed back from a position, and this led to No. 2433 Sepoy Balwant Singh, 90th Punjabis, being awarded an **IOM, 2nd Class**: *When a portion of his line was driven back 250 yards by an enemy counter attack, he, supported by heavy artillery fire, remained behind on his own initiative with a non-commissioned officer and kept up rapid fire till the line was re-established.*

Other recipients of the same award were No. 2136 Lance Naik Shabib Din, 90th Punjabis, (no citation located) and Subadar Mula Singh, 90th Punjabis: *For conspicuous gallantry and devotion to duty on the 28th-29th September 1917. He commanded two platoons and greatly inspired his whole company by his coolness, judgement and initiative. His conduct under heavy fire and in difficult circumstances was most praiseworthy.*

The Turkish surrender

Some Turkish cavalry escaped by swimming across the Euphrates, and a few infantrymen infiltrated through the British cavalry positions only to be captured by cavalry and armoured car patrols later. But 3,456 enemy prisoners, 13 guns, 12 machine guns, 2 armoured launches, 2 barges and large quantities of arms, ammunition and stores were captured. The British had suffered 995 casualties, the vast majority being wounded, but had gained an important victory.

The 30th Punjabis at Tandamuti Hill and Nakadi Ridge East Africa February – October 1917

Introduction

The 30th Punjabis started the war as a Class Company Regiment containing 4 companies of Sikhs, 2 companies of Dogras and 2 companies of Punjabi Mussulmans; this composition was later reorganised by halving the number of companies to four, each having 4 platoons. A 14-month stay in the Daryaganj Lines, Delhi, resulted in much sickness from malignant malaria, and twice in late 1914 the regiment reported itself unfit for service in France. The regiment was involved in 1915 in operations against the Mohmands on the North-West Frontier, and there Subadar Muhammad Khan, 29th Punjabis attached to 30th Punjabis, and No. 4391 Havildar Sher Khan were awarded the **Indian Distinguished Service Medal**. After a further 11 months spent in India the 30th Punjabis was deployed to East Africa in November 1916.

The situation in early 1917

After the fierce fighting for the crossing of the Rufiji River, described in the article *Fighting For The Rufiji River Crossing: The British 1st East African Brigade in action German East Africa, 1 to 19 January 1917*, (where Subadar Allah Ditta won a posthumous **Indian Order of Merit, 2nd Class**) the 30th Punjabis moved north and in June 1917 the regiment was at Tabora on the German Central Railway that ran from Dar Es Salaam westwards to Lake Tanganyika. Here a newly-arrived draft of 90 Rank & File brought the regimental strength up to 4 British and 6 Indian officers and 259 sepoys. Arriving with the draft was Lieutenant Colonel C.C.R. Murphy who took over command of the regiment from Major W.K.P. Wilson. The 30th Punjabis were then moved by train to

Morogoro, except for a detachment under Lieutenant E.M. Shelverton that was part of a force attempting to stop German raiders moving back into the Lake Victoria region. This detachment re-joined the regiment at Morogoro in July. At Morogoro 2 Lewis light machine guns were issued to each of the four companies and gun teams were trained whilst hand grenades were also issued and selected men were trained to be 'bombers'.

In late July the 30th Punjabis, who had just received another large draft from the regimental depot in India and from the 29th Punjabis, was railed to Dar Es Salaam and shipped south to Lindi, arriving there on 25th July. The strength of the regiment was now 9 British and 14 Indian officers, 774 sepoys and 36 followers. A local depot had been formed and left at Morogoro staffed by 1 British and 3 Indian officers and 43 sepoys.

On 31st July the regiment marched 25 kilometres southwestwards to Mingoyo. News came in that for gallantry displayed at the Rufiji crossing in January Sepoys No. 246 Ghurko and No. 251 Gobind had each been awarded an Italian **Bronze Medal for Military Valour** whilst Lieutenant D. Powell had received a French **Croix de Guerre**.

The desperate fight near Tandamuti Hill

The commander at Lindi, Brigadier General H. De C. O'Grady (52nd Sikhs), wanted to advance from Lindi and the British theatre commander, the South African General J.L. Van Deventer, had sent reinforcements. These were, as well as the 30th Punjabis, the 3rd Battalion of the 4th King's African Rifles (3/4th KAR) from Uganda, the 8th South African Infantry, the 3rd South African Field Battery (two 13-pounder guns), the Kashmir Imperial Service Mountain Battery (six 10-pounder screw guns), and 1,200 porters.

General O'Grady mounted an operation on 2nd August splitting his now-enlarged command into four columns. The immediate objective was to advance up the Lukuledi River to capture Tandamuti Hill which was occupied by the enemy; the hill was overlooked on both flanks by other enemy machine gun posts. The 3rd Battalion of the 2nd King's African Rifles (3/2nd KAR) from Nyasaland advanced on the British right with the objective of attacking and seizing German defended locations along a trolley line that ran from inland agricultural estates to Lindi port. At dawn on 3rd August 3/4th KAR attacked towards Tandamuti Hill whilst 3/2nd KAR continued its advance on the right, but German machine guns on both sides of the valley fired effectively on the Askari of both battalions. 3/2nd KAR began to take casualties without being able to respond satisfactorily.

The Kashmir Mountain Battery came into action in support of 3/2nd KAR, firing 100 rounds at the enemy positions immediately in front of the battalion. In the centre 3/4th KAR and 25th Royal Fusiliers (Frontiersmen) fought up Tandamuti Hill but could not take the German position near the summit; the British artillery could not fire onto the hill as the opposing forces were too close together.

On the left the 30th Punjabis struggled alone through very thick thorn bush before dawn and then moved up the right bank of the Mohambika River. The thick bush prevented sightings of the friendly troops to the right, and the sepoys were isolated from the main battle. However German observation posts on Tandamuti Hill and on the east side of the valley were observing the progress of the Punjabis and telephoning the information to Field Companies near them.

Soon the Punjabis became nearly surrounded by German companies and fought alone without artillery support. Major W.K.P. Wilson, the Punjabis' commander for this operation, was soon severely wounded and captured; 6 other British and 3 Indian officers soon became wounded or missing. Platoons and companies were deployed in bush so thick that they soon became disorientated and lost, or else they walked into enemy ambushes.

The Punjabis held their ground for several hours under intense fire mainly due to the leadership displayed by Lieutenant J.B. Dalison, 30th Punjabis, who having been wounded and evacuated, returned to the firing line to take command when it was needed. Then with most leaders killed or wounded, the young inexperienced sepoys became demoralised and began streaming back to the rear where the Indian officers rallied them. The old soldiers withdrew in a disciplined fashion and Jemadar Sundar Singh, 30th Punjabis, later received an **Indian Order of Merit, 2nd Class**: *For conspicuous gallantry and skill in handling machine gun sections in action on the 3rd August 1917, when the Machine Gun Officer was severely wounded. The enemy were attacking from both flanks and from the front at very close quarters, but he succeeded in withdrawing all the machine guns except one and brought them safely back.*

The porters, seeing the flight of the young sepoys, dropped their ammunition loads in the bush and also fled rearwards. The German 4th

Schutzen Company then surged forward and over-ran the British advanced field hospital but respected it, the German officers removed quinine from the hospital stores but protected the patients from bayonet-wielding German Askari. These Germans then met 1/2nd KAR advancing from its position as force reserve and engaged it, preventing that battalion from becoming involved in the main battle.

Running out of water on Tandamuti Hill, hearing of the punishment inflicted on the 30th Punjabis, and receiving a message from Colonel Phillips stating that 3/2nd KAR was hard-pressed, General O'Grady broke off his action and withdrew his force in relatively good order to Lindi. The Punjabi initial casualty figures were: 1 British officer died of wounds, 4 wounded and 2 missing; 2 Indian officers wounded and 1 missing; 5 Sepoys killed, 4 died of wounds, 104 wounded and 142 missing – a total of 265 casualties. One machine gun and 2 Lewis guns had been lost.

However two days later Captain E.M. Shelverton appeared from the bush where he had been lost, along with 1 Indian officer, 1 Lewis gun and 25 sepoys. As the 30th Punjabis war diary is reticent about the number of missing who were actually killed, it is prudent to refer to the Commonwealth War Graves Commission's records, and they commemorate a total of 132 men from the 29th and 30th Punjabis killed on 3rd August 1917. The officer who died of wounds was Lieutenant Henry St. John Saunders-Jones, 30th Punjabis. Lieutenant D. Powell had been wounded and also captured by the enemy but he was returned by them as was Major Wilson.

No. 3933 Havildar Ali Ahmed and No. 4678 Sepoy Fateh Ali later received the **Indian Distinguished Service Medal**, and it is likely that these were awards for gallantry displayed at Tandamuti.

The action at Nakadi River

After Tandamuti the 30th Punjabis was employed on lines of communication security duties and patrolling whilst it absorbed new drafts and lightly wounded men recovered. In early September Lieutenant Colonel A.H.G. Thomson DSO took over command from Lieutenant Colonel A. Ward DSO who had temporarily come down from his staff job in Dar Es Salaam to command. By now the local conditions had begun to affect the newly-joined sepoys and fever and dysentery became prevalent. But the biggest battle of the East Africa campaign was looming as the British manoeuvred to engage and destroy the German Schutztruppe. A British column was marching down cross-country from Kilwa whilst the British Lindi force moved to attack the enemy simultaneously.

On the 8th October 1917 the 30th Punjabis was deployed into the Lindi No. 4 Column. Also in the column were the:

- 25th Royal Fusiliers (Frontiersmen) now with a strength of about 120 men.

- 3/4th King's African Rifles.

- 259 Machine Gun Company, Machine Gun Corps, formed from ex-Loyal North Lancashire soldiers, some of whom had fought at Tanga in 1914.

- a Trench Mortar Battery manned by the West India Regiment.

- 1st Kashmir Imperial Service Mountain Battery.

The Column Commander was Lieutenant Colonel H.C. Tytler DSO, 17th Infantry (The Loyal Regiment), who took over from a South African colonel who was hospitalised. The strength of the 30th Punjabis was 7 British and 10 Indian officers; 1 Sub-Assistant Surgeon; 656 sepoys; 6 machine guns and 5 Lewis guns.

After marching and manoeuvring whilst trying to trap the Germans, and also whilst attempting to stop the Germans from destroying British columns individually, No. 4 Column was committed to battle on 16th October when Colonel Tytler was ordered to seize a ridge above the Nakadi River. The dry river bed was in a 350 metre-wide U-shaped valley whose sides were 60 metres high. 3/4th KAR attacked in the late afternoon and pushed enemy posts across the river bed to the west ridge; when the KAR left flank was threatened at 1700 hours Major E.C.L. Wallace, 30th Punjabis, took 'C' and 'D' Companies across the valley to support the Askari. But the Germans, commanded by General Kurt Wahle, intended to hold the west ridge and the KAR Askari were repulsed; after dark they withdrew to dig-in on the east ridge. The Kashmir Battery fired 101 rounds in support, and did not cease firing until 2100 hours.

The next day 3/4th KAR attacked again across the valley supported by 'D' Company, 30th Punjabis. At this point No. 3 Column under Brigadier

General O'Grady joined in on the right and a furious battle broke out along the ridge. However the Germans were determined to keep Nos. 3 and 4 Columns on the east side of the ridge to prevent them from relieving two Nigerian battalions that were fighting desperately against other German units. This was bush warfare at its most savage as African Askari on both sides repeatedly flung themselves and their bayonets at their enemies. In the Nigerian position blood dripped from the trees for three days after the battle and it came from the human body parts that had been flung up there by artillery shells. The German commander, General Paul von Lettow-Vorbeck, wore his full dress uniform for the only time in the campaign to signal to his Askari that this was a decisive battle and that defeat was not an option.

On Nakadi Ridge all the Punjabis had crossed the river bed to join the battle. Good fire support came from machine guns, trench mortars and the Kashmir mountain battery on the east side of the valley. But the Germans mounted a fierce counter-attack that pushed 3/4th KAR back from the portion of the ridge that they had gained. The Punjabis' casualties that day were 6 killed and 19 wounded.

On the following day, 18th October, dawn patrols sent by the Punjabis erroneously reported that the enemy had gone. 'A' Company (Lieutenant C.E. Thomas) and 'B' Company (Captain T.A. Digby) attacked the west ridge as the first wave whilst 'C' and 'D' Companies formed the second wave. The first wave came under fire when nearing the top of the west ridge but it pressed on and with its blood up pursued the retreating German Askari for 350 metres. Meanwhile the second wave rapidly dug-in forward of the crest. Colonel Thompson was evacuated with a bullet through the neck. 'A' and 'B' Companies remained forward, covering the trench digging activities of 'C' and 'D' Companies. 3/4th KAR provided support on the left and No. 3 Column provided fire support on the right.

But the Germans were not beaten yet and they mounted two counter-attacks on the first wave that were repulsed. However a third attack was effective when it broke the British line. Both British officers in the first wave were wounded and Jemadar Bahar Khan and Subadars Labh Singh, Lachhman Singh, Maghar Singh, Sundar Singh, and Wahab Khan were all killed (all were 30th Punjabis except Wahab Khan who was 29th Punjabis attached to 30th Punjabis). 'A' and 'B' Companies ran back past 'C' and 'D' Companies, but they were rallied on the old German trench line on the crest which they occupied. 'C' and 'D' Companies now had a rough time from the

Germans who eventually pushed the two companies back to the crest, where they joined 'A' and 'B' Companies in the old enemy trenches. Here the 30th Punjabis stayed, resisting all further attacks, until the enemy withdrew.

Subadar Labh Singh was awarded a posthumous **Indian Order of Merit, 2nd Class**: *For conspicuous bravery and initiative in action on the 17th and 18th October 1917. He was in command of his company on 18th, his company officer having taken command of the battalion. His skilful control of fire and fearless example enabled determined enemy counter-attacks to be repulsed.*

No. 3870 Havildar Gurditt Singh and No. 4479 Lance Naik Said Muhammed were awarded the **Indian Distinguished Service Medal**. Jemadar Prabh Dial also received the same award, and this was probably also for gallantry displayed at Nakadi Ridge.

Later Major Edward Charles Lloyd Wallace, 30th Punjabis, was awarded a **Distinguished Service Order**. **Military Crosses** were awarded to Captain George Gerome Dunlop Kellie, 30th Punjabis; Lieutenants James Shaw, General List attached to 30th Punjabis; and Leonard Adolphus Otto, King's African Rifles attached to 30th Punjabis.

The 30th Punjabi's casualty figures for 18th October 1917 were: British officers 4 wounded; Indian officers 6 killed and 4 wounded; Sepoys 31 killed, and 156 wounded or missing.

The return to India

The result of the battle of Mahiwa-Nyangao, as it was later named, was that both sides caused terrible attrition to each other until they were both exhausted. But the Germans recovered first and General von Lettow-Vorbeck marched his Schutztruppe away, fighting effective rearguard actions against the pursuing British. The Germans moved onto the Makonde Plateau and there they left their wounded Germans and their prisoners plus many unwounded Germans whom their commander did not want to take with him on his next trek. The drastically slimmed-down Schutztruppe then crossed the Rovuma River into Portuguese East Africa, now Mozambique, and continued campaigning until after the Armistice was declared in Europe.

The 30th Punjabis stayed at Nakadi on Lines of Communication duties. However it had been decided that the remaining European and Indian units serving in the East Africa theatre were to be repatriated on health grounds, as now sufficient battalions of the King's African Rifles had been formed to continue the campaign. The African Askari were much more resilient in the face of the challenges that bush warfare presented. On 10th December 1917 the 30th Punjabis embarked at Lindi for Dar Es Salaam, and from there they embarked again, arriving at Karachi on 10th January 1918.

Awards of the Indian Meritorious Service Medal for service in East Africa

For noteworthy service whilst in East Africa the following six members of the 30th Punjabis were awarded the **Indian Meritorious Service Medal**:

> No. 4188 Havildar Devi Singh; No. 3771 Havildar Punjab Singh; No. 118 Naik Sher Singh; No. 65 Sepoy Lakha Singh; No. 3940 Naik Zaman Mehdi; and No. 1095 Sepoy Moti Ram.

The Kuki Rising 1917-1919
Insurrection in north-eastern India and Burma

In 1916 Britain approached the government of India for the supply of a volunteer Labour Corps to serve in both France and Mesopotamia. The Indian government delegated the responsibility to raise separate Corps of 2,000 men to United Provinces, Bihar & Orissa, Assam, North-West Frontier, Burma and Bengal. No central administrative direction was given and each region decided its own terms and conditions. As time passed more and more Labour Corps were needed, and this resulted in an Indian Jail Labour Corps being raised for service in Mesopotamia; the volunteer prisoners worked well and earned wages, but these were lower than the wages of the 'free' workers.

British officers, assisted by senior non-commissioned officers acting as Supervisors, commanded companies of 500 men; they were supported by a number of chiefs or head-men recruited to act as junior officers. When the British command personnel understood and spoke the dialects of their men and appreciated the prevailing culture there were few difficulties and the labourers were self-disciplined, often performing well in adverse or dangerous conditions.

The rulers of the Princely States of India demonstrated their support for the Allied war effort in various ways, and the Hindu Ruler of Manipur in north-eastern India supplied his own labour corps of 2,000 men. However the Ruler did not nominate his Hindu citizens for this service, but he recruited 1,200 Christian or animist Naga tribesmen and 800 similar Kuki tribesmen from the mountainous areas in his state. The head-hunting hill tribesmen were not highly regarded by the Hindus and it is likely that tribal chiefs were just ordered to produce the required numbers of men whether they were volunteers or not.

On the whole the Nagas presented no problems and were pleased to be wage earners, as were the neighbouring Lushai and the Garo and Khasi hill tribesmen from around Shillong in today's Meghalaya state[79]. Further recruitments from these hill tribes ran smoothly as some had experience of working for the British in labour capacities on public works or minor military operations. However when certain of the more remote Kuki chiefs heard that further labour was needed an insurrection broke out that lasted for 18 months. But it should be noted that initially the insurrection was not confined to the Kuki family of tribes, and also that many Kukis remained loyal to the State of Manipur and to the British, some of them assisting the British military effort against their disaffected tribal brethren.

The fighting that took place during the Kuki Rising, as the insurrection was named, was in the hills around the Imphal plain, and British forces were deployed both from the main base at Imphal and from bases in Burma along the Chindwin River. Those readers familiar with the Second World War Battle of Imphal will recognise many place-names and hill features, as during the Rising the Kukis held ground that the British were to fight over 26 years later when Japanese invaders seized it. A legacy of the Kuki Rising was that in 1944 during the Japanese invasion of Manipur many of the Kukis chose to side with the invaders, although others did not.

In both wars the Kukis were the eventual losers, but during the Rising they were able to embarrass the British by a continued resistance, as the military resources available to the British were finite due to overseas wartime commitments. The British were reliant on those military units already in Assam and Burma, the principal units being the Assam Rifles and the Burma Military Police; both of these regiments recruited from Nepal and the Punjab as well as locally. This had an effect on India's contribution to the Allied war effort as the overseas posting of drafts of trained men from Assam and Burma to Gurkha and other regiments was suspended during the Rising.

The Kuki Rising was eventually put down by a combination of British military ruthlessness supported by modern weapons of war, assisted by Kuki pragmatism in submitting when morale was low and further resistance was seen to be futile. The Kuki Rising was not the most glorious of Britain's colonial actions and it was deliberately under-publicised at the time. However

---

79 The 'Tower of France', a memorial to the Khasis who did not return from France, can be seen today in central Shillong.

the exertions and courage of the British sepoys in fighting serious and savage banditry over very hostile terrain deserve recognition.

The start of the Kuki Rising

In 1917 the local Political Officer, Lieutenant-Colonel H.W.G. Cole CSI, advised the Kukis that the Labour Corps needed more men to go to France. The Kuki Chiefs refused this request, and then refused a second similar one. Colonel Cole then went to France with the Lushai Labour Corps and another officiating Political Officer was appointed. This man arranged for a Durbar to be held and invited all the Chiefs to listen to his explanations of why the men were wanted, the nature of the work and the terms and conditions. The leading recalcitrant Chiefs, Ngulkhup of Mombi and Ngulbul of Longya, replied in an insolent manner rejecting the invitation and stating that if force was used against them then they would retaliate with force. The British authorities were suspicious that these Chiefs may have been incited by Bengal seditionists in Sylhet and Cachar who wished to impede the Allied war effort, but proof of this was never found.

As the two Chiefs had defied British authority they had to be dealt with, and in September the officiating Political Officer marched a force of 100 rifles from the Imphal-based 4th (Darrang) Battalion, Assam Rifles, under Captain M.C. Coote[80] to Mombi where after a skirmish the village was burned down. This force then marched on Longya to repeat the process but an instruction from Shillong, the administrative capital of Assam, arrived ordering that no further action should be taken against the Kukis. The punitive operation was cancelled and the troops withdrew, leaving the Kukis to believe that the British did not have the resources or the stomach for a real fight.

Both Chiefs then closed their territories to the British and in December started raiding the Hindu villages on the extremities of the Imphal plain; little mercy was offered to the Hindu subsistence farmers and their families. At that time and due to the fact that both the Assam Rifles and the Burma Military Police had sent thousands of their best men overseas in drafts, leaving the units composed of either very young or very old soldiers, the British were not responding strongly to all the challenges to their authority.

At this point a very brave effort was made by a British lady to keep the peace with the Kukis. Colonel Cole's wife lived in Imphal and she knew

---

80 Captain Coote was attached from the 107th Pioneers.

Chief Ngulkhup personally. She sent him a message asking for a meeting at Shuganoo, and went there with just an interpreter; the journey took four days marching from Imphal. Ngulkhup and a few of his leading men met Mrs. Cole courteously and listened to her pleas for reconciliation. However Ngulkhup had his own agenda and declined the suggestions made by Mrs. Cole, who returned to Imphal having attempted to do more than any British official had done to keep the peace.

The Southern Chin Hills

Meanwhile in Burma a similar resistance to further recruiting for the Labour Corps was being organised in the Southern Chin Hills. This resistance was aggravated by British attempts to suppress slavery, which was a popular custom amongst the southern Chins. This rising took the British authorities in Burma by surprise and Haka was besieged by Chin rebels, so assistance was requested from the Assam Rifles. The Deputy Inspector General of the Assam Rifles, Colonel L.W. Shakespear, obtained authority and despatched Captain H.L.F. Falkland[81], Commandant of 1st (Lushai) Battalion, Assam Rifles, with 150 rifles from Aijal to Haka, 16 days' marching away. A few days later another message arrived from Burma reporting that Falam was also surrounded by rebels. Shakespear now ordered Captain E.C.Montefiore[82] at Kohima with the 3rd (Naga Hills) Battalion, Assam Rifles, to take 150 rifles to Burma. Montefiore's journey involved marching to Manipur Road Station, Dimapur, taking trains to Chittagong, then a river steamer to Rangamatti followed by country boats to Demagiri and finally two weeks' hard marching to Haka. British strength in Manipur was being dispersed even before campaigning against the Manipur Kukis began.

The Rising spreads

As no punitive action was taken against the Kuki raids on isolated Hindu villages, more Kukis from Hinglep and Ukah, south of the Imphal Plain, joined in the fun. Two serious raids, one against the police post near Shuganoo and the second near Moirang, led to two detachments of the 4th (Darrang) Battalion, Assam Rifles, being sent out from Imphal; each detachment was 80 rifles strong. The Political Agent with Lieutenant Halliday marched on

---

81   Captain Falkland was attached from the 13th Rajputs (The Shekawati Regiment).
82   Captain E.C. Montifiori was attached from the 110th Mahratta Light Infantry.

Mombi and Captain Coote with Lieutenant E.J. Hooper[83] marched on Hinglep. Coote's column entered the hills below Moirang and was immediately attacked but fought back fiercely, punishing the Ukah tribesmen with little loss to itself. But after going through Shuganoo Halliday encountered strong stockades at the Chokpi River crossing where he lost three men killed and several wounded; this caused his retirement and Kuki morale soared. Many more villages joined the Rising, closing the Palel-Tamu road to Burma by destroying the rest houses, killing the caretakers and bringing down the telegraph line.

On the Burma side of the border Kukis began attacking posts in the Chindwin Valley and in the northern Chin Hills; Shakespear moved to Imphal to control events. As porters were needed to transport supplies for columns, 800 Nagas were recruited at Kohima and marched to Imphal, escorted by a platoon from the 3rd (Naga Hills) Battalion, Assam Rifles. The 4th (Darrang Battalion), Assam Rifles, was put through a three-week intensive jungle training course, whilst 100 rifles from the 2nd (Sadiya) Battalion, Assam Rifles, were ordered to march from Sadiya through Silchar to Imphal, under Major H.D. Cloete MC[84]. Well-stocked bases were established at Palel and Shuganoo, and two columns each of 120 rifles were formed, with trained Naga porters carrying a 7-pounder mountain gun and ammunition for each column.

Captain Hebbert, with the Political Agent, commanded a column marching from Palel to Tamu to reopen the Burma Road and punish rebel villages in the vicinity. Captain Coote, with Mr. J.C. Higgins, Indian Civil Service and Political Agent Imphal, marched from Shuganoo for Mombi planning to join up with a Burma column under Captain Steadman that was marching north from Tiddim to deal with Longya.

Shakespear accompanied Coote's column and later wrote an account of its actions. The column marched to its base at Shuganoo destroying Aihang village on the way; then Longyin village was destroyed as a punishment for the attack on the nearby Itoll police post. An attack was prepared on the Chokpi River crossing stockades but scouts found them deserted; however nearby were found the bodies of the men killed in Halliday's previous attack.

---

83 Lieutenant Hooper was attached from the Indian Army Reserve of Officers (IARO).

84 Major Cloete was attached from the 90th Punjabis. His Military Cross had been awarded in Mesopotamia. He was murdered at Sadiya in 1920.

These corpses were without heads, hands or feet. As Coote knew that the direct route to Mombi was strongly stockaded his column marched up a ridge to the east of the Tuyang River. But now the column began to take casualties from snipers hidden in the thick jungle who could not be seen. When Mombi could be observed from the ridgeline the 7-pounder gun came into action at 800 metres range, hitting the village and dispersing the armed tribesmen inside it. The next day Coote's men descended to Mombi but found it deserted.

Whilst the Nagas built strongly-defended villages on hill tops the Kukis were more nomadic, building temporary villages until they moved on to the next one. However they often defended the approaches to their villages with thorn or 'punji' stick[85] spiked hedges protecting stout stockades. Log breastworks, loopholed for musket firers, covered likely approach routes. Sometimes leather cannon rolled from buffalo hide were mounted on trees to fire stones or metal fragments at attackers, but these weapons usually burst when fired. The civil authorities were taken by surprise by the number of firearms that the Kukis possessed, and although these were generally old flint-locks and muzzle-loaders they were effective in close-quarter sniping and fighting. However the Kukis rarely stood and fought from a defensive position, preferring to cause some attrition to their attackers and then to quickly withdraw.

Coote rested at Mombi whilst his wounded were carried back to Shuganoo and rations were brought forward. Smoke had been seen rising from the direction of Longya, and heliograph contact with the Lenakot post in the north Chin Hills ascertained that Steadman had burned Longya without opposition. Steadman had then marched towards Khailet, the rendezvous point for him and Coote, but on meeting a long stockade barring his path he had charged it. The result was a serious reverse for Steadman who lost 11 men killed and many wounded including himself, wounded three times. Many of his porters had bolted and Steadman withdrew to Lenakot, much to the joy of the Kukis.

Coote set about his own task of punishing insurgents in the Mombi area. His column marched through thick jungle for five days, incessantly climbing up or descending down steep-sided hills. When halting for the night the jungle had to be cleared and a barbed wire fence run around the perimeter

---

85 A simple spike, made out of wood or bamboo, generally placed upright or at an angle in the ground. Punji sticks are usually deployed in substantial numbers

to deter sudden attacks. On 7th February 1918, having destroyed Nungoinu and other nearby villages, Coote was advancing along a densely-wooded ridge when he was ambushed. Reconnaissance showed that a barrier of rocks ran across the ridge, the narrow track was heavily stockaded and the space before the rocks was covered in felled trees 40 metres deep. Both Shakespear and Higgins led flanking parties but the steep terrain defied their efforts to get behind the stockade and rocks. Meanwhile Coote was losing men killed and wounded from around 70 firearms being discharged through small apertures in the rock barricade.

After 45 minutes of heavy firing from an almost invisible enemy, accompanied by loud drumming and war-chanting, the mountain gun was brought forward and came into action. But after the third round had been fired the gun Havildar and three others of the gun crew were hit, putting the gun out of action. Coote then decided to rush the position with Jemadar Kharga Sing's platoon advancing on the left, accompanied by Shakespear, whilst Coote provided supporting fire on the right from his soldiers' old single-shot Martini Henry rifles. Because of the tree obstacles on the ground a rush was not possible but Kharga Sing methodically walked his men forward across the trees and up the rocks. Both Coote and the enemy ceased firing and Kharga Sing crossed the rocks to find that the Kukis had not chosen to stand and fight but had withdrawn; bloodstains and trails confirmed several Kuki casualties and examination of the excellent defensive position showed that up to 300 tribesmen could have been holding it.

Coote occupied the adjacent Khengoi Village for the night, burning it the next morning after his signallers had heliographed Tamu to arrange for rations to be ready for him at Withok, across the Burma border in the Kale Kabaw valley. At Withok a camp had been prepared for the column and carts came up from Tamu, 35 kilometres away, to evacuate the wounded and sick. Captain Grantham of the Burma Police and Lieutenant C.G. Kay-Mouatt, 1-70th Burma Rifles, rode in with the carts to advise that the Kuki Rising was spreading swiftly. A Burma Column was forming at Tamu to operate against the Chassadh Kukis occupying the hills east of Imphal who were raiding Kangal Thana and Homalin in the Chindwin Valley. Further north and to the west of Imphal the Silchar Road had been closed, rest houses destroyed and anyone seized by the Kukis was being cut up. Major Cloete was in Silchar preparing to reopen the road to Imphal.

Coote marched his column back towards Palel, burning Changpol, Gnarjal and Pantha Villages on the way. The column's final action was on Rekchu Hill where a strong line of breastworks and shelter pits commanded the track upwards. However the Kukis opened fire too soon, and the column's two flanking parties got abreast of the position before the defenders noticed them, causing an immediate Kuki withdrawal. After five weeks of strenuous campaigning Cootes' men, in ragged clothing and worn-out boots, but now fit and experienced, reached Imphal. Here the column found that 100 rifles from the 2/2nd Ghurkas under Major J.E. Cruickshank had been sent to garrison the town, and another 100 were in Kohima under Lieutenant Duff, thus releasing more of the Assam Rifles for operations[86].

Hebbert's column had returned a few days previously having had a less arduous time punishing villages near the Imphal-Tamu road, with only one skirmish being fought near Suampo. Several other columns were now deployed in the hills surrounding the Imphal plain, and Major Cloete's column was on the Silchar Road and had fought a sharp action at Laibol. There was still much work to be done both along the Chindwin and around the Imphal plain.

The Spring and Summer of 1918

In March Shakespear marched to Tamu escorted by 50 rifles from the 4th (Darrang) Battalion, Assam Rifles, under Jemadar Babu Lal. There he met with his Burma counterpart, Lieutenant-Colonel J.J.W. ffrench-Mullen CIE, and a co-operative strategy was devised. Two Chindwin columns starting from Homalin (Major T.D.H. Hackett[87]) and Kangal Thana (Captain Patrick) would work together with Captain Coote's Imphal column against the Chassadh Kukis whilst a fourth column from Kohima (Lieutenants H.C. Prior[88] and Sanderson) operated towards the un-administered Somra Tracts. Meanwhile 100 rifles from 1st (Lushai) Battalion, Assam Rifles, under Subadar Bhowan Singh were to be stationed at Bangmual in south-west Manipur to cooperate with any troops that pursued insurgents into that area. Bhowan

---

86 The 2/2nd Gurkha detachment remained in Imphal and Kohima for four months before returning to its Battalion location at Tank on the North-West Frontier. The Gurkhas did not deploy for operations against the Kukis.

87 Major Hackett was an Indian Army officer serving on the Burma Commission.

88 Lieutenant Prior was attached from the IARO.

Singh was later mentioned in despatches for his leadership on operations in the Bangmual area.

When Coote set off with his column, accompanied by Lieutenant N.E. Parry[89] and Mr. Higgins, the Naga porters suddenly went on strike and refused to carry loads. To quote directly from Shakespear: 'The wholesome spectacle of the 11 ringleaders being publicly flogged soon induced all to think differently and they quietly resumed work'. Coote marched on, punishing those villages that did not submit, and near Kangal Thana he met up with Patrick and they marched together to attack Kamjong, Chief Pachei's principal village. During the fighting around here the columns suffered several casualties but Pachei escaped and moved into the unexplored Somra Tracts. Indecisive skirmishes continued into the summer and the Kukis remained active, recruiting more tribesmen to join the Rising. At Bamakshan village an unexpected and well-planned Kuki night attack killed two men in a column led by Captain Goodall, and the telegraph lines were chopped down again on the Burma road despite previous punitive actions against local villages. Goodall had to move into this area to support a column under Captain Francis Tuker, 2nd Gurkha Rifles, an officer destined for senior appointments in World War II.

In April prompt military support had been provided by the territorial Indian Defence Force unit the Surma Valley Light Horse. A group of 70 or 80 Kukis raided the North Cachar Hills and both the Europeans and the local labour on the tea estates near Haflong lived in fear of losing their heads. Twenty four members of 'B' Troop, Surma Valley Light Horse, forsook their civilian occupations and turned out from Silchar for up to a fortnight to provide a military presence until relieved by 100 rifles of the 2nd (Sadiya) Battalion, Assam Rifles, under Captain J.H. Copeland[90.]

By July both Falkland's and Montefiore's columns had returned from successful operations against the southern Chins in Burma, the latter column returning via Rangoon, Calcutta and Kohima. During his deployment Montefiore had entered Manipur from the south to restore the unfortunate situation that Steadman's withdrawal had created, destroying big stockades at Haika and killing many Kuki including Gnulbul, the Chief of Longya, who was attempting to escape with his little son in his arms. Falkland's column had sustained many casualties in the hard fighting against the Chins, and it

---

89 Lieutenant Parry was attached from THE IARO.
90 Captain Copeland was attached from the IARO.

marched back to Aijal; both columns had experienced a tough seven months of campaigning, and their main source of replacement clothing had been the Ladies' War Society in Rangoon. The southern Chin rebels were now reduced to a small number of activists, and Montefiore was to be awarded an honour for his military prowess in Burma.

As the mid-year hot-weather season commenced both sides felt exhausted and needed to rest. It was now apparent to the British that the Rising could not be put down in the traditional way by dispersed and loosely coordinated columns of troops using antiquated weapons. Additional handicaps were an inadequate transport arrangement and a supply system that prevaricated on grounds of cost whenever worn-out boots and clothing needed replacing. The Chief Commissioner of Assam took Shakespear to Simla for discussions with the Commander in Chief, India.

The arrival of Lieutenant General Sir Henry D'Urban Keary KCB KCIE DSO

Simla wanted to be rid of the embarrassing Kuki Rising and some decisive measures were taken. The old single-shot Martini Henry rifles used by the Assam Rifles and Burma Military Police were replaced with new .303-inch long Lee-Enfield magazine rifles. Lewis guns[91] and rifle grenades[92] were issued and four Stokes trench mortars were supplied to the Burma Military Police; this last weapon was to be a decisive factor in breaking Kuki resistance. New issues of clothing, boots and kit were made to the sepoys, free of charge. More officers from the Indian Army Reserve of Officers were posted into the theatre. The only Political Officer who had been into the Somra Tracts, Mr. W. Street of the Burma Commission, was recalled from his duties with the Chin Labour Corps in France.

Lieutenant General Sir Henry D'Urban Keary KCB KCIE DSO was due to take command of the Burma Division and he was tasked with ending the Kuki Rising. Keary was to command from Burma whilst Colonel C.E.E.F.K. Macquoid DSO commanded in Manipur but reported to Keary; ffrench-Mullen was to be Keary's principal staff officer. General Keary had served in the Third Anglo-Burmese War in 1885 and he later raised a battalion of Burma Military Police; whilst operating in the mounted infantry

---

91 Light machine guns.

92 Fragmentation grenades that are discharged from a rifle muzzle.

role he had been awarded the DSO for gallantry at Wuntho in 1891. He had then commanded a battalion in the operations to suppress insurrection in the Northern Chin Hills in 1892-93. He was a soldier with definite views regarding the efficacy of strong punitive measures against recalcitrant tribes. After making his appreciation of the situation he declared his plan of action to be: '... to put an end to the Kuki revolt by force of arms, break the Kuki spirit, disarm the Kukis, exact reparation and pave the way for an effective administration of their country'.

In Burma the troops that Keary used were the 1/70th and the 85th Burma Rifles, the 62nd Company Burma Sappers & Miners, the 202-man strong Chin Friendly Corps, and detachments of the Military Police battalions from Chin Hills, Bhamo Hills, Monywa Hills, Mandalay Hills, Myitkyina Hills, Taunggyi Hills, Shwebo Hills, Pyabwe Hills, Rangoon Hills and Toungoo Hills. With his headquarters and Supply and Transport personnel his Burma force totalled 3,011 men. In Assam Macquoid commanded the four Assam Rifles battalions already mentioned, one section of 35 signallers from 43rd Signal Company and a company of 150 Friendly Kuki Scouts; this was a total of 3,223 combatants. In the non-combatant role were 310 officers and men comprising a Section of the Gauhati Labour Corps, an officer and 35 men forming a survey detachment and 4,600 local porters.

The signallers from 43rd Signal Company were to make a big impact on future operations on the Manipur side, allowing Keary and his subordinates to closely coordinate column movements. On the Burma side 150 Burma Military Police signallers under Subadar Atta Muhammad provided the requirement and Atta Muhammad was later mentioned in despatches. Carrier pigeons were introduced to carry messages, but the birds were not given enough time to familiarise themselves with their new surroundings.

On the Manipur side transport had to be large gangs of porters as no pack-transport roads existed apart from the cart road from Dimapur via Kohima to Imphal. It took a cart one month to bring a load from Dimapur to Imphal. On the Burma side mules could be used and 1,500 of them were purchased across the Chinese border. Unfortunately surra disease[93] affected these mules on their journey into Burma, and Burman porters had to be hired until the mules recovered. These porters lived along the Burma rivers and were not hill-men, but they were all that could be raised as friendly

---

93 Surra is a disease inflicted by the horse-fly that can be fatal if not treated promptly.

Kukis who had previously offered to do the work were intimidated against performing it by their rebel brethren. The operations mounted from Burma were well supported by steamers plying the Chindwin River.

Keary's tactics

Keary adopted a plan initiated by Major A. Vickers[94], 3rd (Naga Hills) Battalion, Assam Rifles. Seven Areas of Operation were demarcated in which lines of posts were to be established; the posts were to be rationed for three months and manned generously so that small columns could be formed from within them. The Areas were: North East (Somra and North Chassadh); East (Chassadh); South-East (Mombi and Longya); South (Manhlung); South-West (Hinglep and Ukha); North-West (Silchar Road and Jampi).In each Area a base position was nominated to which supplies would be brought and dumped, these dumps would then support both the posts and any columns operating in the area.

Mobile columns in each area were to drive the Kuki onto the lines of posts where they were to be harried until the tribesmen submitted. As some villages in the Kuki heartlands were ostensibly 'friendly' care had to be taken to not attack them. To a degree this problem was solved by the construction of 'concentration camps' on the Manipur plain where the 'friendly' Kukis could reside during operations. Those 'friendlies' that did not come down to the camps had to take the rough with the smooth, and few British tears were shed for them as undoubtedly those villagers would be coerced into helping the rebels in various ways during operations.

Whilst the plans were being made and the new weapons introduced to the troops minor operations continued. Subadar Hanspal Limbu of the 3rd (Naga Hills) Battalion, Assam Rifles, who commanded a post at Niemi received information from 'friendlies' that a large group of Chassadh Kukis was approaching. The Subadar took a party of his men out to meet the rebels and in a sharp fight 30 Kukis were killed; Hanspal Limbu was subsequently awarded the Indian Distinguished Service Medal. Encountering the new British Lewis guns and magazine rifles must have been a distressing experience for many Kukis.

---

94 Major Vickers was attached from the 48th Pioneers.

With hostilities ceasing in France in late 1918 a number of experienced officers were returned to India to join Keary's force. Prominent amongst them was Major H. Douglas of the Surma Valley Light Horse who was to command a column and receive an honour for the way he operated. But the world-wide Spanish influenza epidemic struck some of the Assam Rifles, and an outbreak of cerebral meningitis affected others. Nevertheless in early November 1918 all Keary's columns were on the move and the Kukis were experiencing coordinated pressure from several directions.

The final months of the Kuki Rising

As the British columns advanced they accepted submissions from those villagers who had had enough of war, but the villages that resisted were destroyed along with any cultivated areas that they possessed. As a village submitted it had to surrender its firearms and pay a fine of livestock, and accept the guidance of a Political Officer; if insufficient firearms were surrendered then the cultivation of that village was destroyed. Chiefs considered dangerous were arrested after submission or capture and some were held in detention outside Manipur. Villagers or tribal units attempting to move away from advancing columns were forced back by posts or other columns so that they could not escape retribution for their rebellious acts. Wherever the Kukis went they could see the winking flashes of British heliographs reporting their movements. As the British columns advanced they made bridle paths through the jungle and over the hills, opening up the Kuki territory for the British administrators who followed. The surveyors took their readings in the field and used them to produce the first maps of unexplored areas such as the Somra Tracts.

The main rebel leaders were always on the move attempting to enter new areas to find refuge, but their followers rapidly became dispirited and demoralised by the new firepower of the British columns and posts. In the North West Area Subadar Hari Ram, 3rd (Naga Hills) Battalion, Assam Rifles, commanded the Channachin post and he made a surprise attack on Layang village killing 28 rebels and capturing the entire livestock; Hari Ram was later awarded the Indian Distinguished Service Medal. When the nearby garrison of the Dulin post attacked the rebel village of Sompuram with similar results nearly all organised resistance in the Jampi region ceased, most chiefs submitted, surrendering weapons and paying tribute without further argument. This pattern of the successful use of superior British firepower was repeated in all seven Areas,

With the Burma Military Police columns on the Chindwin side denying the Kukis freedom of movement across the border, Keary had achieved his aim of putting an end to the Kuki revolt by force of arms, breaking the Kuki spirit, disarming the Kukis, exacting reparation and paving the way for an effective administration of their country. His success was undeniable. After four months of operating from the Somra Tracts Chief Pachei found that he was even being pursued and hounded there, and in April he appeared in Imphal and surrendered. By 20th May 1919 nearly all resistance had ceased and operations were terminated. To help the country settle down strong posts were maintained by the Assam Rifles at Ukruhl, Kamjong, Nantiram, Tamenglao, Chura Chandpur, Mombi, Poshing, Chanakin and Kerami.

Totalling the results of military operations between December 1917 and May 1919, 140 rebel villages were destroyed, 112 rebel villages submitted and 15 villages were found deserted. In Manipur 970 muskets were confiscated whilst in the south Chin Hills over 600 were handed in. Large amounts of grain and cattle were also confiscated. The estimated number of Kukis killed was 126 men, but doubtless others died of wounds away from the scenes of action, especially when the new British weapons came into use. The British lost 59 all-ranks killed, 135 wounded and 97 dead from other causes, principally disease.

The whole affair had been an embarrassment to the government of India and the campaign was denied publicity. Participation in the campaign did not qualify for a clasp to the Indian General Service Medal; however troops who served in the field for any period from the start of the Kuki rising until 31st October 1918 qualified for the award of the British Victory Medal. Two Distinguished Service Orders were awarded but the citations were not published.

The last word must go to the Kukis. They led the British on a merry dance for 18 months armed only with ancient muskets, they carried no packs and had no supply trains or medical support but they knew their own country well and how to live off it and fight effectively from it. They were a tough and fierce adversary who commanded the respect of all who went up against them. Shahbash (Well Done!) the Kukis!

Awards made for service during the Kuki Rising

Companion of the Order of the Star of India (CSI).

Lieutenant-Colonel John Lawrence William ffrench-Mullen CIE, Indian Army.

Companion of the Order of the Indian Empire (CIE).

Colonel Leslie Waterfield Shakespear CB and Colonel Charles Edward Every Francis Kirwan Macqoid DSO, both of the Indian Army; Captain Edward Joseph Calveley Hordern, Royal Indian Marine; John Comyn Higgins, John Henry Hutton and John Brown Marshall, all of the Indian Civil Service.

Commander of the Military Division of the Order of the British Empire (CBE).

Lieutenant-Colonel Walter Bulmer Tait Abbey and Major Lindsay Elliott Lumley Burne, both of Indian Army.

Officers of the Military Division of the Order of the British Empire (OBE).

Captain Claud Emanuel Montefiore, Indian Army, Assam Military Police[95]; Captain William Niven Greer MB, Royal Army Medical Corps; Lieutenant Charles George Kay-Mouat, 1/70th Burma Rifles, Indian Army; Major Hannath Douglas Marshall, 2nd Surma Valley Light Horse, Indian Defence Force; Temporary Captain David Vincent O'Malley MB, Royal Army Medical Corps; Captain George Edward Scott, Indian Defence Force; Major (Temporary Lieutenant Colonel) William Blomfield White, 39th Central Indian Horse, Indian Army.

Members of the Military Division of the Order of the British Empire (MBE).

Temporary 2nd Lieutenant Val Ardern Hulme, Indian Army Reserve of Officers; Captain John Hugh Copeland, Indian Army Reserve of Officers attached to 8th Gurkha Rifles; Lieutenant George David Walker, 2/8th Gurkha Rifles; Lieutenant Eric John Wilkinson, Indian Army Reserve of Officers attached to Supply & Transport Corps and Headquarters Staff, Burma Force.

---

95 The Assam Rifles had previously held titles as Military Police Battalions.

Distinguished Service Order (DSO)

Captain William George King Broome, 89th Punjabis and Major Thomas Dalby Hutchison Hackett, both of the Indian Army.

Indian Distinguished Service Medal

Assam Rifles recipients: Subadars Bhawan Sing, 1st Bn, Hiraup Sahi, 1st Bn, Hari Ram, 3rd Bn, Nain Singh Mull, 3rd Bn, Birman Thapa, 4th Bn; Jemadars Hanspal Limbu, 3rd Bn and Satal Singh Cachari, 4th Bn; Havildar 1886 Jangbir Gurung, 2nd Bn; Rifleman 2729 Bhabajit Rhai, 2nd Bn.

Burma Military Police recipients: Subadars Mir Fazal, Mandalay Bn; Arjan Singh, Reserve Bn. and Hpaulula attached 85th Burma Rifles.Jemadars Fateh Muhammad, Mandalay Bn; Mota Suba, Chin Hills Bn; Kulman Lapcha, Bhamo Bn and Tek Bahadur, Myitkyina Bn.Havildars 40 Umardin, Bhamo Bn;5094 Nirbakht Rai, Myitkyina Bn and 1551 Harkabahadur Chettri, attached 85th Burma Rifles.Sepoy 3677 Jasbahadur Ghalle, SSS Bn.

King's Police Medal

Subadar Pokul Thapa, Assam Rifles.

Mentioned in Despatches

90 officers and men[96]

---

96 The names can be seen on Page 7761 of a Supplement to the London Gazette dated 23 July 1920 under the heading KUKI PUNITIVE OPERATIONS.

Fighting the Marris and the Khetrans

Baluchistan in 1918

The Baluchistan Province of British India was a large but thinly inhabited territory that bordered southern Afghanistan, south-east Persia and the approaches to the Straits of Hormuz leading into the Persian Gulf. The Province was administered directly by the Indian Political Service, as was the North-West Frontier Province immediately to the north. During the Great War both of these Provinces were targeted by German agents positioned in neutral Persia who used gold and intrigue to spread disaffection against British rule.

The Marri tribe of eastern Baluchistan had a history of resistance to the British. The tribesmen were long-bearded and long-haired and lived in a remote, barren area that was relatively untouched by economic progress or the war. In 1917 Marri chiefs had travelled to Quetta for a visit by the British Viceroy and there probably they had been led to believe by other more devious chiefs that there were no British soldiers left in India as all had gone to the war. Then the British Political Agent asked for Marri recruits for a tribal levy, this caused anger and the Marris swore to refuse this British request. In February 1918 this anger was translated into action and an attack was mounted on Gumbaz Fort.

The attack on Gumbaz Fort

Thirty men from the 3rd Skinner's Horse were garrisoning Gumbaz Fort when news of trouble brewing in the Marri region was received at regimental headquarters in Lorelai. On 17th February 1918 Major J.R. Gaussen CMG, DSO was despatched with 50 more men to reinforce Gumbaz, and this group arrived at the fort the following day. The fort and surrounding area appeared quiet and the resident Political Officer, Lieutenant Colonel F. McConaghey, was living in his bungalow some distance away. However towards evening

Gaussen sensed impending violence and he persuaded the Political Officer to move into the fort.

Gaussen's appreciation for the defence of the fort with just 80 men had decided him not to attempt a perimeter defence but to concentrate his men in the two flanking towers; he commanded one tower and Lieutenant H.B. Watson (Indian Army Reserve of Officers attached to 3rd Skinner's Horse) commanded the other. At 2300 hours on 19th December several hundreds of mainly sword-wielding Marris suddenly attacked, scaled the fort walls, and then hurled themselves against the towers. Mullahs had promised the tribesmen immunity from infidel bullets and the Marris were fearless. The intensity of the fighting can be gauged from the citations for the two **Indian Orders of Merit (2nd Class)** that were later awarded:

No 786 Dafadar Lal Singh, 3rd Skinner's Horse

This non-commissioned officer showed the greatest gallantry and power of command in action on the night of 19th-20th February 1918. He exposed himself continually to fire, directing fire and rallying his men, till severely wounded. When the non-commissioned officer who had charge of the key of the magazine had been cut down, and the key lost, he at once volunteered to go down and force open the magazine, ammunition being needed. When wounded, he was placed under the little cover available but a second bullet inside the post struck him in the brain and killed him.

No 1334 Lance Dafadar Khem Singh, 3rd Skinner's Horse

When his post was attacked from the rear, he at once rushed out to the head of the ladder and resolutely defended it from a mob of Marris, shooting down several and holding the ladder unaided until the attack was beaten off.

The first assault was halted but minutes later fresh waves of Marris vigorously attacked again until they too were driven out of the fort by rifle fire. A third and final attack was mounted at 0200 hours 20th February but this also eventually withered under the intensive rifle fire of the defenders. As they departed the Marris showered curses on their infidel foes and carried away some of their own casualties, but even so 200 dead or wounded tribesmen were found lying in and around the fort as dawn broke. The regimental history does not record the casualties sustained by 3rd Skinner's Horse.

This had been a very savage action and it was later included in the Official List of Battles and Actions of the Great War. For gallantry displayed in commanding the towers James Robert Gaussen received a **Companionship of the Most Eminent Order of the Indian Empire** (CIE), as did Frank McConaghey who had been fighting alongside him, and Harold Boyes Watson was awarded a **Military Cross**.

The Marri Field Force

The Marris continued attacking government buildings and induced the Khetran tribe to join them; the Khetranis joined in wholeheartedly and burned down buildings at Barkhan on 7th March. But on 28th February the government had sanctioned punitive measures. Lieutenant General R. Wapshare CB, CSI ordered a Field Force to concentrate at two locations: Duki for operations against the Marris and Dera Gazi Khan for operations against the Khetrans. Brigadier General T.H. Hardy commanded at Duki and Brigadier General P.J. Miles commanded at Dera Gazi Khan. Details of the major units that were most active in the two columns can be extracted from the list of recipients of the Battle Honour shown at the end of the article.

The Deri Ghazi Khan (or Rakhni) Column

The 1st Battalion of the 55th Coke's Rifles (Frontier Force), commanded by Lieutenant Colonel H.E. Herdon, de-trained at Deri Ghazi Khan on 4th March 1918. The four rifle companies were class-composed of: Dogras, Sikhs, Punjabi Mussulmans and Pathans; the Pathan company was half Yusufzais and half Khattacks. Colonel Herdon was ordered to move to Fort Munro, 90 kilometres away and on top of a 1,800 metre-high escarpment; the battalion departed on 5th March. The following day news was received of an impending attack on Fort Bhar Khan, 100 kilometres distant. Colonel Herdon marched towards Fort Bhar Khan with half of his battalion but after travelling 16 kilometres further news was received that the Fort Bhar Khan garrison had escaped to Kher. Colonel Herdon now set his compass towards Kher, and by marching through a pitch-black night accompanied by heavy rain and mist his half-battalion reached Kher at 0130 hours on 7th March. The men had no greatcoats or blankets and no food was available, whilst the only huts there were fire-damaged. On the next day the other half of Coke's Rifles reached Kher, and a rudimentary supply line was established. Over the next few days the battalion picqueted the roads to Girdo and Rakhni.

On 15th March around 3,000 Marris and Khetranis, mostly swordsmen, attacked Fort Munro. Coke's Rifles marched hard to get there in time, accompanied by Centre Section (2 guns) of 23rd (Peshawar) Mountain Battery. The tribesmen got into some bungalows near the fort and occupied an adjacent hill. Centre Section was commanded by Captain T.F. Hennessy and he provided fire support, firing 32 rounds at 1550 metres range whilst two companies of Coke's Rifles attacked and dispersed the enemy. Coke's Rifles had four men wounded, one mortally, by sword cuts.

The next day more troops arrived and the Force moved to Rakhni from where punitive columns destroyed villages, cut crops, seized cattle and took many prisoners. The 12th Pioneers, commanded by Lieutenant Colonel J.S. Hooker, supported the infantry by road and camel-track construction, and often by accompanying columns to use pioneer expertise in demolishing villages. The region was dry and very hot by day, but the temperature dropped to freezing conditions by night.

Sapper engineering support

As well as the pioneer support both the Bengal and the Bombay Sappers & Miners provided sub-units for heavier military engineering tasks. Captain H.E. Roome, Royal Engineers, commanded the 52nd Company, Bengal Sappers & Miners, whilst Captain M.G.G. Campbell, Royal Engineers, commanded the 72nd Company, Bombay Sappers & Miners. The sappers improved water supplies and communications generally, bridging ravines, destroying enemy fortified towers and erecting camp defences.

The Duki Column

Units in the column de-trained at Harnai and concentrated at Duki by 18th March, when the order of battle was:

- Column Headquarters
- One Squadron 3rd Skinner's Horse
- One section of 23rd (Peshawar) Mountain Battery
- One section of Sappers & Miners
- 1st Battalion The South Lancashire Regiment

- 107th Pioneers

- 2nd Battalion 2nd King Edward's Own Gurkhas, with one platoon from 3rd Battalion 5th Gurkha Rifles attached

- Detachments from the 71st Punjabis, the only Christian battalion in the Indian Army.

- A Machine Gun Company, motor cycle mounted.

- Two sections of a Field Ambulance.

- A detachment of Mule Corps.

- A detachment of Bikaner Camel Corps, an Imperial Service unit provided by the Princely State of Bikaner.

- Rain fell heavily on Duki and there was little shelter. The South Lancashires, commanded by Lieutenant Colonel A. De Vere Willoughby-Osborne, was an all-British unit on the peace-time ration scale. The battalion suffered because it was impossible to make local purchases as there were no local suppliers in sight. The British soldiers were each issued with half a kilogram of atta flour (milled from semi-hard wheats) with which to make chapatis, but they needed friendly help from the Indian units before anything resembling a chapati appeared. At Duki it was decided to forget about the motor cycles as there were no roads ahead of the column, so the machine gun sections were converted to pack-animal transport and the ammunition belts were carried in packing cases by mules and camels. The former motor cyclist riders had worn the soles off their boots cornering on their bikes, and being in no condition to march a long distance they persevered as far as Kohlu where they stayed as a garrison.

The 107th Pioneers, commanded by Major W.P.M.D. McLaughlin initially picqueted the road by day between Harnai and Ashgara, garrisoning posts along them. One night a company camp at Torkhan was surrounded by hostile Marris, but the pioneers' rifle fire drove off the tribesmen at a loss of one Pioneer wounded. The 107th then marched with the Duki column.

The column advanced on 18th March to Gumbaz, the scene of the February attack, where mules were allocated to carry greatcoats. Meat was driven 'on the hoof' and the herdsmen had to be constantly chivvied to keep up with the column. Next morning Nurhan, the entrance to the Marri country, was reached and a reconnaissance party observed many stone-built sangars (protective firing positions) on the crests of hills controlling the valley that had to be used as a route; however the sangars were not manned. That night heavy rain soaked the greatcoats and blankets which resulted in unstable mule-loads that constantly slipped during the following day; the wet blankets froze stiff during the following night.

Air support

Air co-operation planes had appeared overhead. These were BE2c aircraft from Nos 31 and 114 Squadrons, Royal Air Force; two planes were based at Sibi, two more at Duki and a further five at Deri Ghazi Khan. The first sortie, on 1st March, was a plane armed with a Lewis gun and four small bombs that went looking for a reported 3,000-strong lashkar (fighting group) of Marris approaching from Chandia. The plane made no contact, and this was fortunate as the reported lashkar was in fact the audience dispersing after a sports meeting at Chandia. However operationally the planes could look for enemy groups and drop messages on the columns with details of enemy locations or directions of travel, and they could bomb villages and camps. On 24th March Kahan, capital of the Marri district, was bombed and 14 armed tribesmen were killed. The threat offered by the aeroplanes was a significant deterrent and helped in eventually subduing the inadequately armed belligerents.

Securing Watwangi Pass

On 22nd March the column secured and marched through the very steep-sided Watwangi Pass, leaving half the Gurkhas there to secure the route and operate punitive columns. Lieutenant Colonel A.B. Tillard, the Gurkhas' commanding officer, stayed with his headquarters at Zrind at the top of the pass. The two companies of Gurkhas that marched onwards with the column were commanded by Captain E.J. Corse Scott. Kohlu was reached where the revenue and levy posts had been burned out. Here the column halted for a few days, the motor cyclists in their by-now imitations of boots were left as a Line of Communication garrison whilst infantry columns destroyed local villages and crops and collected any weapons seen.

Confiscated herds of livestock were attached to the column and moved on with it to Bor, where torrential rain all night prevented cooking and allowed the livestock to escape. To recover the stock 40 South Lancashire volunteers who claimed equestrian status were mounted on transport mules, with pack-saddles and rope stirrups, and sent back towards Kohlu. However as soon as the mules decided to move up a gear from walking to trotting the countryside was littered with dismounted soldiers and riderless mules; it took two hours to reform the detachment. The mules were then walked to Kohlu where the herds had faithfully returned, and a sheep or two or three were requisitioned to provide grilled lamb chops with the chapatis that evening.

It took all of the next day to return to Bor as the herds were very hungry and stampeded towards grazing whenever they saw it; by now few of the equestrian volunteers wanted to ever ride again. Bor was totally fly-infested and when eating, speed and dexterity with spoon and fork were essential to prevent the swallowing of swarms of flies. Also the water was brackish and purgative, keeping all ranks on the run. Everyone kept on good terms with the re-supply convoy commander who always brought a barrel of sweet water up with him.

The action at Hadb

As 4th April dawned news came in of a strong lashkar (fighting group) of around 1,500 Marris positioned at Hadb to bar the route to Mamand. The lashkar was occupying sangars on the crest of a long upward-running spur. A reconnaissance was made resulting in a decision to attack directly with two companies of Gurkhas and one company of South Lancashires, supported by the mountain gunners. A Gurkha company and a South Lancashire platoon climbed the spur and the steep ground at its head whilst two other South Lancashire companies manoeuvred to be able to fire into the Marris' flank as they retired.

As the British assault troops crested the ridge and engaged the sangars the Marris broke and retreated, leaving up to 100 dead on the ground; many wounded were carried away. Shells from the mountain guns and the kukhris and bayonets of the assaulting troops had all done deadly work in and around the sangars. This was the only stand made by the primitively-armed Marris against the Duki Column. Five British soldiers had been wounded. Subadar Gamer Sing Gurung and 2403 Lance Naik Dhanraj Gurung, both of 2/2nd King Edward's Own Gurkhas, were later Mentioned in Despatches.

Submission

The Duki Column moved on to the Marri capital of Kahan without further opposition, arriving on 18th April. During the following day the Political staff got to work and on 2nd May accepted the formal submission of the Marri Nawab and tribal headmen. A similar acceptance from the Khetrans was accepted at Barkhan on 7th May. By now hot weather had arrived, with temperatures reading 110 degrees in the shade.

Whilst at Kahan the gunners came across two British 12-pounder howitzers that had been spiked and abandoned after a disastrous encounter with the Marris in 1840. The guns were hauled back to Quetta where one of them adorned the Royal Artillery mess there for several years.

As hostilities had ended the Duki Column marched back towards Duki. The 55th Coke's Rifles was met at Chappi Kach, complete with tents, a proper scale of rations, and beer; the 55th was generous towards its companions-in-arms. At Harnai station a Munro Canteen had been set up, manned by ladies from Quetta; after appreciating the canteen contents and the kindness of the staff the column entrained for Quetta. Uniforms were torn and patched, and boots were disintegrating, but after three months of marching across the unforgiving Baluchistan terrain all ranks were fit, slim, and content.

Lieutenant Colonel Arthur De Vere Willoughby-Osborne, The South Lancashire Regiment, was later Mentioned in Despatches and also received a Companionship of the Most Eminent Order of the Indian Empire (CIE).

Battle Honour

These twelve regiments and units were awarded the Battle Honour **Baluchistan 1918**, but those underlined did not elect to carry the honour; the units and sub-units from these twelve that were employed in the 1918 Marri Field Force are shown bracketed:

- The South Lancashire Regiment (1st Bn);
- The Kent Cyclist Battalion (1st/1st Bn);
- Skinner's Horse (3rd Skinner's Horse);
- The Peshawar Mountain Battery (23rd (Peshawar) Battery);

- The Bengal Sappers & Miners; (52nd Company);

- The Bombay Sappers & Miners; (72nd Company);

- Madras Pioneers (81st Pioneers);

- Bombay Pioneers (12th Pioneers and 107th Pioneers);

- The Frontier Force Rifles (1st/55th Coke's Rifles);

- The 2nd Gurkha Rifles (2nd Bn);

- The 4th Gurkha Rifles (1st Bn).

(An edited version of this article appeared in a recent issue of *Durbar*, the journal of the Indian Military Historical Society http://imhs.org.uk/. Gratitude is expressed to the Royal Geographical Society for the use of their photographs, and to Matthew Broadbridge for drawing attention to the Cradock-Watson article.)

Indian Army units in Dunsterforce North-West Persia in 1918

Introduction

The start of the Russian Revolution in the Spring of 1917 heralded the decline of Russia as an effective member of the alliance that was fighting the Central Powers who were led by Germany and Turkey. By December of that year revolutionaries had seized power in Russia and had signed a separate peace with the Central Powers at Brest-Livotsk. This resulted in the demoralisation and disintegration of the Russian forces that had been confronting Turkey in Anatolia and Persia. Turkey was now able to reclaim territory previously occupied by the Russians, punish those people such as the Armenians who had collaborated with Russia on Turkish soil, and look to expand Turkish influence both in the Caucasus region and eastwards.

The Caucasian states of Armenia, Georgia and Azerbaijan created a Transcaucasian Federation that eventually declared itself to be independent from Bolshevik Russia in April 1918. Initially the Federation sought friendly relations with Turkey but agreement could not be reached on border demarcation and fighting commenced. This situation was compounded by Germany becoming involved on the side of Georgia, that state declaring itself independent from the Federation in May. Turks fighting Georgian troops found themselves fighting Germans who were assisting Georgia. Both German and Turkish eyes and interests were focused eastwards on the Azerbaijani oilfields at Baku on the Caspian Sea.

The Turkish War Minister, Ismail Enver Pasha, had ambitions to unite the Turkic people of Central Asia with Anatolian Turkey. On hearing of the fighting in Georgia Enver quickly went there accompanied by the German Chief of the Turkish General Staff, General Hans Von Seeckt. Differences were resolved between German and Turkish policies in the region, and Enver ordered two weak Turkish armies to prepare to advance eastwards. The Ninth Army was to advance through Persian Azerbaijan with Tabriz as its immediate objective, whilst the Third Army advanced upon Baku to seize the oilfields there. Neither of these Turkish armies contained German troops; the Germans were busy concentrating a weak division at Tiflis and they watched Enver's eastern advances with interest but did not directly support them, preferring to thwart them where they could. But German training missions were already in Persia attempting to achieve a change of government that would bring Persia into the war as an ally of the Central Powers.

The British reaction

During the Autumn of 1917 Britain had observed the decline of Russian military capability on the Caucasian Front with deep concern. It was vital that Caspian oil and cotton (the cotton was used in the manufacture of munitions) be prevented from getting into German hands. Britain also feared that the Central Powers would now move through neutral Persia (previously they had been restrained by an effective Russian military presence in the north of that country) to de-stabilise the Indian North-West Frontier and beyond, and bring Afghanistan into the war against Britain. Stability in India was a vital British requirement as a further half-million Indian soldiers were being recruited and trained at this time, with the aim of establishing 67 more infantry battalions, to be used primarily in overseas theatres.

Some modern historical commentators have derided this British fear. However during the war Germany promoted strong insurrections in Persia and infiltrated small groups of men and weapons through the country to Afghanistan; the Germans and the Turks did not need to move large armies through Persia, as well-led and financed training missions could achieve their aims. During the war German support for the Indian Ghadr revolutionary movement and Turkish calls for a Muslim Holy War caused serious problems in India and Burma, including mutiny in some military units. The Afghanistan threat was potent as was shown in 1919 when that country invaded India, encouraging thousands of border tribesmen to join in the fight against the British.

During late 1917 the War Cabinet in London wanted to move British troops into the Caucasus but none were available. An alternative plan was adopted to send a British Military Mission to the Georgian capital, Tiflis;

this mission would not be a fighting unit but would contain instructors and staff officers capable of financing, training and organising indigenous Caucasian units that would fight the Turks. The only conventional part of the mission was to be a British Armoured Car Brigade. It was determined that the best possible route to Tiflis was overland from Baghdad through Persia to the Caspian Sea, then by boat to Baku, and onwards by train to Tiflis. Unfortunately events in Tiflis were already making this British plan redundant.

Command of the British Mission was given to Major General Lionel Charles Dunsterville CB. He was a well-liked and respected Indian Army officer and a fluent Russian speaker, with operational experience on the Indian North-West Frontier and in China. As Dunsterville states in his account of DUNSTERFORCE, the name by which his mission became known:**'My own knowledge of the Russian language and known sympathy with Russia had probably a good deal to do with my selection for the task'**. His mission was: '**the maintenance of an effective force on the Caucasus front so as to protect the occupied portions of Turkish Armenia and to prevent the realisation of Pan-Turanian designs'**. The then British Military Agent in Tiflis was Lieutenant Colonel G.D. Pike MC, 9th Gurkha Rifles, Indian Army, and Dunsterville was to take over the appointment from him.

Initially Dunsterville's resources were a large treasure chest, the Armoured Car Brigade, a small group of mainly Indian Army staff officers, another small group of Russian officers, and around 200 officers and 200 Non Commissioned Officers selected chiefly from Canadian, Australian, New Zealand and South African units. Many of these men had been decorated for gallantry in the field. This was a Special Forces unit, tasked with a strategic Special Forces mission, long before Special Forces were officially invented, glamorised and awarded cult-hero status.

In the event DUNSTERFORCE did not get to Tiflis, but it was involved in heavy fighting against the Turkish Third Army around Baku and in serious fighting against the Turkish Ninth Army and its Persian allies in northern Persia. In northern Persia two Indian Army units were attached to DUNSTERFORCE and took part in hard fighting, leading to several gallantry awards being received by Indian soldiers.

The Road to and from Enzeli

DUNSTERFORCE men trickled into Baghdad as they arrived from other theatres and Lionel Dunsterville's first major problem was that he could not concentrate his mission before it was deployed; he set off himself first with a small staff hoping that his men and vehicles would quickly follow. In the event some parts of the Armoured Car Brigade did not arrive in Persia until after DUNSTERFORCE had been disbanded. The second major problem was the attitude of the theatre commander in Mesopotamia, Lieutenant General W.R. Marshall KCB, who had succeeded in command after General F.S. Maude's death from illness in Baghdad. Marshall strenuously objected to the concept of DUNSTERFORCE because he had to logistically support it across Persia, but more personally he vehemently objected to the fact that Lionel Dunsterville reported directly to London. From this moment onwards Marshall's somewhat petulant opposition to DUNSTERFORCE grew and Dunsterville's chances of achieving some kind of success receded.

At Kermanshah Dunsterville met up with a group of 1,200 Russian Caucasian Cossacks under the command of Colonel Lazar Bicherakov, a courageous and charismatic Ossetian who was to be a staunch ally of the British in northern Persia and the Caucasus. Bicherakov and his Caucasian Cossacks were fiercely anti-Bolshevik. Lieutenant Colonel C.H. Clutterbuck, 125th Napier's Rifles, Indian Army, was the British liaison officer with the Russians, and he was assisted by New Zealand army signallers manning a Russian wireless set. Clutterbuck was a Russian language specialist and popular with the Cossacks; the New Zealanders were from an Australian and New Zealand wireless squadron.

Dunsterville pushed on the next day, now accompanied by one of Bicherakov's officers acting as a guide. Due to snowfalls the convoy did not reach Hamadan until 11th February but fortunately the road being followed was an ancient trade route and old serais, designed to shelter passing camel caravans, were located along the way. At Hamdan the advance party was waiting as was Brigadier General Offley Shore, CB, CIE, DSO, Indian Army, who was returning from Tiflis and waiting to brief Dunsterville on the current situation there.

Also at Hamadan was the Russian Lieutenant General Nikolai Baratov, commander of the Russian troops in northern Persia. This force had performed well as part of the Imperial Russian Army and had pushed a

Turkish advance into Persia back towards Mesopotamia. But now Baratov's command had disintegrated and most of his remaining soldiers refused to accept orders as they tried to get home. Dunsterville carefully negotiated separately with Bicherakov and Baratov. He paid Baratov for items of military equipment purchased and he paid Bicherakov when he needed the Cossacks to fight.

Dunsterville left Hamadan on 14th February when a pass immediately ahead was cleared of snow and his convoy, now including an armoured car, made good time down an excellent Russian-constructed road to Kasvin. This was an important town of 50,000 inhabitants and the road to Tehran, the Persian capital, forked eastwards from there.

DUNSTERFORCE was now approaching territory controlled by a group of Persians known as the Jangalis because they operated from the heavily forested or jungle-like land in Gilan Province south of the Caspian Sea. The Jangali revolutionary leader, Mirza Kuchik Khan, had vowed not to let the British through his region. Kuchik Khan, like many Persians had felt humiliated by the Anglo-Russian Convention of 1907 that was used to allow 'Spheres of Influence' to be created in Persia, the Russian sphere being almost the entire north of the country and the British sphere being in the south-east, adjacent to the Indian border. So far the Jangalis had resisted attempts by both the Tehran government and the local Russian forces to destroy them. A German mission under Colonel von Passchen was training Kuchik Khan's men who were equipped with rifles and Turkish machine guns.

The British convoy drove on towards the Caspian on 16th February, pushing its way through hordes of Russian pro-Bolshevik soldiers who had demobilised themselves and who just wanted to go home with whatever booty they could carry. The convoy crossed the bridge at Menjil and drove on to Resht, not knowing that both locations would shortly have to be fought over. At Resht Dunsterville met with the British Acting Vice-Consul Charles Maclaren, who was soon to be captured and incarcerated by the Jangalis along with Captain E.W.C. Noel CIE, 91st Punjabis, Indian Army, attached to the Political Department. Noel would be carrying despatches from Tiflis for DUNSTERFORCE at the time of his capture. The cars then drove to Enzeli where trouble started to mount.

At Enzeli, the main Persian port on the Caspian Sea, Dunsterville discovered that the Bolsheviks controlling Baku were not going to let his force operate in or pass through Azerbaijan. Dunsterville withdrew, as his small group was not configured as a fighting unit, and took his convoy of cars back to Hamdan; this was a prudent move as the money that several of his cars were carrying had to be protected.

The Eastern Committee of the War Cabinet in London made an important policy change on 27th May, telegraphing that DUNSTERFORCE was now not to attempt to get to Tiflis but was to reach the Caspian Sea and take control of the shipping fleet there. The military priority was to secure the Mesopotamia-Enzeli road. This instruction was modified to allow Dunsterville or one or more of his officers to go to Baku, at General Marshall's discretion, to reconnoitre the task of demolishing Baku's oil wells. General Marshall was to find the troops needed by DUNSTERFORCE. But Lionel Dunsterville was never to get the troops he needed to complete the tasks that he would undertake, and by now many of his men were dispersed around northern Persia on intelligence, famine-relief and training duties with local levies.

Concurrent with DUNSTERFORCE operations were a British military move into Russian Transcaspia from Meshed in north-eastern Persia and the military operations of the British-sponsored South Persia Rifles in the south of the country. In both these other operations Indian Army units formed the bulk of the British troops involved; Persia had become an important theatre for the Indian Army.

The fight for Resht

On 1st June DUNSTERFORCE moved to Kasvin, leaving Brigadier John Byron in charge of the Line of Communication at Hamadan where Lieutenant Colonel W. Donnan, a re-enlistment from the Indian Army Retired List, was commanding an efficient militia.

On 10th June, negotiations with Kuchik Khan to persuade him to become neutral having failed, DUNSTERFORCE marched out to fight. Bicherakov commanded the fighting troops and his column consisted of two squadrons of Cossack cavalry and a detachment of infantry, a section of Russian mountain artillery plus 'C' Squadron 14th (The King's) Hussars; the column advanced towards Resht with the British squadron leading. In support were two British armoured cars and two British aeroplanes. At Menjil, half way to the Caspian, was a 200-metre long, 5-span girder bridge over the Kizil Uzun River that the Jangalis were defending with an estimated 2,000 men and several machine guns. However the Jangali defences were poorly sited and vital ground was not occupied despite the presence of Colonel von Passchen. The effective and co-ordinated use of British aircraft, Russian mountain artillery and both Cossack and British cavalry overcame the Jangali defenders and their German mentors, and the Persians finally broke and hastily withdrew.

Dunsterville needed to get more men forward from Hamadan before he could secure his line of communications whilst he advanced. General Marshall had sent from Mesopotamia a composite battalion, half 1/4th Hampshires and half 1/2nd King Edward's Own Gurkha Rifles (The Sirmoor Rifles), under the command of Lieutenant Colonel C.L. Matthews, Durham Light Infantry attached to and commanding 1/4th Hampshires. This unit was accompanied by Right Section (two guns) of 21st Kohat Mountain Battery (Frontier Force), Indian Army. The battalion and the gunners were titled 'Matthews' Column'. Some of the composite battalion now joined Dunsterville but the Jangalis, their morale recovered, gave them a warm welcome by mounting two successful ambushes.

Then the Gurkhas became involved and the fight-back began. On 29th June Captain Knightley Holler Coxe, Indian Army Reserve of Officers attached to 1/2nd Gurkhas, won a **Military Cross** at Imam Zadeh Hachem: **For conspicuous gallantry and devotion to duty near Stahmd Bridge, Persia, on 29th June 1918. He organised and executed a brilliantly successful attack on an enemy position, inflicting heavy losses on the enemy at very slight cost to his own force. He displayed marked ability and initiative, coolly meeting every contingency that arose with marked courage and skill.**

The prominent use of Gurkha kukris during this action gave the Jangalis something to think about, but they were still prepared to attack as events in Resht during the next month demonstrated. Elsewhere at this time there were reported to be around 2,000 Turkish soldiers in Tabriz, and the DUNSTERFORCE troops observing that route were ordered to establish a post at Mianeh and to patrol westwards from there.

On 20th July around 2,500 Jangalis supported by a number of Turks and Germans under von Passchen attacked Resht. Colonel Matthews had with him 300 rifles from his 1/4th Hampshires, 150 Gurkha rifles under Captain G.M. McCleverty, 1/2nd Gurkha Rifles, two guns of 21st (Kohat) Mountain battery transported in Ford vans, and two armoured cars. Most of the British troops were in their base camp outside the town which was heavily attacked but detachments were inside Resht guarding buildings. At the base the enemy were driven back, leaving over 100 dead on the ground. Fifty enemy soldiers surrendered to the British troops, including some Austrian and Hungarian former prisoners of war who had been released by the Bolsheviks from camps around Tashkent in Central Asia.

However and more seriously another large group of Jangalis had entered Resht and attacked the small British posts at the British Consulate, the telegraph office and the bank, which contained bullion. Colonel Matthews dispatched Captain McCleverty with 100 rifles and the armoured cars to withdraw the guards at the Consulate and reinforce the other posts within the town. This was easier said than done in the maze of alleys within the town and bitter street-fighting started that was to last for several days.

Two Military Crosses were awarded to officers of the Motor Machine Gun Corps and one to a Hampshires' officer. Another **Military Cross** was awarded to Subadar Major Tulsiram Gharti, 1/2nd Gurkhas: *For conspicuous gallantry and devotion to duty at Resht on 20th July 1918. During the attack by an enemy on a town he led his men with exceptional ability and dash, and by the rapidity of his advance inflicted heavy casualties on the enemy, taking a number of prisoners. Later he displayed marked initiative and daring in the relief of a besieged garrison. His conduct throughout the operation was splendid.*

Two men of the 1/2nd Gurkhas received **Indian Orders of Merit**.

3695 Havildar Kule Thapa: *He was in command of a small guard that was in a house surrounded by the enemy. Although heavily attacked and hard-pressed for nine hours, he beat off all attacks until relief arrived. He behaved throughout with the greatest coolness and resource, inspiring his men by his magnificent example. This non-commissioned officer has previously done good work in carrying out daring patrols and bringing back valuable information.*

3966 Lance Naik Kuman Singh Gurung: *It was largely due to the skill and initiative with which this non-commissioned officer used his Lewis Gun that his platoon was able to advance as rapidly as it did. On one occasion when heavy enfilade fire from* *a house was delaying the advance, he left two men with a Lewis gun to give covering fire and with the remainder of his section rushed the house, killing a number of the enemy, including an officer, and taking several prisoners.*

For the operations in Resht and at Imam Zadeh Hachem a month previously awards of the **Indian Distinguished Service Medal** were made to nine officers and men of 1/2nd Gurkhas: Subadar Aiman Rana; Jemadar Nandbir Thapa; 3489 Havildar Tilakchand Gurung; 199 Lance Naik Kalu Gharti; 3222 Lance Naik Maniraj Gurung; 1833 Lance Naik Balbir Rai; 1234 Rifleman Singbir Thapa; 455 Rifleman Kahar Sing Rana and 4535 Rifleman Jagia Khattrie.

Two men of Right Section 21st (Kohat) Mountain Battery also won **Indian Distinguished Service Medals** for gallant and resourceful actions at Resht: 403 Havildar Jaggat Singh and 152 Gunner Kishen Singh. The Section had lost an officer, Lieutenant Maurice Richard Wheatley Johnson, Indian Army Reserve of Officers, in late June when he was ambushed and captured on the Enzeli road, and then murdered by Jangalis.

A **Distinguished Service Order** was awarded to Captain Guy Massy McCleverty MC, 1/2nd Gurkhas: *For conspicuous gallantry and devotion to duty at Resht, Persia, on 20th July, 1918. He was in command of a relief party sent to extricate a force besieged in a building. He displayed great courage and initiative, and it was mainly due to his resource and daring leadership that the relief was successfully accomplished. His work throughout the operations was of a very high order.*

Matthews' Column had taken over 50 casualties but by the end of July Resht was cleared of all enemy troops and Kuchik Khan negotiated for peace; hostilities with the Jangalis ceased on 12th August. Attacks by the Martinsyde aircraft of 'B' Flight, No 72 Squadron, Royal Air Force, operating from Khasvin had been instrumental in demonstrating to the Jangalis that they could not compete with DUNSTERFORCE. The British hostage Edward Noel was released, Vice-Consul Charles McClaren having escaped earlier, and Kuchik Khan quickly changed sides and became the largest contractor supplying rice for the British forces in Gilan Province.

Turkish movement forward from Tabriz

On the 20th August the DUNSTERFORCE post at Mianeh, commanded by Major Lewis Wagstaff CIE, 2nd Queen's Own Rajput Light Infantry, Indian

Army, reported that Turks were advancing from Tabriz, where the Turkish 11th Caucasian Division was believed to have recently concentrated. This was unwelcome news as the enemy's intentions could have been to disrupt the British line of communication between Mesopotamia and the Caspian Sea. Wagstaffe had a platoon of 1/4th Hampshires and 650 levies with DUNSTERFORCE instructors forward of the Kuflan Kuh ridgeline; in the rear at Zenjan there was the by now weak squadron of 14th Hussars and 50 rifles of 1/2nd Gurkhas.

Reinforcements for Wagstaffe were sent from Kasvin on 21st and 22nd August. The artillery component consisted of a section each from the 44th and C/69th Field Batteries that had come up from Mesopotamia, and a section of 21st (Kohat) Mountain Battery. The infantry troops despatched were 100 more rifles from the Hampshires and 50 more from the Gurkhas. British air reconnaissance verified an enemy advance to Yusufabad, whilst a British intelligence report indicated that the Turks also proposed advancing from Sauj Bulag on the two roads through Saqqiz and Sain Kaleh. This intelligence assessment led to guns and infantry from 39th Brigade being held back at Hamadan and Kasvin, and this fact was to lead to a refusal of immediate reinforcements for Dunsterville in Baku at the end of the month.

The fighting along the Tabriz-Kasvin Road

On 5th September up to 2,000 Turks advanced from Yusufabad and engaged the British observation screen at Tikmedash. The British screen was commanded by Wagstaffe's second-in-command a DUNSTERFORCE officer named Captain H.E. Osborne, 2nd King Edward's Horse. Osborne, who had previously reconnoitred up to the outskirts of Tabriz, had under his command locally recruited levies, stiffened by 'C' Squadron 14th Hussars (60 sabres) and small detachments of Gurkhas and Hampshires. When the Turks used artillery against Tikmedash the levies soon became demoralised and fled, as did the local mule train drivers who cut the loads loose and rode off on the mules. The Medical Officer Captain Jordan Constantin John, Indian Medical Service, attempted but failed to stop this flight although he did manage to evacuate the wounded, and he was later appointed **Officer of the Order of The British Empire(OBE).**

During the withdrawal from Tikmedash 1032 Lance Naik Sherbahadur Ghale, 1/2nd Gurkha Rifles, displayed gallantry that earned him an **Indian Distinguished Service Medal**. Osborne's next fight was at Turkmanchai a day later and here he was supported by the two mountain guns that had come forward; the mounted enemy unsuspectingly rode within range and suffered from accurately fired shrapnel shells. Here 4848 Lance Naik Bahadurman Rai, 1/2nd Gurkhas, also won an **Indian Distinguished Service Medal**. Osborne's troops, now joined by Guy McCleverty who had reinforced him with 100 Gurkha rifles, reached Mianeh on 9th September. Here Colonel Matthews had come forward to take command from Lewis Wagstaffe. A further withdrawal was made to a defensive position at the pass over the Kuflan Kuh ridgeline. Throughout the withdrawal from Tikmedash 'C' Squadron 14th Hussars had fought continuously as the rearguard, and it was due to the Hussars' professionalism that the Turks were held back, allowing the infantry to make clean breaks from the fiercely-fought actions.

The defensive position on the Kuflan Kuh was strong in artillery as the 18-pounders and the howitzers were in support along with a platoon of the 9th Battalion the Worcestershire Regiment, but with only about 60 sabres and 300 rifles there was insufficient infantry for Matthews to defend the feature satisfactorily. After repulsing a very determined enemy attack, during which his levies again fled whilst the Worcesters saved the day with a bayonet charge forward from their reserve position, Matthews ordered a withdrawal back to Zinjan. Here the situation stabilised as the Turks had by now appreciated the firepower of the British artillery and of the armoured cars that had engaged them on the Zinjan road. Commonwealth War Graves Commission records suggest that two Gurkha riflemen were killed as the British pulled back from Tikmedash to Zinjan; all the British wounded were evacuated safely.

The disbanding of DUNSTERFORCE

In early August 1918 Dunsterville sailed to Baku from Enzeli with a small headquarters and a few British Army units either accompanied or followed him. In Baku Dunsterville tried to put some backbone into the local Azerbaijani and Armenian forces but without success. The local attitude was that now that the British had arrived the Azerbaijanis could relax. The Turks attacked Baku and the British fought back but were short of troops, Dunsterville urgently requested reinforcements but General Marshall refused them. In mid-September Dunsterville re-embarked his troops and returned to Enzeli; the Turks took Baku and the local Azerbaijanis massacred many of the Armenians in the town.

General Marshall immediately disbanded DUNSTERFORCE and sent Lionel Dunsterville back to India. All the British units in north-western Persia were subordinated to a new formation titled NORTH PERSIA FORCE that was commanded by Temporary Brigadier General H.F. Bateman-Champain CMG, 9th Gurkha Rifles, Indian Army. The individuals previously in DUNSTERFORCE were re-assigned to other duties in Persia or Mesopotamia such as the training of the new Urmia Brigade that consisted of battalions of Assyrian and Armenian Christians who had fled from Turkish attacks.

However the Indian Army units in North Persia stayed where they were, even though by early November 1918 Armistices had been agreed with Germany and Turkey. These Indian units were the 21st Kohat Mountain Battery (Frontier Force), 36th Sikhs, 1/2nd King Edward's Own Gurkha Rifles (The Sirmoor Rifles) and 1/6th Gurkha Rifles. In mid-November 1918 General Marshall sent British troops to re-occupy Baku but Indian units were not involved. Due to the Russian civil war North Persia remained a volatile location for the next three years and in 1920 Russian Bolshevik troops landed at Enzeli to confront the sepoys, but finally in the Spring of 1921 all British and Indian units still in the region withdrew.

Reforming and Redeploying The 120th Rajputana Infantry in Southern Persia and Seistan 1918 – 1920

Introduction

In 1914 the 120th Rajputana Infantry was a Class-Company Regiment headquartered at Belgaum, India. The regiment was composed of two companies each of Rajputana Gujars, Mers, Rajputana Rajputs, and Hindustani Mussalmans. The unit was part of 18th (Belgaum) Brigade in the 6th (Poona) Division that was deployed to Mesopotamia in November 1914. The regiment fought up the River Tigris to Ctesiphon, withdrew to Kut and there surrendered with the remainder of that besieged garrison on 29th April 1916. The victorious Turks brutally marched their prisoners to Anatolia for the duration of the war, and 117 Sepoys and followers of the regiment died either on the march or in prison camps.

In early 1917 the battalion was reformed at its Depot at Ahmednagar, India. Regimental officers who had been on leave or employed elsewhere when Kut fell were joined by others from the Indian Army Reserve of Officers whilst men were enlisted from the traditional recruitment areas. After a brief reorganisation the Commanding Officer, Lieutenant Colonel C.H. Ward, moved his new battalion to Kohat leaving the Depot under the command of Captain C.O.R. Mosse MC. Half of the battalion was posted to Thal and nine months of strenuous training in mountain warfare, combined with the movement of mobile columns between Kohat and Thal, resulted in the battalion becoming operationally efficient for deployment overseas. Orders for two companies to proceed to Persia were received on 15th March 1918, and 'A' and 'B' Companies were nominated. Major J.H.V. Barr, 109th

Infantry, was posted in to command in place of Lieutenant Colonel Ward on March 27th 1918.

Before long the whole battalion was in or near southern Persia where it experienced some operational activity, but also great hardship due to the harsh conditions that prevailed and the prevalence of an infectious disease that killed over 150 men.

Persia in 1918

Throughout the Great War the Central Powers employed well-financed European specialists, many of them pre-war residents of Persia, in continuous attempts to bring both Persia and Afghanistan into the war as allies of Germany and Turkey. If such alliances had occurred then India would have been faced with serious military problems. The North-West Frontier had been almost denuded of its pre-war garrisons as regular units had been deployed to overseas theatres; training depots proliferated but experienced infantry battalions and artillery units did not.

Persia had a very weak central government and the Germans were able to induce several Persian war-lords and their tribal followers to attack British commercial and military locations. The British riposted by moving troops into eastern Persia and by forming an indigenous formation named the South Persia Rifles (SPR), commanded by Sir Percy Sykes. The SPR operated around Shiraz in the west of southern Persia. The 120th Rajputana Infantry was initially deployed into the SPR orbit of operations, but on detached duty securing the eastern SPR flank.

Saidabad

'A' Company (Captain E.J. Cumming) and 'B' Company (Captain C.O.R. Mosse MC), a total of 553 men, sailed from Karachi on the *S.S. Bamora*, disembarking at Bandar Abbas on 29th March 1918. The ship had to anchor nearly 5 kilometres off-shore, and the sepoys were taken off in mahailas (light off-shore or river boats), wading through the last 50 metres of surf. Captain Cumming, the senior officer, was ordered on 19th April to march northwards to Saidabad escorting a convoy of over 1,300 camels and strings of donkeys. The convoy departed at midnight but a dust-storm then swept in causing the camels to stampede and throw their loads, leaving Lewis guns, ammunition, grenades and stores littering the countryside; a downpour of rain swiftly followed. Order was restored at dawn and one camel had to be retrieved from the well that it had fallen down. Saidabad, 320 kilometres distant, was reached 19 days later after a spectacular trek through wild mountainous country.

Saidabad's importance was that it controlled the route from Shiraz to Kirman and the route south to Bandar Abbas. It lay nearly 1,750 metres above sea level and at that time contained around 10,000 inhabitants. A large fort outside the town was held by a SPR Garrison. The Rajputs were first quartered in the town but quickly moved out when cholera in the town water supply killed some of the inhabitants; a camp was set up away from the town.

The main British military activity was taking place around Shiraz where Sir Percy Syke's Mission was located. As the SPR were judged to be unreliable the Mission was supported by one squadron 15th Lancers, the 23rd Peshawar Mountain Battery (Frontier Force), Headquarters and two companies 16th Rajputs, the 3/124th Duchess of Connaught's Own Baluchistan Infantry, one squadron of Burma Mounted Infantry, plus detachments from 108th, 161st and 162nd Indian Field Ambulances and 21st Mule Corps.

The SPR garrison at Khan-i-Zinian, 40 kilometres from Shiraz, mutinied on 25th May killing the two British soldiers there, Captain A.W. Will, an interpreter on the Special List, and No. 9162 Sergeant A.W. Coomber, Royal Sussex Regiment. The mutineers then surrendered to a large insurgent group from the Qashqai tribe that had been surrounding the post.

On hearing of this mutiny it was decided to evict the SPR from Saidabad Fort. This was accomplished using stealth rather than force as when the SPR were on parade the 120th Rajputana Infantry quietly entered the fort and took charge.

Action on the Saidabad – Bandar Abbas road

In July the remainder of the 120th Rajputana Infantry sailed from Bombay along with other Indian units sent to support the Sykes Mission. As most of the sepoys had never seen the sea before the eight-day voyage was an experience in itself, particularly as rations were unavailable on the leg between Bombay and Karachi. Disembarkation over the surf took place on 12th July and Major Barr and his men camped on the Bandar Abbas beach for over a fortnight during the hottest time of the year in the Persian Gulf. With distinct relief the march northwards started on 29th July; accompanying the 120th were sections from the 35th Mountain Battery and the 174th Field Ambulance. The troops escorted another large convoy of 1,400 camels carrying supplies to Shiraz.

But the climate took its toll on the young sepoys, two of whom collapsed and died from the heat; this event resulted in a 24 hour rest period to allow recovery for all ranks. Conditions improved as the road climbed higher and Saidabad was reached after 19 marches. During the remainder of the hot season the 120th garrisoned posts along the Bandar Abbas – Shiraz route and patrolled between these posts. Many of the officers were recently-promoted havildars and nearly all the soldiers were recent recruits, but all ranks performed their tasks admirably under very trying conditions.

One day No. 2 Platoon under Jemadar Jawar Singh was patrolling from Chah Chaguk to Saidabad when it was ambushed by around 400 tribesmen. The enemy opened fire at dusk, killing three and wounding three more sepoys of the leading rifle section. Jawar Singh and his men fought back fiercely, killing ten and wounding 20 of the enemy. The platoon went into perimeter camp for the night but were not attacked again.

For gallantry displayed during this action No. 2883 Lance Naik Mukand Singh and Langri (Cook) Ganga Singh were awarded Indian Distinguished Service Medals. Gangha Singh, although a non-combatant, saved a wounded man and two rifles from falling into enemy hands and insisted on carrying the rifle and equipment of a wounded man on the march back to Saidabad. Ganga Singh had previously petitioned to be a sepoy but had been rejected because of his small stature, however within hours of his arrival at Saidabad he was accepted as a soldier by the regiment that he so gallantly served.

Death by influenza

During 1918 the very virulent Spanish Influenza swept around the world and in Shiraz it killed one fifth of the 50,000 inhabitants. The disease was brought to Saidabad by camel drivers and passed on to the sepoys. Interestingly those living under canvas were hardly affected but 75% of those living in buildings were afflicted. On Armistice Day, 11th November 1918, the routine communications from the 120th garrison at Niriz suddenly ceased. Three days later when no further communications had been received Lieutenant C.

Hunnybun took two platoons from Saidabad to Niriz, accompanied by the Medical Officer Captain J.B. Hance MB, Indian Medical Service.

As the platoons approached the Niriz camp they were struck by the dead silence and absence of movement that prevailed. The post commander, Captain Cumming, was found dead in his tent; the post Lewis gun was under his bed and his confidential papers were beside him, evidently torn into pieces as his last living act. The guard all lay dead in the Quarter Guard tent, their rifles by their sides. Also in the tent were the detachment's rifles and a small treasure chest; initially Lieutenant Hunnybun was surprised that the tent had not been looted but a reconnaissance into Niriz town found that only corpses remained there. In the lines the sepoys were in a state of collapse, many being beyond human aid. The total death count of the Niriz 130-man detachment proved to be Captain Cumming, Jemadar Balu Ram and 93 sepoys and followers. Hostile tribesmen had cut the communications cables and forced messengers back into the camp. The weather was bitterly cold and firewood and medical stores had run out, whilst nearby inhabitants did not help as they were concerned with their own survival.

A tablet was afterwards set into the wall of Niriz Fort with the inscription:

120th Rajputana Infantry

To the memory of Major E.J. Cumming, Jemadar Balu Ram, 91 Rifles and two followers of the above Regiment, who died of influenza in this post, November 1918; this tablet is erected by his comrades.

The total deaths caused by Spanish influenza in the 120th Rajputana Rifles totalled the two officers already named and 157 others, and sadly one of these was Langri Ganga Singh whose decoration was later sent to his family[97].Edward John Cumming, gazetted to major after his death, is commemorated on the screen wall at the West Norwood Cemetery and Crematorium, London, whilst the Indian names are recorded on the Tehran Memorial within the British Embassy Compound, Gulhak, Tehran, Iran.

---

[97] The Commonwealth War Graves Commission records Ganga Singh as being a son of Baldeo of Lawa, India.

India briefly, and then Seistan

After ten months on Field Service in Persia the 120th returned to the Depot, now in Deesa, India, in April 1919 – but only for a week. Because of the Afghan War leave and demobilisation were both cancelled and the battalion was ordered to garrison Nasratabad, the largest town in Seistan[98] in south-eastern Persia. Although leave was over-due particularly for many former prisoners of war taken at Kut and now returned to the Depot, there was immense enthusiasm amongst the ranks for the new deployment. The battalion less 'E' and 'F' Companies[99] was shipped from Bombay to Karachi and then sent by train to Duzdab. From there a 160 kilometre march was made across soft sand that came up to the ankles and constantly blew into the sepoys' faces. Because of intense daytime heat marching was done at night, but this caused navigational difficulties and often halts had to be made until the Seistan Levy[100] guides could pick up their bearings again[101]. Despite these problems Nasratabad was reached after five days of marching, with only one casualty being recorded.

Seistan was a sensitive issue between Afghanistan and Persia; it was a fertile region that had been claimed by both countries but Britain as arbitrator had awarded most of it to Persia. It was thought in Delhi that now that the Afghans were fighting against India they might move into Seistan to attack British troops. Lieutenant Colonel W.E. Pye, 98th Infantry, commanded the Nasratabad garrison which also contained No. 1 Kashmir Imperial Service Mountain Battery and the Kapurthala Imperial Service Infantry. The 120th provided all the required picquets for the mud-hut military camp and the British Consulate, whilst the Adjutant, Lieutenant A.B.C. Piper, commanded a camel-mounted mobile column of two officers and 50 sepoys.

---

98 Seistan was at the southern end of the East Persia Cordon that had been established within Persia by the British during the war to hopefully prevent German arms convoys from entering Afghanistan.

99 'E' and 'F' Companies 120th Rajputana Infantry, under Captain J.L.K. Kane, 109th Infantry attached to 120th Rajputana Rifles, were sent to Nushki on the Baluchistan frontier. They were employed on Line of Communication security duties including manning an armoured train.

100 At this time the Seistan Levy Corps was composed of around 1,400 men mounted on camels or horses.

101 During the following month a party of the Kapurthala Infantry lost its way on this route, resulting in eight men dying of thirst.

The mobile column was tasked with scouting duties and with reacting to raiders. On one occasion the column followed-up raiders for nine hours until the camels had to be rested, just inside the Afghan border. The men then had to march the 55 kilometres back to base on minimal water and rations, leading the worn-out camels. For displaying endurance and excellent discipline on this pursuit Captain Piper mentioned Subadar Nur Mahomed, Seistan Levy Corps; and from the 120th No. 3190 Havildar Mati Kathat[102], No. 3909 Sepoy Lilla[103], and No. 3947 Sepoy Bhura Rawat.

The Afghan War ended on 26th July 1919, convoy-guarding ceased and duties in Seistan became more uneventful and relaxed, with sporting competitions playing a significant part of regimental life. The sepoys were moved from their mud huts to excellent quarters in a new fort that was built. However the climate remained challenging, summer winds could blow constantly at speeds of over 200 kilometres per hour, and in the winter blizzards sometimes appeared and standing water froze. In September 1919 leave was allowed for 25% of the officers and 40% of the men, and in early 1920 training programmes were run for the large drafts that arrived to replace men on leave.

But all deployments eventually come to an end and the 120th Rajputana Infantry left Seistan on 1st November 1920, arriving in Deesa 20 days later to commence demobilisation of sepoys enlisted for war-service. Lieutenant Colonel P.F. Pocock DSO, a survivor of the Mesopotamian Campaign, had taken over command from Major Barr on 14th August 1920. Sadly the Adjutant, Lieutenant Albert Benjamin Charles Piper, was taken ill on the return journey and died of pneumonia at Quetta on 6th December; he was buried in the Quetta Government Cemetery and is commemorated on the Delhi Memorial (India Gate).

Awards to the 120th Rajputana Infantry for service in Persia 1918 – 1920

Indian Distinguished Service Medal

2833 Lance Naik Mukand Singh; Langri Ganga Singh.

---

102 See Indian Meritorious Service Medal Award.
103 See Indian Meritorious Service Medal Award.

Indian Meritorious Service Medal

Acting Havildars 3190 Mote Kathat and 2570 Nanda Rawat; 3909 Sepoy Lilla Ram.

Mentioned in Despatches

Lieutenant (Acting Captain) T.G. Howdle, attached South Persia Rifles; Langri Ganga Singh; 3184 Sepoy Kan Singh; 2833 Lance Naik Mukand Singh; 2255 Sepoy Rewat Singh; 2299 Sepoy Seo Singh.

Also Mentioned was Captain (Acting Lieutenant Colonel) J.B. Hance MB, Indian Medical Service attached South Persia Rifles.

Death on a Dark Desert Night
Manchester Column Disaster
Mesopotamia, July 1920

The 35th Scinde Horse in Mesopotamia

After spending a quiet war serving on home defence duties in India the 35th Scinde Horse was posted to Mesopotamia in March 1920. In India squadrons of the regiment had been on detached duty, whilst many drafts of good men had been sent to regiments in other theatres, and officers had been detached elsewhere as directed by the staff. Immediately after the war ended surplus men were demobilised and effective training programmes were introduced, but detachments continued; in April 1919 squadrons were at Calcutta, Bombay, Lucknow and Jubbulpore with large detachments at Remount Depots in Bangalore and Sehore. Therefore the concentration of the regiment for a move to Mesopotamia was welcomed by all, although Palestine would have been preferred as a destination.

The regiment was a class squadron regiment comprising 2 squadrons of Derajat Mussalmans, 1 squadron of Pathans and 1 squadron of Sikhs. After landing at Basra the regiment moved by rail to Diwaniyah on the Hillah branch of the Euphrates River, and from there two squadrons were detached to join the 7th Cavalry Brigade at Hinaidi, near Baghdad. Regimental headquarters and the other two squadrons also moved to Hinaidi in early June. To its surprise, as it had not been told before it left India, the regiment discovered that it should have a machine gun section as part of its establishment, and training on this weapon began hurriedly.

The regiment was not impressed by the indiscipline and lack of cooperation existing in many of the British units and depots scattered around Mesopotamia at that time; in particular large-scale racketeering was being practised with military stores and funds, and depots were obstructive rather than cooperative when issues were requested. The regimental history comments: *'One could almost feel the miasma of lethargy, apathy and corruption that pervaded the whole country'*. Regrettably the regiment had not been able to draw its full scale of equipment before operations commenced.

The 1/32nd Sikh Pioneers

The 1st Battalion of the 32nd Sikh Pioneers had landed at Basra in May 1917, and for the duration of the Great War campaign in Mesopotamia it was fully employed on repairing and constructing roads and railway lines. The 32nd Sikh Pioneers was a class regiment composed of Mazbi Sikhs. The battalion remained in Mesopotamia after the Armistice and worked on road construction in the Mosul area and on building encampments around Baghdad and up in the cooler Persian hills at Karind, where army headquarters personnel and their families spent the hot summers. As soon as the Arab Revolt broke out the battalion was concentrated and deployed at posts along the Euphrates River.

The Manchester Column

Details of why and how the Arab Revolt started in Mesopotamia in July 1920 have been described in the article *'A Close-Run Thing - The Fight to Relieve Rumaitha'*. A situation then developed in the Kifl – Kufah area on the Euphrates River south of Baghdad. A 30-inch (0.76 metre) guage railway line ran from Hillah to Kifl and on 23rd July Kifl station was attacked by insurgents and the railway staff were held captive. The local Political Officer requested a show of force in the area and the British commander at Hillah sent a small column. This column, known as the Manchester Column, contained:

- **35th Scinde Horse** – Regimental Headquarters and 2 squadrons.
- **39th Battery Royal Field Artillery** - 2 sections (4 guns).
- **2nd Battalion Manchester Regiment** – Battalion Headquarters and 3 companies.
- **1/32nd Sikh Pioneers** – 1 company ('A' Company).
- **24th Combined Field Ambulance** – 1 section.

The column commander was Brevet-Lieutenant Colonel R.N. Hardcastle DSO, The Manchester Regiment. The column burdened itself unnecessarily with 150 transport carts carrying tentage, stores for messes and personal kits, but despite the high summer temperature no extra water above the normal scale was carried except by the Scinde Horse who carried full chagals as well as water bottles. Before leaving Hillah Lieutenant Colonel Hardcastle had been led to believe that he was the advance guard of a larger force that would follow his column, and he was instructed: *"If opposed by large hostile forces, you will avoid becoming so involved as to necessitate reinforcements, and should occasion arise you will fall back on the position you now occupy."*

On the second day of the march, the 24th July, the column reached the Rustumiya Canal at 1235 hours. The heat was causing problems and 60% of the Manchester Regiment soldiers were so exhausted that the Medical Officer recommended a 24-hour rest period. Two cavalry troops were deployed as standing patrols on the Kifl road whilst the infantry and pioneers made camp. The camp site was tactically sound with earth banks bordering three sides. An observation post was placed on a line of mounds that ran outside the west side of the camp.

At 1745 hours when trench-digging on the open north side of the camp had just begun, a messenger from the cavalry standing patrols returned to report that 10,000 insurgents were advancing from Kifl and were ripping up the rail track. A few minutes later the figure of insurgents was decreased to 500 or so, but in fact between 2,000 and 3,000 were approaching the camp. As the enemy came in sight the artillery was ordered to engage them, but the artillery signallers were elsewhere tapping into the telegraph line in order to send messages to Hillah and some time elapsed before the guns opened fire.

The insurgents advanced at some points up to 135 metres from the camp and fire was exchanged. The two Political Officers with the column now approached Lieutenant Colonel Hardcastle and advised him that if the column remained where it was then all the Arabs between the camp site and Hillah would join the insurrection the next day, whilst others would attack and capture Hillah. Lieutenant Colonel Hardcastle called for all the company, battery and squadron commanders. He did not present them with a set of orders but instead he held a Council of War, where everyone could comment on the situation. The Political Officers urged an immediate retreat, and this was agreed, orders being issued 30 minutes later. The encampment was left standing whilst the Arab enemy watched and waited.

The Retreat

One company of the Manchesters acted as advanced guard whilst the other two companies marched on the flanks. The mass of transport followed the first company, then came the guns escorted by the Sikh Pioneers, and finally the two squadrons of Scinde Horse acted as rearguard. The column headed towards Hilla, and what happened on the march is best told through the gallantry citations that were awarded later. At 2040 hours the retreat started. Very soon the transport stampeded, charging through the Manchesters and splitting them up into small groups. Out of the darkness swarmed mounted Arabs who cut down many transport animals and their drivers. Chaos ensued, some men ran but some stood and fought.

39th Battery's guns now came into action at close quarters and one 18-pounder gun was lost in a canal. One artillery officer was seen fighting a lone hand-to-hand action at the rear of a lorry until his revolver ammunition was expended and he was cut down. But the gunners manned their remaining guns and whilst withdrawing frequently came into action and drove off hordes of the enemy.

Indian soldiers were driving teams of horses pulling wagons and No. 18535 Naik Kala Khan, 39th Battery, 19th Brigade, Royal Field Artillery, was responsible for a team of horses for one of the ammunition wagons. He was posthumously awarded an **Indian Order of Merit, 2nd Class**: *When the gun of his sub-section had limbered up and was about to move off to follow the column, this Naik, as coverer of one of the ammunition wagon teams, took his team up to get the waggon away from the position which was under heavy fire. He, the three team drivers and all six horses of the team were killed in attempting to do this. He set a magnificent example of devotion to duty to all ranks.*

Through gallant acts by some infantry officers and men, one of whom was later awarded a posthumous Victoria Cross, and by the firepower of the guns and the charges of the cavalry a measure of order was restored. The Commander-in-Chief later wrote:

> *'The officers of the 39th Battery and those of the cavalry behaved like heroes and it is thanks to their fine example and the discipline of those under their command that a complete disaster was averted.'*

Meanwhile the two cavalry squadrons under the command of Major H.E. Connop were fighting fiercely in their rearguard action and on each rear flank. Many charges, mounted using the sword and dismounted using the bayonet, were made to drive the enemy back and to protect stragglers who would suddenly appear out of the night having been stripped off their clothing, equipment and weapons by the Arabs. Ressaldar Major Mahomed Azim was conspicuous in protecting the flanks of the guns until he was mortally wounded by a shot in the stomach. Lieutenant Francis George Bott, 35th Scinde Horse, was also mortally wounded early in the fight as he tried to steady the transport drivers. The company of Sikh Pioneers fought on foot to protect the guns but their vulnerability to mounted attack cost them many casualties, and if captured they were immediately killed for being non-Muslims.

James Hay Graham Knox, attached to 35th Scinde Horse, won a **Military Cross**: *He commanded a squadron which was acting as rearguard to a column withdrawing at night, and, by his skilful dispositions, kept the enemy in check. Whilst leading his men he was wounded, but quickly rallied the squadron and repeatedly charged the enemy, thus enabling the rearguard to fall back.*

2nd Lieutenant William Eric Dixon Robinson, 35th Scinde Horse, also gained a **Military Cross**: *By skilful handling of his Vickers gun and by judicious control of fire, he prevented a very determined attempt to break through the line. His courage and initiative were a splendid example to his squadron. It was mainly due to his bold leadership and coolness in action that the enemy were driven back.*

Ressaidar Dur Khan, 35th Scinde Horse, was awarded an **Indian Order of Merit, 1st Class** (his Indian Order of Merit, 2nd Class, had been won in Palestine in July 1918 when he was attached to the 36th Jacob's Horse): *During a rear guard action at night he led his troop with ability and courage. When both squadron officers were wounded he took command and led three successive charges against the enemy. His bravery and initiative throughout the operations were most marked.*

Jemadar Muhammad Niwaz Khan, 35th Scinde Horse, and No. 24126 Driver Surej Bhan, 39th Battery Royal Field Artillery attached to 35th Scinde Horse, were both awarded **Indian Distinguished Service Medals** for gallantry displayed during the night.

Due to the disorder generally prevailing on the battlefield a portion of the Manchesters lost its way in the darkness and fell into the hands of the

Arabs. Some were killed immediately whilst others were taken prisoner, to be later killed or released depending on the whims of their captors. But the main body carried on retreating in an organised manner.

But the Arab insurgents could not resist the temptation of the loot waiting in the abandoned transport carts and waggons, plus the discarded rifles lying on the ground, and they now concentrated their efforts on acquiring as much booty as they could carry away. This allowed the battered survivors of the Manchester Column to withdraw the last 15 kilometres into Hillah without serious interference. The gun in the canal was recovered by the insurgents. The breech-block and sights had been removed by the gunners, but an Arab blacksmith forged a rough replacement breech-block and the gun was later used to sink the British vessel *Firefly* on the Euphrates River.

Conclusion

The immediate British casualty count was 20 men killed, 60 men wounded and 318 missing. Only 79 British and 81 Indian missing soldiers were later released by the Arabs (and some of these had been captured previously), so the count of men dead was in fact over 180. The 1/32nd Sikh Pioneers lost 30 men killed. The Manchester Regiment lost 3 officers and 131 NCOs and men killed; it is believed that around 100 prisoners from the Manchester Regiment were taken to Najaf and killed there. The 35th Scinde Horse lost 23 men killed in action or died from wounds, 16 others wounded, and lost around 100 horses killed or put down, with more animals suffering light wounds.

The column commander later stated that without the gallant actions of the Scinde Horse there would have been many more casualties. As Major Connop submitted the applications for gallantry awards for the Scinde Horse he did not include his own name, but later in the campaign at Kufah he was to be awarded admission to the **Distinguished Service Order**.

The insurgents had won a great victory. The British, through ignorance of the land, its inhabitants and the effects of the climate, paid the price for breaking many rules of warfare that had been learned the hard way on the Indian North-West Frontier.

Fierce fighting continued in Mesopotamia until the insurgency began to run out of steam towards the end of the year. British reinforcements arrived from India allowing harsh punitive measures to be applied against dissident tribes. The last action took place in February 1921. After a very shaky start Britain had finally enforced its authority over the Mesopotamian tribes living near the Euphrates and Tigris Rivers.

Clasp to the General Service Medal

A clasp titled **IRAQ** was issued to the General Service Medal (1918 – 1962) to those present on the strength of an establishment within the Boundaries of Iraq, between 1st July and 17th November 1920.

Gallantry awards made later in the campaign

35th Scinde Horse

- **Distinguished Service Order** – Major Harry Ernest Connop.

- **Indian Distinguished Service Medal** - Ressaldar Dur Khan, IOM.; 4164 Lance-Dafadar Ali Khan.

- **Mention in Despatches** – Ressaldar Abdul Karim; Major Charles Richard Henry Landon.

1/32nd Sikh Pioneers

- **Indian Distinguished Service Medal** - 4297 Company Havildar Major Arjan Singh; 4051 Havildar Bur Singh; 4909 Sepoy Udham Singh.

Bibliography

Chapter 1: Military Operations in Aden during 1914 and 1915

- Anonymous article. *Combined Naval and Military Operations Against Sheikh Seyd, Southern Arabia.* (The Naval Review online: http://www.naval-review.com/tblcont.asp).

- Betham, Lieutenant Colonel Sir G. and Geary, Major H.V.R. *The Golden Galley. The Story of the Second Punjab Regiment 1761-1947.* (Oxford University Press 1956).

- Chhina, Rana. *The Indian Distinguished Service Medal.* (InvictaIndia 2001).

- Condon, Brigadier W.E.H. *The Frontier Force Regiment.* (Gale & Polden Aldershot 1962).

- Condon, Brigadier W.E.H. *The Frontier Force Rifles.* (Naval & Military Press reprint).

- Connelly, Mark. *The British Campaign in Aden, 1914-1918.* (Journal of the Centre for First World War Studies 2005).

- Duckers, Peter. *Reward of Valour. The Indian Order of Merit, 1914-1918.* (Jade Publishing Ltd Oldham 1999).

- Farndale, General Sir M. *History of the Royal Regiment of Artillery. The Forgotten Fronts and the Home Base, 1914-18.* (The Royal Artillery Institution 1988).

- Hayward, J.B. & Son, Medal Specialists (re-publishers). *Honours and Awards Indian Army, 1914-1921.* (Originally published in *1931 as Roll of Honour Indian Army, 1914-1921*).

- Lucas, Sir Charles. *The Empire at War.* (Oxford University Press 1921).

- Lord, Cliff and Birtles, David. *The Armed Forces of Aden 1839-1967*. (Helion & Company)

- MacMunn, Lieut. General Sir George. *The History of the Sikh Pioneers. 23rd, 32nd, 34th*. (Sampson Low, Marston & Co Ltd, London 1936).

- MacMunn, Lieutenant General Sir George and Falls, Captain Cyril (compilers).*Official History. Military Operations Egypt & Palestine from the Outbreak of War with Germany to June 1917*. (Battery Press Nashville reprint 1996).

- Maxwell, R.M. *Jimmie Stewart – Frontiersman. The Edited Memoirs of Major General Sir J.M. Stewart KCB, CMG*. (Pentland Press 1992).

- McKenzie, F.A. The Defence of India (article) in The Great War edited by H.W. Wilson, Volume 7, Chapter 128 (available on Internet Archive).

- Nath, Ashok. *Izzat. Historical Records and Iconography of Indian Cavalry Regiments, 1750-2007*. (Centre for Armed Forces Historical Research, United Services Institute, Delhi 2009).

- Pickering, Peter (website). *Perim Island. The Last Colonial Outpost*. http://www.peterpickering.com/perimisland.com/page25/page54/page54.html

- Qureshi, Major Mohammed Ibrahim. *The First Punjabis. History of The First Punjab Regiment 1759-1956*. (Gale & Polden Aldershot 1958).

- Sandes, Lieutenant Colonel E.W.C. *The Indian Sappers and Miners*. (Institution of Royal Engineers, Chatham 1948).

- Younghusband, Major General Sir G. *Forty Years a Soldier*. (G.P. Putnam's Sons, New York 1923).

- War Diaries: 23rd Sikh Pioneers (WO 95/5438); 109th Infantry (WO 95/5438); 26th Light Cavalry (WO 95/5437); Aden Troop; various medical units (WO 95 5439).

- Despatches from Commander-in-Chief India in the *London Gazette*.

Chapter 2: Military Operations on the North-West Frontier and in Baluchistan – October 1914 – March 1917

- Anonymous. *History of the Guides 1846-1922*. (Naval & Military Press reprint).

Bibliography

- Anderson, Lieutenant Colonel R.H. *Regimental History of the 45th Rattray's Sikhs during the Great War and after.* (Naval & Military Press reprint.)

- Campbell, Major General F. CB DSO. *Report to the Chief of the General Staff, Army Headquarters, India, on the action in the vicinity of Landekai Spur 28th, 29th August 1915.* Kindly provided by Cliff Parrett.

- Chinna, Rana. *The Indian Distinguished Service Medal.* (InvictaIndia 2001).

- Condon, Brigadier W.E.H. *The Frontier Force Regiment.* (Gale & Polden, Aldershot 1962).

- D'Souza, Major General E. *Valour to the Fore. A history of the 4th Battalion the Maratha Light Infantry.* (ARB Communications, India 2000).

- Daniels, Major A.M. *The History of Skinner's Horse.* (Naval & Military Press reprint).

- Duckers, Peter. *Reward of Valour. The Indian Order of Merit, 1914-1918.* (Jade Publishing, Oldham 1999).

- Dunsterville, Major General L.C. *Stalky's Reminiscences.* (Jonathan Cape, London 1928.)

- *Hart's Annual Army List 1915.*

- *Indian Army List January 1919.* (Naval & Military Press reprint).

- Lawford Lieutenant Colonel J.P. and Catto, Major W.E. *Solah Punjab. The History of the 16th Punjab Regiment.* (Gale & Polden, Aldershot 1967).

- *London Gazette Supplements.* No. 29514, page 3037 dated 20th March 1916; No. 29652, page 6695 dated 4th July 1916; No. 30360, page 11269 dated 31st October 1917.

- Petre, F. Loraine. *The 1st King George's Own Gurkha Rifles. The Malaun Regiment. 1815-1921.* (Royal United Service Institution, London 1925.)

- Sandes, Lieutenant Colonel E.W.C. *The Indian Sappers and Miners.* (The Institute of Royal Engineers, Chatham 1948).

- Trench, Charles Chenevix. *The Frontier Scouts.* (Jonathan Cape, London 1985).

- Walker R.W. *Recipients of the Distinguished Conduct Medal 1914-20.* (Midland Medals, Birmingham 1981).

- Ward, S.G.P. *Faithful. The Story of the Durham Light Infantry.* (Thomas Nelson & Sons Ltd, London 1962).

- Woodyatt, Major General N. *Under Ten Viceroys.* (Herbert Jenkins Limited, London 1922 and available on Internet Archive.)

Chapter 3: The Actions at Shimber Berris, Somaliland, November 1914 to February 1915

- Official History, Military Operations Egypt and Palestine by Macmunn and Falls.

- The National Army Museum Book of the Turkish Front 1914-18 by Field Marshall Lord Carver.

- Sir John Maxwell's Despatch dated 16th February 1916.

- British Campaigns in the Nearer East 1914 – 1918 Volume I by Edmund Dane.

- 100 Years of the Suez Canal by R.E.B. Duff. Orientations by Ronald Storrs.

- Honours and Awards Indian Army 1914-1921. Published by J.B. Hayward & Son.

- The Times History of the War.

Chapter 4: The 36th Sikhs at the fall of Tsingtao, China - October to November 1914

- de Rouen Forth, Nevill. *A Fighting Colonel of Camel Corps.* (Merlin Books Ltd, UK 1991).

- Farndale, General Sir Martin. *History of the Royal Regiment of Artillery. The Forgotten Fronts and the Home Base, 1914-18.* (The Royal Artillery Institution 1988).

- Graham, C.A.L. Brigadier General. *The History of the Indian Mountain Artillery.* (Gale & Polden Ltd, Aldershot, UK 1957 and downloadable here:https://archive.org/details/IndianMountainArtillery).

- Lucas, Sir Charles. *The Empire at War.* (Oxford University Press 1926).

- MacMunn, Sir George and Falls, Captain Cyril. *History of the Great War. Military Operations Egypt & Palestine*, three volumes. (Imperial War Museum and The Battery Press 1996).

- Renfrew, Barry. *Forgotten Regiments. Regular and Volunteer Units of the British Far East.* (Terrier Press, Amersham, UK 1909).

- Robertson, John. *With the Cameliers in Palestine.* (A.H. & A.W. Reed, Dunedin, New Zealand, 1938, or Naval & Military Press reprint).

- Rollo, Denis. *The Guns and Gunners of Hong Kong.* (Gunners Roll of Hong Kong, 1991).

- Walker, R.W. *Recipients of the Distinguished Conduct Medal 1914-1920.* (Midland Medals, Birmingham, UK 1981).

- Wavell, Lieutenant General A.P. The Palestine Campaigns. (Constable, London 1941).

- *London Gazette* entries and Medal Index Cards.

Chapter 5: The Suez Canal 1914-15

- Colvin, Ian: *The Life of General Dyer.* (William Blackwood & Sons Ltd, Edinburgh and London 1929).

- Dickson, Brigadier-General W.E.R.: *East Persia. A Backwater of the Great War.* (Edward Arnold & Co., London 1924).

- Dyer, Brigadier-General R.E.H.: *The Raiders of the Sarhad.* (Witherby, London 1921 and online: https://archive.org/details/raidersofsarhadb00dyerrich).

- Graham, Brigadier-General C.A.L.: *The History of the Indian Mountain Artillery.* (Gale & Polden, Aldershot 1957 and online: https://archive.org/details/IndianMountainArtillery).

- Head, Richard and McClenaghan, Tony: *The Maharajas' Paltans. A History of the Indian State Forces (1888-1948).* (Manohar, Delhi 2013).

- Hopkirk, Peter: *Like Hidden Fire. The Plot to Bring Down the British Empire*, first published as *On Secret Service East of Constantinople.* (Kodansha International paperback 1994).

- James, F.: *Faraway Campaign. Experiences of an Indian Army Cavalry Officer in Persia and Russia during the Great War.* (Leonaur paperback 2007).

- Kreyer, Major J.A.C. and Uloth, Captain G.: *The 28th Light Cavalry in Persia and Russian Turkistan.* (Slatter & Rose Ltd., Oxford 1926).

- London Gazette Supplement dated 31 October 1917, page 11270 and online: https://www.thegazette.co.uk/London/issue/30360/supplement/11270).

- Moberly, Brigadier-General F.J.: *Operations in Persia 1914-1919*. (Imperial War Museum 1987.)

- Pigot, G. compiler: *History of the 1st Battalion 14th Punjab Regiment, Sherdil-Ki-Paltan, (Late XIX Punjabis)*. (Naval & Military Press reprint).

- Sabahi, Houshang: *British Policy in Persia 1918-1925*. (Frank Cass 1990).

- Sandes, Lieutenant-Colonel E.W.C.: *The Indian Sappers and Miners*. (The Institution of Royal Engineers, Chatham 1948).

- Tugwell, Lieutenant-Colonel W.B.P.: *History of the Bombay Pioneers 1777-1933*. (Naval & Military Press reprint).

Chapter 6: The Hong Kong-Singapore Mountain Battery in Egypt, Sinai and Palestine 1915 – 1918

- *Operations in Persia 1914 – 1919* Official History compiled by Brigadier General F.J. Moberley CB CSI DSO *psc* (Imperial War Museum 1987).

- *The Transcaspian Episode* by C.H. Ellis (Hutchinson & Co Ltd 1963 and available on Internet Archive).

- *The 28th Light Cavalry in Persia and Russian Turkestan 1915 – 1920* by Major J.A.C. Kreyer DSO and Captain G. Uloth (Slatter & Rose Ltd 1926).

- *History of the 1st Battalion 14th Punjab Regiment, Sherdil-Ki-Paltan (Late XIX Punjabis)* by an anonymous compiler.(Naval & Military Press reprint).

- *History of the Guides 1846-1922* by an anonymous compiler (Naval & Military Press reprint).

- *Faraway Campaign* by F. James (Leonaur paperback 2007).

- *On Secret Patrol In High Asia* by Captain L.V.S. Blacker (John Murray London 1922 and available free on Internet Archive).

- *Mission to Tashkent* by Lieutenant Colonel F.M. Bailey (The Travel Book Club, London 1946).

- *History of the Royal Regiment of Artillery. The Forgotten Fronts and the Home Base, 1914-18* by General Sir Martin Farndale KCB. (The Royal Artillery Institution 1988).

- *The Times History of The War Volume XX* (The Times, London 1919)

- *Like Hidden Fire* (first published as *On Secret Service East of Constantinople*) by Peter Hopkirk (J. Murray 1994).

- *The Spy Who Disappeared* by Reginald Teague Jones alias Ronald Sinclair (Victor Gollancz Ltd 1990).

- *Honours and Awards Indian Army August 1914-August 1921* (J.B. Hayward & Sons London). Originally published in 1931 as Roll of Honour Indian Army 1914-1921.

- *Reward of Valor. The Indian Order of Merit, 1914-1918* by Peter Duckers (Jade Publishing Ltd Oldham 1999).

- *The Indian Distinguished Service Medal* by Rana Chinna (InvictaIndia 2001).

- *The London Gazette.*

Chapter 7: The East Persia Cordon and the Sarhad Operations, 1915 – 1917

- Brigadier General F.J. Moberly, *Official History. Operations in Persia 1914-1919*, Imperial War Museum 1987.

- General Sir John Nixon KCB, *Despatch dated 15th January 1916*, London Gazette No 29685, page 7456, 27 July 1916.

- General Sir H.E. Blumberg KCB, *Britain's Sea Soldiers. A record of the Royal Marines during the War*, Naval & Military Press.

- Lieutenant Colonel J. de L. Conry, compiler: *Regimental History of the 2/19th Hyderabad Regiment (Berar)*, Gale & Polden 1927.

- Conrad Cato, *The Navy Everywhere, Chapter XIII*, http://archive.org/details/navyeverywhere00cato

- Rana Chhina, *The Indian Distinguished Service Medal*, InvictaIndia 2001.

- Peter Duckers, *Reward of Valour. The Indian Order of Merit, 1914-1918*, Jade Publishing, Oldham 1999.

- M.S. Leigh OBE ICS, *The Punjab and the War*, Sang-E-Meel, Lahore 1997.

- *Honours and Awards, Indian Army 1914-1921*, J.B. Hayward & Son (reprint of *Roll of Honour, Indian Army 1914-1921*, 1931).

- Antony Wynn, *Persia in the Great Game*, John Murray paperback 2004.

- Sean McMeekin, *The Berlin-Baghdad Express*, Penguin Paperback 2011.

- Commonwealth War Graves Commission records and British National Archives Medal Index Cards.

Chapter 8: Indian Military Transport units in Macedonia 1916 – 1918

- Falls, Cyril (compiler): *History of the Great War.Military Operations Macedonia*. Two Volumes. (Battery Press reprint 1996).

- Head, Richard and McClenaghan, Tony: *The Maharajas' Paltans. A History of the Indian State Forces 1888-1948, Part 1*. (Manohar, India 2013).

- J.B. Hayward & Son (publisher): *Honours and Awards Indian Army August 1914 - August 1921*.

- *Indian Army List 1919*. (Naval & Military Press reprint).

- *London Gazette Supplement* dated 28th November 1917, page 12490.

- Nicholls, Brian. *The Military Mule in the British Army and Indian Army. An Anthology*. (D.P. & G. Military Publishers, Doncaster 2006).

- Wakefield, Alan and Moody, Simon. *Under the Devil's Eye. The British Military Experience in Macedonia 1915-1918*. (Pen & Sword Military 2011).

- War Diaries: 3rd (Cavalry Brigade) Mule Corps; 31 Mule Cart Corps Bharatpur Imperial Transport Corps; Indore Imperial Transport Corps. (All WO 95/4813).

Chapter 9: The 25th Cavalry (Frontier Force) in German and Portugese East Africa– September 1917 – February 1918

- *War Diary 25th Cavalry, October 1917-January 1918*. (WO95/5321).

- *Record of the 3rd Battalion The King's African Rifles During The Great Campaign in East Africa 1914-1918*. (WO106/273).

- *Extract from the Gazette of India* re-published in the London Gazette Second Supplement dated 20th March 1916, pages 3037-38.

- Bruce, Norman S. *Reminiscences of being the Medical Officer to the 25th Cavalry in the East Africa Campaign.* (Liddle Collection, Leeds University).

- Chhina, Rana. *The Indian Distinguished Service Medal.* (InvictaIndia, Delhi, 2001).

- Clifford, Sir Hugh. *The Gold Coast Regiment in the East African Campaign.* (On-line at Internet Archive).

- Fraser-Tytler, W.K. MC. *Cavalry in Bush Warfare.* (Article in The Cavalry Journal Volume 15, 1925, pp 501-13).

- Nath, Ashok. *Sowars and Sepoys in the Great War 1914-1918, Cavalry and Infantry Regiments.* (Nath Foundations, Dhaka, 2014).

- Paice, Edward. *Tip & Run. The Untold Tragedy of the Great War in East Africa.* (Weidenfeld & Nicolson, London 2007).

- Medal Index Cards and London Gazette notifications.

Chapter 12: The Gurkha Action at Tor, Sinai - The 2/7th Gurkhas in action on 12th February 1915

- *London Gazette No 29632, page 6169, dated 21st June 1916.*

- Macmunn, Lieutenant General Sir George and Falls, Captain Cyril:*Official History, Military Operations Egypt & Palestine, From the Outbreak of the War with Germany to June 1917,* page 53. (Imperial War Museum in association with The Battery Press, Nashville.)

- The War Diary of the 2/7th Gurkha Rifles from the 10th to 13th of February 1915, kindly provided by Mr Gavin Edgerley-Harris of The Gurkha Museum, Winchester.

- Winstone, H.F.V. (editor): *The Diaries of Parker Pasha.* (Quartet Books.)

- Article: *A daring Commando Raid on the Suez Front* by Mehmet Fatih Bas.

- Research notes kindly provided by Per Finsted of Denmark.

Chapter 13: Atonement: The 5th Light Infantry in German Kamerun - August 1915 to February 1916

- *War Diary 5th Light Infantry August 1915 – January 1916* (The National Archives WO95/5388);

- *Official History. Togoland and the Cameroons,* (compiled by) Brig. F.J. Moberley CB, CSI, DSO;

- *The History of the Royal West African Frontier Force,* Col. A. Haywood CMG, CBE, DSO and Brigadier F.A.S. Clarke DSO;

- *The Great War in West Africa,* Brig.-Gen. E. Howard Gorges CB, CBE, DSO;

- *From a Diary in the Cameroons,* Maj. C.S. Stooks DSO, 5th Light Infantry, downloadable at (refer to page 380): http://www.archive.org/details/newcornhill47londuoft; *Turmoil and Tragedy in India 1914 and After,* Lt.- Gen. George MacMunn KCB, KCSI, DSO;

- *Fidelity & Honour. The Indian Army from the Seventeenth to the Twenty-first Century;* Lt-Gen. S.L. Menezes;

- *Small Wars and Skirmishes 1902-1918,* Edwin Herbert;

- *The Indian Distinguished Service Medal,* Rana Chhina; "London Gazette" Supplement of 31 May 1916, *Despatches of Major-General C.M. Dobell and of Brigadier-General F.J. Cunliffe.*

Chapter 14: The 5th Light Infantry in East Africa - March 1916 – January 1918

- *5th Light Infantry War Diaries March 1916-January 1918* (WO95 5369 and WO95 5324).

- *Unpublished Draft Chapter XVII of Official History* (CAB 44/9).

- *East African General Routine Orders* (WO 123/288).

- Hordern, Lieutenant Colonel Charles. *Official History, Military Operations East Africa August 1914 – September 1916.* (Battery Press, Nashville 1990.)

- Duckers, Peter. *Reward of Valour. The Indian Order of Merit 1914-1918.* (Jade Publishing, Oldham 1999.)

- Chinna, Rana. *The Indian Distinguished Service Medal.* (Invicta India 2001).

- *Honours and Awards Indian Army 1914-1921* compiled by J.B. Hayward and Sons, London.

Chapter 15: Lake Victoria, German East Africa, 6th December 1915

- Official History. East Africa. August 1914 to September 1916 compiled by Lieutenant Colonel Charles Hordern (pages 224 – 225).

- 98th Infantry War Diary for 6th December 1915 plus Montford's report (WO95/5333)

- Nairobi Area HQ War Diary for 9th December 1915 (WO95/5360).

- Die Operationen in Ostafrika by Ludwig Boell.

- The Battle of Tanga 1914 by Ross Anderson.

- Hart's Annual Army List for 1915 and Medal Index Cards.

- A Backwater. Lake Victoria Nyanza during the campaign against German East Africa an article in the Naval

Chapter 16: The 15th Ludhiana Sikhs and the Senussi - The Egyptian Western Desert, November - 1915 to February 1916

- Russell McGuirk, The Sanusi's Little War;

- The 15th Sikhs War Diary (copy kindly provided by Russell McGuirk);

- Lieut.-General Sir George Macmunn & Captain Cyril Falls, Official History of the War, Military Operations Egypt and Palestine, from the outbreak of war with Germany to June 1917;

- Field Marshall Lord Carver, The National Army Museum Book of the Turkish Front 1914-18;

- Peter Duckers, Reward of Valor, The Indian Order of Merit 1914-1918;

- Rana Chhina, The Indian Distinguished Service Medal.

Chapter 19: Kisangire and Kisiju – Operations north of the Rufiji River - Delta, German East Africa October and November 1916

- *Official History. Volume I. Military Operations East Africa August 1914 to September 1916* compiled by Lieutenant Colonel Charles Hordern.

- *Draft Chapter XIII of the Official History Volume II.* (CAB 44/5 in the UK National Archives.)

- *High Noon of Empire* edited by B.A. 'Jimmy' James.

- *Regimental History of the 4th Battalion 13th Frontier Force Rifles (Wilde's).* Anonymous author, printed privately by Butler & Tanner Ltd around 1930.

- *Tip & Run. The untold tragedy of the Great War in Africa* by Edward Paice.

- *Die Operationen in Ostafrika* by Ludwig Boell.

- *The Indian State Forces. Their Lineage and Insignia* by His Highness the Maharaja of Jaipur.

- *Honours and Awards, Indian Army, 1914-1921* published by J.B. Hayward & Son.

- *Reward of Valour. The Indian Order of Merit, 1914-1918* by Peter Duckers.

Chapter 20: The 129th DCO Baluchis at German East Africa - October 1916 to January 1917

- *The 4/10th Baluch Regiment in the Great War* by W.S. Thatcher.

- *War Diary 129th Duke of Connaught's Own Baluchis October – November 1916* (WO 95/5341).

- *War History – 1st/2nd King's African Rifles* (WO 161/75).

- *War Diary 2nd/2nd King's African Rifles* (WO95/5341).

- *Draft Chapters XIII and XIV of Part II of the Official History, East African Campaign* (CAB 44/5).

- *Tip & Run. The Untold Tragedy of the Great War in Africa* by Edward Paice.

- *A Hull Sergeant's Great War Diary* by Dan Fewster. Edited by Robert B. Sylvester.

- *So Many Loves* by Leo Walmsley.

- *Shells & Bright Stones. A biography of Leo Walmsley* edited by Nona Stead.

- *Reward of Valour. The Indian Order of Merit, 1914-1918* by Peter Ducker.

- *The Indian Distinguished Service Medal* by Rana Chhina.

- *East African General Routine Orders* (WO123/288).

- *The Cross of Sacrifice Volume I* compiled by S.D & D.B. Jarvis.

- *London Gazettes* and *Medal Index Cards* and *Commonwealth War Graves Committee* records.

BIBLIOGRAPHY

Chapter 21: The 22nd Derajat Mountain Battery (Frontier Force) - in East Africa – December 1916 to December 1918

- *Historical Record of 22nd Derajat Mountain Battery (Frontier Force)*.Anonymous compiler (Naval & Military Press reprint).

- *The History of the Indian Mountain Artillery* by Brigadier-General C.A.L. Graham.(Available on Internet Archive.)

- *The Gold Coast Regiment in the East African Campaign* by Sir Hugh Clifford. (Available on Internet Archive.)

- *The King's African Rifles* by Lieutenant-Colonel H. Moyse-Bartlett. (Gale & Polden Ltd 1956.)

- Selected papers from British National Archives files prefixed CAB 44 and CAB 45 (draft chapters of the unpublished Part II of the Official History of the Great War East African campaign).

Chapter 22: Indian Army Battalions in the Battle of Ramadi, Mesopotamia,

- *Official History. The Campaign in Mesopotamia. Volume IV.* Compiled by Brigadier F.J. Moberley CB, CSI, DSO, psc.(Battery Press reprint).

- *History of the 5th Royal Gurkha Rifles (Frontier Force) 1858-1928.* Anonymous compilers.(Naval & Military Press reprint).

- *Historical Record of the 6th Gurkha Rifles* compiled by Major D.G.J. Ryan DSO, Major G.C. Strahan OBE and Captain J.K. Jones.(Published privately in Simla in 1926).

- *War Diary of 1/4th Battalion The Dorsetshire Regiment February 1916 – February 1919.* (Public Records Office reference: WO 95/5196).

- *The Neglected War: Mesopotamia 1914-1918* by A.J. Barker (Faber & Faber 1967).

- *The Long Road to Baghdad Volume II* by Edmund Candler (Cassell & Co Ltd 1919).

- *Reward of Valor. The Indian Order of Merit, 1914-1918* by Peter Duckers. (Jade Publishing Limited, Oldham 1999).

- *British Campaigns in the Nearer East Volume II* by Edmund Dane (Hodder & Stoughton 1919).

- *The London Gazette* and *Medal Index Cards.*

Chapter 23: The 30th Punjabis at Tandamuti Hill and Nakadi Ridge, East Africa – February – October 1917

- *Solah Punjab. The History of the 16th Punjab Regiment* by Lieutenant Colonel J.P. Lawford MC and Major W.E. Catto (Gale and Polden 1967).

- *War Diaries of the 30th Punjabis, January to November 1917* (WO95 5332, 5327 and 5324).

- *Draft Chapter XVIII of the unpublished Part II of the Official History, Military Operations East Africa* (CAB 44/10).

- *Reward of Valor.The Indian Order of Merit* by Peter Duckers (Jade Publishing, Oldham 1999).

- *The Indian Distinguished Service Medal* by Rana Chhina (InvictaIndia 2001).

- *Honours and Awards Indian Army 1914-1921* published by J.b Hayward, London).

- *Commonwealth War Graves Commission on-line records.*

- *How the Great War Razed East Africa* by Edward Paice: http://www.africaresearchinstitute.org/publications/counterpoints/how-the-great-war-razed-east-africa/

Chapter 24: The Kuki Rising 1917-1919 - Insurrection in north-eastern India and Burma

- Kearey, Lieutenant-General Sir H. D.U.: *'Kuki rising, 1917-1919'*, L/PS/10/724, Oriental and India Office Collections (OIOC), British Library, London

- Lisam, Khomdon Singh: *Encyclopedia of Manipur.* (Kalpaz Punblications, Delhi 2011. The relevant chapter can be found on-line.).

- Parratt, John: *Wounded Land. Politics and Identity in Modern Manipur.* (Mittal Publications, Delhi 2005.The relevant chapter can be found on-line.).

- Shakespear, L.W. Colonel: History of the Assam Rifles. (Naval & Military Press re-print).

- Shakespear, L.W. Colonel: *History of the 2nd King Edward's Own Goorkhas (The Sirmoor Rifle Regiment), Volume II 1911-1921.* (Naval & Military Press).

BIBLIOGRAPHY

- Shakespear, L.W.: The Lushei Kuki Clans. (Macmillan & Co Ltd, London 1912 and on-line: https://archive.org/details/lusheikukiclans00shak).

- Starling John & Lee Ivor: *No Labour, No Battle. Military Labour During the First World War.* (Spellmount, UK 2009).

- Wood, Reverend W.H.S.: Through Fifty Years. A History of the Surma Valley Light Horse. (Naval & Military Press reprint).

Chapter 25: Fighting the Marris and the Khetrans - February to April 1918

- *Frontier and Overseas Expeditions from India, Volume III, Baluchistan and the First Afghan War* (http://archive.org/details/frontieroverseas03indi)

- *The History of Skinner's Horse* by Major A.M. Daniels.

- *History of the 2nd King Edward's Own Goorkhas (The Sirmoor Rifle Regiment), Volume II, 1911-1921.* By Colonel L.W. Shakespear.

- *History of the Bombay Pioneers* by Lieutenant Colonel W.B.P. Tugwell.

- *The Frontier Force Rifles, 1849-1946* by Brigadier W.H. Condon OBE.

- *Official History. The War in the Air, Volume Six* by H.A. Jones.

- (The above six titles are available as re-prints from The Naval & Military Press Ltd.)

- **Unattributed Article** in the Queen's Lancashire Regiment Museum Archives, *The Marri Field Force 1918.*

- *Ich Dien: The Prince of Wales's Volunteers (South Lancashire Regiment) 1914-1934* by Captain H. Whalley-Kelly.Gale & Polden, Aldershot 1935.

- Regimental Journal Article: *The Defence of Fort Gumbaz February 1918* by Lieutenant Colonel K.C. Cradock-Watson, Skinner's Horse.

- *Reward of Valour. The Indian Order of Merit, 1914-1918* by Peter Duckers.Jade Publishing Limited, 1999.

- *The Indian Political Service . A Study in Indirect Rule* by Terence Creagh Coen KBE, CIE.Chatto & Windus, London, 1971.

- *The History of the Indian Mountain Artillery* by Brigadier General C.A.L. Graham DSO, OBE, DL, *psc.*Gale & Polden Ltd, Aldershot, 1957. (http://archive.org/details/IndianMountainArtillery)

- *The Indian Sappers & Miners* by Lieutenant Colonel E.W.C. Sandes DSO, MC.

- *The Battle Honours of the British and Indian Armies 1662-1982* by H.C.B. Cook. Leo Cooper, London, 1987.

- *Indian Army List, January 1919.*

- *London Gazettes Nos 31235 (pages 3586-87) of 17 March 1919, and 31903 (pages 5581-83) of 18 May 1920.*

Chapter 26: Indian Army units in Dunsterforce - North-West Persia in 1918

- Moberley, Brigadier General F.J., *Official History. The Campaign in Mesopotamia 1914-1918, Volume IV.* Imperial War Museum and Battery Press reprint.

- Moberley, Brigadier General F.J., *Official History. Operations in Persia 1914-1919.* Her Majesty's Stationery Office. Facsimile Edition 1987.

- Jones H.A., *The War in the Air, Being the Story of the part played in the Great War by the Royal Air Force, Volume VI.* Naval & Military Press reprint.

- Dunsterville, Major General L.C., *The Adventures of Dunsterforce.* Naval & Military Press reprint. Available on-line at: http://archive.org/details/adventuresofduns00dunsrich

- Dunsterville, Major General L.C., *Stalky's Reminiscences.* Jonathan Cape, London 1928.

- Donohoe, Major M.H., *With The Persian Expedition.* Naval & Military Press reprint. Available on-line at: http://archive.org/details/abx3721.0001.001.umich.edu

- Shakespear, Colonel L.W., *History of the 2nd King's Own Goorkhas, Volume II 1911-1921.* Naval & Military Press reprint.

- Graham, Brigadier General C.A.L., *The History of the Indian Mountain Artillery.* Gale & Polden, Aldershot 1957. Available on-line at: http://archive.org/details/IndianMountainArtillery

- Farndale, General Sir Martin, *History of the Royal Regiment of Artillery. The Forgotten Fronts and the Home Base 1914-18.* The Royal Artillery Institution 1988.

- Townshend, Charles.*The British Invasion of Mesopotamia and the Creation of Iraq 1914-1921*.Faber and Faber, London 2010.

- Hopkirk, Peter, *Like Hidden Fire. The Plot to Bring Down the British Empire*. First Published as *On Secret Service East Of Constantinople* by J. Murray 1994.

- Encyclopedia Iranica, *Jangali Movement*. http://www.iranicaonline.org/articles/jangali-movement

- Duckers, Peter.*Reward of Valour. The Indian Order of Merit 1914-1918*. Jade Publishing Limited, 1999.

- Chhina, Rana.*The Indian Distinguished Service Medal.*Invicta, India, 2001.

- Hypher, P.P.*Deeds of Valour Performed by Indian Officers and Soldiers during the period from 1860 to 1925*. Liddell's press, Simla 1927.

Chapter 27: Reforming and Redeploying - The 120th Rajputana Infantry in southern Persia and Seistan 1918 – 1920

- Dickinson, Brigadier General W.E.R. CMG CIE: *East Persia. A Backwater of the Great War*. (Edward Arnold, London 1924).

- Kreyer, Major J.A.C. DSO and Uloth, Captain G: *The 28th Light Cavalry in Persia and Russian Turkistan 1915-1920*. (Slater & Rose, Oxford 1926).

- Moberly, Brigadier General Frederick James CB CSI DSO: *Operations in Persia 1914-1919*. (Imperial War Museum 1987).

- Palit, Major General D.K. VrC: *Jammu and Kashmir Arms. History of the J&K Rifles*. (Palit & Dutt, Dehra Dun 1972).

- Rawlinson, H.G. CIE: *The History of the 2/6th Rajputana Rifles (Prince of Wales's Own)*. (Oxford University Press 1936).

- Chhina, Rana. *The Indian Distinguished Service Medal*. (InvictaIndia 2001).

- *Hart's Annual Army List for 1915* and *India Army List January 1919*.

- *Honours and Awards Indian Army 1914-1921*. (J.B. Hayward & Son, London).

- Supplement to the London Gazette, 23 July 1920, pages 7758-776

Chapter 28: Death on a Dark Desert Night - Manchester Column disaster., Mesopotamia, July 1920

- *The Insurrection in Mesopotamia 1920* by Lieutenant General Sir Aylmer L. Haldane (Battery Press reprint).

- *Prince of Wales's Own, The Scinde Horse, 1839-1922* by Colonel E.B. Maunsell (Naval & Military Press reprint).

- *History of the Royal Regiment of Artillery.Between the Wars, 1919 – 39* edited by Major General B.P. Hughes.

- *The Indian Distinguished Service Medal* by Rana Chhina (Invicta India 2001).

- *Honours and Awards Indian Army August 1914 – August 1921* (published by J.B. Hayward and Sons, London).

- *The London Gazette.*

Index

A

Adye, Lieutenant Colonel D.R. 165

Aitken, Major-General A.E. 194

Al Darb Village 13

Annenkovo 112, 115, 116, 117

Apthorp, Captain Shirley East 126

Arab Rifles 159, 179

Armenian infantry 103, 106, 108, 113

Arnold, Lieutenant Colonel A.S. 12

Astrakhan 100

Australian and New Zealand Corps (ANZACs) 49

Australian & New Zealand Mounted Division 59

Austro-Hungarian 62

B

Bab El Mandib 2

Bakhtiari tribesmen 76

Ball, Major Lionel Plomer 163

Bandar Abbas 291, 292, 293

Barlow, Captain C.E. 135

Battle Honour Baluchistan 1918 276

Battle Honour "MERV" 119

Battle of Annenkovo 112

Battle of Dushak 106

Battle of Gaza 61

   First Battle 61

   Second Battle 63

Battle of Ramadi vi, 236, 317

Beersheba 64

Beynon, Brigadier General W.G.L. 22

Bir Gerawla 176

Black Water Fever 87

Boulton, Lieutenant C.E. 143, 157

Boyle, Commander Patrick James 126

Brooking, General H. T 128, 129, 130, 132

Broughton, Major William George 117

Brownlow, Colonel Charles 141

~ 325 ~

Brownlow's Punjabis 28

Bukerebe Island 166

Bulgarian Flying Corps 88

Bushire v, 120, 121, 122, 123, 126, 127, 128, 129, 130, 131, 132

C

Campbell, Captain M.G.G. 272

Carrigan, Major Dreyer. Robert William 231

Caspian Sea 99, 100, 105, 116, 121, 278, 280, 282, 283, 287

Caucasus 99

Chindwin River 254, 264

Chirimba Hill 232, 233

Chokpi River 257

Companion of the Order of Saint George 46

Companion of the Order of Saint Michael 46

Companion of the Order of Saint Michael and Saint George 80

Companion of the Order of the Bath 80

Convent of Saint Catherine 134, 136

Cossipore Artillery Volunteers 195

Cotton, Lieutenant Colonel W.L. 142, 147, 157

Cox, Brigadier-General H.V. 2

Crocker, General S.F. 16

Croix de Guerre 25, 28, 90, 190, 246

Cruickshank, Major J.E. 260

D

Damascus Djemal Pasha 50

Dar Es Salaam 97, 98, 159, 162, 181, 182, 183, 184, 192, 197, 202, 208, 209, 210, 211, 212, 215, 228, 234, 245, 246, 248, 252

Davies, Lieutenant Colonel C.H., DSO 10

Davies, Lieutenant Owen Gilbert 233

Dehan-i-Baghi 75

Dekhani Mussulmans 76

Derajat Mountain Battery vi, 186, 229, 233, 234, 235, 317

Deri Ghazi Khan 271, 274

Deversoir 51

Dickson, Captain A.N. 221

Diyala River 236

Dobell, Lieutenant General Sir C.M. 61, 62, 63, 64, 144, 146, 314

Douglas, Captain G.S. 180

Drummond, Major J.G.P. 113, 114, 117

DUNSTERFORCE 100, 101, 105, 110, 280, 281, 282, 283, 284, 286, 287, 288, 289

Durham Light Infantry 23, 26, 284, 308

E

Earl of Lucan 172

El Arish 57, 58, 59, 134, 324

El Burj 65

El Ferdan 51

El Kubri posts 52

Exham, Captain H. 136, 137

F

Farfan, Major A.J.T. 222

Faridkot Sappers & Miners 204

Fort Turba 3

G

Gallipoli ix, 47, 83, 84, 86, 90, 171

Gamshadzais 77, 78, 79

Gaussen, Major J.R. 269, 270, 271

Gaza War Cemetery 71

Geneffe 51

German Usambara Railway 181, 195

Ghulam Ali, Subedar M.C 189

Golam-Hossain, Captain H.S. 181

Gold Coast Regiment 95, 185, 186, 187, 188, 222, 232, 313, 317

Gordon, Lieutenant-Colonel J.L.R. 26, 172, 173, 174, 175, 176, 177

Gumbaz Fort 269

Gusht Fort 78

H

Hafiz Khor 18, 19, 20, 21, 26

Haflong 261

Haldane, Lieutenant Colonel C.L. 136, 137, 138, 139, 322

Hannyngton, Brigadier-General J.A. 203

Hazara Pioneers 24, 25, 78, 80, 81

Hazara Shiite 105

HMIMS Dalhousie 123

HMIMS Lawrence 123

HMS Clematis 174, 175

HMS Duke of Edinburgh 3

HMS Hyacinth 169

HMS Juno 123, 124, 128

HMS Kavirondo 165

HMS Minerva 135, 136, 138

HMS Nyanza 165

HMS Pyramus 123, 124, 129

HMS Winifred 165

Holland-Pryor, Brigadier General Pomeroy, DSO MVO 242

Hoskins, Major-General A.R. 203

Howarth, Lieutenant G.D. 209

Hulseberg, Lieutenant Colonel H., DSO 216, 217, 224

Hutchison, Captain H.S. 4

I

Imperial Camel Brigade 59

Imperial Camel Corps 65

Imperial Camel Corps Memorial 71

Imphal-Tamu road 260

Ingle, Lieutenant Louis Sobaux 81, 113, 117

J

Jebel Habeita 52

Jerusalem 64

Jhalawan 23, 24

Jimmie Stewart, Brigadier-General J.M. 194

K

Kaakha 103, 104, 105, 106, 107, 109, 117

Kagera River 166

Kalamaria Camp 84

Kamaran Island 5

Kantara War Memorial Cemetery 71

Keary, Lieutenant General Sir Henry D'Urban KCB KCIE DSO 262

Kemondo Bay 164, 166, 168

Khedive Abbas Hilmi 48

Khelat-i-Ghilzal Regiment 73, 80

Kiaochow Bay 41, 42

Kibata 185, 186, 187, 213, 216, 217, 218, 219, 220, 221, 222, 224, 225, 227, 228, 230

Kilwa Kivinje military cemetery 228

King's African Rifles 31

Kisangire vi, 208, 209, 211, 315

Kisiju vi, 208, 211, 212, 315

Kohat 284, 285, 286, 287, 289, 290

Krasnovodsk 99, 100, 102, 103, 105, 110, 117

Kreyer, Major John Arthur Claude 117

Kuki Rising 253

Kurram Militia 15

L

Lahej 5, 6, 7, 8, 9, 10, 12, 13, 14

Lake Flotilla 164, 165, 170

Lake Victoria vi, 164, 165, 166, 170, 181, 195, 246, 314, 315

Lakkatigga Post 15

Landakai Pass 22

Lao Shan Bay 43

Laramba Pass 78

Latema-Reata Nek 195

Lettow-Vorbeck, Colonel Paul von 92, 94, 95, 96, 191, 193, 208, 213, 214, 216, 225, 228, 232, 250, 251

Listermann, Doctor 121

Lord Kitchener 48

Lubembe peninsula 164, 165, 166

INDEX

Lukuledi River 246

M

Macedonia v, ix, 82, 85, 86, 87, 88, 89, 156, 312

Macedonian Campaign 82

MacMunn, Lieutenant General Sir George 141

Mahomed Bin Abdulla Hassan 30

Makonde Plateau 96, 251

Malleson, General 101, 102, 103, 109, 111, 116, 195, 196, 198

Malleson Mission 101

Malone, Captain E.M. 159

Manchester Column 299

Mastung Road 24

Maude, Lieutenant General Sir Frederick Stanley 236

Mbemkuru River 94

Mbindia Hill 226

Mehrab Din, Subedar MC 185

Merua River 145

Mhumbira water holes 93

Mitchell, Lieutenant Colonel J.W. 179

Mockler, Lieutenant Colonel G.H.G. 22

Mombasa 157, 158, 159, 164, 179, 195, 214

Montford, Lieutenant 165, 167, 315

Morpeish Hills 78

Mount of Moses 134

Mudros Island 83

Mule Corps 83

Mushaid Ridge 238

Mwu River 144

N

Nanyati 230, 231

Narungombe 190, 191, 230, 231

Narungombe battle 190

Nasratabad 74, 75, 76, 295

Natha Singh, Major General 209

Nawaz, Lieutenant Mohamad 117

Nkam River 144

Nogal Valley 33

North Cachar Hills 261

O

Oliphant, Major H.E. 122

O'Neill, Captain H.J.D. 201

P

Palin, Lieutenant C.W. 218

Pangani River valley 199

Parker, Lieutenant Colonel Alfred Chevallier 135, 136, 139, 313

Pennington, Major William Herbert 130, 132

Perim Island 4

Persian Gulf 120, 126, 155, 269, 292

Pigot, Captain G. MC 107, 112, 113, 114, 117, 118, 310

Port Amelia 232, 234

Port Said 51, 57, 83

Port Tewfik 51, 70

Prince Hussein Kamal Pasha 48

R

Rafah 59, 60, 61

Ramadi Ridge 238, 239, 241, 242

Ranking, Captain G.J.L. 123

Rasthaus Hill 198

Red Sea 1, 2, 5, 134, 136

River Ramisi 157

Robat 73

Robert, Lieutenant V.G. 216, 227

Rothwell, Major R.S. 128, 132

Royal West Kent Regiment 26

Rufiji River Delta 193, 208

Ruwu River 199, 200, 202, 204, 206

S

Sango Bay 166

Sarhad Operations 72

Sarhad Tribes

   Gamshadzais 77

Ismailzais 77

Rekis (friendly tribe) 77

Yarmuhammadzais 77

Sarwekai Fort 28

Schutztruppe 91, 96, 97, 142, 146, 157, 162, 181, 184, 191, 192, 193, 194, 198, 202, 203, 206, 208, 213, 215, 216, 228, 232, 233, 234, 249, 251

Sea of Galilea 68

Senussi invasion 56

Serapeum 52

Shakespear, Colonel L.W. 256, 319

Sheikh Said 2, 3, 5

Shimber Berris, Somaliland v, 30, 32, 33, 34, 35, 36, 37, 38, 39, 40, 308

Shute, Captain George Eric FitzGerald 118

Sidi el Barrani 56, 171

Sinai Desert 49, 50, 52, 57

Sinai Peninsula 134

Sistan 73, 74, 80, 81

Smuts, General J.C. 208

Somaliland v, ix, 30, 31, 33, 34, 36, 37, 39, 40, 159, 162, 308, 325

Somaliland Camel Corps (SCC) v, 30, 31, 36, 39

South Persia Rifles (SPR) 291

Star of Bokhara 112

Stewart, Lieutenant Francis William 104, 118

Stewart, Major General J.M. 11

Stooks, Captain Charles Sumner 158

Straits of Hormuz 269

Suez Canal v, 1, 48, 49, 50, 56, 57, 134, 154, 308, 309

Surma Valley Light Horse 261

Swat Valley 22

T

Tandamuti Hill vi, 245, 246, 247, 248, 318

Tangistan 121

Tel-el-Kebir 83

The Malaun Regiment 22

Thorburn, Lieutenant Robert 160

Tighe, General Michael J., D.S.O 196

Tillard, Lieutenant Colonel A.B. 274

Tochi Valley 15, 16, 91, 325

Tochi Valley Operations 15, 91

Toussoum post 53

Transcaspia 80, 99

Trench warfare 222

Tsingtao v, 41, 42, 43, 44, 45, 46, 47, 308

Turcoman cavalry 102, 104, 105, 106, 108, 109, 110

Turkish Fourth Army 50

Tyndale-Biscoe, Brigadier-General J.D.T. 172

Tyndall, Major J.W.H.D. 161

U

Umm Rakham 174

W

Wadi El Ghazze 63

Wadi Hasheifat 173

Wadi Majid 174, 176

Wadi Senab 172

Wallace, General 172, 175, 176, 178, 249, 251

Watwangi Pass 274

Whigham-Teasdale, Lieutenant Dennis George 185

Willans, Lieutenant Colonel T.J. 210

Wilson, Major W.K.P. 245, 247

Wintle, Major 122, 124, 125, 126, 127

Wintle, Major C.E.H. 122, 127

Wooldridge, Lieutenant Colonel H.C. 6

Y

Yarmuhammadzais 77, 78

Younghusband, Major General Sir George 8, 9, 13, 306

www.ingramcontent.com/pod-product-compliance
Lightning Source LLC
Chambersburg PA
CBHW031722230426
43669CB00007B/210